The Cambridge Companion to Writing of the English Revolution

This collection of fifteen essays by leading scholars examines the extraordinary diversity and richness of the writing produced in response to, and as part of, the upheaval in the religious, political and cultural life of the nation which constituted the English Revolution. The turmoil of the civil wars fought out from 1639 to 1651, the shock of the execution of Charles I, and the uncertainty of the succeeding period of constitutional experiment were enacted and refigured in writing which both shaped and was shaped by the tumultuous times. The various strategies of this battle of the books are explored through essays on the course of events, intellectual trends and the publishing industry; in discussions of canonical figures such as Milton, Marvell, Bunyan and Clarendon; and in accounts of women's writing, of lyric poetry and of fictional and non-fictional prose. A full chronology, detailed guides to further reading and glossary are included.

CAMBRIDGE COMPANIONS TO LITERATURE

THE CAMBRIDGE
COMPANION TO

WRITING OF THE
ENGLISH REVOLUTION

EDITED BY

N. H. KEEBLE

CAMBRIDGE
UNIVERSITY PRESS

PUBLISHED BY THE PRESS SYNDICATE OF THE UNIVERSITY OF CAMBRIDGE
The Pitt Building, Trumpington Street, Cambridge, United Kingdom

CAMBRIDGE UNIVERSITY PRESS
The Edinburgh Building, Cambridge CB2 2RU, UK
40 West 20th Street, New York, NY 10011-4211, USA
10 Stamford Road, Oakleigh, VIC 3166, Australia
Ruiz de Alarcón 13, 28014 Madrid, Spain
Dock House, The Waterfront, Cape Town 8001, South Africa

http://www.cambridge.org

© Cambridge University Press 2001

First published 2001

Printed in the United Kingdom at the University Press, Cambridge

Typeface Adobe Sabon 10/13pt   *System* QuarkXpress®   [SE]

A catalogue record for this book is available from the British Library

Library of Congress Cataloguing in Publication data
The Cambridge companion to writing of the English Revolution / edited by N. H. Keeble.
p.   cm. – (Cambridge companions to literature)
Includes bibliographical references and index.
ISBN 0 521 64252 3 (hardback) – ISBN 0 521 64522 0 (paperback)
1. Great Britain – History – Puritan Revolution, 1642–1660 – Literature and the
revolution. 2. English literature – Early modern, 1500–1700 – History and criticism.
3. Christianity and literature – Great Britain – History – 17th century. 4. Politics and
literature – Great Britain – History – 17th century. 5. Literature and history – Great
Britain – History – 17th century. 6. English literature – Puritan authors – History and
criticism. 7. Revolutionary literature, English – History and criticism. 8. Royalists in
literature. 9. Puritans in literature. I. Title: Companion to writing of the English
Revolution. II. Keeble, N. H. III. Series.
PR435 .C36 2001
820.9′358–dc21   00-054175

ISBN 0 521 64252 3 hardback
ISBN 0 521 64522 0 paperback

CONTENTS

Part 3: Female voices

Part 4: Conservative voices

Part 5: Rethinking the war

ILLUSTRATIONS

CONTRIBUTORS

SHARON ACHINSTEIN, University of Maryland
THOMAS N. CORNS, University of Wales Bangor
MARTIN DZELZAINIS, Royal Holloway, London
RICHARD L. GREAVES, Florida State University
ELAINE HOBBY, University of Loughborough
DAVID LOEWENSTEIN, University of Wisconsin Madison
JOHN MORRILL, Selwyn College, Cambridge
DAVID NORBROOK, University of Maryland
SHEILA OTTWAY, University of Groningen
ANNABEL PATTERSON, Yale University
ISABEL RIVERS, St Hugh's College, Oxford
ALAN RUDRUM, Simon Fraser University
PAUL SALZMAN, La Trobe University
NIGEL SMITH, Princeton University
HELEN WILCOX, University of Groningen
SUSAN WISEMAN, Birkbeck College, London

CHRONOLOGIES

Events and texts

In England, Scotland, Ireland and most Protestant countries of Europe the old Julian calendar, instituted by Julius Caesar in 45 BC, was still followed in the seventeenth century. All Roman Catholic, and some Protestant, countries, however, used the reformed calendar introduced by Pope Gregory XIII in 1582. This was not adopted in Britain until 1752. During the intervening period, British dates were ten days behind those of the New Style calendar. Dates given below are according to British usage, that is, Old Style.

In England, the official calendar year began on Lady Day (the Feast of the Annunciation), 25 March, but in the seventeenth century this was gradually being superseded by the continental practice of beginning the year on the previous 1 January. This was adopted in Scotland from 1 January 1600, but officially not until 1752 in England. Until then, for dates falling between 31 December and 25 March, the year was often given according to both reckonings (so Charles I was executed on 30 January 1648/9). In this Chronology and the following chapters, the year is taken as beginning on 1 January.

1599	Birth of Oliver Cromwell, afterwards Lord Protector
1603	Death of Elizabeth I
	Accession of James VI of Scotland as James I of England
1612	Birth of Thomas, 3rd Baron Fairfax
1625	Death of James I
	Accession of Charles I
	Publication of the first of Lady Eleanor Douglas' sixty tracts
1626	Birth of Richard Cromwell, afterwards Lord Protector
1628	William Laud becomes bishop of London
	Assassination of George Villiers, 1st Duke of Buckingham, favourite of Charles I
1630	Birth of Charles, Prince of Wales, afterwards Charles II (29 May)

1630s	Period of Charles I's personal rule without a Parliament
1633	Laud becomes archbishop of Canterbury
	Birth of James, Duke of York, afterwards James II (14 October)
1634	Performance of Milton's masque *Comus*
1637	Trial and punishment of the Puritan activists William Prynne, John Bastwick and Henry Burton
	Star Chamber Decree concerning Printing
1638	Trial and punishment of John Lilburne, afterwards leader of the Levellers
	National Covenant signed in Scotland
1639	First Bishops' War
1640	Second Bishops' War
	George Thomason begins his collection of tracts and books
	Long Parliament assembles (3 November)
	Impeachment of Archbishop William Laud (December)
1641	Abolition of Court of Star Chamber (July); collapse of censorship regulations
	Parliamentarian *Diurnall Occurrences*, the first English printed newsbook, begins publication (November)
	News of the Irish Rebellion reaches London (November)
	Grand Remonstrance presented (1 December)
	Publication of Milton's anti-prelatical tracts (1641–2)
1642	Charles I's attempted arrest of five members of the House of Commons (2 January)
	Charles I withdraws from London to York (19 March)
	Charles I raises his standard at Nottingham (22 August)
	Battle of Edgehill (23 October; inconclusive)
1643	Abolition of episcopacy (January)
	John Birkenhead's Royalist newsbook *Mercurius Aulicus* begins publication (January)
	Marchamont Nedham's *Mercurius Britanicus* begins publication in reply to *Mercurius Aulicus*
	Ordinance for the Regulating of Printing (14 June)
	Battle of Adwalton Moor (30 June; Royalist victory under William Cavendish, Marquis (afterwards Duke) of Newcastle)
	Battle of Roundway Down (13 July; Royalist victory)
	First Battle of Newbury (20 September; Parliamentarian victory)
	Commons takes Solemn League and Covenant (25 September); Scots enter the war on Parliament's side
	Publication of Milton's divorce tracts (1643–5)

1644 Battle of Marston Moor (2 July; Parliamentarian victory over Newcastle)

Second battle of Newbury (27 October; Parliamentarian victory)

Publication of Milton's *Areopagitica* (November)

1645 Ordinance prohibiting the Book of Common Prayer and prescribing the Directory for Public Worship (4 January)

Execution of Laud for treason (10 January)

Self-Denying Ordinance (3 April), by prohibiting MPs (with the exception of Cromwell) from holding military office, creates the New Model Army determined to prosecute the war to a conclusion

Battle of Naseby (14 June; decisive Parliamentarian victory)

Charles' correspondence captured at Naseby published in *The King's Cabinet Opened*

Publication of Milton's *Poems . . . both English and Latin*

Publication of Francis Rous' *The Ancient Bounds, or Liberty of Conscience, Tenderly Stated, Modestly Asserted, and Mildly Vindicated*

Publication of Henry Hammond's *A View of the New Directory*

1646 Charles surrenders to the Scots (5 May)

First Civil War ends with surrender of Oxford (20 June)

Sir John Temple's *The Irish Rebellion* published

Gangraena, Thomas Edwards' Presbyterian denunciation of sectarian practices, published

Levellers' *Remonstrance of Many Thousand Citizens* published

1647 Failing to come to terms with Charles I, the Scots, for £200,000, hand him over to the English (30 January)

Charles imprisoned in Holmby House, Northants (16 February)

Army removes Charles from Parliament's keeping at Holmby House (4 June) to Hampton Court (24 August)

Putney debates between Levellers and officers of the New Model Army (28 October–1 November)

Publication of Levellers' manifesto and draft constitution, *An Agreement of the People for a firme and present peace, upon grounds of common-right and freedom*

Charles escapes from Hampton Court to the Isle of Wight and is confined by the Army in Carisbrooke Castle (11–14 November)

Charles secretly signs Engagement with the Scots agreeing to recognize Presbyterianism in England in return for his restoration to power (26 December)

Publication of Thomas May's *History of the Long Parliament*

Publication of Richard Lovelace's *Lucasta: Epodes, Odes, Sonnets*

Publication of Elizabeth Poole's *A Vision* and *An Alarum of War*

Publication of Abiezer Coppe's *A Fiery Flying Roll* and *A Second Fiery Flying Roule*

1650   Cromwell returns from Ireland (May)

Nedham's *Mercurius Politicus*, the official newsbook of the Commonwealth, begins publication (13 June)

Cromwell invades Scotland (22 July)

Cromwell's victory at Dunbar (3 September)

Publication of Nedham's *The Case of the Common-Wealth of England*

Publication of Jacob Bauthumley's *The Light and Dark Sides of God*

Unauthorized publication of Anne Bradstreet's collection *The Tenth Muse Lately Sprung up in America*

Composition of Marvell's 'Horatian Ode upon Cromwel's Return from Ireland'

Publication of Vaughan's *Silex Scintillans*

Publication of Taylor's *The Rule and Exercise of Holy Living*

1651   Charles II crowned at Scone in Scotland (1 January)

Publication of Milton's *Defence of the English People* (February)

Charles II and Scots army enter England (6 August)

Cromwell's victory over Charles II and Scots at Worcester (3 September)

Charles II flees, eventually landing in France (16 October)

Publication of Hobbes' *Leviathan*

Publication of Vaughan's *Olor Iscanus*

Publication of Taylor's *The Rule and Exercise of Holy Dying*

Publication of Sir William Davenant's *Gondibert*

Publication of first part of Roger Boyle's *Parthenissa*

1652   First Dutch War (June)

Publication of Herbert's *Remains* (including *A Priest to the Temple*)

Publication of Vaughan's *The Mount of Olives*

1653   Cromwell forcibly turns out Rump Parliament (20 April)

Nominated Parliament ('Barebones Parliament') meets (4 July)

Nominated Parliament resigns (12 December); Protectorate established, with Cromwell as Lord Protector

Publication of Margaret Cavendish's *Poems and Fancies*

Publication of An Collins' *Divine Songs and Meditations*

First Quaker tracts published

Publication of Milton's *Readie and Easie Way to Establish a Free Commonwealth* (February; 2nd edn April)

Convention meets (25 April)

Convention votes to recall Charles II (1 May)

Charles II lands at Dover (25 May)

Charles II enters London on his birthday (29 May)

Act of Oblivion receives royal assent (29 August)

Convention dissolved (31 December)

1661 Bunyan imprisoned for refusing to desist from preaching (January)

Coronation of Charles II (23 April)

Cavalier Parliament meets (8 May)

Hyde created Earl of Clarendon

Savoy Conference fails to reach agreement on revision of Prayer Book

Publication of Sir Percy Herbert's *The Princess Cloria*

1662 Act of Uniformity, outlawing Puritan opinion in the Church of England, schools and universities, comes into effect on 24 August; approximately 2,000 ministers are ejected

Publication of Katherine Evans' and Sarah Cheevers' *Short Relation of Cruel Sufferings*

1664 Conventicle Act prohibits religious gatherings save according to the Prayer Book

The widowed Lucy Hutchinson may now begin composition of her biography (completed 1671) of her regicide husband

In exile, Ludlow may now be composing his *A Voyce from the Watch Tower*

Publication of Philips' *Poems*

1665 Five Mile Act prohibits ejected ministers from living in any corporation

Great Plague

Second Dutch War (July)

Publication of Bunyan's *The Holy City*

1666 Fire of London

Publication of Bunyan's *Grace Abounding*

1667 Treaty of Breda concludes Second Dutch War (July)

Dismissed from office and under threat of impeachment, Clarendon is driven into exile, where he resumes work on his *History*

Hobbes writes *Behemoth, or the Long Parliament*(?)

Publication of Milton's *Paradise Lost*

Publication of *Poems by Mrs Katherine Philips, the Matchless Orinda*

Composition of Marvell's *Last Instructions to a Painter*

1669	Publication of Cowley's *Works*
1670	Publication of Milton's *History of Britain*
1671	Death of Fairfax
	Publication of Milton's *Paradise Regained* and *Samson Agonistes*
1672	Charles II's Declaration of Indulgence permits Nonconformist and Roman Catholic worship
	Bunyan released from prison
	Anonymous publication of Marvell's *The Rehearsal Transpros'd*
1673	Pressure from Parliament forces withdrawal of the Declaration of Indulgence
	Publication of second part of Marvell's *The Rehearsal Transpros'd*
1674	Publication of second edition of Milton's *Paradise Lost*
1677	Anonymous publication of Marvell's *Account of the Growth of Popery and Arbitrary Government*
	Publication of Anne Wentworth's *A Vindication*
1678	Allegations of a 'Popish Plot' to assassinate Charles II whip up anti-Roman feeling
	Publication of Bunyan's *The Pilgrim's Progress*
	Publication of revised and expanded edition of Bradstreet's *Tenth Muse*
1679–81	During the prolonged 'Exclusion Crisis' successive Parliaments seek unsuccessfully to compel Charles to exclude his Roman Catholic brother, James, from the succession
1680	Publication of Bunyan's *The Life and Death of Mr Badman*
1681	Publication of Marvell's *Miscellaneous Poems*
1682	Publication of Bunyan's *The Holy War*
1684	Publication of the second part of Bunyan's *The Pilgrim's Progress*
1685	Death of Charles II (6 February)
	Accession of James II
1688	'Glorious Revolution' (deposition of James II (11 December) and accession of Charles I's grandson William III and of William's cousin and wife, James II's daughter Mary II (13 February 1689))

Writers' lives

Richard Braithwait	1588?–1673
Thomas Hobbes	1588–1679
Sir Robert Filmer	1588–1653
Lady Anne Clifford (Anne Sackville, Countess of Dorset; Anne Herbert, Countess of Pembroke)	1590–1676

Lady Eleanor Douglas (*née* Touchet; Lady Eleanor Davies)	1590–1652
Robert Herrick	1591–1674
Izaak Walton	1593–1683
John Bramhall, Archbishop of Armagh	1594–1663
Thomas May	1595–1650
Lady Brilliana Harley (*née* Conway)	1600?–1643
Henry Hammond	1605–1660
Sir William Davenant	1606–1668
Edmund Waller	1606–1687
John Milton	1608–1674
Edward Hyde, Earl of Clarendon	1609–1674
Sir John Suckling	1609–1642
Gerrard Winstanley	1609–1676
Sir James Harrington	1611–1677
Anne Bradstreet (*née* Dudley)	1612–1672
John Cleveland	1613–1658
Jeremy Taylor, Bishop of Down & Connor	1613–1667
Margaret Fox (*née* Askew; Margaret Fell)	1614–1702
John Lilburne	*c.* 1614–1657
Richard Baxter	1615–1691
Laurence Clarkson	1615–1667
Sir John Denham	1615–1669
Sir John Birkenhead	1616–1679
Edmund Ludlow	1617?–1692
Abraham Cowley	1618–1667
Richard Lovelace	1618–1658
Abiezer Coppe	1619–1672
Lucy Hutchinson (*née* Apsley)	1620–1681
Marchamont Nedham	1620–1678
Roger Boyle, Baron Broghill and Earl of Orrery	1621–1679
Andrew Marvell	1621–1678
Henry Vaughan	1622–1695
Anna Trapnel	1622?–
Margaret Cavendish (*née* Lucas), Duchess of Newcastle	1623–1673
George Fox	1624–1691
Ann, Lady Fanshawe (*née* Harrison)	1625–1680
Anne Audland (*née* Newby)	1627–1705
Dorothy Osborne (afterwards Lady Temple)	1627–1695
John Bunyan	1628–1688
Hester Biddle	1629–1696

(1) Works by Bunyan, Clarendon, Marvell and Milton

Bunyan, *GA*	John Bunyan, *Grace Abounding to the Chief of Sinners*, ed. Roger Sharrock (Oxford: Clarendon Press, 1962)
Bunyan, *HW*	John Bunyan, *The Holy War*, ed. Roger Sharrock and James Forrest (Oxford: Clarendon Press, 1980)
Bunyan, *MW*	John Bunyan, *Miscellaneous Works*, gen. ed. Roger Sharrock, 13 vols. (Oxford: Clarendon Press, 1976–94)
Bunyan, *PP*	John Bunyan, *The Pilgrim's Progress*, ed. James Blanton Wharey, 2nd edn, ed. Roger Sharrock (Oxford: Clarendon Press, 1960)
Clarendon, *HR*	Edward, Earl of Clarendon, *The History of the Rebellion and Civil Wars in England*, ed. W. Dunn Macray, 6 vols. (1888; rptd Oxford: Clarendon Press, 1992)
Clarendon, *LC*	Edward, Earl of Clarendon, *The Life of Edward, Earl of Clarendon . . . in which is included a Continuation of his History of the Grand Rebellion, from the Restoration in 1660 to his Banishment in 1667*, 2 vols. (Oxford, 1857)
Marvell, *P&L*	Andrew Marvell, *Poems and Letters*, ed. H. M. Margoliouth, 3rd edn, rev. Pierre Legouis and E. E. Duncan-Jones, 2 vols. (Oxford: Clarendon Press, 1971)
Milton, *CPW*	*Complete Prose Works of John Milton*, gen. ed. Don M. Wolfe, 8 vols. (New Haven, Conn.: Yale University Press, 1953–83)
Milton, *PL*	John Milton, *Paradise Lost* (cited from *Milton:*

Paradise Lost, ed. John Carey, 2nd edn (Harlow: Longman, 1998)); Milton's other poems are cited from *Milton: Shorter Poems*, 2nd edn ed. John Carey, (Harlow: Longman, 1997)

(2) Standard historical works

DNB	*Dictionary of National Biography*
Firth & Rait, *A&O*	C. H. Firth and S. R. Rait (eds.), *Acts and Ordinances of the Interregnum, 1642–1662*, 3 vols. (1911)
Gardiner, *CDPR*	S. R. Gardiner (ed.), *Constitutional Documents of the Puritan Revolution, 1625–1660*, 3rd edn (Oxford: Clarendon Press, 1906)
Gardiner, *HCP*	S. R. Gardiner, *History of the Commonwealth and Protectorate,1649–56*, 4 vols. (1903; rptd Adlestrop, Glos.: Windrush Press, 1988–9)
Gardiner, *HGCW*	S. R. Gardiner, *History of the Great Civil War*, 4 vols. (1893; rptd London: Windrush Press, 1987)

(3) Journal titles

CHJ	*Cambridge Historical Journal*
EcHR	*Economic History Review*
EHR	*English Historical Review*
ELH	*English Literary History*
ELR	*English Literary Renaissance*
HJ	*Historical Journal*
HR	*Historical Review*
JBS	*Journal of British Studies*
JEH	*Journal of Ecclesiastical History*
JHI	*Journal of the History of Ideas*
P&P	*Past and Present*
PMLA	*Publications of the Modern Language Association*
RES	*Review of English Studies*
TRHS	*Transactions of the Royal Historical Society*

The place of publication for seventeenth-century texts is London unless otherwise stated.

Introduction

Writing in November 1648, the Puritan minister Richard Baxter exclaimed in dismay that '*Every ignorant, empty braine (which usually hath the highest esteem of it selfe) hath the liberty of the Presse . . . whereby the number of bookes is grown so great that they begin with many to grow contemptible*'.[1] By 1653, he had come to fear the '*Luxuriant Fertility, or Licentiousness of the Press of late*' as '*a design of the Enemy to bury and overwhelm in a croud . . . Judicious, Pious, Excellent Writings*'.[2] Baxter's disquiet was fuelled by his recent experiences as a chaplain to a regiment of the New Model Army. Like the vast majority of those Presbyterian Puritans who sided with Parliament, he was 'unfeignedly for King and Parliament', and was committed to the Civil War aim of bringing the King to a reconciliation with Parliament. When, in 1645, he joined the Army, he was appalled to find the mood of Cromwell's forces far more extreme. To him it appeared that those he described as 'hot-headed Sectaries' intended no less than 'to subvert both Church and State': 'they took the King for a Tyrant and an Enemy, and really intended absolutely to master him, or ruine him'.[3] Baxter's Puritanism valued order, tradition and authority; the revolutionary and radical wing of the movement, as represented by Levellers, Anabaptists, Ranters and, later, Quakers, disclosed to him a prospect of anarchy. Within the Army itself, these anarchic ideas were spread by word of mouth, through preaching, oral discussion and disputation; but it was the prolific output of the press which spread them through the country at large.

While we may dispute Baxter's assessment of the dire consequences of this '*Luxuriant Fertility*', there is no disputing either the productivity or the influence of the press during the middle decades of the seventeenth century. Both were unprecedented in our cultural history. In the century and a half since the printing press had first been established in England by William Caxton in 1476 its output had steadily increased, but during the middle of the seventeenth century this strengthening flow of publications became a torrent. An annual output of fewer than 300 titles in 1600 had become 3,000 in 1642.

A unique record of this output is preserved in the extraordinary collection of broadsides, tracts, pamphlets and books assembled by the bookseller George Thomason, who, between 1640 and 1661, amassed 22,000 publications.[4] Never before had so many people turned to writing, never before had so many seen their thoughts into print, and never before had what they printed generated such extensive interest and public debate.

For this output there were two, related, causes. First, the civil wars which engulfed the kingdoms of Britain in the mid seventeenth century differed from earlier medieval conflicts in one crucial respect.[5] Unlike the fifteenth-century Wars of the Roses, they were not fought over who should be King, nor, unlike the thirteenth- and fourteenth-century Scots Wars of Independence, over who owed allegiance to whom: at the outbreak of hostilities, everyone agreed that Charles I should be King and that subjects owed him allegiance. What men fought over was rather what kind of king he should be, over the idea of kingship, over the place, rights and prerogatives of monarchy within the constitution and over the extent of the subject's obligation of obedience to a sovereign. How far the monarch might, or might not, disregard the will of his people voiced in Parliament, and how far the state was, or was not, entitled to coerce individual consciences in matters of religious faith, were the points at issue. It was, that is to say, an ideological conflict, a war of ideas, and, in that sense, the first modern war in our history. When in due course it became apparent that, though defeated, Charles would never modify his conception of divine right kingship by acknowledging obligations to his subjects or by respecting the will of Parliament, Charles' right to rule did become the issue, but at a theoretical, not a personal, level. What, in politics, had been a conflict between notions of unlimited (or despotic) and limited (or constitutional) monarchy became a conflict between monarchy and republicanism; and what, in religion, had been a challenge to episcopalianism from Presbyterianism became the repudiation of a national state church (whatever its complexion) and of state-imposed uniformity of religious practice by Independent advocates of 'liberty of conscience' (that is, toleration of the right of individuals to follow their own beliefs).[6] At every stage of their development, these competing notions required articulation and defence. They required, that is to say, publication. Hence, the many battles of the Civil War included a battle of the books, fought, in Clarendon's phrase, with 'paper skirmishes'.[7]

Secondly, in 1641, just at the outset of hostilities, the apparatus of pre-publication censorship, which had been in place since the time of Henry VIII and by which the state sought to control the dissemination of ideas, collapsed. For the first time since the introduction of printing into England, there was no restriction upon what might be published. Although this freedom was neither entirely novel (state censorship had never been efficiently or universally enforced) nor of long duration (the Long Parliament soon re-imposed the old legislation), it was an incentive and encouragement to publication which could not thereafter be restrained. The result was not merely an increase in volume of publication, but a huge extension of the range of published material and a diversification of the social background and opinions of its authors. John Bunyan is only the most famous of a host of marginal and socially disadvantaged people for whom the turmoil of the mid-century for the first time provided both the incentive and the means to express themselves publicly in print.[8] In Bunyan, there is a discernible wariness of the monied and of the social elite – Mr Worldly-Wiseman and most of the dubious characters in *The Pilgrim's Progress* are 'gentlemen', Giant Despair is a great landowner – but the radicalism of these marginal voices could reach much further. It is epitomized in the remarkable democratic conviction of Colonel Thomas Rainsborough that the franchise should be extended far beyond those propertied classes to whom it was then confined, since 'the poorest he that is in England hath a life to live, as the greatest he . . . every man that is to live under a government ought first by his own consent to put himself under that government'.[9] Such ideas were hardly to be voiced again until the nineteenth century, and not to be fully enacted until the twentieth.

Among the voices now heard in numbers for the first time are those of women. The challenge to traditional hierarchies in public affairs was matched by a challenge in domestic and private affairs to received gender roles and to traditional notions of sexual difference. 'Man is made to govern commonwealths, and women their private families' was the traditional view.[10] For almost the first time, that is now challenged by defences of women's right of access to public spheres of activity (including publication) which, though the word was not then available, might be described as feminist. Above all, woman's dignity and potential as God's creature is affirmed in repudiations of the standard inferences drawn from Genesis: that, created after Adam from his rib, woman is secondary and subordinate to man, and that, the occasion of his fall from perfection and of humanity's expulsion from Paradise, she is both prone to, and the vehicle of, temptation. Women, pronounced Bunyan, 'when-ever they would perk it and Lord it over their Husbands, ought to remember, that both by Creation and by Transgression they are made to be in Subjection' and therefore 'to the Worlds end, must wear tokens of her *Underlingship*'.[11] By contrast, women such as the Independent Katherine Chidley allowed a wife's conscience equal authority to her husband's, and the Quaker Margaret Fell (afterwards the wife of the Quaker leader, George Fox) vigorously defended the right of women to a public voice like men.[12] There are, of course, far more conservative female voices, and women's publications frequently carry deferential prefaces, but for any woman to appear in print at all was a sufficiently remarkable thing in an age when it could be asserted – with rhetorical and satirical emphasis, certainly, but nevertheless with disturbingly serious intent – that 'whore is scarce a more reproachful name / Than poetess'.[13]

With such searching ideas abroad, those of more conservative temper were put upon explaining and defending their allegiance to traditional modes. That traditionalism focused its commitment on the figure of the executed Charles I and on the banned Book of Common Prayer: these became the potent symbols and badges of loyalism.[14] Theirs was a grievous and all but incomprehensible loss. From having had control of every lever of church and state, they found themselves deprived of all access to power largely by those who, in pre-revolutionary England, had counted for very little. Cromwell's achievement was certainly unprecedented in English history, inconceivable to conservative tempers and inexplicable to traditional patterns of thought. The struggle to come to terms with it marks Royalist literature of the mid century, and not only Royalist literature. It is one of the many fascinations of Marvell's 'Horatian Ode' to watch the figure of Cromwell breaking free from conventional patterns of praise; the poem is both fascinated and appalled, overwhelmed and apprehensive, as it recognizes that Cromwell's career can be contained neither within received constitutional ideas nor within the tropes of panegyrical rhetoric. Cromwell all but defeats words, as he defeated his military foes: ''Tis Madness to resist or blame / The force of angry Heavens flame'.[15] Marvell's ode opens with the rival claims of the active and the retired life: for Royalists and episcopalians, withdrawal from public life, and even exile, were their lot during the 1650s. As in 1660, when Charles II was restored to his throne, the Puritans would have to try to understand their defeat,[16] so, during the 1650s, Royalists and episcopalians had to come to terms with the apparent loss of their cause. In the poetry and prose of the period, retirement, retreat and isolation become the contexts for reflection and retrenchment. There is an elegiac note, and an unmistakable regret and longing, in the poetry of a Herrick, of a Vaughan, or a Philips, but there is hardly submissiveness.[17] Similarly, what we might be tempted to think of as fanciful excursions into the remote world of romance on the part of Royalist writers of fiction, and as escapism in their readers, prove to be resilient re-engagements with contemporary political affairs.[18]

The context for this political and religious speculation and debate, and in part the explanation for it, was the uncertainty and unpredictability of the times. Contemporary experience was overwhelmingly of disruption, disorder and disorientation; of, in the frequently cited words of Acts 17:6, a 'world turned upside down'.[19] For some, such as Gerrard Winstanley's Diggers, this overturning was rich with possibilities, possibilities of recovering Eden, or of building the New Jerusalem, perhaps even of welcoming King Jesus for his millennial reign.[20] Similarly, by Milton, the disputatious ferment which so distressed Baxter was construed as vital to continuing Christian commitment: 'Truth', he wrote in *Areopagitica* (1644), referring to Psalm 85:11, 'is compar'd in Scripture to a streaming fountain; if her waters flow not in a perpetuall progression, they sick'n into a muddy pool of conformity and tradition.'[21] Stability and security are deeply suspect to such a cast of mind; radical interrogation of received customs and beliefs – the pursuit, rather than the possession, of truth – is the mark of the true Christian. Such positive notes are resoundingly struck, but perplexity, if not anxiety and apprehension, even despair, are more often to be met with than radical fervour. Cromwell and the power of the Army ruined, in Marvell's words, 'the great Work of Time, / And cast the kingdome old / Into another Mold', but it was far from clear quite what that mould would be or how durable it would prove.[22] The state, as well as Charles I, lost its head on 30 January 1649; there ensued increasingly desperate efforts to heal the body politic. The 1650s are a period of constitutional experimentation, and of attendant uncertainty, as Commonwealth gives way to Protectorate, and its first constitution to its second; as offers of the crown are made to Cromwell; and as, in the eighteen months following his death, constitutions and governments change every few months, if not every few weeks. This was a world without the traditional assurances of security and stability, without readily recognizable emblems of order, a world in which customs, precedents, traditions and authorities could no longer be relied upon.

This uncertainty generated on every side an increasing public desire, and concern, to know what was afoot. Since what was happening in the formerly distant world of politics now bore immediately and directly on everyday lives, current affairs came to matter in a new, and urgent, way. The 'news' hence assumed its modern sense and importance. Newsbooks, the forerunners of the newspaper, were first printed in the 1640s, seeking both to inform and to give a partisan gloss to their reporting of events: John Birkenhead's Royalist *Mercurius Aulicus* was answered by Marchamont Nedham's *Mercurius Britanicus*.[23] (Subsequent historical, autobiographical and biographical accounts would have a similar eye to justifying party allegiances.)[24] As that implies, public opinion now comes to count as never before. Ordinary people (at least, ordinary literate people) were empowered by the uncertainty of the times and the competing claims to their allegiance of rival factions: what they thought, which side they took, mattered. Readers came to assume a new importance as the warring sides sought to enlist public support through the press; reading itself now becomes a critical activity. Attempts to promote one side and to discredit the opposition led to propaganda publications, such as Parliament's publication in *The King's Cabinet Opened* (1645) of the highly damaging correspondence of Charles I, captured at the battle of Naseby. This battle of the books is nicely exemplified by the direct engagement between the presentation of Charles I as a martyr to truth and justice in *Eikon Basilike* (1649) and its direct contradiction in Milton's *Eikonoklastes* (1649).[25]

Whether this disorder was the consequence of deep-seated constitutional and religious causes or of short-term frictions, whether it had the inevitability and radicalism of a revolution or the arbitrary contingency of war, historians debate. The older Whig view was that the century presented a steady march towards constitutional democracy. In the 1960s and 70s, the work of Christopher Hill, drawing out the long-term causes of the conflict and focusing on its radical wing, discerned in it the first European revolution in the Marxist sense of that word. It was, indeed, his books which established the term *English Revolution* to cover the period which had previously been referred to as the Great Rebellion, or the Civil War, and the Interregnum.[26] During the last twenty or thirty years, 'revisionist' historians, attending to the immediate experience of war in provincial lives unremarkable for political action or intellectual daring, have been less impressed by either the idealistic fervour of the participants or the clear-headedness of their aims. While not denying the motivating power of religious fervour or libertarian aspirations, their work registers the confusion and haphazardness of the course of events as strongly as ideological commitment.[27]

Debates about the appropriateness of the term *revolution*, or about its nature, do not, however, affect the sensitivity of the writing of the period to the turmoil of the times. This engagement with current affairs was not confined to such obviously topical genres as newsbooks. Early twentieth-century accounts of the literature of the period were accustomed to making a firm distinction between, on the one hand, ephemeral tracts and pamphlets which were 'merely' political or topical in their interest, and, on the other, works of literature which rise above immediate particularities to engage with universal truths. The contributors to this volume are among those scholars who, since the 1970s, have challenged and finally discredited this distinction. They have done so in two ways. First, by demonstrating that rhetorical skills are not confined to any particular form of writing, they have greatly extended the range of what falls within the purview of the literary scholar. Whereas older critical discussion had admitted to the canon from among the artisan class only Bunyan, and then with some embarrassment at his ignorance of literary decorum, critics now engage with the writing of an Abiezer Coppe, of Quaker pamphleteers, and, most signally, of numerous women writers of every religious and political persuasion. This admission of controversial and topical prose is evident, too, in reappraisals of Milton, who is now recognized not merely as an epic poet but as a writer of extraordinary prose.[28]

Secondly, recent historically sensitive critics have demonstrated that no genre, however sophisticated or elitist, is free from the pressure of its time. It is now recognized that the century's disputes, forcefully articulated in controversial prose, and the experience of war, were rhetorically refigured and imaginatively refracted in all genres, however seemingly distant from the conflict. There is no doubting that Marvell's 'Horatian Ode' is inspired by, and engages with, the constitutional crisis of the mid century; but it is there, too, in the pastoral retreat of Herrick and in the devotional exercises of Jeremy Taylor. Similarly, *Paradise Lost* is now read against Milton's times, as well as against Virgil or St Augustine. Far from rising majestically and timelessly above the seventeenth-century fray, Milton's epic is as deeply marked by contemporary experience as by Classical precedent, as implicated in revolutionary politics as in Christian theology. His portrayal of the War in Heaven owes as much to the Civil War, his Satan as much to the Stuarts, as do either to Homer or to the Book of Revelation.[29] It may be Biblical history which is revealed to Adam in Books 11 and 12, but it is seventeenth-century history which has resonated throughout the epic, as throughout all the writing of the period.

The chapters in this Companion are exercises in such historically sensitive reading. They seek to introduce students to the centrality of literary production in the English Revolution, to the generic range of literature's engagement with the revolutionary times, to the extraordinary number and variety of men and women who expressed themselves in print, and to the rhetorical power, imaginative daring and multi-vocal richness of their texts.

NOTES

1 Richard Baxter, *Aphorismes of Justification* (1649), pref. ep., sigs. A1–A1v.

2 Richard Baxter, *The Right Method for a Settled Peace of Conscience* (1653), pref. ep., sig. A11. The 'Enemy' is, of course, Satan.

3 Richard Baxter, *Reliquiae Baxterianae* (1696), 1.50–1, §§ 73, 74.

4 The productivity of the press is discussed more fully in John Morrill's and Sharon Achinstein's chapters below, pp. 21–3, 50–68.

5 For the occasion and course of these wars, see John Morrill's chapter below, pp. 13–31.

6 These issues are discussed in more detail in Martin Dzelzainis' chapter below, pp. 32–49.

7 Clarendon, *HR*, II:13, 206. For Edward Hyde, Earl of Clarendon, and his *History of the Rebellion*, see David Norbrook's chapter below, pp. 241–6.

8 On Bunyan, see Richard L. Greaves' chapter below, pp. 268–85.

9 A. S. P. Woodhouse (ed.), *Puritanism and Liberty: Being the Army Debates (1647–49) from the Clarke Manuscripts*, 3rd edn (London: Dent, 1986), p. 53, cited and discussed in Thomas N. Corns' chapter below, pp. 74–5.

10 Margaret Cavendish, *The Worlds Olio* (1655), preface, in N. H. Keeble (ed.), *The Cultural Identity of Seventeenth-Century Woman* (London: Routledge, 1994), pp. 47–8.

11 John Bunyan, *An Exposition on the Ten First Chapters of Genesis* (first published in Bunyan's *Works* (1692)), in *MW*, XII:147; Bunyan, *A Case of Conscience Resolved* (1683), in *MW*, IV:325.

12 Katherine Chidley, *Justification of the Independent Churches of Christ* (1641) and [Margaret Fell], *Women's Speaking Justified* (1666), excerpted in Keeble (ed.), *Cultural Identity*, pp. 201–3. See further Elaine Hobby's chapter, below, pp. 162–78.

13 John Wilmot, Earl of Rochester, 'Artemisa to Chloe', lines 26–7 (written 1674?), in Frank H. Ellis (ed.), *The Complete Works of John Wilmot* (Harmondsworth: Penguin, 1994), p. 49. See further the chapters by Susan Wiseman and by Helen Wilcox and Sheila Ottway, below, pp. 127–61.

14 These and their literature are discussed in Isabel Rivers' chapter below, pp. 198–214.

15 Andrew Marvell, 'An Horatian Ode upon Cromwel's Return from Ireland', lines 25–6, in *P&L*, 1:92. Marvell's view of Cromwell is discussed in Annabel Patterson's essay below, pp. 107–23.

16 This is one of the themes pursued in David Norbrook's chapter below, pp. 233–50.

17 See Alan Rudrum's chapter below, pp. 181–97.

18 See Paul Salzman's chapter below, pp. 215–30.

19 Cf. the title of Christopher Hill's seminal study of radical culture during the 1640s and 1650s, *The World Turned Upside Down* (London: Maurice Temple Smith, 1972).

20 For discussion of Winstanley, and of other varieties of radical optimism, see Thomas N. Corns' chapter below, pp. 71–86.

21 Milton, *CPW*, II:543. See further David Loewenstein's chapter below, pp. 87–106.

22 Marvell, 'Horatian Ode', lines 34–6, in *P&L*, 1:92.

23 See Sharon Achinstein below, pp. 58–60.

24 See David Norbrook's chapter below, pp. 233–50.

25 *Eikon Basilike* is discussed in Isabel Rivers' chapter below, pp. 205–6.

26 Cf. such titles as *Puritanism and Revolution* (London: Secker and Warburg, 1958); *The Century of Revolution, 1603–1714* (London: Nelson, 1961); *The Intellectual Origins of the English Revolution* (Oxford University Press, 1965). In the seventeenth century, the word *revolution* signified cyclical movement or rotation, rather than (as in the modern sense) abrupt change; it was hence not used of contemporary events. Contemporaries were more likely to describe as *innovation* what we might call a revolution in politics or religion (as noted by Michael Wilding, *Dragons Teeth: Literature in the English Revolution* (Oxford: Clarendon Press, 1987), p. 91). However, in 'The Word "Revolution"', in his *A Nation of Change and Novelty*, rev. edn (London: Bookmarks, 1993), pp.

100–20, Christopher Hill argues that anticipations of the modern sense can in fact be detected in seventeenth-century usage.

27 For a fine summary account of the differences between this position and Hill's, see John Morrill's chapter 'Christopher Hill's Revolution', in his *The Nature of the English Revolution* (Harlow: Longman, 1993), pp. 274–84. Historians of the 'revisionist' stamp include, besides Morrill himself (see his chapter in this volume, pp. 13–31), Anthony Fletcher, Conrad Russell, Kevin Sharpe and Blair Worden. For a useful introduction to the issues, see Ann Hughes, *The Causes of the English Civil War*, 2nd edn (Basingstoke: Macmillan, 1998); William Lamont, *Puritanism and Historical Controversy* (London: UCL Press, 1996); R. C. Richardson, *The Debate on the English Revolution,* 3rd edn (Manchester University Press, 1998).

28 See David Loewenstein's chapter below, pp. 87–106.

29 See the discussion in Nigel Smith's chapter below, pp. 251–67.

I
CONTEXTS

I

JOHN MORRILL

The causes and course of the British Civil Wars

Introduction

An assiduous reader of everything published in England or in English in the 1630s would find little evidence of a polity crumbling into civil war. The modern editors of the exhaustive catalogue of all such publications list around 750 titles a year for the decade, and it was pretty tame stuff compared with the publications of the final quarter of the sixteenth century when a virulent Catholic campaign was waged against the heretic-bastard-tyrannical Elizabeth, a campaign which called for her to be deposed in favour of the Queen of Scots (before that queen's execution in 1587) or a string of less plausible Catholic candidates thereafter. Furthermore, the Puritan polemic against bishops and against the 'innovations' of Archbishop William Laud and his henchmen – the restoration of stone altars against the East walls of churches, the insistence on the faithful kneeling at an altar rail to receive holy communion, the clamp-down on preaching by unbeneficed clergymen and so on – was turgid and uninspired in comparison to the vitriolic and effective polemic of the Martin Marprelate Tracts of the 1580s. Historical treatises, play-texts, ballads might ponder the evils of tyrannical government in the distant past or in places geographically remote from Britain, but the application to the Stuart realms was veiled and indirect: much more so than in the more vigorous historiographical and theatrical worlds of the decades straddling the turn of the sixteenth and seventeenth centuries.

Only a small part of this can be explained by censorship.[1] There was a licensing system for all published work, operated by the Stationers' Company (more concerned to protect their monopoly than to police anything but the grossest content of what they licensed), or (for religious works) by the bishops and their chaplains – more pro-active, but with plenty else to occupy them. There was blue-pencilling of religious works, and some authors were required to add glosses to their work, which they found irksome. This may have considerably heightened the amount of self-censorship (just as printers who wanted government business would be keen not to be seen to be printing material the court found deeply irritating), but there is no evidence of widespread suppression of work. One measure of all this was that those who wrote in Latin could be much more blunt than those who wrote in English. No-one was punished in early Stuart England for taking up extreme views in Latin, since such works were accessible only to an elite intellectually equipped to evaluate them. If Richard Montagu had written *A New Gag for an Old Goose* (1624) – with its attempt to make the doctrine and practice of the Church of England closer to Catholic teaching and practice than continental reformed Protestant teaching and practice – in Latin, there would have been no furore. It was, however, another matter to write it in the vernacular, to be read by the undiscriminating multitude. A handful of men who stepped over the line – and it really is only a handful of five men – were hauled before the courts and were whipped with knotted cords through the streets of London or were branded and disfigured by knife and hot iron. But those who could not live by widely recognized rules of limited self-censorship had the option of publishing abroad and smuggling their tracts into England; and *that* was subversive and resented by those around Charles I. So we return to our starting point. An assiduous reader of everything published in England or in English in the 1630s would find little evidence of a polity crumbling into civil war.

And yet by 1642 there was civil war in England. It is important to say 'by' 1642, because the raising of armies and the creation of the bureaucracies and engines of war was the culmination of a short but severe and acute crisis throughout Charles I's dominions, following on from the outbreak of civil war in Scotland and a Scots 'invasion' of England, and the outbreak of civil war in Ireland and an English and Scottish 'invasion' of Ireland. It is that which unlocks the mystery of how England could have an acute crisis in the 1640s without a chronic crisis preceding it.

The problem king

In 1625, Charles I's accession to the thrones of England, Scotland and Ireland was the most untroubled in any of those kingdoms since the fourteenth century. He was only the second of eight Stuart rulers in 250 years to have reached his twenty-first birthday at the time of his succession; most of the others had not even reached their twenty-first month. He was the first ruler of England since Henry V in 1410 to have a completely uncontested succession, with the partial exception of the seventeen-year-old Henry VIII in 1509. This was a great strength and removed the greatest single cause of civil war in the early modern period – a disputed succession. Paradoxically, it meant that although civil war was less likely than at any point in the six-teenth century, if there *was* a civil war it would get much nastier. To get rid of Charles I, one had to think of replacing not *him* but monarchy itself: hence the crisis of 1649. If only he had had a younger brother who did not get on with him.

Yet Charles I was a problem King. He had very strong and high-minded views of the nature of his office and the nature of the confessional state he was destined by God to protect and develop, but very few of his subjects shared his particular views. He was naturally authoritarian, seeking to develop policies not in the cut-and-thrust of conciliar debate and the give-and-take of Parliamentary management (the Houses would give him money if he would address their concerns, many of them neutral to royal author-ity), but in the internal forum of his own conscience, informed only by the advice of the ghostly fathers he chose to listen to. He would not listen to, let alone weigh up, any advice he did not want to hear. He had a strong sense of what was right; a poor sense of what was feasible. Hence, rather than reach uncomfortable accommodations with the English Parliament, from 1629 he suspended it *sine die*. Hence, rather than get the best diplomatic deal he could with the Spanish in order to give military support to the French Huguenots, or make the best diplomatic efforts he could for the Huguenots while fighting the Spaniards, he took on both super-powers simultaneously between 1626 and 1629 with predictable consequences. It was just as well for him that the eyes and arms of Habsburg and Bourbon were so fixed on the Rhineland and North Italy that thoughts of new Armadas were not enter-tained. Charles' supreme folly in this regard was his determination to impose his will militarily on the Scots in 1640 when he lacked any of the necessary cash, and the country lacked the political will to make it possible. Few if any believed the King to be a classical tyrant. However, self-righteous haughti-ness and a penchant for authoritarian ('wicked') counsellors like Thomas Wentworth, 1st Earl of Strafford, and William Laud, archbishop of Canterbury, induced a high level of anxiety within the political elite. A pref-erence for surrounding himself with first- or, at most, second-generation peers and for ignoring or cold-shouldering the older aristocratic families, with their wealth of land, cash and connections, compounded the problem. Not the least of Charles' problems in the early 1640s was a revolt of these *consiliarii nati*, those entitled by their ancient lineage to be his advisers.

Charles presided over a court that was less riddled with sexual and finan-cial scandal than that of his father. He was a puritan with a very small 'p' or, more accurately, a prude. There was a straitlacedness, an obsession with decorum about Charles' court; but much of the new regulation and cere-mony he introduced derived from continental *Catholic* models and that fed into the growing conviction of large numbers of his subjects that Charles was – deliberately, as a few thought; through inadvertence and the cunning of others, as many thought – a Catholic *Risorgimento*, or revival. A Catholic Queen, a beguiling Papal nuncio who had become the King's chess partner, secret (but known to the great-and-the-good) Catholics in the Privy Council and Household, high-profile converts, a Catholic chapel allocated to the Queen but packed with courtiers – there was much for anti-Catholic para-noiacs to fret about. By the later 1630s, the old Elizabethan and Jacobean fear of the enemy-without, conniving with a fifth column in the darker corners of the land, had been fatefully replaced by a fear of a conspiracy at the heart of the state, with the King as its dupe or complaisant agent.

And popery seemed to be implanted into the heart of the established epis-copal Church of England. The promotion of William Laud, first to the see of London (1628) and then of Canterbury (1633), with his own mentor and close ally Richard Neile at Winchester (1628) and then York (1632), trans-formed the agenda of the established church. The group they headed, with the full support of the King, were sacerdotal ceremonialists: they believed in the autonomy, dignity and divinely conferred authority of the priestly caste, in the restoration to the church of much of the jurisdiction and wealth 'plun-dered' (their word) from it during and since the Reformation. They believed in a strict (and at times strained) enforcement of the words and *rubrics* of the Book of Common Prayer. Episcopal adjudication was to replace parochial self-determination over the appropriate furnishing of the church and the precise forms of worship and of religious ritual. Most obviously, it was to be the bishop and not the vestry that decided where the communion table / altar should be (and that was normally against the east wall and to be made of stone, and railed off); and episcopal visitors would ensure that men and women knelt to receive the body and blood of Christ rather than sat around a table to commemorate Christ's death and resurrection: 'once offered, a full, perfect and sufficient sacrifice, satisfaction and oblation for the sins of the whole world'. Such a programme generated a rainbow-coalition against it: all the self-consciously godly believed that the Reformation was being betrayed; liberal intellectuals, whose thought was nurtured as much by Christian Humanism as by hardline Calvinism, disliked the clerisy; and common lawyers resented the challenge to their monopoly. Laudianism had few friends beyond the clerical estate and it was swept away in 1640–1.

A central plank of the Laudian programme was the restoration of the wealth of the Church. In England this amounted to little more than a series of legal challenges to agreements reached by borough corporations and the Church in the mid sixteenth century which commuted tithe payments (that is, the church tax of one-tenth raised on parishioners' incomes) for fixed (and non-inflation-proofed) sums. In Scotland and Ireland, however, it meant a much more substantial attempt to cancel many of the transfers of church land, including former monastic estates, or at the least to re-negotiate the terms and conditions on which they had been transferred, so as effectively to ensure that a proportion of the revenues were restored to the Church; and there was widespread fear that the same was intended for England. It was for this reason that an overwhelming majority of the descendants of those who had acquired church lands in the sixteenth century supported Parliament in the Civil War.

This fear for the security of former church lands was part of a more generalized fear that property rights were not safe under Charles I. His attempt to lay royal claim to lands reclaimed from the sea, his aggressive policy of securing crown interests in relation to the disafforestation of large areas of the west country, his encouragement to the Court of Chancery to interfere in areas that the common lawyers thought to be their preserve, and declining public confidence in the probity and independence of the judiciary (revealed by the blizzard of appeals to the House of Lords against their judgements in 1641), also reveal a serious deterioration of trust in the political system during the 1630s. The King's determination to keep himself free of Parliament by excessive use of his discretionary power to raise money by prerogative action was the coping stone on this process. Monarchs had for many decades been able to call on coastal counties to provide them with ships to defend the realm when there was a sudden threat of naval attack, but to convert this into an annual renewable charge on *all* counties under the pretence of on-going threats from Barbary corsairs was all too thin an attempt to use the letter of the law against its spirit.

It does not follow that anyone was planning a civil war. As we have seen, despite the inefficiency and complaisance of the engines of censorship, the perceived misgovernment did not produce a literature as violent in its clamour for change and for direct action as the events of the 1580s and 1590s had done. There was no literary campaign for the King's assassination or deposition; there was no direct call to resistance. More than 30,000 men, women and children migrated to the New World in the course of the 1630s, almost one per cent of the population, and a lot of more substantial men – future leading Parliamentarians including William Fiennes, Viscount Saye & Sele, and Robert Greville, Lord Brooke, and at least ten future radical MPs, including Oliver Cromwell – seem to have been very close indeed to emigrating; and certainly they discussed how to demonstrate their dissent by acts of passive disobedience – refusal to pay Ship Money and challenging the charges levied for the war with Scotland in 1639 and 1640 being the most obvious. England, however, was a long way from civil war in 1640.

A British crisis

The Scots were worse treated than the English. At the outset of his reign Charles had arbitrarily cancelled all the land grants made by his predecessors over the past 200 years. Although his intention was not to reclaim the lands but to re-negotiate the terms on which they were granted away, the principle of an inalienable grant being summarily cancelled caused true alarm, and not just north of the border. It was a Scottish Chancellor who observed that the King's actions rendered insecure every title to land from the time of King Fergus, the fabled first King of the Scots. Widespread passive disobedience broke the policy and it had to be abandoned as unenforceable. The Scottish Council ceased to make policy – it was made in London and delivered to Edinburgh for enforcement – and appointments in Scotland owed everything to patronage at Whitehall, and this caused deep resentment, while a belief grew that the Union of the Crowns had led to the end of Scottish self-government under a Scots King who happened to live in England. It was the attempt to promote the assimilation of the government, liturgy and practice of the Scottish Church to that of England which created the first great crisis of Charles' reign. Following Charles' calamitous visit to Scotland in 1633 for a coronation that exceeded his English coronation in popish flipperies (bishops in rochets and golden copes, a great crucifix woven into a tapestry screen behind the high altar, holy communion according to the full English rite), Charles proceeded to introduce new canons, a new ordinal and finally a new prayer book (based on the 1549 English Prayer Book, more conservative even than the Elizabethan Prayer Book of 1559). The contents of all three were inflammatory, but they were introduced without any of the appropriate consultative stages – they were not submitted to a General Assembly of the Presbyterian Church of Scotland, to a Parliament or even to the Scottish Council. This provoked a constitutional crisis as well as a religious crisis; and the Scots reacted by binding themselves into a Covenant of passive disobedience – a collective promise not to accept the cuckoo-worship. Just such a general protest had wrecked Charles' Act of Revocation cancelling his predecessors' land grants, but the signing of the National Covenant in 1638 had a different outcome. Charles did not capitulate: he set out to impose his will by force.

There was a war between the King of England and the Parliament of Scotland from the summer of 1639 to the autumn of 1641, and the King was the protagonist. It was Charles I who decided in 1639 to make use of those Scottish noblemen who remained loyal to him – principally the Catholics of the North East – together with the army of loyal Irish Catholics controversially assembled in recent years by Lord Deputy Wentworth and a scratch army scrambled together in England. It obviously took time to co-ordinate this multi-national force from across Charles's dominions, and the Scots were nimbler in their preparations, so that when the English lumbered up to the Borders the Scots were able to outface them in a stand-off. The resulting truce included clauses that required the King to accept the abandonment of every crown-sponsored church reform since the turn of the century. It was an ignominy Charles could not abide, and so he called an English Parliament to finance a second war. That Parliament offered him unprecedented sums of money in exchange for a guarantee of regular English Parliaments and the abandonment of the most offensive aspects of 'fiscal feudalism'. Charles, though, had no intention of dishonouring his agreement with the Scots by making what he considered dishonourable concessions to his English sub-jects; and so he dissolved Parliament after just two weeks and attempted to invade Scotland from England without the cash or a credit-line to support it. The Scots were nimbler yet this time, and headed south across the border before the English could cross it heading north. The disintegration of Charles' army left the Scots in control of Northumberland as far south as Newcastle (and thereby in control of London's coal supply) and they made it clear they would not return home until they had their war costs met and their Presbyterian religious reformation guaranteed by an English Parliament, and a new federal constitution in place that ensured an effective self-government for Scotland. From November 1640 to September 1641, the English 'Long Parliament', as it afterwards came to be styled, was under intense pressure from an occupying power to introduce changes to the government of church *and* state in England. The Long Parliament, however, was also in a unique position in English history. It was a Parliament that the King had lost the power to dissolve. Until the Scots were satisfied and went home, they were an occupying power insisting on the continuance of the Parliament. This gave the MPs a once-and-for-all opportunity to settle grie-vances. They could not afford to waste it. They spent several months driving 'wicked counsellors' from office – into exile, into the Tower, or onto the block; they passed a law ensuring that henceforth there were Parliamentary sessions at least every third year; they passed a law transferring to themselves the right to determine the length of their own sitting; they moved to restore to the Houses the authority to vet and to veto senior royal appointments – an authority spasmodically exercised in the fourteenth century but not since; they dismantled the Laudian regime but fell out comprehensively about what to put in its place. The King's ill will in giving his constrained assent to all this, his feckless attempts to use the remnants of his army to stage coups against them, his manifest determination to reverse as much as possible as soon as possible, radicalized many members. The breakdown of order around the country led some to call for an end to innovation and others to blame the King.

In the autumn of 1641, the Scots believed they had got all they wanted: payment by the English, a new constitutional *and* religious framework *within* Scotland, and the expectation of radical reform of church and state both *within* England and *between* England and Scotland. Scotland was now a self-governing kingdom with a fully Presbyterian church; and the English had agreed to developing a confederal constitution for Britain. Then, just as the Scots pulled out, there was a rebellion by the Catholic communities of the Pale in and around Dublin. It too seemed to come out of clear sky.

The early Stuart period had seen a significant drop in the levels of violence, of rebellion and of enforced plantation that had marked the period 1570–1610 in Ireland. However, it had not seen any diminution in levels of resentment and injustice. Nonetheless, the 1630s were a strange decade. The King's Lord Deputy, Thomas, Lord Wentworth (created Earl of Strafford only in January 1640), was sent to Ireland with one overwhelming objective: to make it less of a drain on the English Exchequer. To that end, he granted more freedom of religion to the Catholics than they had enjoyed for decades, and he raised revenues mainly by going after the New English and making them disgorge some of their ill-gotten gains. In the long run, his aim was to resume an aggressive policy of plantation that would have hit the native population; but in the short term, the Catholics did better than they had come to expect, and they watched Wentworth seek to rebuild *royal* and Protestant *clerical* power and authority at the expense of the colonial-settler interest. When he was attaindered and executed by the Long Parliament, the Protestant colonists sought to take their revenge; and the Catholic groups faced the bleak prospect of renewed religious persecution and expropriation at the hands of those very families and their English comrades who had already taken so much from them in earlier plantations. With English government paralysed in the autumn in 1641, and the Long Parliament solidly behind the Protestant interest, the old English Catholic leaders who had suffered most from the plantations saw not only the necessity but the opportunity for a pre-emptive strike to secure their own control, within the kingdom of Ireland, of the institutions of that kingdom. They launched a failed coup in Dublin. Alongside that, however, there was a second uprising, by the dispossessed Catholics of Ulster against those who had expropriated them a generation before, and either driven them abroad (whence many now returned) or reduced them to labouring on the land they had once farmed. Many personal scores were settled. Over time, as the repossessions got out of control, many hundreds, perhaps as many as 3,000, Protestants were killed and perhaps as many again fled to England, a sight as harrowing and inflaming as any modern refugee column. The stories, dreadful enough, were grotesquely exaggerated (and gruesomely illustrated in woodcuts) by the English press. Enough copies of atrocity stories were printed for every literate household in England to receive a dozen different accounts. It seared the English conscience and an Anglo-Scottish army was despatched to protect the remaining British-Protestant communities. To pay for this army, Parliament passed an act guaranteeing one fifth of the land mass of Ireland to those who lent £2 million – just over 1,000 so-called 'Adventurers' quickly raised the full sum. That army could protect the remaining Protestant settlers, but it became just one party in a bitter series of ethnic and religious wars that would see the population of Ireland drop by one third, and see nearly half the productive land of Ireland change hands.

The massacres in Ireland fed back into the growing sense of panic and recrimination in England. From the summer of 1641 parties began to form at the centre and in the localities, first around the future of the bishops and the Prayer Book, then around the control of the army needed to suppress the rebellion in Ireland, and finally over the King's summons of MPs to join him away from his capital. The Civil War no-one had planned and no-one really wanted came upon the nation largely unawares.

As the nation polarized, it did so in a way that had never been possible before. Men (and it was essentially a male choice) across the social spectrum, or at any rate the *literate* social spectrum, made free political choices. The economic ties between landlord and tenant were weakening, and many tenants defied the political preference of their lords. In towns all over England, men of the second rank took power from long-established oligarchies. Preachers in pulpits had an influence that had no precedent. Above all, the free choice of sides was possible because there was a revolution in the production of, and access to, the printed word.

A war of words

The paper war began with a flood of Scottish tracts pouring into England in 1638–9 seeking to explain to the English that what Charles had imposed on Scotland was not only wicked and ungodly of itself, but was a foretaste of what he would seek to impose on the English. Even more dramatic was the coverage of the massacres of Protestant settlers in Ulster in 1641–2, and, even more, the gross and grossly exaggerated accounts of those massacres and of the plight of thousands of destitute refugees who fled across the Irish Sea played on English anti-Catholic prejudices. Of the 1,500 pamphlets appearing in the months from November 1641 to the raising of standards and the outbreak of Civil War in England in August 1642, 1 in 6 focused on the Irish Rebellion, many describing atrocities (in lurid detail and with woodcuts more graphic than anything that would be presented photographically today). These were the bedrock upon which rested a polemic that portrayed Charles I and his bishops as, at best, the dupes, and, at worst, the passive agents of a Papist plan to recover Britain and Ireland. In the course of 1641 more than 200 pamphlets were published calling for the abolition of bishops, or at the very least their 'reduction' to the status of chairmen of diocesan boards of governors. About two-thirds of that number were published in defence of the Elizabethan and Jacobean order (shorn of Laudian 'innovations'). Rather less was published for and against the Book of Common Prayer; but the debate generated was still significantly larger than the debate on any single secular political issue. More than half the English counties drew up petitions to Parliament and/or the King calling for the retention of bishops and Prayer Book, and almost as many lobbied against (28 counties all told). There was no great pamphlet debate about the Annual Parliaments Bill (which became the Triennial Act); about the Grand Remonstrance; about the Attempt on the Five Members; about the Militia Bill; even about the Nineteen Propositions.[2] In January 1642, for example, there was a fierce literary debate about the protest of the bishops that their absence from the Lords (enforced by mass picketing of the Parliament by Puritan apprentices) invalidated the votes taken on those days, which generated five times as many items as discussion of the King's attempt to arrest the leading 'incendiaries'.

The paper war of 1640–2 was intense and it generated several new genres of literary text.[3] The systematic printing of religious petitions (and later of petitions for peace and a negotiated settlement) was the first. The widespread reporting of speeches by MPs, many of them fabricated (some ascribed to non-existent MPs; others put into their mouths by ghost-writers, perhaps with their collusion – as in the case of 15 of the 33 printed speeches by John Pym) was another; another, short 4- to 8-page graphic narratives of disturbances in particular parts of the country – many of them, too, invented, like the narrative of the Papist uprisings in Cheshire in the spring of 1642 or pitched battles in the Welsh marches in the late summer. In the twelve months from the autumn of 1642, the King's press corps and the Parliamentary press corps issued over 200 *official* declarations helpfully gathered together at the close of the year as Edward Husband's *Exact Collection of all Remonstrances, Declarations, Votes, Orders, Ordinances, and Proclamations, Petitions, Messages and Answers*. All this material was available across the kingdom. It could be supplemented by the four Parliamentary sermons (two in each House) delivered on the day of fasting and humiliation which was held each month. We know of a Cheshire MP who sent a large package home every month of all these kinds of material, with instruction that they be passed round the country houses and read out in churches and market squares – and the material he sent was from both sides; and we know of a Suffolk yeoman who received on subscription the fast-day sermons with their powerful political messages and demand for personal and national reformation. They were not alone.

As the war took hold, there were changes in the literary output. From mid 1643 there were weekly newspapers, normally in 8-page quarto, describing the course of the war and reporting major votes in Parliament (though not individual speeches). Initially these took a straightforward Royalist or Parliamentarian standpoint, but by 1646 the Royalist press was collapsing, while the Parliamentarian press took on factional hues, reflecting the tensions within a movement that had won the war but did not know how to win the peace. Hundreds of pamphlets described particular events, or contained reports from generals (Cromwell's battle letters were censored by Parliament, his pleas for religious liberty being excised).

The war of the three kingdoms

The Irish Civil War broke out in November 1641 and continued spasmodically until it merged with the full-scale Cromwellian invasion in August 1649 (leading to a conquest effectively completed by 1652, to be followed by outbreaks of banditry or guerrilla war down to 1660 and beyond). The English Civil War broke out in the high summer of 1642 and lasted until the King surrendered in May 1646; and was followed by a series of regional rebellions in the spring and summer of 1648 (and by Scots 'invasions' in August 1648 and August/September 1651); and the Scottish Civil War broke out in 1644 and lasted until late 1645 and then started up in a rather different form in 1649, lasting until 1651, when it was superseded by an English conquest and occupation that lasted down to 1660. There were civil wars in each of the kingdoms, but there was for much of the time *in addition* a single war being fought out across all three kingdoms.

The numbers of men in arms were immense – certainly a higher proportion of the adult male population than in the wars of the twentieth century. In the summers of 1643, 1644 and 1645 there were probably 150,000 Englishmen in arms (perhaps 11 per cent of the 1.4 million males between the ages of 16 and 50 in a population of 4.5 million). The proportions of adult male Scots and of males resident in Ireland in arms was almost certainly higher. At some point in the 1640s, perhaps 1 in 4 of all adult males probably bore arms. At least 1 in 20 males died as a direct consequence of the clash of arms, and as many again of the diseases characteristic of military encampment and confinement in barracks. These were traumatic wars.

The wars were fought in different ways and according to different rules in each of the kingdoms. In England, the death rate even on the losing side of a battle was rarely more than 10% and most usually about 5%, while something between 15% and 25% were taken captive. Officers might be ransomed, or exchanged, or released on a promise of not rejoining the war. Common soldiers were invited to change sides – and many, like most of the 3,000 Royalists who surrendered after the battle of Naseby (June 1645), did so. Others were simply disarmed and sent home. When a town surrendered at the end of a siege, the garrison and inhabitants would often negotiate terms which were usually honoured (typically the garrison was allowed to march forth with their colours but without their weapons, and the inhabitants would secure guarantees that they would not be plundered or required to pay the costs of the siege, and would be granted special exemptions from, or reductions of, the heavy fines levied by Parliamentary ordinance on all those who had assisted the King's cause). Occasionally towns (the two main examples are Bolton in 1644 and Leicester in 1645), or strongly defended houses (the most notorious example is Basing House in Hampshire), were stormed and massacres ensued, but even then the massacres were perpetrated in *hot blood*. There are very few examples in England and Wales of disarmed soldiers or prisoners, let alone civilians, being massacred in *cold blood*. Most of the small number of atrocities in the English Civil War involved a strong religious motivation.

It was very different in Ireland. There prisoners were routinely massacred, garrisons and civilians killed even when a town was surrendered on a promise of quarter; and much of the killing was in cold blood. Cromwell's notorious killing of perhaps 3,000 soldiers and an unknown number of civilians during the sack of Drogheda in September 1649 and of slightly fewer at Wexford a month later were the largest but not the most vicious episodes in which many hundreds were killed in cold blood, often clubbed to death to save bullets. The story of the wars in Scotland lies somewhere between the English and Irish stories, although both the maverick Royalist commander James Graham, Earl of Montrose, with his largely Irish Catholic army, and his Presbyterian opponents left few alive who bore arms against them and who fell into their grasp.

It was a war of fluctuating viciousness, then, but cumulatively a war which created tens of thousands of widows and orphans and many more thousand war invalids – a county like Cheshire was issuing war pensions to 453 certificated Parliamentarian 'maimed soldiers' as late as 1656. The national figure might be as high as 15,000, excluding the Royalists (many of whom took over the pensions after the return of the King in 1660).

The price of war

Wars are first of all expensive in lives; but at a lesser level they are greedy for resources. Many people had felt that Ship Money was an insupportable burden; and indeed more was collected from Ship Money in five years in the 1630s than from all the Parliamentary subsidies raised in the 1620s to support simultaneous wars against France and Spain. Yet at the height of the civil wars, Parliament alone was raising the equivalent of a Parliamentary subsidy every fortnight, or a full Ship Money levy every six weeks. In addition to that, there were many direct taxes for local and specific purposes (for the refugees from the Irish Rebellion, for the maintenance of Parliament's Scottish allies, for maimed soldiers). The King was asking for rather less, but relying more heavily on free quarter as a result. Some disputed regions were paying both sides simultaneously; and a 'liberated' region would be back-taxed. To supplement the taxes on land and income, both sides introduced (for the first time in English history) an excise, levying it on staple products such as beer and other beverages, on salt (the necessary preservative for all food) and on meat. Needless to say, each side expected their opponents to pay for the war. Wherever the King was in control, he asked grand juries to indict Parliamentarian activists of treason so that he could confiscate their estates; the Parliamentarians passed an Ordinance giving local committees the power to confiscate the estates of all they considered Royalists. In due course those 4,000 Royalists who had been 'sequestered' were divided into two groups: nearly 80 per cent were deemed to be 'delinquents' or lesser offenders, and were allowed to resume their estates on payment of fines that averaged two years' income and after taking oaths of loyalty to the Parliament; and the remaining 750 were deemed to be 'malignants' (such as the King's closest adherents and all 'Papists in arms') and their estates were to be confiscated and sold outright. Royalist land flooded the market in the wake of the sale of the lands previously held by bishops and cathedral chapters and the lands of the Crown. This was not an asset sale on the scale of the 1540s when the monastic estates were sold off; and it paled into insignificance in comparison with the confiscation and redistribution of 40 per cent of the land of Ireland from (Irish) Catholic to (English) Protestant proprietors, or the greater part of the estates of the Scottish aristocracy. Nevertheless, it was not negligible.

It was a war that affected regions and social groups very differently. Virtually no blood was shed, no battle fought, no siege endured in Cambridgeshire or Suffolk (except for some 'stirs' during the second civil war of 1648). The far north west, parts of mid Wales, Kent and Surrey witnessed only spasmodic violence. On the other hand, the Severn and Upper

Thames Valleys saw almost constant fighting and towns like Bristol, Chester, Newark and Worcester experienced several prolonged sieges. The most devastated areas were almost certainly the western and the West Midlands counties: divided at the outset, these were the battlegrounds where the Royalists made their major advances in 1643 and then steadily lost ground thereafter. The north-eastern counties of Northumberland and Durham experienced little fighting, but three years of military occupation by a Scots army that had to live off the country since the English Parliament failed to honour its obligation to pay and supply them made them feel (and certainly complain) as though they had the worst time of all. Counties like Cambridgeshire sent their young men off to war; they had to pay huge sums in taxation to sustain the war effort, and more was expected of an area free of fighting; but at least they only had to pay one side, crops were not trampled underfoot, town suburbs were not pulled down to make medieval walls more effective as barriers, and absent troops could not demand free quarter. Across the Midlands and West, many householders had to put up with unwelcome guests staying overnight or for much longer periods, eating what they wanted and taking whatever they pleased when they moved on: 'taken by the troopers when they left us, six yards of hose, a bible and other necessaries', recorded one farmer when those quartered on him moved away; while in the West Midlands another farmer complained that soldiers had requisitioned not only his calf, but the chair to which it had been tethered. Several parishes along the Welsh Border formally complained when Parliamentarian troops melted down their organ pipes to make bullets; and at Devizes Sir Ralph Hopton, finding his troops short of 'match', the greased smouldering rope used to fire 'matchlock' rifles, ordered the cords impregnated with human sweat to be torn out of the mattresses of the better-off citizens, for emergency use.

Most people's material world was falling to pieces in the 1640s, but so was their mental and spiritual world. Few people approved of the religious changes of the 1630s, but most people wanted a return to the comfortable patterns of Jacobean religious practice. The rhythms of the liturgies written for the Prayer Book by Archbishop Thomas Cranmer in the 1540s – with known and recognized patterns of prayer and response, with a liturgical year that fell in with the seasons and gave shape to a life of feast and fast, with high-points in midwinter, early spring and early summer – and with scope for local parish communities to adapt and develop the forms of the Prayer Book, had been disrupted by the autocratic centralism of the Laudian regime which commanded people to reorder their churches as they were instructed by their bishop, required them not only to follow the Prayer Book services in a particular way but to restrict themselves to those services laid out in the

Prayer Book, and reversed a century of inexorable lay expropriation of the wealth and jurisdictions bequeathed by the medieval church. What most Royalists, and initially most Parliamentarians, wanted, was the end of Laudianism, and the introduction of reforms of church structures that would hobble episcopacy so that it could never rise again, and a return to a sort of Anglican Congregationalism, local self-determination within the broad framework of the 1559 Elizabethan church settlement. Those who made the war happen, however, and who took control of the armies and the local war-time civil administration were committed Puritans, determined to discard the discredited half-way reformation, and to build on the experience of Geneva, Presbyterian Scotland and, above all, New England and the non-separating Congregationalist way. The need for military assistance from the Scots in 1640–1 and 1644–6 required a dialogue with the champions of the Scottish way, but a full-blown Presbyterianism was favoured by few in England. In the event, the Puritans could agree on what they would not have, but not what they would have, and the system hammered out by the Anglo-Scottish Westminster Assembly and diluted by the Long Parliament (what Robert Baillie famously christened 'a lame, Erastian presbytery') had no admirers within the Puritan cause and many opponents who began to clamour for the right of the righteous to gather in covenanted communities outside the national system. The issue of religious liberty and the benefit/catastrophe of religious pluralism became the new burning issue of the years 1645–8.

Within the national, parish-based church, much changed. One in three of all ministers were expelled from their livings; use of the Prayer Book and the celebration of the great Christian Festivals of Christmas, Easter and Pentecost were proscribed; churchwardens were placed under duress to remove all 'monuments of idolatry and superstition' from their churches, and in Suffolk and Cambridgeshire William Dowsing undertook the task of a roving commissioner and kept a remarkable diary of his bureaucratic icon-oclasm. Soldiers often anticipated or completed the minimalist response of the wardens. Cathedrals were closed down and converted into prisons, shop-ping precincts or preaching centres. The church courts vanished and their jurisdiction was transferred to justices of the peace (their office having been restored after suspension during the war years). In at least a third of the par-ishes, liturgy continued to be based on pared-down versions of proscribed Prayer Book forms, especially in the administration of the sacraments. Elsewhere, worship tended to be designed and dominated by the godly min-isters, who chose the readings, articulated the extempore prayer, and preached. This converted few. Meanwhile, Baptist churches were flourish-ing, and freer forms of experiential worship were spreading wherever the

New Model Army was stationed. For in the absence of chaplains, many officers, and later many troopers, had taken to breaking the Word themselves and encouraging prophetic and apocalyptic utterance by one and all. The venom and bitter self-righteous anger of the orthodox Puritan was no longer directed at 'Laudians' or even Papists; it was directed against sectarians. William Prynne, who had lost the tips of his ears for criticising the Queen for taking part in stage plays and the stumps of his ears for accusing the bishops of usurping the King's supremacy over the Church, now inveighed against the sects and against the 'atheism' of the Army; while the more irenic Richard Baxter – sheltering in Coventry, having been driven by popular Royalist feeling from Kidderminster where he had been town preacher – was profoundly shocked by the inappropriate religious enthusiasm of the New Model Army in the wake of its great victory at Naseby: 'a few, proud, self-conceited, hot-headed Sectaries had got into the highest places', he later recalled, 'and by their very heat and activity bore down the rest or carried them along with them, and were the Soul of the Army'.[4]

Baxter would not be reassured by what was issuing from the presses. From late 1645 in a crescendo down to early 1649 came passionate advocacy of religious liberty, and then the claim that there could be no religious liberty until there was political liberty. The group who came – from the autumn of 1647 – to be known as the Levellers demanded manhood suffrage, or at any rate the active political participation of all not in personal service or in receipt of alms, a constitution that itemized a set of natural rights – religious liberty and freedom from conscription foremost amongst them – which no King and no Parliament could touch, and an end to professional lawyers, professional clergymen, all who claimed a superiority of knowledge to lord it over others. They wanted an end to the discriminatory consequences of primogeniture, the granting to all tenant farmers of greater security of tenure, and the reversal of much recent enclosure, so that the poor could be endowed with the land taken from them by the greed of landlords. It fell short of the strict egalitarianism of Winstanley and the Diggers in the heady days of 1649–50, but it was menacing stuff to those who had gone to war to safeguard existing property rights and to create a Puritan confessional state.[5]

By 1646 the war in England was won. It was not a victory for better generals, more advanced military technology or tactics. It was a victory for the side that could keep its soldiers paid by ruthless taxation and sounder credit; and which had control of the seas (and therefore supply lines) and a cause that more of its soldiers were passionately committed to. More Parliamentarians than Royalists truly believed that God was on their side. The Scots were fed up and ready to go home; and there was stalemate in

Ireland, with the Protestants in control of the Pale and substantial parts of Ulster and the Catholic Confederacy in control of the other two-thirds of the island. A half-hearted expeditionary force sent in 1647 made little headway. Conquest was left to the greatest Ironside of them all, Oliver Cromwell, but only after the King's death.

Revolution

The Tacitean epigram 'they made a desert and they called it peace' was something of an exaggeration, but it was an exaggeration that informed many hearts and minds in 1646–7. Parliament had won, but at immense material cost and they had to build a new world on the rubble of the old. They had defeated the King but how could they stop him from being his old self once the general disarmament everyone clamoured for had been achieved? They told him their terms for the post-war settlement, and he ignored or spurned them. They modified them and it made no difference. A majority were willing to commit themselves to the disbandment of the Army without its arrears being guaranteed, without an adequate promise of a binding and comprehensive indemnity for the soldiers' actions in war (that chair attached to a calf was in someone's mind and perhaps on their conscience and there were many hundreds of worse cases); and they included the confirmation of the lame, Erastian but Presbyterian confessional state that most in the Parliamentarian Army abominated. And so the Army refused to stay silent. It petitioned and bullied the Parliament, and was faced by resentful denials and a serious attempt by a majority of MPs to raise a second force to compel it into early disbandment. The Army occupied London, purged Parliament a first time (in August 1647, of eleven 'incendiaries') and offered their own terms to the King, placing fewer restrictions on his powers, demanding a far more limited exemption from pardon for his own closest supporters, and permitting the return of the 1559 ecclesiastical settlement so long as the episcopate was jurisdictionally emasculated. In return they insisted on the senior officers and their civilian allies securing control of his Council, and they asked him to concede the principle of religious liberty to all species of Protestants. Charles saw it as a good deal, but he also saw in the disunity of his opponents the prospects for an even better one. As Army unity in turn disintegrated, and as calls grew within it for a settlement without him at all, he fled to the Isle of Wight and called for a second war to purge the kingdom of those who had drenched it in blood. He promised a Scottish faction that he would allow a Presbyterian experiment for three years, and a confederal union of the kingdoms, and he sought to build a rainbow coalition of Catholic and Protestant-landowner interests in Ireland. For several months the outcome of the renewed fighting in 1648 was unclear. The King's friends, however, each followed their own timetable and not an agreed one. Rebellions in the south east, in Wales and in the North followed one another in series and not in parallel, and the Scots delayed their invasion until the major rebellions in England had been dealt with. By the autumn the second war was over. Gradually the Army leaders, who had come to believe in late 1647 that the King must be replaced by one of his sons, but who doubted their own moral authority to be the agents of his deposition and death, became convinced that Charles I was a 'man of blood' as defined in the Book of Numbers (35:33), one who had shed innocent blood on whom God would have vengeance, and that he deserved to be deposed and probably executed. Yet still they hesitated. Could they handle the domestic and international fury that would result from the act of regicide? For weeks the Army leadership pressurized the King to abdicate in favour of his younger sons. They threatened him with trial and execution, but they delayed setting up the court. Miscalculating to the end, he called their bluff and he was indeed convicted before a court made up of the Army's closest friends and he was executed on 30 January 1649. If they were to stand their ground against all comers, the Generals had to establish a free Commonwealth; but few of those who signed the King's death warrant were strict republicans; and most of the true believers in kingless government – Henry Vane, Algernon Sidney, the more radical of the Levellers – refused to do so. This kangaroo court was not their high-minded route to the restoration of civic virtue. The blighted attempt to build that republic of virtue in the 1650s began with a public relations catastrophe.[6]

NOTES

1 See further the discussion in chapter 3 below, pp. 56–8.
2 These documents from 1641–2 are printed in Gardiner, *CDPR*, pp. 144–55, 202–32, 245–7, 249–54.
3 For further discussion of this topic, see chapter 3 below, pp. 58–64.
4 Cf. Introduction, p. 1, and the references there given.
5 For further discussion of the Levellers and Diggers, see chapter 4 below, pp. 72–80.
6 For the part played in this catastrophe by the publication of *Eikon Basilike*, see chapter 11 below, pp. 205–6.

FURTHER READING

Bennett, Martyn, *The Civil Wars in Britain and Ireland*, Oxford: Blackwell, 1997.
Carlin, Norah, *The Causes of the English Civil Wars*, Oxford: Blackwell, 1999.
Gardiner, S. R., *History of the Great Civil War*, 4 vols., London: Windrush Press, 1987.

Hughes, Anne, *The Causes of the English Civil War*, 2nd edn, Basingstoke: Macmillan, 1998.

Kenyon, J. P., *The Civil Wars of England*, London: Phoenix, 1996.

Morrill, John, *The Nature of the English Revolution*, Harlow: Longman, 1993.

   Revolt in the Provinces: The English People and the Tragedies of War, 1634–1648, Harlow: Longman, 1999.

   (ed.), *The Impact of the English Civil War*, London: Collins and Brown, 1991.

Ohlmeyer, Jane (ed.), *The Civil Wars: A Military History of England, Scotland and Ireland, 1638–60*, Oxford University Press, 1999.

   (ed.), *Ireland: From Independence to Occupation, 1641–1660*, Cambridge University Press, 1995.

Russell, Conrad, *The Causes of the English Civil War*, Oxford: Clarendon Press, 1990.

Stevenson, David, *King or Covenant? Voices from the Civil War*, Edinburgh: Tuckwell, 1996.

Young, J., *Celtic Dimensions of the English Civil War*, Edinburgh: John Donald, 1997.

2

MARTIN DZELZAINIS

Ideas in conflict: political and religious thought during the English Revolution

Liberty, absolutism and the ancient constitution

When the philosopher Thomas Hobbes (1588–1679) published *The Questions concerning Liberty, Necessity, and Chance* in 1656, he was attempting to close the debate on human freedom in which he had been engaged with Bishop John Bramhall (1594–1663) since 1645 when they were both exiles in France. As a materialist and determinist (that is, as one who believed that the universe consists of nothing but matter in motion, and that all movements are caused by the impact of other moving bodies, and so on in a sequence that leads back ultimately to a first cause or unmoved mover, namely God) Hobbes could not subscribe to orthodox notions of free will; for him, human mental processes were physically *caused*, just like everything else. Indeed, the 'occasion' of his debate on free will with Bramhall is itself wittily posited as the outcome of a causal sequence which began when the 'doctors of the Roman Church' first

> brought in a doctrine that not only man but also his will is free, and determined to this or that action not by the will of God, nor necessary causes, but by the power of the will itself. And though by the reformed Churches instructed by Luther, Calvin and others, this opinion was cast out; yet not many years since it began again to be reduced by Arminius and his followers, and became the readiest way to ecclesiastical promotion; and by discontenting those that held the contrary, was in some part the cause of the following troubles; which troubles were the occasion of my meeting with the Bishop of Derry at Paris, where we discoursed together of the argument now in hand.[1]

The Arminian Bramhall might dismiss the view 'that outward objects do determine voluntary agents by a natural efficacy' (*Hobbes and Bramhall*, p. 48), but to Hobbes' mind the course of his own life – including the fact of becoming a spokesman for free will – bore witness to the 'natural efficacy' of outside forces.

Despite his facetious tone, Hobbes was profoundly concerned about the power of ideas to shape events. The Civil War, he thought, was actually caused by a professor of theology at Leiden, Jacobus Arminius (1560–1609), who rejected the Calvinist teaching on salvation according to which God had predestined from all time those who would be saved and those who would be damned, arguing instead that individuals were free to accept or reject God's universal offer of saving grace. The ensuing dispute between the Arminians, backed by the republicans, and their Calvinist opponents, backed by the supporters of the House of Orange, led the United Provinces to the brink of civil war.[2] In 1619, the Calvinists triumphed at the Synod of Dort, where divines had gathered to resolve the issue, but the Arminians prospered in England under the leadership of Archbishop William Laud (1573–1645), who was already a key figure in the Caroline regime by 1629. The subsequent 'Arminianisation of the Church of England' alienated Puritans, for whom Arminianism was virtually indistinguishable from popery.[3] However, when the King and Archbishop tried to impose a set of canons and a liturgy upon the Presbyterian Scots, they provoked an outright rebellion – the so-called Bishops' Wars of 1639 and 1640 – which ended the eleven years of Charles I's personal rule without a Parliament and led, in due course, to the collapse of the monarchy.

Hobbes' analysis of the historical course of events cannot be discounted as the product of an idiosyncratic if powerful intellect. Not only did contemporaries adopt it (for example, Andrew Marvell in *The Rehearsal Transpros'd* (1672)), it has also been followed in its essentials by several modern historians such as Nicholas Tyacke and Conrad Russell. However, others at the time – including Hobbes himself elsewhere in his writings – focused upon the secular rather than the religious origins of the English Revolution.

One of the most powerful forms of political argument in the early modern period was that of appealing to the ancient constitution. This doctrine was, paradoxically, a recent invention – largely the work of François Hotman who, in his *Francogallia* (1573), concluded from research into the ancient laws and institutions of France that the monarchy must originally have been elective, and that the assembly of the Three Estates had the power not only to elect but also to depose.[4] This new mode of argument was widely adopted, and Pocock cites the examples of Holland, Sweden and Sicily to show that by 1600 'there was hardly any constitutionalist movement without its accompanying myth'. Nowhere was this truer than in England, where both the common law and Parliament were asserted to be 'immemorial and therefore beyond the king's power to alter or annul'.[5]

The English version of the myth was vulnerable in two ways. In the first place, the Norman Conquest appeared to represent a fatal breach in the continuity of these ancient rights. Not only had William I brought with him an alien law based on feudal principles, but he had also imposed it on the natives by virtue of his absolute power as conqueror. The common lawyers responded by denying that there had been a conquest at all: William arguably had a valid claim to the throne; had not changed English laws and institutions since most feudal usages antedated the Conquest; and had in any case sworn to confirm the laws of the Saxon king, Edward the Confessor (the first of many such supposed 'confirmations', including Magna Carta and the Petition of Right). The second challenge was mounted on abstract rather than historical grounds by absolutists, who held that the power of the monarch was not legally constrained and who hoped in this way to by-pass the ancient constitution altogether. Although they conceded that the law ordinarily circumscribed the king's power, they went on to point out that this could have no bearing on his *extra-legal* prerogative. In exceptional circumstances, it would actually be in the public interest for him to override the known law, regardless of how fundamental or ancient it was alleged to be. The king was, moreover, the sole judge of when such a state of emergency existed. This did not mean, however, that he was free to rule arbitrarily; on the contrary, the absolutists insisted that he was obliged at all times to observe natural and divine law (though accountable only to God for any transgressions).

John Selden (1584–1654) was too sophisticated a lawyer and historian to subscribe uncritically to either of these positions. Nevertheless he placed the blame for the constitutional crisis of the early 1640s squarely on the absolutist policies of the preceding two decades: 'So 'tis with the incendiaries of the state: they that first set it on fire (by monopolizing, forest business, imprisoning Parliament men *tertio Caroli* [the third year of Charles's reign], &c.) are now become regenerate, and would fain quench the fire; certainly they deserved most to be punished for being the first cause of our distractions.'[6] Charles I's inflammatory disregard for the liberty and property of his subjects was evident from the use of extra-Parliamentary means of raising money, such as monopolies (the exclusive right to trade in certain commodities), the exploitation of 'feudal' devices such as fines for encroaching on royal forests, and the imprisoning of political dissidents such as the MPs (including Selden) gaoled after Parliament was dissolved in 1629. All of these practices were among those condemned in the Grand Remonstrance presented to the King by the Commons in December 1641.[7] When the advisers who had formerly been responsible for these policies also disowned them and joined in the chorus of condemnation, Selden reminded them that it was they who had been 'the first cause of our distractions'.

Hobbes had no time for these defectors either, but, in his case, this was from the point of view of an unrepentant absolutist. The first statement of his political philosophy, *The Elements of Law Natural and Politic* (circulated in manuscript in 1640), was a systematic attempt to destroy the intellectual premises upon which opposition to the Personal Rule had been based.[8] Considering the causes of rebellion, Hobbes traces the 'false and pernicious belief' that tyrannicide is lawful to 'the writings of those moral philosophers, Seneca and others, so greatly esteemed amongst us'. The mistaken 'doctrine' that subjects could judge their sovereign 'proceedeth from the Schools of Greece, and from those that writ in the Roman state, in which not only the name of a tyrant, but of a king, was hateful'. The reason why these modern 'authors of sedition' are 'ignorant of the right of state' is because of their misplaced reliance on 'Aristotle, Cicero, Seneca, and others'.[9] Although Hobbes still cites Aristotle and Sallust approvingly in the *Elements*, he seems already to have formed the view that the humanist curriculum taught in the schools and universities was politically subversive.[10] As he later puts it in *Leviathan* (1651), nothing could possibly be 'more prejudiciall to a Monarchy, than the allowing of such books to be publikely read'. He even likens the 'Venime' (venom) imparted to the body politic by these classical authors to the hydrophobia contracted from the bite of a rabid dog:

> For as he that is so bitten, has a continuall torment of thirst, and yet abhorreth water; and is in such an estate, as if the poyson endeavoured to convert him into a Dogge: So when a Monarchy is once bitten to the quick, by those Democraticall writers, that continually snarle at that estate; it wanteth nothing more than a strong Monarch, which nevertheless out of a certain *Tyrannophobia*, or feare of being strongly governed, when they have him, they abhorre.[11]

Republicanism is, in short, a species of madness.

At the level of ideology therefore the conflict between Parliamentarians and Royalists appears to be replicated several times over in the opposition between Calvinists and Arminians, constitutionalists and absolutists, and republicans and monarchists. In each case, it seems, we find progressives and reactionaries squaring up to each other. However, these impressions can be misleading and may actually get things the wrong way round. For example, it is true that Arminian clerics tended to promote an inflated view of the royal prerogative, but since their Dutch counterparts sided with republicans, there was clearly nothing about Arminian theology as such which dictated an alliance with absolutism in England.[12] Equally, there was no necessary connection between Calvinism and political radicalism since we later find supporters of Parliament like Milton and John Goodwin abandoning Calvinist orthodoxy in favour of Arminian doctrines. The categories of progressive and reactionary simply fail to work out as expected. For, as Tyacke remarks, 'the Arminians and their patron King Charles I were undoubtedly the religious revolutionaries in the first instance' for abandoning the Calvinist foundations of the Elizabethan church, while it was their Calvinist opponents who were 'initially conservative and counter-revolutionary'.[13]

The confrontation between those who attributed to the royal prerogative the authority to dispense with the law and those upholding the rights and liberties of the subject is another case in point. In 1637, these were the stances adopted by the prosecution and the defence respectively in the trial of John Hampden for refusing to pay Ship Money (a levy on inland as well as coastal counties to equip a fleet). By 1642, however, and the time of the militia controversy over who controlled the raising of troops in the counties, the positions had been reversed. Now it was the two Houses and their apologists who used arguments from necessity to justify overriding the letter of the law, while the King's propagandists condemned these arbitrary doctrines and declared their allegiance to the known laws.[14] Thus not all absolutism was Royalist. Conversely, Charles' success in disowning absolutism and draping himself instead in the borrowed robes of the ancient constitution helps to explain how he was able to gather enough support to go to war at all.

'Mixarchy'

We need to be no less cautious when dealing with republicanism. Whereas Hobbes maintained that the humanists had been turning out classical republicans for years, many scholars have found few signs of this before the outbreak of the conflict in 1642 or even when it reached a climax in 1649. According to Zagorin, if republicanism is defined as 'a doctrinaire antagonism to all forms of kingship', then those 'who created the revolutionary government were not, for the most part, republicans. They put Charles I to death, not out of an antagonism to kingship, but because they had concluded that no other alternative was left them.'[15] 'English republican theory' was therefore 'far more the effect than the cause of the execution of the King in 1649'.[16] Indeed, the main spur to the 'republican speculation' of the 1650s was not so much the failings of the monarchy as the 'impermanence of the successive improvised regimes of the Interregnum' set up to replace it.[17] The consensus is that republican thought only came of age in England with the appearance of James Harrington's *The Commonwealth of Oceana* in 1656. How can Hobbes' claims about the headway made by republicanism before the war be reconciled with these findings of its belatedness?

The answer lies in how republicanism is defined. If taken in the strict sense of a doctrinaire opposition to monarchy as such, then there were far fewer republicans than Hobbes suggests. The picture changes, however, if what republicanism entails is a less strenuous commitment to a mixed constitution, in which a monarchical element is still present but combined with aristocracy and democracy. For the classical idea – derived from Plato, Aristotle and, especially, Polybius – that the best form of government consists of a balance between the one, the few, and the many was frequently articulated by English humanists from the sixteenth century onwards. This is why Sir Robert Filmer (1588–1653) was indulging in hyperbole rather than succumbing to paranoia when he complained in *The Anarchy of a Limited or Mixed Monarchy* (1648) that even the 'meanest man of the multitude' believes that 'the government of the kingdom of England is a limited and mixed monarchy'. It could hardly be otherwise 'since all the disputes and arguments . . . from the pulpit and the press do tend and end in this confusion'. What had given rise to this 'scandal' in the first place was the habit of seeking 'the original of government from the inventions or fictions of poets, orators, philosophers and heathen historians'.[18] Similarly for Hobbes in 1640 this 'error concerning mixed government' was another of the causes of rebellion (*Elements*, p. 167). Ten years later, he was sure that, but for the 'opinion received of the greatest part of *England*, that these Powers were divided between the King, and the Lords, and the House of Commons', there would never have been a civil war, 'first between the temporall factions of Parliamentarians and royalists . . . and since between the doctrinall faction of Presbyterians and Independents' (*Leviathan*, p. 127). Even long after the event, in *Behemoth* (published in 1682, but written in about 1638), he was still blaming 'the whole nation' for having been 'in love with *mixarchy*, which they used to praise by the name of mixed monarchy, though it were indeed nothing else but pure anarchy'.[19]

Further evidence of the diffusion of these ideas is provided by the fact that the most authoritative and influential statement of the theory of mixed government was issued not by Parliament or any of its apologists but by the Royalists themselves on the eve of the Civil War. In June 1642, two of the King's counsellors, Sir John Colepepper and Lucius Cary, Viscount Falkland, drafted and published *His Majesty's Answer to the Nineteen Propositions*, in which they argued that, there

> being three kinds of government among men, absolute monarchy, aristocracy and democracy, and all these having their particular conveniences and inconveniences, the experience and wisdom of your ancestors hath so moulded this out of a mixture of these as to give to this kingdom (as far as human prudence can provide) the conveniences of all three, without the inconveniences of any one, as long as the balance hangs even between the three estates.[20]

Colepepper and Falkland were trying to do two things at once: to identify the King more closely still with the ancient constitution and to translate that constitution into the classical idiom of the one, the few and the many. However, in doing so they gave several hostages to fortune, apparently abandoning the bishops, who until recently had sat in Parliament as one of the three estates (lords spiritual, lords temporal, and commons), and demoting the King from ruling over the three estates to being merely one of them. Paradoxically, it was the King's *Answer* that 'imported the possibility of a republican alternative into English political thinking'.[21]

The Parliamentary coalition

Clearly, these opposed sets of religious and political ideas cannot be mapped directly onto the conflict between Royalists and Parliamentarians. Not only did constant ideological repositioning make that conflict more complicated than is often supposed, but there were also several struggles for supremacy going on; between the King and Parliament, of course, but also *among* Royalists and *among* Parliamentarians. Indeed many of the most important and intense ideological debates took place within these armed camps rather than between them, with the result that there are lines of argument which make sense only when we realize that they were fashioned in response to internal clashes of opinion. What shaped the ideological landscape was not just a single fault-line but multiple fissures.

One such point of division, upon which the Parliamentary coalition eventually broke apart, was the question of whether the war was being fought to preserve or destroy the ancient constitution. In mounting their opposition to Charles I's religious policies, the Scottish Presbyterians, or Covenanters, naturally turned to the theory of popular sovereignty developed by their sixteenth-century Calvinist predecessors in France and Holland. According to this 'monarchomach' theory, the people are originally free by nature and, for their own benefit, merely delegate their power to those whom they thereby create their rulers. Should rulers employ these powers for their own ends rather than the welfare of the public, then they may be resisted and even deposed by the people, who remain ultimately sovereign.[22] Accordingly, when Alexander Henderson drew up 'Instructions for Defensive Arms' to be read from Scottish pulpits in 1639, he reaffirmed the monarchomach axioms that 'Princes principally are for the people and defence, and not the people principally for them', that 'the safety and good of the people is the supreme law', and that 'the people maketh the magistrate, but the Magistrate maketh not the people'. These 'common principles of Policie', he argued, were sufficient to justify resistance to Charles; indeed, nothing would 'excuse the people if they resist not his violence pressing them against the Covenant of God'.[23]

This militant tone was rather at odds with the caution which otherwise characterized Henderson's arguments and which was underscored when his work was published for the benefit of an English readership in 1642 as *Some Speciall Arguments which Warranted the Scottish Subjects Lawfully to Take up Armes in Defence of their Religion and Liberty*. For, in discussing the lawfulness of what subjects might do, Henderson did not wish to imply that the people either individually or collectively have the right to take matters into their own hands. Instead, he followed his Calvinist predecessors in specifying that the right to act against a tyrant belongs exclusively to the people's representatives, the so-called inferior magistrates. This was because the right to resist was like the entitlement to bring a legal action; since the magistrates rather than the people as a whole had been parties to the original contract with the king, it fell to them rather than the people to act upon any breach of its conditions. What all these theorists assumed therefore was that 'the constitution always remains intact'; provided that resistance was properly led there could be no question of a 'return to the equality and freedom of the first political society'.[24] The belief that a resort to arms need not dissolve the constitution also underpinned the Solemn League and Covenant of 1643; although this set out the terms on which the Scots would enter the Civil War on the Parliamentary side, its third article nevertheless consisted of an undertaking 'to preserve and defend the King's Majesty's person and authority'.[25]

For the Scots and their Presbyterian allies in England, the aim of the war was to secure some version of the mixed monarchy derided by Filmer and Hobbes, but other members of the Parliamentary coalition, especially in the New Model Army, saw much less call for a settlement that accommodated kingship. The most powerful spokesman for the officers and the Independents was Commissary-General Henry Ireton (1611–51), later denounced by the Leveller John Lilburne as 'the cunningest of Machiavilians'.[26] The *Heads of the Proposals*, drafted by Ireton and published in August 1647 after lengthy debates in the General Council of the Army at Reading, did retain a king, but only as a figurehead whose executive functions were assigned to a Council of State.[27] Even this was unacceptable to the regimental agitators and their civilian allies in the Leveller movement, who sought to commit the Army instead to a complete remodelling of the constitution.

Richard Overton (*fl.* 1631–64) had already set out the Levellers' thinking with exemplary clarity in a sequence of pamphlets. Thus in *A Remonstrance of Many Thousand Citizens and Other Freeborn People of England to their own House of Commons* (1646), he referred contemptuously to 'king-waste', and demanded that the Commons at least declare 'the intolerable inconveniences of having a kingly government'. He also condemned the Lords as 'monarchical', and urged that they be stripped of their 'negative voices' (the discretionary power of veto) since this was 'a perpetual prejudice in our government neither consisting with freedom nor safety'. Nor were the Commons exempt, being sharply reminded that all they had 'of us was but a power of trust – which is ever revocable, and cannot be otherwise – and to be employed to no other end than our own well-being' – a fine example of the Leveller tactic of turning Parliamentary propaganda back on its authors. And insofar as he did appeal to ancient liberties, this was only to point out that they had been lost at the Conquest: 'we remain under the Norman Yoke of an unlawful power, from which we ought to free ourselves'. Despite the common lawyers' denials, William had 'introduced the Norman laws', while Magna Carta was no confirmation of pre-Conquest laws but 'a beggarly thing containing many marks of intolerable bondage'.[28]

At this stage, the Levellers still hoped to achieve reforms through petitioning the magistracy, but when the Commons ordered the burning of their petitions in May 1647, they concluded that the constitution had in effect dissolved (rather as if the state of affairs that the Calvinist theory of resistance was designed to preclude had actually come about). Starting from here, the only way of 'setling an equall just Government' would be on the basis of their proposed constitution, *An Agreement of the People*.[29] This was drafted in time for a meeting of the Army General Council at Putney in October 1647, and at the centre of the scheme was a reformed legislature, elected on a new franchise, and answerable only to the people. There was no mention of the King and the Lords.

The premise of making a fresh start proved one of the more controversial features of the *Agreement* since the debate at Putney was initially dominated by the question of how far the participants were bound by existing engagements in the form of the Army's *Representation* of 14 June 1647[30] and the *Heads*. John Wildman (1623–93) summed up the issue from a Leveller point of view: that 'whereas it is desired that engagements may be considered, I shall desire that only the justice of the thing that is proposed may be considered'. Justice took precedence in any case, he argued, since unjust engagements 'could lawfully be broken'. Replying for the officers, Ireton agreed that 'if a man have engaged himself to a thing that is not just', then he could not be 'bound to perform' it. The catch was that the question of whether something was just or unjust could not be resolved – or even be meaningfully formulated – outside the conceptual framework of contract. For the fundamental rule of justice, the 'general ground of righteousness', was simply 'that we should keep covenant one with another' (*Army Debates*, pp. 24–6).

Underlying the procedural wrangle was a basic difference of outlook. The strong notion of contract with which Ireton worked meant that he was unwilling to describe as unjust any government to which the people might conceivably have agreed:

> The government of Kings, or of Lords, is as just as any in the world, is the justest government in the world. *Volenti non fit injuria.* Men cannot wrong themselves willingly, and if they will agree to make a King, and his heirs [their ruler] there's no injustice. They may either make it hereditary or elective. They may give him an absolute power or a limited power. Here hath been agreements of the people that have agreed with this. There hath been such an agreement when the people have fought for their liberty, and have established the King again.

Whatever the agreed arrangement, however, it was binding: 'Any man that makes a bargain, and does find afterwards 'tis for the worse, yet is bound to stand to it' (*Army Debates*, p. 122). This was one of Ireton's most telling speeches but essentially he was going over old ground. Thus on the opening day, Wildman singled out a 'dangerous' principle, 'spreading abroad in the Army *again*' (my emphasis), that

> when persons once be engaged, though the engagement appear to be unjust, yet the person must sit down and suffer under it; and that therefore, in case a Parliament, as a true Parliament, doth anything unjustly, if we be engaged to submit to the laws that they shall make, though they make an unjust law, though they make an unrighteous law, yet we must swear obedience.
>
> (*Army Debates*, p. 24)

Indeed, it was precisely in order to rule out the possibility of this kind of Parliamentary absolutism that article four of the *Agreement* insisted that 'all future representatives of this Nation' would be barred from legislating on a range of 'reserved' matters such as 'religion and the wayes of Gods Worship'.[31]

Liberty of conscience

Religion, and in particular the question of the form a state church should take, proved no less divisive for the Parliamentary coalition. Once again, the Presbyterians' aims were enshrined in the Solemn League and Covenant: firstly, 'to bring the churches of God in the three kingdoms to the nearest conjunction and uniformity', and, secondly, to 'endeavour the extirpation of Popery, prelacy . . . superstition, heresy, schism, profaneness'.[32] This drive towards doctrinal and organizational uniformity was opposed by the Independents, who favoured a looser form of association between congregations of like-minded believers. They found it easy to embarrass the Presbyterians by turning on them the arguments they themselves had used against the Laudian church (analogous to the way in which the Levellers recycled Parliamentary materials in their struggles with the Lords and Commons). Potentially, however, there was no end to this kind of outflanking manoeuvre, as the Independents found when their form of governance was criticized in turn by the radical separatists.

Several works were shaped by these developments, including Milton's *Areopagitica* (1644), but few are more revealing than *The Ancient Bounds, or Liberty of Conscience, Tenderly Stated, Modestly Asserted, and Mildly Vindicated* (1645), attributed to Francis Rous the Elder (1579–1659). Remarkably, more than half a century separates Rous' publication of his Spenserian poem *Thule* in 1598 from the time when, as Provost of Eton, he came into contact with Marvell, who arrived as a tutor in 1653. As a Parliamentary campaigner against Arminianism, Rous was prominent in the attack during the 1628 session on Roger Manwaring (one of the King's chaplains who had delivered a pair of controversial sermons on *Religion and Allegiance* the year before). He led the debate on Arminianism with his stepbrother John Pym in 1629, and in 1641 presented to the Lords the articles impeaching Bishop John Cosin for his Arminianizing policies at Durham and elsewhere. Pro-Scottish as well as anti-Arminian, Rous nevertheless began to shift his position towards Independency in the mid 1640s, finding himself 'strangely led' by 'the instinct of *Providence*' in a direction 'contrary to those prae-engagements' (*Ancient Bounds*, sig. A3v).

Reacting to Presbyterian assertions of the magistrate's duty to suppress departures from nationally established norms of religious practice, Rous produces a variety of arguments 'against all externall compulsion in Religion' to demonstrate that it must be misplaced or ineffectual or both. Firstly, since 'the Magistrate cannot reach the *mind*', it follows that 'he ought not to punish the *outward* man'. Man is both a natural and spiritual creature, and since 'they are *men* before they are *Christians*', Rous warns, 'for faultinesse in Christianity, you must not destroy the *man*'. The individual is also compartmentalized in his religious and political capacities, such that he may hold 'some heterodox opinions' and still be 'a good subject'. Admittedly, the magistrate could intervene if he 'disturbed the publique peace by the turbulent managing of his opinion', but to violate his '*politick* beeing or priviledges' on account of his religious beliefs alone would be 'to punish *one* man for *another* mans fault' (*Ancient Bounds*, pp. 18, 22–3).

Rous also seeks to undermine his opponents' dogmatism by drawing extensively on *Of Wisdom* (1608), a translation of *De la sagesse* (1601) by the French sceptic Pierre Charron.[33] Rous converts Charron's central argument – that since we lack a way of arriving at the truth of any proposition the wisest course is to suspend our judgement – into an attack on Presbyterian certitude. How, he asks (quoting Charron),

> should we be capable to know more, if we grow *resolute* in our opinions, settle and repose ourselves in certain things, and in such manner, that we seeke no farther, nor examine any more, that which we thinke we *hold*. – They know not that there is a kind of ignorance and *doubt*, more learned and certain, more noble and generous then all their *science* and certainty.   (*Ancient Bounds*, p. 37)

Rous is careful to insist from the outset that '*I contend not for variety of opinions, I know there is but one truth*' (sig. A4v). In the absence of certainty, however, there can be no resting secure in the possession of the truth, only a *process* of truth-seeking in which its apprehension is constantly deferred:

> The running water keeps pure and cleare, when the standing poole corrupts; that's the sense of the Proverbiall speech, *An Academick, or Pyrrhonian was never heretick*. While men *sleep* in a carnall recumbency upon their Doctors and Teachers, the Devill *sowes tares*; the true temper and proper imployment of a Christian, is always to be working like the Sea, and purging ignorance out of his understanding, and exchanging notions and apprehensions imperfect for more perfect, and forgetting things behinde to presse forward. (p. 34)

Here, at least, Rous recreates some of the sublime restlessness of *Areopagitica* (cf. Milton, *CPW*, II: 543, 551).

However, his commitment to these principles was not open-ended. For although, as Coffey has recently shown, the number of those 'within the puritan community who argued passionately for the toleration of *false* religion' was greater than has been supposed, Rous was not one of them.[34] Thus he excluded, for example, 'the doctrines of the *Papists*' from toleration on the grounds that the magistrate could punish infringements of the law of nature that were capable of being discerned as such by natural reason. Polytheism, atheism and idolatry arguably fell in this category, being things 'which a *Heathens* light should not tolerate', but Rous also wanted the magistrate to restrain specific 'errors' such as Arianism, Socinianism and Familism by having the 'publique preaching or printing' of them 'interdicted'. At this point, however, his argument began to collapse because, as he conceded, the doctrines at issue – 'the article of the *Trinity*, or the *person* and *Office* of Jesus Christ' – are not discernible 'by the light of Nature' but are culturally acquired. After suggesting, unconvincingly, that these articles of faith are at least quasi-natural because 'Custome or Education is another nature', Rous abandoned this aspect of his case altogether (*Ancient Bounds*, pp. 2, 4, 7, 8).

The dilemma for Rous (as for many Independents) was that in maintaining against the Presbyterians that doubt is better than certainty he opened the door to beliefs he found objectionable, and that in setting limits to toleration which excluded these beliefs he implied that there are certainties after all, so undermining the anti-Presbyterian case. Nothing had been resolved when the officers met at Whitehall in December 1648 to debate 'Whether the magistrate have, or ought to have, any compulsive and restrictive power in matters of religion'. Colonel Nathaniel Rich was sure no-one present thought the magistrate should 'persecute any honest man that walks according to his conscience in those things that are really religious', but the problem was 'that we cannot find out any way to discriminate this [liberty] from that exorbitant liberty which those that are not religious, but would pretend to be so, would take'. Once again Ireton and Wildman confronted each other, with Ireton insisting that any actions which are contrary to the first four Commandments 'are things against which there is a testimony in light of nature, and consequently they are things that men as men are in some capacity [to judge of]' *(Army Debates,* pp. 125, 149, 154). Wildman replied that

> it is not easy by the light of nature to determine [more than that] there is a God. The sun may be that God. The moon may be that God. To frame a right conception or notion of the First Being, wherein all other things had their being, is not [possible] by the light of nature . . . And therefore the magistrate cannot easily determine what sins are against the light of nature, and what not.
>
> (p. 161)

A state based on this minimalist account of the light of nature would have no investment in one form of religion rather than another – or even in any religion at all.

Royalist reactions

The defeated Royalists did not merely look on in horror. Charles I's surrender in 1646 was the prelude to negotiations with the various groups in the victorious coalition, a process which was complicated by – and in turn exacerbated – ideological splits among the Royalist exiles.[35] One faction urged the King to reach an agreement with the Independents by conceding toleration, while the policy of Queen Henrietta Maria's circle was for him to settle with the Scots by agreeing to introduce Presbyterianism. Yet another faction led by Edward Hyde (1609–74), chief architect of the Royalist constitutionalism of the early 1640s, vehemently opposed any deal whatsoever at the expense of the Anglican Church. Early in January 1647 Hyde was still hoping the King would keep to 'a resolution of riding out this storm by those principles which will better defend him (whatever new politicks are read) than a union with either faction', but, only days before, Charles had signed up to the Covenant in return for the Scots' military intervention.[36] However, neither Charles' defeat in the second Civil War nor his execution in 1649 ended Royalist divisions for, by 1650, the Scots were again making overtures, this time to Charles II.

The most prominent exponent of the 'new politicks' was Hobbes, whose patron William Cavendish, Marquis (and afterwards Duke) of Newcastle, was a member of Henrietta Maria's circle. A willingness to sacrifice the Anglican interest distanced Hobbes still further from Hyde and Bramhall. Even before their debate on free will, Bramhall had sent Hobbes 'sixty exceptions' to his *De cive* [*On the Citizen*] (1642), a Latin version of the *Elements of Law*.[37] Though these have been lost, one topic they differed on was the theory of conquest, which was mainly used by Royalists to establish the non-elective nature of the English monarchy and thereby remove one of the grounds on which resistance was based. Thus Bramhall had argued in *The Serpents Salve* (1643) that 'His Majesties originall Title to this kingdome was not Election, either of the Person, or of the Family, but Conquest'. However, he dissociated himself from the stronger argument that because the monarchy originated in conquest it was therefore absolute. He had no wish 'to enslave our Nation as Conquered Vassals. It is a grosse fallacy to dispute . . . from the right of absolute Conquerers to His Majesty now, as if so many good Lawes, so many free Charters, so many acts of Grace in so long a succession had operated nothing' (p. 8). Even so, since the rights of the subject were a royal gift, they could not be pleaded against the King. In *De cive*, Hobbes did not regard conquest and consent as incompatible. Indeed his account of how men were able to leave a state of nature actually depended on assuming that agreements 'extorted by fear' are binding, because otherwise those agreements 'by which men unite in civil life are invalid (for one's submission to government by another person is motivated by fear of mutual slaughter)'. Voluntary submission and fear were as compatible as liberty was with necessity.[38]

Fundamentally, what marked Hobbes off from most Royalists was the assumption he shared with theorists of popular sovereignty that mankind was originally free and equal. Other Royalists argued that the premise of original freedom is mistaken because men were not born free but subject to paternal power which in turn derived from God's gift of dominion to Adam, but this was an argument Hobbes consistently undermined by maintaining that children in fact belong to their mothers (see *Elements of Law*, pp. 130–1, and *On the Citizen*, pp. 108–10). The most noted exponent of the patriarchalist thesis was Filmer, who in his *Observations Concerning the*

Originall of Government (1652) strikingly conjoined Hobbes, Milton and Grotius as representatives of the opposing school of thought. As this conjunction suggests, Hobbes was ideologically better placed than any other Royalist to come to terms with the new regime in England. In the Review and Conclusion to *Leviathan* he set out the grounds for submission to the Commonwealth, and by 1656 was claiming that this had 'framed the minds of a thousand gentlemen to a conscientious obedience to present government, which otherwise would have wavered in that point'.[39] Still in exile, Hyde observed that Hobbes 'could not abstain from bragging in a Pamphlet ... that he alone, and his doctrine, had prevail'd with many to submit to the Government', and added it to the list of 'the Enormities of Mr *Hobbes* and his *Leviathan*'.[40]

One of those whose minds were framed to obedience (and who also incurred Hyde's wrath) was Abraham Cowley, who had known Hobbes from his time in Paris as the Queen's secretary. In 1656, with the Royalist cause extinguished, and with Cromwell immovably established as Protector, Cowley thought the time was right to propose ideological disarmament in the Preface to his *Poems*.

> Now though in all *Civil Dissentions*, when they break into open hostilities, the *War* of the *Pen* is allowed to accompany that of the *Sword*, and every one is in a maner obliged with his *Tongue*, as well as *Hand*, to serve and assist the side which he engages in; yet when the event of battel, and the unaccountable *Will* of *God* has determined the controversie, and that we have submitted to the conditions of the *Conqueror*, we must lay down our *Pens* as well as *Arms*, we must *march* out of our *Cause* it self, and *dismantle* that, as well as our *Towns* and *Castles*, of all the *Works* and *Fortifications* of *Wit* and *Reason* by which we defended it.[41]

While Cowley may have been aware of the depth of republican opposition to Cromwell, led by Harrington and others, he could not have foreseen how quickly the regime would collapse in the later 1650s. Like other proclamations of the end of ideology, this one turned out to be distinctly premature.

NOTES

1 Vere Chappell (ed.), *Hobbes and Bramhall on Liberty and Necessity* (Cambridge University Press, 1999), p. 70.
2 See Richard Tuck, *Philosophy and Government, 1572–1651* (Cambridge University Press, 1993), pp. 181–4.
3 Nicholas Tyacke, 'Puritanism, Arminianism and Counter-revolution', in Richard Cust and Anne Hughes (eds.), *The English Civil War* (London: Arnold, 1997), p. 149.
4 See Quentin Skinner, *The Foundations of Modern Political Thought*, 2 vols. (Cambridge University Press, 1978), II: 270, 311–15.

5 J. G. A. Pocock, *The Ancient Constitution and the Feudal Law* (Cambridge University Press, 1987), pp. 16–17. For differences between English and European constitutionalism, see Glenn Burgess, *The Politics of the Ancient Constitution* (Basingstoke: Macmillan, 1992), pp. 15–18.

6 John Selden, *The Table-Talk* (1800), p. 51, *s.v.* 'Incendiaries'.

7 See Gardiner, *CDPR*, pp. 209–12.

8 See further Martin Dzelzainis, 'Edward Hyde and Thomas Hobbes's *Elements of Law, Natural and Politic*', *HJ*, 32 (1989), 303–17.

9 Thomas Hobbes, *The Elements of Law Natural and Politic*, in J. C. A. Gaskin (ed.), *Human Nature and De Corpore Politico* (Oxford University Press, 1994), pp. 168–70.

10 See Quentin Skinner, *Reason and Rhetoric in the Philosophy of Hobbes* (Cambridge University Press, 1996), pp. 250–93.

11 Thomas Hobbes, *Leviathan*, ed. Richard Tuck (Cambridge University Press, 1996), p. 226.

12 See Burgess, *Ancient Constitution,* pp. 181–9.

13 See Tyacke, 'Puritanism, Arminianism and Counter-revolution', p. 138.

14 See Michael Mendle, *Henry Parker and the English Civil War* (Cambridge University Press, 1995), pp. 70–89.

15 Perez Zagorin, *A History of Political Thought in the English Revolution* (Bristol: Thoemmes Press, 1997), pp. 146, 148.

16 J. G. A. Pocock and Gordon J. Schochet, 'Interregnum and Restoration', in J. G. A. Pocock (ed. with the assistance of Gordon J. Schochet and Lois G. Schwoerer), *The Varieties of British Political Thought 1500–1800* (Cambridge University Press, 1993), p. 148.

17 Blair Worden, 'Milton's Republicanism and the Tyranny of Heaven', in Gisela Bock, Quentin Skinner and Maurizio Viroli (eds.), *Machiavelli and Republicanism* (Cambridge University Press, 1993), p. 226.

18 Sir Robert Filmer, *Patriarcha and Other Writings*, ed. Johann P. Sommerville (Cambridge University Press, 1991), p. 133.

19 Thomas Hobbes, *Behemoth or the Long Parliament*, ed. Ferdinand Tönnies, introduced by Stephen Holmes (University of Chicago Press, 1990), pp. 116–17.

20 In J. P. Kenyon (ed.), *The Stuart Constitution 1603–1668* (Cambridge University Press, 1976), p. 21.

21 Pocock, *Ancient Constitution*, p. 310.

22 See Skinner, *Foundations*, II: 318–48.

23 Ian Michael Smart, 'The Political Thought of the Scottish Covenanters, 1638–88', *History of Political Thought*, 1 (1980), 169, 171.

24 David Wootton (ed.), *Divine Right and Democracy: An Anthology of Political Writing in Stuart England* (Harmondsworth: Penguin, 1986), p. 45.

25 Gardiner, *CDPR*, p. 269.

26 William Haller and Godfrey Davies (eds.), *The Leveller Tracts 1647–1653* (Gloucester, Mass.: Peter Smith, 1964), p. 423.

27 See Gardiner, *CDPR*, p. 320.

28 Andrew Sharp (ed.), *The English Levellers* (Cambridge University Press, 1998), pp. 33, 35, 36, 38, 45, 46–7.

29 G. E. Aylmer (ed.), *The Levellers in the English Revolution* (London: Thames and Hudson, 1975), p. 93.

30 For which, see A. S. P. Woodhouse (ed.), *Puritanism and Liberty. Being the Army Debates (1647–9)*, 3rd edn (London: Dent, 1986), pp. 403–9.
31 Aylmer, *Levellers*, p. 90.
32 Gardiner, *CDPR*, pp. 268–9.
33 See Tuck, *Philosophy and Government*, pp. 83–8.
34 John Coffey, 'Puritanism and Liberty Revisited: The Case for Toleration in the English Revolution', *HJ*, 41 (1998), 962.
35 Tuck, *Philosophy and Government*, pp. 270, 320–1.
36 'Martin Dzelzainis, '"Undouted Realities": Clarendon on Sacrilege', *HJ*, 33 (1990), 517; see Gardiner, *CDPR*, pp. 347–52.
37 Chappel (ed.), *Hobbes and Bramhall*, p.15.
38 Thomas Hobbes, *On the Citizen* [*De cive*], ed. Richard Tuck and trans. Michael Silverthorne (Cambridge University Press, 1998), pp. 38–9; see Chappell (ed.), *Hobbes and Bramhall*, pp. 30, 54.
39 Johann P. Sommerville, *Thomas Hobbes: Political Ideas in Historical Context* (Basingstoke: Macmillan, 1992), p. 67.
40 Edward Hyde, Earl of Clarendon, *A Survey of Mr Hobbes His Leviathan*, in G. A. J. Rogers (ed.), *Leviathan: Contemporary Responses to the Political Theory of Thomas Hobbes* (Bristol: Thoemmes, 1995), pp. 237, 297.
41 Abraham Cowley, *The Essays and Other Prose Writings*, ed. A. B. Gough (Oxford: Clarendon Press, 1915), p. 9.

FURTHER READING

For individual editions of primary texts cited or discussed, please see the notes above.

Aylmer, G. E. (ed.), *The Levellers in the English Revolution*, London: Thames and Hudson, 1975.
Burgess, Glenn, *The Politics of the Ancient Constitution: An Introduction to English Political Thought, 1603–1642*, Basingstoke: Macmillan, 1992.
Chappell, Vere (ed.), *Hobbes and Bramhall on Liberty and Necessity*, Cambridge University Press, 1999.
Coffey, John, 'Puritanism and Liberty Revisited: The Case for Toleration in the English Revolution', *HJ*, 41 (1998), 961–85.
Dzelzainis, Martin, 'Edward Hyde and Thomas Hobbes's *Elements of Law, Natural and Politic*', *HJ*, 32 (1989), 303–17.
'"Undouted Realities": Clarendon on Sacrilege', *HJ*, 33 (1990), 515–40.
Haller, William, and Godfrey Davies (eds.), *The Leveller Tracts, 1647–1653*, reprint. Gloucester, Mass.: Peter Smith, 1964.
Kenyon, J. P. (ed.), *The Stuart Constitution 1603–1668: Documents and Commentary*, Cambridge University Press, 1976.
Mendle, Michael, *Henry Parker and the English Civil War: The Political Thought of the Public's 'Privado'*, Cambridge University Press, 1995.
Peltonen, Markku, *Classical Humanism and Republicanism in English Political Thought 1570–1640*, Cambridge University Press, 1995.
Pocock, J. G. A., *The Machiavellian Moment: Florentine Political Thought and the Atlantic Republican Tradition*, Princeton University Press, 1975.

The Ancient Constitution and the Feudal Law: A Study in English Historical Thought in the Seventeenth Century. A Reissue with a Retrospect, Cambridge University Press, 1987.

Pocock, J. G. A., and Gordon J. Schochet, 'Interregnum and Restoration', in J. G. A. Pocock (ed. with the assistance of Gordon J. Schochet and Lois G. Schwoerer), *The Varieties of British Political Thought 1500–1800*, Cambridge University Press, 1993, pp. 148–79.

Rogers, G. A. J. (ed.), *Leviathan: Contemporary Responses to the Political Theory of Thomas Hobbes*, Bristol: Thoemmes, 1995.

Russell, Conrad, *The Causes of the English Civil War*, Oxford: Clarendon Press, 1990.

Sharp, Andrew (ed.), *The English Levellers*, Cambridge University Press, 1998.

Skinner, Quentin, *The Foundations of Modern Political Thought*, 2 vols., Cambridge University Press, 1978.

Reason and Rhetoric in the Philosophy of Hobbes, Cambridge University Press, 1996.

Liberty before Liberalism, Cambridge University Press, 1998.

Smart, Ian Michael, 'The Political Thought of the Scottish Covenanters, 1638–88', *History of Political Thought*, 1 (1980), 167–93.

Sommerville, Johann P., *Thomas Hobbes: Political Ideas in Historical Context*, Basingstoke: Macmillan, 1992.

Tuck, Richard, *Philosophy and Government, 1572–1651*, Cambridge University Press, 1993.

Tyacke, Nicholas, 'Puritanism, Arminianism and Counter-revolution', in Richard Cust and Anne Hughes (eds.) *The English Civil War*, London: Arnold, 1997, pp. 136–59.

Woodhouse, A. S. P. (ed.), *Puritanism and Liberty: Being the Army Debates (1647–9) from the Clarke Manuscripts with Supplementary Documents*, 3rd edn, London: Dent, 1986.

Wootton, David (ed.), *Divine Right and Democracy: An Anthology of Political Writing in Stuart England*, Harmondsworth: Penguin, 1986.

Worden, Blair, 'Milton's Republicanism and the Tyranny of Heaven', in Gisela Bock, Quentin Skinner and Maurizio Viroli (eds.), *Machiavelli and Republicanism*, Cambridge University Press, 1993, pp. 225–46.

Zagorin, Perez, *A History of Political Thought in the English Revolution*, reprint. Bristol: Thoemmes Press, 1997.

3

SHARON ACHINSTEIN

Texts in conflict: the press and the Civil War

In 1640, the bookseller George Thomason purchased 22 printed titles; in 1642, he purchased well over 2,000. To him, something new and extraordinary was happening in the press no less than in politics or on the battlefield. With a passion that was historical and not strictly bibliographical, Thomason collected as many specimens as was possible of each publication emerging in the volatile Civil War period. Thomason, a Presbyterian and friend of the poet and polemicist John Milton, was a leading stationer who sympathized with Parliament during the Civil War. Though Thomason was rewarded by Parliament for his importation of foreign books, he became increasingly royalist from 1647 onwards, as did many Presbyterians in the wake of the King's surrender. Arrested in 1651, he was imprisoned for seven weeks in connection with a Presbyterian plot to bring in Charles II; after 1651 he played no role in politics. With the coming of the Restoration, Thomason pledged his oath of allegiance to the monarchy. Thomason ended his collection of pamphlets soon after the coronation of Charles II, 23 April 1661, with a few pamphlets dribbling in until the last in December of that year, as if Thomason was recognizing, or hoping, that an era had come to an end.

Thomason's collection, amassed between 1640 and 1661 'for the Use of Succeeding Ages', is our most extensive source of literary and political information for the period. It contains over 22,000 pamphlets. Although the collection is not a sum of total production, it gives an indication of the range of output of the press during these years. The average yearly consumption for this bookseller in the 1640s was around 1,500 items; numbers were cut to under 1,000 annually between 1650 and 1653, reflecting Cromwellian censorship. Thomason sought out copies of all the pamphlets he could get his hands on which had appeared in London during those years, and his collection includes partisan writing from across the spectrum as well as illicit publications. His careful notation of the date when each tract came into his possession, or in some cases the date of publication, is an invaluable help to the student of the English revolutionary press during its most prolific and colourful years. His collection is held in the British Library, much of it now microfilmed for the use of students and scholars.[1]

The English Revolution inaugurated a new era in the dissemination of political information in England. From the outbreak of hostilities between King and Parliament, the press was instrumental in the conflict; the press was also a medium, as well as a primary exhibit, of social transformation in the early modern period. Consider the following figures: in 1600, the output of the English press was 259 separate items. By 1642, that figure exploded to 2,968, a more than tenfold increase. The 22,000 pamphlets collected by Thomason between 1640 and 1660 represent a rate of publication which far outstrips anything previously known in England. Although many of the books published were only short tracts and pamphlets, the frequency with which they appeared evinces a vital engagement with current events and a desire to rush ideas and opinions into print. For the first time in English history, the press became the vehicle for open political conflict. Freed from the constraints of censorship, the press was the means for expression of ideas not only of elites in power but also of a variety of oppositional viewpoints. In this most extraordinary of political circumstances – where a parliament warred against a king; where a king was tried and executed; where radicals sought a restructuring of social relations – the press was made to serve as a public forum in which political debate over vital issues could be conducted. Printing enabled the rise of a new conduct of politics in England, the development of a political culture that extended far beyond the perimeters of the court and the royal household. In the fabric of the lives of ordinary English citizens, printing refashioned political consciousness.

Can a medium make a qualitative change in history? Historians have argued that the coming of the printed book in early modern Europe was a force for changes that were both political and psychic.[2] Printing was not simply a technological revolution, but a shift with many consequences. In addition to technological innovation, there are several long-term factors which bear on the conditions of the press at the outbreak of the English Civil War that help explain the potency of the medium. These are the shift to vernaculars in the printing culture of the Renaissance; the Protestant Reformation; the rise of literacy; the situation of London; and the existence of a strong culture of manuscript dissemination. The explosion in the press, like the Revolution itself, should be seen as the consequence of these long-term causes, and not merely the result of the breakdown of censorship during a period of political turmoil. In this chapter, we will explore these several factors as preconditions to the Civil War press, and then we shall look to printed output during the revolutionary years.

Print culture

In Europe, the arrival of the printed book around 1500 entered a culture of Renaissance humanism, and it displaced the manuscript in library collections as well as in international scholarly communication. The figures tell part of the story of a shift to a more democratic readership. Before 1500, a high proportion of books printed were in Latin – about 77 per cent.[3] The transmission of classical literature as well as the Bible was the legacy of the first great era of printing in Europe. An audience for the classics, though restricted to educated elites, was on the rise, as Latin authors were soon followed by Greek and then Hebrew in this new medium. When Thomas Hobbes looked back on the English Civil War he saw as one of its causes the wide transmission of classical authors that had given young men an appetite for tyrannicide![4] This feeling could only have been possible given the spread of such classical literature through the medium of print.

In the long view, the greatest sea change in printed output over the early modern period was the shift from ancient languages to vernaculars. Benedict Anderson has argued that language forms the basis for the 'imagined community' one calls a nation.[5] Indeed, national self-consciousness was born in the Renaissance in no small part due to the rising respect for the vernacular. Print helped with the regularization of national languages around a fixed set of rules. Translations of the major classical authors into English were accomplished in the sixteenth century; during this period, an audience arose that was also interested in works by modern authors in native tongues. By the seventeenth century, languages were assuming their modern forms. Printing, of course, was not the only factor in this evolution; but its importance cannot be underestimated in the process of the fashioning of a uniform national language and thus a national political community. Scientific thinking may also be a consequence of this new format with its tendency towards standardization.[6]

In technical terms, the printing press had been continuously improved since its use by Gutenberg in the fifteenth century, when the most it was capable of producing was 300 impressions in a day. By 1620, Dutch innovations had enabled the production of one press to reach 250 impressions an hour.[7] In England, the effects of printing were speeded by the Protestant Reformation, which from the beginning was a Bible-centred, literate movement. As early as 1538 English parish churches had been ordered to equip themselves with an English Bible for public reading; and in 1539 an official translation was published. By putting the Bible into the common people's hands, printing assisted the ideology of the Reformation in its transfer of spiritual authority away from priests towards individual consciences. Access to the Bible, as well as to John Foxe's *Book of Martyrs,* had been ensured by an Elizabethan edict commanding that copies of both should be chained within each church in the land. For the humblest of writers in the English Revolution – for instance, the Diggers – Foxe's book and the Bible were the only texts cited; John Bunyan too relied heavily upon these most widely accessible books.

Another long-term issue contributing to the importance of printing in the English Revolution was the spread of literacy. Although formal education was heavily socially restricted during the early modern period, there was a substantial progress in reducing illiteracy amongst all social groups in the seventeenth century. Literacy in early modern England was a marker of social and economic position, with the lowest orders, including husbandmen and agricultural labourers, lacking opportunities to acquire the ability to read. Historians have estimated that 30% of adult males could read, with a much lower rate for women. The figures may be considerably higher in London, with an estimated 60% of adult male literacy.[8] Despite this rate which may appear low by today's standards, on the contrary, England's was the highest rate across Western Europe. More could read than could write, and the many interconnections between oral and printed culture gave rise to the overlapping genres of the ballad, newssheet, sermon and metrical psalm. In many ways then, even without achieving full comprehension, English men and women could participate in a culture of print.

The spread of the printed word down the social scale is a remarkable story of the early modern period. Print runs for individual works were roughly 1,500 copies, and prices were low, as pamphlets cost from one to six pence. For those with the barest literacy, there were ballads, newsbooks, single-sheet broadsides, chapbooks, jestbooks; a variety of religious materials – Bible stories, sermons, catechisms, primers, devotional works; and almanacs – by 1640, sales of almanacs had reached 400,000 copies, sufficient to supply one quarter of all households. During the civil war period, ballads gave news accounts, scurrilous gossip, prognostications and moralizing, covering a range of opinions from avid support for the King to sympathy for Parliament, reaching out to an audience of literate and illiterate alike. Oral culture was alive to the currents of the day, and not just through song; texts were read aloud, at a time when habits of reading aloud were far more pre-valent than they are today. Further, the experience of this textualized culture led many from social groups to whom literacy was alien to wish to participate.

Another factor facilitating the tremendous outpouring of the press was the consolidation of the printing industry within the nation's capital city. The place of London as a metropolitan setting cannot be underestimated in exploring the consolidation of a political culture. The population of London had grown with startling speed over the seventeenth century, from some 200,000 in 1600 to 400,000 in 1650.[9] Almost all Civil War pamphlets were produced in London, and the sheer volume of what was published underscores the existence of a large number of readers. John Milton, urging press freedoms in *Areopagitica* in 1644, gave a rousing image of that city in upheaval:

> a City of refuge, a mansion house of liberty, encompast and surrounded with his protection; the shop of warre hath not there more anvils and hammers waking, to fashion out the plates and instruments of armed Justice in defence of beleaguer'd Truth, then there be pens and heads there, sitting by their studious lamps, musing, searching, revolving new notions and idea's wherewith to present, as with their homage and their fealty the approaching Reformation: others as fast reading, trying all things, assenting to the force of reason and convincement.   (*CPW*, II: 553–4)

Civil war was to be conducted by means of the pen. Although English printing was permitted only in London, Oxford and Cambridge, London was an exceptional locality, the national centre of finance, entertainment, law and, of course, politics. By 1641, 300 ballad sellers hawked their wares on London street corners. The main locale for bookselling in revolutionary London was in the vicinity of St Paul's Cathedral, a churchyard where a great number of printer–publishers rented a small shop or stall, with their main printing house in some less expensive district; John Stow had recorded that text writers had kept shops there since well before the invention of printing. Another locale for production within the city walls was the Royal Exchange on Cornhill, but there were other places in this metropolis for book production and consumption. Many printers had shops outside the walls, near West Smithfield and further north-east in Redcross Street and Grub Street. Nonconformist religious and political groups set up their own printing presses, often in secret, some even within their own houses. Mercury women sold pamphlets in the street; in 1648 John Hall gave a salacious image of the young men of the Inns of Court buying their newsbook *Mercurius Elencticus*, their transaction like that of seeking the services of a prostitute: 'But who would think so admired an author as *Elencticus* should be found lurking under a womans petticoats? Commonly the young Gentleman, who *softly* enquires for them, feels and findes them in her *placket*, and when he hath got him, hastily pockets up his *two penyworth of lyes*'.[10] Pamphlets were also produced in the Netherlands, especially those of Puritans, who communicated with sectaries in London to smuggle them into the kingdom.[11]

Alehouses were other significant venues for the creation and dissemination of revolutionary political texts; the 'pot-poet', thought to take his inspiration from alcohol, became a particular object of satire. Chapbooks might
have been sold in alehouses, and pamphlets were read aloud there.
Coffeehouses, first known in the 1650s, spread widely during the 1660s, and
from the earliest period they became the sites for communication and
exchange, as well as serving as semi-public places for the conducting of business. Jurgen Habermas describes the coffeehouse as where 'private people
came together as a public' in his account of the rise of the public sphere in
early modern Europe.[12] Newsbooks in these coffeeshops were provided by
the proprietor. There were numerous other spaces for consumption: Paul's
Walk, the court, the universities, colleges and inns, even on Civil War battle-
fields, in chapel, or in prison. Both inmates and their captors at the Fleet were
remarked to be splendid sources of 'good intelligence of state occurrences'
as well as 'wise discourse'.[13]

Manuscript publication

Publication in the early modern period included not only the reproduction of
texts through movable type; publication had also long taken place in manuscript. The existence of a tradition of scribal publication meant that the
arrival of mass printing in the early 1640s was a development and not a
wholly new departure. In underground circulation of manuscripts all through
the 1630s, libellous satires and politically targeted verse expressed political
challenges to crown and state leaders. The King's minister, Buckingham,
plagued by an extraordinary number of vicious satires, even offered a £1,000
reward for the recovery of the identity of one of his libellers. Underground
manuscript writers were more difficult to track down than seditious printers.
In times of political crisis, notably during the controversy over the Spanish
match, as well as during the imprisonment of William Laud, Archbishop of
Canterbury, there emerged a cadre of hired pens, amongst whom were such
lights as John Suckling, Thomas Carew, William Davenant and John
Denham, who engaged in savage 'guerrilla war in manuscript'.[14] National
conflict was sharpened by this antagonistic culture of manuscript raillery.

With English national news banned from print circulation until the breakdown of censorship in 1641, manuscript publication had also been the
means by which political documents – notably, state papers, polemical
tracts, reports of Parliamentary proceedings – were circulated; and these
genres were copied in larger quantities than any other kind of scribally published text. A well-organized manuscript newsletter writer, who had built up
good sources of information, developed a roster of subscribers who paid to

receive the letters. Manuscripts were also rented, as Simonds D'Ewes attests. John Pory received the whopping sum of £20 a year from Lord Scudamor for his weekly letters in 1631–2. Transcriptions of the Commons debates in the notorious 1629 Parliament were circulated in manuscript form, and there are at least forty-eight contemporary manuscripts of the scribally published proceedings which differ one from the other in many details.[15]

Even if serving an important political role, manuscript dissemination was, however, different from that in print for it involved a privileged, and thus limited, audience. This difference will be crucial in our thinking about the cultural impact of print in the Civil War years in transforming political consciousness. Scribal publication consolidated bonds to a small community. That same end could be achieved through the medium of print, as can be seen in the writing of Cavaliers during the Civil War period. However, though print and scribal publication alike produced reading communities, the difference in scale and authorship presents a difference in social meaning. To be sure, even to obtain a printed text, one had to know where to find it, what it was and to pay for it. Unlike manuscripts, however, printed texts were available on the open market, and thus authors had no way of excluding readers. A key difference was access: a printed diurnal cost a penny, whilst a manuscript diurnal could cost 4 or 5 shillings. Indeed many authors who leapt into print sought the widest possible audience for their work. Knowledge was no longer to be the reserve of a privileged, self-selected few, but was to be available to the many. Printing during the English Revolution bridged audiences of high and low, and linked local to national politics.

Censorship

If these long-term conditions had given rise to a print-friendly culture, what then were the immediate precipitants of this extraordinary burst of publication in the early years of conflict between Parliament and Crown? Milton's vision in *Areopagitica* of a cacophony of hammers and anvils of the press, and his optimism about the press's role in spreading knowledge, were twin consequences of the fall of the Star Chamber in 1641, an event of real significance in the history of publishing. This was the lapse of the 1637 Star Chamber Decree Concerning Printing. The 1637 Decree, promoted by the Company of Stationers for tighter control of their monopoly, had served the political needs of the government by limiting production, dissemination and content of published material. Before 1641 there were no legally printed newspapers and the publication of domestic news was a criminal offence.[16] State censorship of public political debate led political opposition to emerge

in other forms and other media, including literature, drama, Biblical interpretation, and translations of the classics.[17]

All this changed when the Court of Star Chamber was abolished in July
1641 and Parliament took control of the press. Not only did printers and
booksellers go into revolt against the strictures of the Company and Crown,
with a resulting chaos in the printing industry, but this was a situation that
reflected serious assaults on royal authority and church power in other areas
with Parliament's effort to curtail the prerogative powers of the crown.
Though the Company struggled to retain its lost authority, it confronted
numerous challenges, both from within and from without all through the
Civil War period. The Long Parliament set up in 1641 a Committee of
Printing to deal with particular claims about disorderly publications, and on
14 June 1643 an Ordinance for the Regulating of Printing was passed. All
books were to be officially licensed, and the Government and the Stationers
were once again in partnership, on terms similar to those of 1637. John
Milton exposes the intolerance of the 1643 Ordinance in his *Areopagitica*,
published on 23 November 1644, and charges that it is a return to the repressive Decree of 1637. The attack on licensing by Milton and others led to no
change in the Long Parliament's policy; but the effectiveness of the
Parliamentary Ordinance itself crumbled as the government lost the ability
to control the scale of publishing. Political and religious partisans took
advantage of this chaos and entered their ideas into the public arena through
unauthorized printing.

What happened once state control was lifted in 1641? The contents of the
outpouring of the press are the subject of the ensuing chapters in this
Cambridge Companion: the political thought of James Harrington, Thomas
Hobbes and John Milton; radical pamphleteering of the Levellers, Diggers,
Ranters and other sects and religious groupings; women's prophecy and petitioning along with imaginative literature by Margaret Cavendish and Anne
Bradstreet; Royalist reflections and counterattack; the King's successful
propaganda defence, the *Eikon Basilike*; as well as demotic forms such as
the hymn, ballad and popular religious handbooks. Joseph Frank has estimated that prose works comprise more than 94 per cent of the titles published between 1640 and 1660 in England.[18] Though a 1649 Printing Act
clamped down on publication and its severe penalties led to a drop in publication into the 1650s, the culture had adapted to the expansion of political opportunities in the press. Even though Wing lists only about 1,000 items
per year between 1650 and 1659 and from 1655 to 1659 only 2 newspapers,
both edited by Marchamont Nedham and both officially sanctioned, this
was a greater output than in any year prior to 1641 and was comparable to
yearly output all through the 1660s and '70s.[19] Though the governments

followed the 1649 Act with a second Act for better regulation of printing in 1653, enforcement proved more and more difficult in the tumultuous days of the civil wars. The Printing Act of 1653 remained the basis for authority in the print industry until after the Restoration of monarchy in 1660, but that control was more in name than in deed. Many of the titles for the period 1640–60, perhaps 60 per cent, were anonymously authored, and this convention of anonymity extended to printers and even to booksellers. Such anonymity and failure to seek licence to publish were common ways of avoiding detection and apprehension by authorities for having published politically or theologically sensitive material.[20]

Newsbooks

What was in this tremendous outpouring of print? Since other chapters will treat the many genres proliferating at the time, we shall look here at the most politically involved of the new publications: newsbooks and propaganda. The spread of news was a major cause and consequence of political turmoil, and printed propaganda surrounding the Irish massacre as well as the doings of the King and his wife sought to change people's minds in the court of public opinion. The Parliamentary propaganda piece *The White King* was claimed to have sold 1,800 copies in three days in 1644. Pamphlets describing war atrocities helped to create images of a ruthless enemy. Prince Rupert earned his reputation as the 'Prince Robber' in part because of the Parliamentary pamphlets that narrated the brutality of his military actions.

The first English printed newsbook was published in November 1641 with the records of Parliamentary proceedings, entitled *Diurnall Occurrences*, which had been appearing in manuscript circulation before then. Printed newsbooks were in the format of an eight-page quarto booklet, with two of those pages serving as the title page and its blank verso. News publishers adopted a weekly schedule and their common day for the newsbooks to appear was Monday, so that newsbooks could be sent out from London with the weekly posts on Tuesday. A weekly government postal service had only been established in 1637, but a second weekly post was added in 1649 and then a third in 1655. What may surprise modern readers is that the definition of 'news' for the revolutionary period is quite different from today, with no agreed standards of impersonality or 'equal time' for a balanced view of events. Instead, news readers came to see that their chosen publication contained an editorial viewpoint, sometimes muffled, but very often apparent even from the titles. *Mercurius Aulicus*, first appearing in January 1643, for example, was the court's Mercury. Though the first few issues of this periodical served as a showcase for its author John Birkenhead's latinate, academic, style, it soon shifted in tone to adopt a livelier, wittier style more in keeping with the popular press. The degree of suspicion about impartiality may be observed in the prodigious number of pamphlets purporting to offer a 'true' account. Newsbooks soon catered to particular niches in the market, mapping onto ideological niches as well. *Mercurius Civicus* would be a metropolitan paper, tracking London local politics; the *Parliament Scout* aimed for a less sophisticated readership of countrymen and lower orders in London. The *Moderate* was associated with the Leveller political organization. Marchamont Nedham, whose *Mercurius Britanicus* was instigated to counteract the effects of the Royalist *Mercurius Aulicus*, took both sides over the course of the revolutionary period. Nedham's publication was answered by the caustic *Mercurius Anti-Britanicus*.[21]

With Nedham, we see how the newsbook could take on the role of educating a public in how to become politically literate. Nedham's own political career traverses the span from pro-Parliamentary radical in the 1640s to his attaining a royal pardon in 1647, when he was appointed editor of the Cavalier *Mercurius Pragmaticus*. After the regicide, Nedham was imprisoned in Newgate for printing in April 1649 an issue of *Mercurius Pragmaticus (For King Charles II)*, and was given an offer to write for the Commonwealth in exchange for liberty. Nedham published *The Case of the Common-Wealth of England* in 1650, a bold republican defence that was both pragmatic and idealistic, and he was the author of *Mercurius Politicus*, the official newsbook of the Commonwealth which ran until 1660, for which Milton was licenser. It presented 'a crash course in republican education', using a jocular tone to attract readers as well as to editorialize in a radical republican mode, educating readers and creating political awareness.[22] Nedham's political reversals have earned him the scorn of history; however, they also reveal how quickly positions were shifting in this volatile time.

Nowhere was the power of the press more evident than in the reporting of events from Ireland. News of the Irish Rebellion reached London on 1 November 1641 in a letter to the Earl of Leicester, the new Lord Lieutenant; however, within days, the pamphlet press seized upon rumour to present an account of bloody massacres and dangerous popish uprising, and that information, however tainted, was a part of Parliament's deliberations and a spur to their presenting the Grand Remonstrance to the King. The Irish rebellion galvanized English opinion; Parliamentarians took it as evidence of the international conspiracy to enslave England in popish chains. *A Remonstrance of Divers Remarkable Passages Concerning the Church and Kingdome of Ireland*, issued in London in 1642 and written by the Church of Ireland Bishop Henry Jones, published lurid accounts of atrocities and confrontations in an attempt to earn support for beleaguered Irish Protestants. This was a highly partisan interpretation disguised as impartial fact; a response came from the pen of Irish Catholics to counter these fabrications and exaggerations. Sir John Temple's *The Irish Rebellion* became the official interpretation published in 1646, and republished many times thereafter, citing evidence from the 1641 depositions and reports to support the view of a long-term Papist conspiracy. The rising numbers of reported Protestant deaths over the course of the period attest to the elaboration in print of rumour: from 154,000 in 1642 to 250,000 in 1644; John Milton's estimate in 1649 in *Eikonoklastes* was a much over-inflated 600,000 (*CPW*, III: 470).[23]

The shadow of Ireland loomed over the reporting of domestic Civil War news. For instance, *Marleborough's Miseries,* appearing in 1642 after the sacking of Marlborough by the Royalist army, presented the 'most exact and true relation of the Beseiging, Plundering, Pillaging, Burning', with the sub-title, *England Turned Ireland, by the Lord Digby and Daniel O'Neale*, accusing the Royalist commanders of the most inhumane actions, and arousing fears that the massacres reported to be taking place in Ireland might indeed have come to England. Ireland figured in the Parliamentarian propaganda coup, the publication of the King's correspondence captured at Naseby, *The Kings Cabinet Opened* (1645). This publication, whose effect was enormous (Milton drew heavily upon it in his *Eikonoklastes*), presented documentation of the eagerness of the Stuarts to collaborate with 'all the Papists in *Europe* almost, especially the bloody Tygers of *Ireland*' (sig. A3v). The memory of the Irish massacre fired the Cromwellian campaign in Ireland, and is present in Marvell's 'Horatian Ode' as well as in Milton's *Observations upon the Articles of Peace*, published to justify the Cromwellian conquest in 1649.

Pamphlets and polemics

'Having more news meant, for many, not more but less truth': so observes one literary historian.[24] Printers worked quickly to produce low-grade work, and authors and publishers responded to a new market by outdoing each other in competitive sensationalism, scurrility and daring attack. The sobriquets for the 'diurnal' were many: 'lie-urnal', 'urinal', etc. Lies as well as truths were produced in great quantity, not only in relation to the Irish rebellion. Readers were being confronted with such an array of fantastic stories they had to develop reading abilities to cope with the quantity and quality of material. This did not prevent the very effective deployment of atrocity stories and scare-propaganda. There were hired pens available for each side. Royalist literary activity was controlled by the court. The King from the start, as Lois Potter has shown, 'was strongly committed to printing and publishing'.[25] The best-selling *Eikon Basilike* shows how well the Royalist propaganda machine understood the uses of the printing press. Well-known popular writers such as John Taylor the Water-Poet and the ballad writer Martin Parker were enlisted for the Royalist cause. The Presbyterian John Hacklyt started the Royalist journal *Mercurius Melancholicus* in 1647, though it was soon taken over by (probably) Taylor and Parker. Other Royalist newsbook writers included John Birkenhead, Samuel Butler, George Wharton and John Cleveland, all successful in avoiding arrest. After the execution of Charles, Royalist newsbooks went quiet for a while, but reappeared in support of Charles II as early as April 1649.

These conditions, political and literary, produced new kinds of authors, not only in their ability to make a living from the services of their pen, but in their social role as producers of political information and public knowledge. The leaders of the young republic especially saw that its future depended upon its being able to transform their image from regicides to virtuous liberators, and they attempted this in the medium of print. In December 1650 Parliament was presented with an account of the trial of the King; and the Rump ordered that a copy of the trial record be kept in all the great courts, also to be held amongst the records of every county. Pamphleteers adopted rhetorical strategies that not only set out political positions, but constructed an image of an ideal reader for them. Hostile reporting of the activities could also consolidate a readership, and such animosity led to an effusion of literary response, some of it of lasting value, as poets including Lovelace and Herrick, trained in a courtly tradition, now sought a new audience by putting their works into print and engaging in subtle polemic through literary means. The Leveller tracts show an extraordinary sophistication in their use of the print medium to expound their message.[26] Hymns composed by John Goodwin and Vavasor Powell that were sung to celebrate Cromwellian victories were printed in 1650. Gerrard Winstanley, spokesperson for the Diggers, also availed himself of print in order to take his case above the heads of his persecutors to a wide audience. Publication may not have been the chief medium for the Diggers, given the illiteracy level in rural England of about 70 per cent; instead word-of-mouth and itinerant activism were used to spread the message of this group.[27] Nonetheless, in 1649, *The Diggers' Song* appeared in print and was also meant to be sung, with the rousing call to action, 'Stand up now, Diggers all!' Print was perceived even by these most humble of political activists as vital to their cause.

Printing thus attracted authors from all across the political spectrum, and Royalists no less than Parliamentarians were swift to avail themselves of this potent medium. Even the King was alleged to have had a hand in the anti-populist poem by Peter Hausted, *Ad Populam: Or, a Lecture to the People*. Polemical pamphlets were not the only format for ideological warfare; poetry no less than prose served in a civil warfare of the pen. The Royalist poet Abraham Cowley wrote satires for the scurrilous press, 'The Puritans Lecture' and 'The Puritan and the Papist', published in 1642. Even in his 'high' poetic mode, however, he continued in this polemical spirit when he published his collection of his *Poems* in 1656, noting in his preface the keenness of the political stakes of his publication: 'Now though in all *Civill Dissentions*, when they break into open hostilities, the *War* of the *Pen* is allowed to accompany that of the *Sword*, and every one is in a maner obliged with his *Tongue*, as well as *Hand*, to serve and assist the side which he engages in.'[28] This is a poetry in which bloody contest will take place by other means.

Women's voices were among those newly heard in the printing press. The breakdown of ecclesiastical control led to women's participation in the public religious and political life of the nation no less than in the press. Women engaged in ecclesiastical controversy, as Katherine Chidley argued for the right of separation from the Church of England in her *Justification of the Independent Churches of Christ* (1641), where she debated with the Presbyterian minister Thomas Edwards. Appearing in printed form were collective petitions by Leveller women against the imprisonment of Leveller leaders. Radical women sectarians represented their prophecies and accusations against leaders; indeed, well over half the works published by women between 1649 and 1688 were prophecies.[29] In 1650, the first volume of poetry from the New World was published in London as Anne Bradstreet entered the fray with a poem 'A Dialogue between Old *England* and New, concerning their present troubles. Anno 1642'. Bradstreet railed against the 'Usury, Extortion, and Oppression' of the Stuart monarchy, lamenting 'poore *Ireland* bleeding out her last'.[30] Women's involvement in printing spread beyond their roles as authors. One of the mercury women, dubbed 'Parliament Joan', was in the pay of Parliament as an informant, and she sold counterfeit Royalist papers in an effort to locate the identities and whereabouts of the real distributors. This was one Elizabeth Alkyn, whose husband had been hanged by the Cavaliers. Although women were excluded from position and power in the Stationers' Company, they were also involved in the book trade and in seditious printing, often having inherited businesses from husbands. For the period 1540 to 1730, Maureen Bell has identified about 300 women as connected with the trade, many of whom were active after 1640.[31]

Sects were also amongst those seeking broad appeal through the printed media. Among the many radical groups to whom the press gave new voice, few were more vigorous and compulsively productive than the Quakers. From their beginnings in the Interregnum, they adopted an activist role in which they defined their community through print. The Quaker doctrine of the inner light accessible to all promoted an extraordinary production of writing, by men and women who felt called to speak. Quaker output is astonishing. Over 500 Quaker pamphlet titles appeared in the years 1653–7 and another 500 in 1658–60. Quakers were extraordinarily efficient in coordinating and organizing their printing and dissemination of texts, and printing may have been more than merely a way to express their personal relationships with their God; it may have been a means to consolidate community identity and to create a legacy through sustained acts of shared imagination. The revolution in textual production thus enabled a religious sect to spread its ideas, but also created needs for new forms of bureaucratic organization.[32]

One sect's existence may have been only textual, as historians have quarrelled over whether such a group as the 'Ranters' ever existed as an organized collective, or whether they were just a figment of their enemies' imaginations.[33] Cromwell and his officers wanted nothing to do with the Ranters, whose social and political antinomianism posed a real threat to the young government. Ranters made use of the idiom of print to defend themselves against printed attacks from government propagandists. It is uncertain whether the Ranter pamphlets are 'black propaganda', that is, tracts written by their enemies posing under false identities to discredit them. Laurence Clarkson in his autobiography, *The Lost Sheep Found* (1660), described how he gained admission to a secret group called My One Flesh, where free love was justified on Biblical grounds. Even if these pamphlets were written by detractors, as an attack on the unthinkable, nonetheless it is difficult to overestimate the impact of these words appearing in print, a medium which gave such socially radical actions a sort of existential meaning.

Politics and the press

Political theory found its way to the public through the medium of the press, and many who appealed to the common people were also strong advocates of a free press. The Levellers, who had urged that the law be printed in English, leapt into print in their hopes to raise popular consciousness about English politics. In his 1649 trial, for instance, the Leveller leader John Lilburne appealed to the public to vindicate himself from charges of treason, making the press into a forum in which to solicit public opinion. A political education for the many was both his goal and the means to attain that goal. Levellers understood the place of the press in a more inclusive political culture, and they coupled attacks on the political tyranny of leaders with attacks on their silencing of the press.

Although republicanism has been understood as a political ideology of aristocratic elites, there is evidence in the press of a demotic republicanism. The printer John Streater believed that the manipulation of knowledge and information was the key to creating a commonwealth, and he published his republican ideas in pamphlet form. Streater, who had served in the New Model Army and taken up freedom in the Stationers' Company in 1644, was imprisoned in 1653 for his anti-Protectorate views by order of the Council of State. After his release he produced in serial form a periodical intended for the common reader, *Observations Historical, Political, and Philosophical, upon Aristotles first Book of Political Government*, a sort of newsbook defending a free state against the tyranny of single-person rule, which appeared in eleven weekly instalments from 4 April until 4 July 1654. This was a pointed commentary on Cromwell's coup, and Streater had to go into hiding for months to evade further arrest. In clandestine co-operation with other printers, Streater was to be the printer for James Harrington's great republican work, *The Commonwealth of Oceana*, printed in 1656.[34]

During the English Revolution, people were drawn into political conflict through the medium of the press. Through printing, ordinary English citizens, tradesmen, labourers, women, rich and poor, were being drawn into a common world whose borders were no longer fixed by the geographical or social constraints of land, parish or household; they began to participate in a national sphere for cultural exchange of ideas and information. They could communicate over long distances with people with whom they had never made acquaintance; through the impersonality of print, they could utter dangerous speech which could elicit active political response. Within the sphere of elite politics, recent revisionists have argued, Parliament-men may have regarded division as anathema, and conducted their politics as a matter of consensus. However, the public sphere witnessed another kind of political arena, a rough-and-tumble pattern of combative, partisan publication. The political nation, which in the Tudor age had been an elite men's club, expanded to encompass a literate populace in the revolutionary period. Once we look beyond the corridors of power of elite politics, we can see that the explosion of controversial political material in the press yielded a potent and lasting transformation in the conduct of politics. Not only were the pace of news and information increasing and a variety of opinions disseminated in public; but also a wider range of citizens were involved in the chain of political communication through processes that had been in motion for over a century. The printing revolution in the seventeenth century was vital not only to the political conflict; it was indeed a revolution in English culture.

NOTES

1 For Thomason's collection see [G. K. Fortescue (ed.)], *Catalogue of the Pamphlets, Books, Newspapers, and Manuscripts Relating to the Civil War, the Commonwealth, and Restoration, Collected by George Thomason, 1640–1661*, 2 vols. (London, 1908).

2 Lucien Febvre and Henri-Jean Martin, *The Coming of the Book: The Impact of Printing, 1450–1800*, tr. D. Gerard (London: NLB, 1990); Elizabeth Eisenstein, *The Printing Press as an Agent of Change: Communications and Cultural Transformations in Early Modern Europe*, 2 vols. (Cambridge University Press, 1979).

3 Febvre and Martin, *Coming of the Book*, p. 249.

4 David Norbrook, *Writing the English Republic: Poetry, Rhetoric and Politics 1627–1660* (Cambridge University Press, 1999), pp. 34–5. See above, p. 35.

5 Benedict Anderson, *Imagined Communities: Reflections on the Origin and Spread of Nationalism*, 2nd edn (London: Verso, 1991).

6 On the sociology of the print revolution, see Walter Ong, *Orality and Literacy: The Technologizing of the Word* (London: Methuen, 1982), p. 127; Eisenstein, *Printing Press as an Agent of Change*; Adrian Johns, *The Nature of the Book: Print and Knowledge in the Making* (University of Chicago Press, 1998).

7 On the book trade and development of the press see Marjorie Plant, *The English Book Trade: An Economic History of the Making and Sale of Books*, 3rd edn (London: Allen and Unwin, 1974); and H. R. Plomer, *A Dictionary of the Booksellers and Printers who were at Work in England, Scotland, and Ireland from 1641–1667* (London: Bibliographical Society, 1907).

8 On literacy, see Margaret Spufford, *Small Books and Pleasant Histories: Popular Fiction and its Readership in Seventeenth-Century England* (London: Methuen, 1981); David Cressy, *Literacy and the Social Order: Reading and Writing in Tudor and Stuart England* (Cambridge University Press, 1980); and Thomas Laqueur, 'Cultural Origins of Popular Literacy in England 1500–1800', *Oxford Review of Education*, 2 (1976), 55–75.

9 Keith Wrightson, *English Society 1580–1680* (New Brunswick, N.J.: Rutgers University Press, 1986), p. 128.

10 Cited in Lois Potter, *Secret Rites and Secret Writing: Royalist Literature, 1641–1660* (Cambridge University Press, 1989), p. 25.

11 See, on the printing and dissemination of books, Dagmar Freist, *Governed By Opinion: Politics, Religion and the Dynamics of Communication in Stuart London* (London: Tauris Academic, 1997); Jerome Friedman, *Miracles and the Pulp Press during the English Revolution: The Battle of the Frogs and Fairford's Flies* (New York: St. Martin's Press, 1993); Johns, *Nature of the Book*.

12 Jurgen Habermas, *The Structural Transformation of the Public Sphere: An Inquiry into a Category of Bourgeois Society*, tr. Thomas Burger (Cambridge, Mass.: Harvard University Press, 1989), p. 27; and Christopher Hill, 'Censorship and English Literature', in *Collected Essays of Christopher Hill*, vol. 1: *Writing and Revolution in 17th-Century England* (Brighton: Harvester, 1985), pp. 32–72.

13 Thomas Cogswell, 'Underground Verse and the Transformation of Early Stuart Political Culture', in Susan Amussen and Mark Kishlansky (eds.), *Political Culture and Cultural Politics in Early Modern Europe* (Manchester University Press, 1995), p. 285.

14 On manuscript opposition, see Cogswell, 'Underground Verse', pp. 285, 286; James Holstun, '"God Bless thee, Little David!": John Felton and his Allies', *ELR*, 59 (1992), 513–52; and Alastair Bellany, '"Rayling Rymes and Vaunting Verse": Libellous Politics in Early Stuart England, 1603–1628', in Kevin Sharpe and Peter Lake (eds.), *Culture and Politics in Early Stuart England* (Stanford University Press, 1994), pp. 285–310.

15 See Harold Love, *Scribal Publication in Seventeenth-Century England* (Oxford: Clarendon Press, 1993), pp. 9–10, 70, 17.

16 Cyprian Blagden, *The Stationers' Company: A History, 1403–1959* (London: Allen and Unwin, 1960), p. 118; Frederick S. Siebert, *Freedom of the Press in England, 1476–1776* (Urbana: University of Illinois Press, 1952).

17 Annabel Patterson, *Censorship and Interpretation: The Conditions of Writing and Reading in Early Modern England* (Madison: University of Wisconsin Press, 1984), p. 57.

18 Joseph Frank, *The Beginnings of the English Newspaper, 1620–1660* (Cambridge, Mass.: Harvard University Press, 1961), p. 5.

19 Wilmer G. Mason, 'The Annual Output of Wing-Listed Titles 1649', *The Library*, 5th ser. 29 (1974), 219–20; and Edith Klotz, 'A Subject Analysis of English Imprints for Every Tenth year from 1480 to 1640', *Huntington Library Quarterly*, 1 (1938), 417–19.

20 There were also economic reasons for publishers to resist licensing their publications as well, since an increase in the number of titles published along with a reduction in their length may have led them to believe they would not be worth protecting via copyright. See D. F. McKenzie, 'The London Book Trade in 1644', in John Horden (ed.), *Bibliographia: Lectures 1975–88 by the Recipients of the Marc Fitch Prize for Bibliography* (Oxford: Leopard's Head Press, 1992), p. 137.

21 On the development of newsbook culture, see Joad Raymond, *The Invention of the Newspaper: English Newsbooks 1641–1649* (Oxford: Clarendon Press, 1996); C. John Sommerville, *The News Revolution in England: Cultural Dynamics of Daily Information* (New York: Oxford University Press, 1996); Carolyn Nelson and Matthew Seccomb, *British Newspapers and Periodicals: A Short-Title Catalogue* (New York: MLA, 1987); Richard Cust, 'News and Politics in Early Seventeenth-Century England', *P&P*, 112 (1986), 60–90; and Folke Dahl, *A Bibliography of English Corantos and Periodical Newsbooks 1620–1642* (London: Bibliographical Society, 1952).

22 Norbrook, *Writing the English Republic*, p. 223.

23 T. C. Barnard, '1641: A Bibliographical Essay', in B. MacCuarta (ed.), *Ulster 1641* ([Belfast]: Queen's University Institute of Irish Studies, 1993).

24 Potter, *Secret Rites*, p. 5.

25 Potter, *Secret Rites*, p. 7.

26 W. Haller and G. Davies (eds.), *The Leveller Tracts, 1647–1653* (New York: Columbia University Press, 1944).

27 Thomas Corns, *Uncloistered Virtue: English Political Writing, 1640–1660* (Oxford: Clarendon Press, 1992), p. 160.

28 Abraham Cowley, cited in James Loxley, *Royalism and Poetry in the English Civil Wars: The Drawn Sword* (Basingstoke: Macmillan, 1997), p. 97.

29 For women's participation, see Patricia Crawford, *Women and Religion in England, 1500–1720* (London: Routledge, 1996), p. 132; Elaine Hobby, *Virtue*

of Necessity: English Women's Writing 1649–88 (London: Virago, 1988); Hilary Hinds, *God's Englishwomen: Seventeenth-Century Radical Sectarian Writing and Feminist Criticism* (Manchester University Press, 1996), p. 26; Sharon Achinstein, 'Women on Top in the Pamphlet Literature of the English Revolution', *Women's Studies*, 24 (1994), 131–64; and Phyllis Mack, *Visionary Women: Ecstatic Prophecy in Seventeenth-Century England* (Berkeley: University of California Press, 1992).

30 Anne Bradstreet, *The Tenth Muse* (1650), pp. 184, 185.

31 Maureen Bell, 'A Dictionary of Women in the London Book Trade, 1540–1730', unpublished Master of Library Studies thesis, Loughborough University, 1983; and see her 'Hannah Allen and the Development of a Puritan Publishing Business, 1646–1651', *Publishing History*, 26 (1989), 5–66.

32 Kate Peters, 'Patterns of Quaker Authorship, 1652–56', in Thomas N. Corns and David Loewenstein (eds.), *The Emergence of Quaker Writing: Dissenting Literature in Seventeenth-Century England* (London: Frank Cass, 1995), pp. 6–24.

33 J. C. Davis, *Fear, Myth and History: The Ranters and the Historians* (Cambridge University Press, 1986); and on the controversy, see Christopher Hill, 'Abolishing the Ranters', in his *A Nation of Change and Novelty: Radical Politics, Religion and Literature in Seventeenth-Century England* (London: Routledge, 1990), pp. 152–94; and Nigel Smith (ed.), *A Collection of Ranter Writings from the Seventeenth Century* (London: Junction Books, 1983).

34 On Streater, see Johns, *Nature of the Book*, pp. 271–97; and Nigel Smith, 'Popular Republicanism in the 1650s: John Streater's "heroick mechanicks"', in David Armitage, Armand Himy and Quentin Skinner (eds.), *Milton and Republicanism* (Cambridge University Press, 1995), p. 140.

FURTHER READING

For individual editions of primary texts cited or discussed, please see the notes above.

Achinstein, Sharon, *Milton and the Revolutionary Reader*, Princeton University Press, 1994.

Anderson, Benedict, *Imagined Communities: Reflections on the Origin and Spread of Nationalism*, 2nd edn, London: Verso, 1991.

Blagden, Cyprian, *The Stationers' Company: A History, 1403–1959*, London: Allen and Unwin, 1960.

Cogswell, Thomas, 'Underground Verse and the Transformation of Early Stuart Political Culture', in Susan Amussen and Mark Kishlansky (eds.), *Political Culture and Cultural Politics in Early Modern Europe*, Manchester University Press, 1995, pp. 277–300.

Cressy, David, *Literacy and the Social Order: Reading and Writing in Tudor and Stuart England*, Cambridge University Press, 1980.

Cust, Richard, 'News and Politics in Early Seventeenth-Century England', *P&P*, 112 (1986), 60–90.

Eisenstein, Elizabeth, *The Printing Press as an Agent of Change: Communications and Cultural Transformations in Early Modern Europe*, 2 vols., Cambridge University Press, 1979.

Febvre, Lucien and Henri-Jean Martin, *The Coming of the Book: The Impact of Printing, 1450–1800*, trans. D. Gerard, London: NLB, 1990.

Frank, Joseph, *The Beginnings of the English Newspaper, 1620–1660*, Cambridge, Mass.: Harvard University Press, 1961.

Freist, Dagmar, *Governed By Opinion: Politics, Religion and the Dynamics of Communication in Stuart London*, London: Tauris Academic, 1997.

Friedman, Jerome, *Miracles and the Pulp Press during the English Revolution: The Battle of the Frogs and Fairford's Flies*, New York: St Martin's Press, 1993.

Habermas, Jurgen, *The Structural Transformation of the Public Sphere: An Inquiry into a Category of Bourgeois Society*, trans. Thomas Burger, Cambridge, Mass.: Harvard University Press, 1989.

Hill, Christopher, 'Censorship and English Literature', in *Collected Essays of Christopher Hill*, vol. 1: *Writing and Revolution in 17th-Century England*, Brighton: Harvester, 1985, pp. 32–72.

Holstun, James (ed.), *Pamphlet Wars: Prose in the English Revolution*, London: Frank Cass, 1992.

Johns, Adrian, *The Nature of the Book: Print and Knowledge in the Making*, University Press of Chicago, 1998.

Lambert, Sheila, *Printing for Parliament, 1641–1700*, London: Swift Printers, 1984.

Lamont, William, 'Pamphleteering, the Protestant Consensus and the English Revolution', in R. C. Richardson and G. M. Ridden (eds.), *Freedom and the English Revolution*, Manchester University Press, 1986, pp. 72–92.

Love, Harold, *Scribal Publication in Seventeenth-Century England*, Oxford: Clarendon Press, 1993.

Nelson, Carolyn, and Matthew Seccomb, *British Newspapers and Periodicals: A Short-Title Catalogue*, New York: MLA, 1987.

Ong, Walter, *Orality and Literacy: The Technologizing of the Word*, London: Methuen, 1982.

Patterson, Annabel, *Censorship and Interpretation: The Conditions of Writing and Reading in Early Modern England*, Madison: University of Wisconsin Press, 1984.

Peters, Kate, 'Patterns of Quaker Authorship, 1652–56', in Thomas N. Corns and David Loewenstein (eds.), *The Emergence of Quaker Writing: Dissenting Literature in Seventeenth-Century Literature*, London: Frank Cass, 1995, pp. 6–24.

Plant, Marjorie, *The English Book Trade: An Economic History of the Making and Sale of Books*, 3rd edn. London: Allen and Unwin, 1974.

Raymond, Joad, *The Invention of the Newspaper: English Newsbooks, 1641–1649*, Oxford: Clarendon Press, 1996.

(ed.), *Making the News: An Anthology of the Newsbooks of Revolutionary England, 1641–1660*, Moreton-in-Marsh, Glos.: Windrush Press, 1993.

Siebert, Frederick S., *Freedom of the Press in England, 1476–1776*, Urbana, University of Illinois Press, 1952.

Sommerville, C. John, *The News Revolution in England: Cultural Dynamics of Daily Information*, New York: Oxford University Press, 1996.

Spufford, Margaret, *Small Books and Pleasant Histories: Popular Fiction and its Readership in Seventeenth-Century England*, London: Methuen, 1981.

Watt, Tessa, *Cheap Print and Popular Piety, 1550–1640*, Cambridge University Press, 1991.

2

RADICAL VOICES

4

THOMAS N. CORNS

Radical pamphleteering

On 18 April 1638 John Lilburne, future Leveller, future Quaker, was whipped at the cart's tail from the Fleet prison to Westminster, where he was pilloried; he was afterwards imprisoned in dire circumstances.[1] His offence was to arrange for the production in the Netherlands of a radical Puritan tract by John Bastwick, and its subsequent importation and distribution. While resisting the particular charge, he made in a moment of great extremity an endorsement of the place of radical oppositional writing in the process of reformation he believed he served. In the pillory he advised the largely sympathetic crowd on appropriate reading: 'If you lease to read the second and third parts of Doctor *Bastwicks Letany* . . .'[2] Gagged by his tormentors, he reached into the pockets of his breeches where, showing a wise anticipation, he had concealed copies of tracts by Bastwick which he threw into the crowd.

The suffering of Lilburne, following as it did the pillorying and mutilation (by ear-cropping) of Bastwick, William Prynne and Henry Burton for seditious writing attacking the ceremonialism of the Church of England, illustrates a number of important aspects of radical pamphleteering in the 1640s and 1650s. Certainly, in the Civil War period, it was generally easier to publish; whatever forms of pre-publication censorship existed, they were infrequently applied with the rigour of the late 1630s. Spectacular punishment designed publicly to humiliate the victim was rarely meted out for oppositional publication, though the soldier Ranter Jacob Bauthumley had his tongue bored under the application of military justice, and Ranter and Quaker activists were sometimes flogged and often beaten up and imprisoned. Soldier Levellers were shot (for mutiny) and civilian Levellers were imprisoned. The Blasphemy Ordinance of May 1648, designed specifically to halt the dissemination of radical religious ideas, included provision for imprisonment, facial branding and even execution for promulgating heretical opinions. The spirit of the 1630s lived on in other ways. Publishing what the government – whether the Long Parliament, the Rump or the

Protectorate – wanted to suppress still required courage. Moreover, publishing retained a high priority among oppositional groups. Levellerism developed ideologically through a series of published manifestos or position statements; Diggerism found eloquent expression in the writings of Gerrard Winstanley, a writer and thinker of abiding significance; Ranter writings tested the tolerance of Republican government beyond breaking point; and Quakers professionalized and institutionalized the production of radical pamphlets to an unprecedented degree, matching the Protectorate's own attempts to dominate the work of the press. At the same time, for all four groups, publication was an active (rather than reflective) process integrated into other modes of propaganda. Lilburne in the 1630s not only wrote about his own suffering but also engineered a system of underground publication and dissemination, making a symbolic testament of his faith through the extremity of what he endured. Similarly, for the radical groups of the 1640s and 1650s, publishing was integral to their larger programmes, though in ways which, as we shall see, were subtly different in each case.

Levellers

I have chosen to concentrate on four groups, which in complex ways related to each other and to other radical organizations. Most of the more prominent civilian Levellers had a history of activism as religious radicals. Lilburne, once a promoter of Bastwick (himself a rather conservative figure by the 1640s), progressed through Particular Baptism to his more radical destinations. William Walwyn was active in a radical Arminian congregation, and Richard Overton was a General Baptist,[3] whose personal initiation into radical pamphleteering may well have been writing a brilliant but heretical tract, which argues that the soul 'sleeps' in the dead body in the grave, awaiting its sentence at the last judgement (the so-called 'Mortalist heresy').[4] That heterodox religious milieu rapidly came under the scrutiny and attempted control of the new and largely Presbyterian establishment, which monitored it through the information-gathering of divines like Thomas Edwards, who published, in three massive instalments, *Gangraena: Or a Catalogue and Discovery of many of the Errours, Heresies, Blasphemies and Pernicious Practices of the Sectaries of this Time* (1646). Overton had responded to the new repression in a brilliant series of 'Marpriest' pamphlets.[5]

In the late 1640s, however, religious radicalism for these activists gave way to a new and challenging campaign that was wholly secular in character, though no doubt the ethical values and the confident oppositionalism of their earlier enthusiasms did much to inform their writings and conduct. As the first Civil War ended, Leveller activists formulated a document, *A*

The Ranters Declaration, 2

WITH

Their new Oath and Protestation ; their strange Votes, and a new way to
get money ; their Proclamation and Summons ; their new way of Ranting,
never before heard of ; their dancing of the *Hay* naked, at the white *Lyon* in
Peticoat-lane ; their mad Dream, and Dr.*Pockridge* his Speech, with their
Trial, Examination, and Answers : the coming in of 3000. their Prayer and
Recantation, *to be in all Cities and Market-towns read and published* ; the
mad-Ranters further Resolution ; their Christmas Carol, and blaspheming
Song ; their two pretended-abominable Keyes to enter Heaven , and the
worshiping of his little-majesty, the late Bishop of *Canterbury* : A new and
further Discovery of their black Art, with the Names of those that are pos-
sest by the Devil, having strange and hideous cries heard within them, *to*
the great admiration of all those that shall read and peruse this ensuing subject.

Licensed according to order, and published by M.*Stubs*, a late fellow-Ranter

Imprinted at London , by J. C. MDCL.

1 Titlepage of *The Ranters Declaration*, 1650, a tract hostile to radical Puritanism; this same
woodcut was used of the Quakers, to the same effect, as the titlepage of *The Quakers Dream*
(1655).

Remonstrance of Many Thousand Citizens (1646); H. N. Brailsford, the most vivid chronicler of the Levellers, dates the inception of the movement from this event.[6] The text was probably written by Overton and Walwyn, together with Henry Marten, a Leveller fellow-traveller and future regicide, but like many Leveller publications it is both anonymous and collective, speaking for and on behalf of the many. Decisively – one may say, revolutionarily – it opens up the political debate between Parliament and King to include a discussion of the rights of those currently excluded from the franchise, which was extended only to the minority of males who could satisfy a quite high property qualification. It offers a radically different notion of the political nation, calling on Parliament to justify its conduct to 'the Universallity of the People, their Soveraigne LORD from whom their power and strength is derived'.[7]

The national significance of Levellerism increased hugely as Parliament quarrelled with the New Model Army, the Parliamentary force which had beaten the armies of the King. As Parliament sought ways to reduce the expense of the Army (it was suspected, by reneging on back pay and cashiering now redundant troops), both the senior officers around Oliver Cromwell and junior officers and other ranks identified common ground in resisting them. However, while the civilian Levellers saw among the lower ranks potential recruits and supporters, the senior officers recognized the necessity of keeping their loyalty till Parliament had been brought round or otherwise dealt with. These conditions supported the most far-reaching debate about the basis of political life to take place in any European nation before the French Revolution. And it was literally a debate, most significantly at the meetings of the senior officers, representatives of the lower ranks, and some civilian Levellers in the parish church at Putney, on 28 and 29 October and 1 November 1647. Henry Clarke, a secretary to the Council of War, made a transcription which may be read today as one of the most scintillating and dramatic texts of the Civil War period, no less dramatic for the fact that it records real people speaking in a real event. There are passages of fine eloquence, undercut by opposing voices, as in:

> RAINSBOROUGH[8]: . . . I think that the poorest he that is in England hath a life to live, as the greatest he; and therefore truly, sir, I think it's clear, that every man that is to live under a government ought first by his own consent to put himself under that government; and I do think that the poorest man in England is not at all bound in a strict sense to that government that he hath not had a voice to put himself under; and I am confident that, when I have heard the reasons against it, something will be said to answer those reasons, insomuch that I should doubt whether he was an Englishman or no, that should doubt of these things.

IRETON[9]: . . . Give me leave to tell you, that if you make this the rule I think you must fly for refuge to an absolute natural right, and you must deny all civil right; and I am sure it will come to that.[10]

This exchange, like others, animatedly defines the limited social radicalism of those close to Cromwell and suggests the larger principles espoused by Levellerism. Those principles probably defied a final precise enunciation – it was never really clear whether the male franchise should be extended to all adults or just to all adults who, unlike servants, were not directly dependent on others for their livelihood. While the dialogue with the senior officers lasted, and for some while afterwards, a new model for sovereignty and extended democracy was articulated, characteristically not in discursive or polemical form (an absence that makes the Putney debates all the more valuable) but in quasi-legal form in successive versions of *An Agreement of the People for a Firme and Present Peace, upon grounds of common-right and freedome*, which show a very literal-minded approach to the concept of a contract between government and the governed.[11] These manifestos found considerable support among the Army rank and file, who on occasion wore them in their hatbands as a gesture of solidarity and defiance: the contract for Levellers approached a talismanic significance. As the group around Cromwell purged Parliament ('Pride's Purge', December 1648) and brought the King to trial, so its temporary alliance with those to its left lost its usefulness; civilian Levellers were arrested and imprisoned; Leveller-sympathizing regiments who drifted into mutiny were suppressed; one group, captured near Burford in Oxfordshire, were punished by the execution of three members chosen by lot. As the second Civil War broke out and as the Cromwellian campaign to re-establish the English possession of Ireland was launched, Levellerism expired as a political force. In its declining days, however, some of its leading activists produced personal accounts of their mistreatment that are witty, defiant and poignant. These pamphlets are well exemplified by *The Proceedings of the Councel of State against Richard Overton, now Prisoner in the Tower of London* (1649), in which the language of *religious* radicalism inspires an eloquent expression of political defiance:

I am now in Bonds, a protestor against the Aristocratical Tyrannie of the Counsel of State, scorning their Mercy, and bidding defiance to their Crueltie, had they ten millions more of Armies, & Cromwels to perpetrate their inhumanities upon me; for I know they can pass but to this life; when they have done that, they can do no more; and in this case of mine, he that will save his life shall loose it; I know my life is hid in Christ, and if upon this accompt I must yeild it, Welcome, welcome, welcome by the grace of God.[12]

Diggers

'The Levellers' were thus named by their enemies, to suggest that they sought to level all the social distinctions and rights of property on which society in early modern England was perceived to be founded. It was a term they disliked and disputed. The Diggers, however, willingly took up the name – as in the title of an early Digger manifesto, *The True Levellers Standard Advanced* (1649) – and organized around a more sweeping programme not of political but of economic radicalism. Unlike the many-voiced Leveller movement, Diggerism found almost exclusive expression in the writings of Gerrard Winstanley, a failed cloth-merchant, who from 1648 had published a series of original and challenging theological treatises, and whose career as political activist began early in 1649.

At the centre of Winstanley's life, as of his writing, lies a bold praxis, in which theory and practice become indivisible. On 1 April 1649 a number of activists began the process of communally cultivating common land on St George's Hill in Cobham, Surrey. This was a symbolic action, but it was also practical and potentially deeply subversive. The Digger commune gave its members a possible means to live, and in its egalitarianism it functioned as a paradigm for how society could function, liberating all its participants, despite their propertilessness, to participate in the government of their own economy and the determination of their own lives. Most crucially it vividly united the principal elements in Winstanley's political philosophy. Surrey in that cool spring was the site on which the propertiless of England could set aside the curse under which they laboured and attain that pristine purity that Adam and Eve had enjoyed in their classless Edenic society before the Fall. George's Hill, the hill of England's saint, the ploughman saint, was where paradise would be regained.

Winstanley's tracts from the spring of 1649 glow with a remarkable assurance. Winstanley's career is sometimes made sense of through an interpretative strategy that distinguishes the pre-Digger from the Digger and post-Digger tracts. Thus, George Juretic argues that 'Winstanley's social radicalism can become intelligible only by seeing him as a product of two virtually distinct phases: a pre-Digger and a Digger period.'[13] Such a dichotomy severs Winstanley's politics from his philosophy and theology, valorizing the social perspective at the expense of his earlier thought, the route by which he arrived at George's Hill. Christopher Hill's account, recognizing the conceptual continuities of the oeuvre, is much more cogent.[14]

Winstanley's theological writing takes root in a singularly radical inflection of contemporary millenarianism. The notions that the end of the world was at hand, that the thousand-year reign of the saints was imminent, and the Last Judgement with its rewards and punishments could shortly be expected, were commonplace in England in the early modern period across the political spectrum. A more radical interpretation, however, saw last things as a transformation of present things, and the new heaven and the epoch of the saints as mutations of current, immediate and material circumstances. In Winstanley's case, the millennium consists of a sweeping transformation of the political and social consciousness of all people. The godhead is equated with 'Reason' (or sometimes 'Righteousness') and the second coming of Christ is the spread of that Reason in a spontaneous explosion of revolutionary consciousness. Thus, he writes in *The New Law of Righteousness*, published several days before the execution of Charles I:

> *This new Law of righteousnesse and peace, which is rising up, . . . is now coming to raign, and the Isles and Nations of the earth shall all come in unto him; he will rest every where, for this blessing will fill all places . . . he will throw all the powers of the earth at your feet, and himself will be your governour and teacher, and your habitations on earth shall be in peace, that so you that are the Citie of the Lord, New Jerusalem, the place of his rest, may be the praise of the whole earth.*
>
> *If any one say: The glory of Jerusalem is to be seen hereafter, after the body is laid in the dust; it matters not to me what they say, they speak in their imagination, they know not what.*
>
> *I know that the glory of the Lord shall be seen and known within the Creation.*[15]

Winstanley recognizes and emphasizes his radical deviation from those who see the millenarian transformation in purely posthumous terms, '*after the body is laid in the dust*' or after the end of the created world. His notion is animated with a further political inflection of that radical privileging of the spirit so characteristic of antinomianism and central to early Quakerism. Simply expressed, this concept, as old at least as the teaching of Joachim of Fiore, an Italian mystic, in the twelfth century, postulated three ages: the age of the Father, when the Law of the Old Testament had authority; the age of the Son, when Christ's Gospel had authority; and the age of the Spirit, when the Holy Ghost within each believer has authority. No heresy could be more subversive of the social fabric of the early modern state in that it empowers the conscience of each individual to stand against any received wisdom and against any social or ecclesiastical authority. In the thinking of Winstanley, it allows the poorest he to stand against the mighty of the earth, validated by the godhead within; this internalized political consciousness may be equated with the second coming of Christ: 'the same Spirit . . . should in these last dayes be sent into whole mankind . . . man-kind shall be made onely subject to this one Spirit, which shall dwell bodily in every one, as he dwelt bodily in the man Christ Jesus' (*Works*, p. 161). Thus the godly share in the same kind of godliness as was within 'the *man* Christ Jesus' (my emphasis).

Winstanley represents the origins of private property (and thus sin) in Edenic terms, but mythically and symbolically, rather than historically:

> The Apple that the first man eats [he means Adam], is not a single fruit called an Apple, or such like fruit; but it is the objects of the Creation; which is the fruit that came out of the Seed, which is the Spirit himself that made all things: As riches, honours, pleasures, upon which the powers of the flesh feeds to delight himself . . .
>
> Therefore when a man fals, let him not blame a man that died 6000 years ago, but blame himself, even the powers of his own flesh, which lead him astray; for this is *Adam* that brings a man to misery, which is the man flesh, or the strong man within that keeps the house, till the man of Righteousnesse arise and cast him out, who is the second *Adam*.   (*Works*, p. 177)

Winstanley speaks of 6,000 years because that approximates to the best estimate in the mid seventeenth century for the age of the world: James Ussher, Archbishop of Armagh, using calculations based on internal Biblical evidence, postulated a date for the creation of 4004 BC. Winstanley makes an equation between the risen Christ and the spirit of righteousness spreading through humankind. This rising spirit allows humankind to take up the curse of Adam, that by the sweat of his brow he would have to live, and to set aside the sin of Adam, the appropriation of property through covetousness into private hands, through the construction of a new kind of Eden:

> When this universall law of equity rises up in every man and woman, then none shall lay claim to any creature, and say, *This is mine, and that is yours, This is my work, that is yours*; but every one shall put to their hands to till the earth, and bring up cattle, and the blessing of the earth shall be common to all . . . There shall be no more buying or selling, no fairs nor markets, but the whole earth shall be a common treasury for every man, for the earth is the Lords.
>   (*Works*, p. 184)

Thus the eminently practical option for the rural poor, of living together in the marginal lands, on the uncultivated waste and the undercultivated commons, is infused with the energy of a political philosophy that in turn feeds off the millenarian vigour of radical and heretical theology.

The elements that make up Winstanley's political idiom can thus be disentangled. More elusive, critically, but really what makes Winstanley a great prose writer in the greatest age of English non-fictional prose, is a unique fusion of lyricism, vigour and vision, as in the following passage which works to negotiate great truths while retaining a direct contact with the external realities of a cold English winter and the prospect of a long awaited spring:

The windows of heaven are opening, and the light of the Son of Righteousnes, sends forth of himself delightful beams, and sweet discoveries of truth that wil quite put out the covetous traditional blear-eyes . . . Light must put out darknesse; the warm Sun wil thaw the frost, and make the sap to bud out of every tender plant, that hath been hid within, and lain like dead trees all the dark cold cloudy daies of the Beast that are past, and silence every imaginary speaker, and declare their hypocrisie, and deceit openly.

Now the tender grasse will cover the earth, the Spirit will cover al places *with the abundance of fruit* . . . there shal be lesse talking, preaching and prating, and more righteous acting.   (*Works*, p. 207)

Of course, the most immediate and significant righteous acting and the keystone of his symbolic universe was that incursion by the Digger commune onto the common land of St George's Hill.

Unsurprisingly the propertiless of England did not follow the Digger paradigm in overwhelming numbers (despite concerted efforts to send out missionary groups to other communities, in a manner which in some ways anticipates the role of Quaker missionaries in the 1650s). They were harassed from the initial site by local landowners and their dependants, and were brought to court for trespass. In or before August 1649 they moved to Cobham Heath, but were further prosecuted and their property was destroyed. Though the itinerant propagandists evidently had some success, since other Digger colonies were beginning to appear by early 1650, the Cobham Heath group was dispersed by April, though it survived in some form, probably as a gang of itinerant agricultural workers, late into 1650.

In the crisis Winstanley suddenly adds other, complementary elements to his already formidable literary repertoire. Now he starts to write pamphlets which purposefully and guilefully address those in power, a polemical strategy designed to secure a breathing space for the venture. Besides addressing tracts to the Army, to the House of Commons, and to the City of London, he most assiduously addresses Lord Fairfax, commander in chief of the New Model Army and in 1649, in effect, military governor of southern England. Thus Winstanley addresses to him *A Letter to the Lord Fairfax and his Councell of War* in the midsummer of 1649, releasing the text for publication, after presenting the case to him in person in late April and after meeting with him when Fairfax visited St George's Hill in May for a site-inspection. *Two Letters to Lord Fairfax*, less rhetorical this time and seemingly not published by Winstanley, date from December 1649. What Winstanley was trying to do, especially in the first *Letter*, was both to excite an interest in the theoretical basis for the Digger action and to convince Fairfax, a man who owned a large part of the North Riding, that the cultivation of common and marginal land posed no sustained threat to property. Initial toleration by Fairfax was followed, either through neglect or design, by a gradual involvement of his troops with the destruction of the Digger community.

In those pamphlets relating directly to the persecutions of the Diggers, Winstanley vividly offers a direct representation of experience (or at least the simulation thereof), and an ear for the resonant phrase. This is from *A Watch-word to the City of London and the Armie* (late summer, 1649):

> Then they came privately by day to *Gerrard Winstanleys* house, and drove away foure Cowes; I not knowing of it and some of the Lords Tenants rode to the next Town shouting the diggers were conquered, the diggers were conquered. Truly it is an easie thing to beat a man, and cry conquest over him after his hands are tied, as they tyed ours. (*Works*, p. 328)

Winstanley's ambition exceeds mere journalism, however; the particular is always tied to the larger mythic struggle. The dull repetition, 'the diggers [are] conquered', of his assailants is made to stand against his larger vision in a telling epiphany of rural idiocy and a celebration of Digger heroism: 'I will . . . return again to the Dragons Den, or Hornets nest, the selfish murdering fleshly Lawes of this Nation, which hangs some for stealing, and protects other in stealing' (*Works*, p. 329).

Ranters

Ranters attached themselves to the Diggers, and Winstanley was at pains to distinguish his group from them, publishing a disclaimer of any connections, called *A Vindication of those, whose endaevours is only to make the earth a common treasury, called Diggers or, Some Reasons given by them against the immoderate use of creatures, or the excessive community of women, called Ranting; or rather Renting* (1650).[16] His embarrassment at the unlooked-for association is evident. 'Ranters' were the principal media sensation of the early years of the English republic, and their notoriety served the interests of opponents of the new regime, who suggested its laxness had permitted such licence, and eventually served the interests of the regime itself, which could claim credit by suppressing its excesses (which was fairly easily done).

Ranterism is a much looser phenomenon than Levellerism, with its party organization and its manifestos, or Diggerism, with its practical implementation of an economic agenda – so loose, in fact, that J. C. Davies has wondered whether it ever existed as more than a 'sensation'.[17] Certainly the term was used of various antinomians, who would seem to have used a belief in the spirit within them and in the redundancy of the Ten Commandments for saints like themselves as the basis for 'ranting', outrageous behaviour characterized by swearing, smoking and 'lewdness' (particularly sexual promiscuity). (Of course, most of what we 'know' about them comes from hostile reports.) Contemporaries identified a handful of brilliant prose-writers as Ranters: Laurence Clarkson, Joseph Salmon and, the two I shall consider more fully, Jacob Bauthumley and Abiezer Coppe.

Bauthumley wrote only one book, *The Light and Dark Sides of God* (1650), rightly hailed by John Carey as 'a neglected masterpiece of seventeenth-century devotional prose'.[18] It is a work of high seriousness and patient, eloquent exposition, but its ideas are profoundly challenging to orthodoxies of the Protestant tradition:

> God loves the Being of all Creatures, yea, all men are alike to him, and have received lively impressions of the divine nature, though they be not so gloriously and purely manifested in some as in others, some live in the light side of God, and some in the dark side; But in respect of God, light and darkness are all one to him; for there is nothing contrary to God, but onely to our apprehension. *(Ranter Writings*, p. 234)

Densely written and sometimes paradoxical, Bauthumley's text operates at the leading edge of theological speculation, pondering such issues as the immanent and pervasive nature of God, the notion that heaven is not 'any locall place, because God is not confined', and the idea that sin 'is a nothing', other than 'the defect of Grace', 'the Cloud that interposes betwixt God and us'.[19]

In idiom and, to an extent, in doctrine there are parallels between Bauthumley's text and Winstanley's theological writings, and both authors could have been prosecuted under the Blasphemy Ordinance (1648). Winstanley was not pursued; Bauthumley, however, as a serving soldier, was subject to military discipline, and met with the full rigour of military law: his book was burnt, his tongue was bored through with a red hot iron, and he was cashiered from the service; thereafter, for decades, he fell silent.

Abiezer Coppe is a more ludic writer than Bauthumley (and Winstanley), but like the latter he has a strong social commitment, though he casts it into a most exuberant expression. His most notorious publications, *A Fiery Flying Roll* and *A Second Fiery Flying Roule* (1649), were evidently conceived as companion pieces, since the former contains the contents page of the latter (*Ranter Writings*, pp. 84–5).

Coppe writes himself into the narrative as a challenging wise fool, wandering the streets of London to confront hypocrisy and injustice:

> charging so many Coaches, so many hundreds of men and women of the greater rank, in the open streets, with my hand stretched out, my hat cock't up, staring on them as if I would look thorough them, gnashing with my teeth at some of them, and day and night with a loud voice proclaiming the day of the Lord throughout London and Southwark. *(Ranter Writings*, p. 105)

He courts the media image of antinomians, playing with it, subverting it while seemingly substantiating it, though the social critique remains uncompromised:

> we (holily) scorne to fight for any thing; we had as live [i.e. lief] be dead drunk every day of the weeke, and lye with whores i'th market place, and account these as good actions as taking the poore abused, enslaved ploughmans money from him . . . we had rather starve, I say, then take away his money from him, for killing men.
> (*Ranter Writings*, p. 89)

Coppe anatomizes the conflicting morality of the new republic, that speaks so highly of its defence of ancient liberties but, like kingly rule, founds itself on the systematic exploitation of most English people, and is as driven by simple self-interest as Charles and his court: 'For this Honour, Nobility, Gentility, Propriety, Superfluity, &c, hath (without contradiction) . . . the cause of all the blood that ever hath been shed, from the blood of righteous *Abell*, to the blood of the last Levellers that were shot to death [a reference to the suppression of the Burford mutiny]' (*Ranter Writings*, p. 88). However, whereas Levellers proposed constitutional reform and Winstanley an economic programme, Coppe offers only an ironized, ludic perspective and a theological exposition of an evasive kind.

Not evasive enough for his own good, though: Coppe, too, drew the attention of the authorities, who imprisoned and interrogated him. His release would seem to have depended on a printed recantation, *Copp's Return to the Wayes of Truth* (1651).

Quakers

Lilburne ended his life as a Quaker, as most probably did Winstanley, and many ex-Ranters were among the earliest to be converted to Quakerism (or 'convinced', to use the Quakers' own preferred word). It was a movement which retained a basically egalitarian value system and a belief in the supremacy of the spirit within, though even in its earliest years it did not engage the prevailing political structure in a programmatic way. Nevertheless, in the 1650s Quakers were more persecuted than any other religious group. In October 1656, one early leader, James Nayler, to demonstrate that the individual with the spirit within may aspire to emulate Christ, entered Bristol on horseback with adulating followers in imitation of Jesus' entry into Jerusalem in Matthew 21:1–11. He was punished with a life-threatening flogging, with branding, with spectacular humiliation, and with years of prison under extreme duress. Quakerism (again, the name comes from their enemies; they preferred 'the Religious Society of Friends') only grew under hardship, and by the early 1660s certainly numbered between 35,000 and 40,000 nationally, and possibly as many as 60,000.[20]

As Kate Peters has demonstrated, publication was central to the rise of Quakerism, in complex ways. Because they published and distributed their tracts in focused, efficient ways, proselytizing was successful, and because it was successful, publishing expanded accordingly. Titles far outnumber those by the other groups we have considered. Quaker publication began in 1652. There are 27 extant tracts from 1653, 64 from 1654, and 101 from 1655; though many Quaker activists wrote a tract or two, quantitatively output is dominated by a handful of principal leaders, who were also most prominent in travelling and preaching to spread the movement. Publications helped to keep the coherence of a denomination that seemingly lacked all the infrastructural advantages of more orthodox denominations, such as church buildings and a beneficed ministry. Itinerant preachers travelled equipped with tracts to distribute, and pamphlets often related to particular missions to specified places, and the successes and tribulations of those initiatives. [21] Early Quaker writing is sometimes elevated and indeed messianic, as David Loewenstein has argued, [22] but elements of the newsbook and of the martyrologies of the sufferings of the protagonists are also important. Women played a major role in the dissemination of early Quakerism, as missionaries and as writers. As Elaine Hobby remarks, and as others have noted, 'the first Quakers to preach in London and the English university towns, in Turkey, and in various parts of the Americas were female'.[23] Patricia Crawford estimates that the published works of female Quakers made up as much as 20 per cent of all seventeenth-century women's publications.[24]

Yet amongst all the Quaker writings of the 1650s there is probably no one individual tract to interest a literary critic in the ways in which *The New Law of Righteousness* or *A Fiery Flying Roll* so easily may, though in the Restoration and later there are complex and fascinating Quaker texts, pre-eminently perhaps George Fox's posthumously published *Journal*.[25]

Nevertheless, those Quaker pamphlets of the 1650s resonate with the spiritual – and practical – indomitability of their authors. These are writers who make a virtue of their rhetorical limitations, contrasting their spiritual simplicity with the corrupt sophistication of the professional clergy (and in this example making a deeply subversive point about gender politics):

> Therefore know you, that you may be, and are ignorant, though you think yourselves wise: Silly men and women may see more into the mystery of Christ Jesus, then you: for the Apostles, that the Scribes call illiterate, and *Mary* and *Susanna* (silly women, as you would be ready to call them, if they were here now) these know mor of the Messiah, then all the learned Priests and Rabbies; for it is the Spirit that searcheth all things, yea, the deep things of God . . .[26]

Moreover, such tracts demonstrate, poignantly perhaps, that, whereas the creative genius of a Coppe or a Winstanley had only slight impact on the world around them, more modest talents, courageously applied and incorporated into a larger, purposeful and disciplined organization, succeeded in establishing a denominational movement of abiding significance.

NOTES

1 My account rests heavily on Lilburne's own narrative, *The Christian Mans Triall*, 2nd edn (1641).

2 *Christian Mans Triall*, p. 27.

3 William Lamont reviews the religious background of civilian Levellers in 'Pamphleteering, the Protestant Consensus and the English Revolution', in R. C. Richardson and G. M. Ridden (eds.), *Freedom and the English Revolution: Essays in History and Literature* (Manchester University Press, 1986), pp. 83–4.

4 R. O. [attrib. Richard Overton], *Mans Mortallitie* (Amsterdam, 1643).

5 Discussed by Nigel Smith in 'Richard Overton's Marpriest Tracts: Towards a History of Leveller Style', *Prose Studies*, 9 (1986), 39–66, reprinted in Thomas N. Corns (ed.), *The Literature of Controversy: Polemical Strategy from Milton to Junius* (London: Frank Cass, 1987), pp. 39–66.

6 See H. N. Brailsford, *The Levellers and the English Revolution*, 2nd edn (Nottingham: Spokesman Press, 1983), p. 96.

7 *A Remonstrance of Many Thousand Citizens* (1646), titlepage.

8 I.e., Colonel Thomas Rainsborough, the most senior officer to join the Levellers.

9 I.e. Commissary-General Henry Ireton, Cromwell's son-in-law and the most argumentative of the senior officers at the Putney debates.

10 A. S. P. Woodhouse (ed.), *Puritanism and Liberty: Being the Army Debates (1647–9) from the Clarke Manuscripts with Supplementary Documents*, 3rd edn (London: Dent, 1986), p. 53.

11 See Thomas N. Corns, *Uncloistered Virtue: English Political Literature 1640–1660* (Oxford: Clarendon Press, 1992), pp. 134–5.

12 In A. L. Morton (ed.), *Freedom in Arms: A Selection of Leveller Writings* (London: Lawrence and Wishart, 1975), p. 221.

13 George Juretic, 'Digger no Millenarian: The Revolutionizing of Gerrard Winstanley', *JHI*, 36 (1975), 280.

14 Christopher Hill, *The Religion of Gerrard Winstanley*, *P&P* supplement 5 (1978). The issues he raises are much debated: for a deradicalizing view, see L. Mulligan, J. K. Graham and J. Richards, 'Winstanley: A Case for the Man as He Said He Was', *JHI*, 28 (1977), 57–75; for Hill's response and the subsequent exchange, C. Hill, L. Mulligan, J. K Graham and J. Richards, 'Debate: The Religion of Gerrard Winstanley', *P&P*, 89 (1980), 144–6; also, G. E. Aylmer, 'The Religion of Gerrard Winstanley', in J. F. McGregor and B. Reay (eds.), *Radical Religion in the English Revolution* (Oxford University Press, 1984; rept 1986), pp. 91–119. There are useful caveats against a secularizing of spiritual discourse in Nicola Baxter, 'Gerrard Winstanley's Experimental Knowledge of God', *JEH*, 39 (1988), 184–203.

15 George H. Sabine (ed.), *The Works of Gerrard Winstanley* (Ithaca, N.Y.: Cornell University Press, 1941), pp. 152–3.

16 In *Works*, pp. 399–403.

17 J. C. Davies, *Fear, Myth and History: The Ranters and the Historians* (Cambridge University Press, 1986), pp. 11, 83. For a different view, see: A. L. Morton, *The World of the Ranters: Religious Radicalism in the English Revolution* (1970; London: Lawrence and Wishart, 1979); Christopher Hill, *The World Turned Upside Down: Radical Ideas during the English Revolution* (London: Temple Smith, 1972), especially chs. 9 and 10; Nigel Smith (ed.), *A Collection of Ranter Writings from the 17th Century* (London: Junction Books, 1983), pp. 7–39.

18 John Carey, 'Foreword' to Smith (ed.), *Ranter Writings*, p. 2.

19 *Ranter Writings*, pp. 235–6, 242–3. See also Corns, *Uncloistered Virtue*, pp. 180–1.

20 Barry Reay, *The Quakers and the English Revolution* (London: Temple Smith, 1985), p. 27.

21 Kate Peters, 'Patterns of Quaker Authorship, 1652–1656', *Prose Studies*, 17 (1994), 21 n.11, 17, 9. This issue is reprinted as Thomas N. Corns and David Loewenstein (eds.), *The Emergence of Quaker Writing: Dissenting Literature in Seventeenth-Century England* (London: Frank Cass, 1995).

22 David Loewenstein, 'The War of the Lamb: George Fox and the Apocalyptic Discourse of Revolutionary Quakerism', *Prose Studies*, 17 (1994), 25–41.

23 Elaine Hobby, 'Handmaids of the Lord and Mothers in Israel: Early Vindications of Quaker Women's Prophecy', *Prose Studies*, 17 (1994), 88.

24 Patricia Crawford, 'Women's Published Writings 1600–1700', in Mary Prior (ed.), *Women in English Society 1500–1800* (London: Methuen, 1985), pp. 211–28; cited and discussed by Ann Hughes, ' Early Quakerism: A Historian's Afterword', *Prose Studies*, 17 (1994), 145–6.

25 For recent critical responses, see Thomas N. Corns, '"No Man's Copy": The Critical Problem of Fox's *Journal*', *Prose Studies*, 17 (1994), 99–111, and the introduction to Nigel Smith (ed.), *George Fox: The Journal* (Harmondsworth: Penguin, 1998).

26 Priscilla Cotton and Mary Cole, *To the Priests and People of England, we discharge our consciences, and give them warning* ([1655]), p. 3. On Cotton and Cole, see Elaine Hobby, *Virtue of Necessity: English Women's Writing 1646–1688* (London: Virago, 1988), pp. 43–5.

FURTHER READING

For individual editions of primary texts cited or discussed, please see the notes above.

Brailsford, H. N., *The Levellers and the English Revolution*, 2nd edn, Nottingham: Spokesman Press, 1983.

Braithwaite, William C., *The Beginnings of Quakerism*, 2nd edn rev. Henry J. Cadbury, 1955; rptd York: William Sessions, 1981.

The Second Period of Quakerism, 2nd edn. rev. Henry J. Cadbury, 1961; rptd York: William Sessions, 1979.

Corns, Thomas N., *Uncloistered Virtue: English Political Literature 1640–1660*, Oxford: Clarendon Press, 1992.

Corns, Thomas N., and David Loewenstein (ed.), *The Emergence of Quaker Writing: Dissenting Literature in Seventeenth-Century England*, London: Frank Cass, 1995.

Davies, J. C., *Fear, Myth and History: The Ranters and the Historians*, Cambridge University Press, 1986.

Firth, K. R., *The Apocalyptic Tradition in Reformation Britain, 1530–1645*, Oxford University Press, 1979.

Haller, William, and Godfrey Davies (eds.), *The Leveller Tracts, 1647–1653*, New York: Columbia University Press, 1944.

Hill, Christopher, *The World Turned Upside Down: Radical Ideas during the English Revolution*, London: Temple Smith, 1972.

Loewenstein, David, *Representing Revolution in Milton and his Contemporaries: Religion, Politics and Polemics in Radical Puritanism*, Cambridge University Press, 2001.

McGregor, J. F., and B. Reay (ed.), *Radical Religion in the English Revolution*, Oxford University Press, 1984; rept 1986.

Morton, A. L, *The World of the Ranters: Religious Radicalism in the English Revolution*, 1970; rptd London: Lawrence and Wishart, 1979.

(ed.), *Freedom in Arms: A Selection of Leveller Writings*, London: Lawrence and Wishart, 1975.

Reay, Barry, *The Quakers and the English Revolution*, London: Temple Smith, 1985.

Smith, Nigel, *Perfection Proclaimed: Language and Literature in English Radical Religion 1640–1660*, Oxford: Clarendon Press, 1989.

(ed.), *A Collection of Ranter Writings from the 17th Century*, London: Junction Books, 1983.

Watkins, Owen C., *The Puritan Experience: Studies in Spiritual Autobiography*, London: Routledge and Kegan Paul, 1972.

Woodhouse, A.S.P. (ed.), *Puritanism and Liberty: Being the Army Debates (1647–9) from the Clarke Manuscripts with SupplementaryDocuments*, 3rd edn, London: Dent, 1986.

5

DAVID LOEWENSTEIN

Milton's prose and the Revolution

For nearly twenty years of his career, during the 'tumultuous times' of the English Revolution (*CPW*, 1:807), Milton invested his exceptional literary talents in polemical prose as he struggled with urgent issues of ecclesiastical, civic and domestic liberty. Scholars have sometimes divorced the writer of occasional, fiercely polemical tracts during the Revolution from the visionary author of sublime, lofty poetry. The two, poet and revolutionary polemicist, were, however, closely connected. Milton contributed actively – and imaginatively – to the vital textual dimension of the English Revolution and its crises: as he put it in his *Defensio Secunda* (*Second Defence of the English People*; 1654), at the beginning of a retrospective account of his revolutionary writings, he would 'devote to this conflict all [his] talents and all [his] active powers' (IV:622).

Antiprelatical polemic and religious conflict

Milton's zealous prose in the early 1640s was stimulated by the collapse of the Church of England. Religious and political tensions were fuelled during this period by a series of major religious factors and events: these included godly fears of increased popery within the established episcopal church and at court; the Root and Branch Petition to abolish episcopacy (supported by 15,000 citizens); the assault on the ecclesiastical order and Archbishop Laud (impeached in December 1640); the outbreak of the Irish Rebellion in October 1641; the Grand Remonstrance (an apocalyptic manifesto defining Parliament's grievances against King Charles I and his ministers); debates about matters of church government and liturgy; the increase of Puritan militancy and the desire for godly reformation; and the escalation of apocalyptic rhetoric stimulated by the political/religious crisis. In the midst of these heated developments, and on the threshold of civil war, Milton produced his combative antiprelatical tracts (1641–2), culminating with *The Reason of Church-Government* and *An Apology against a Pamphlet*.

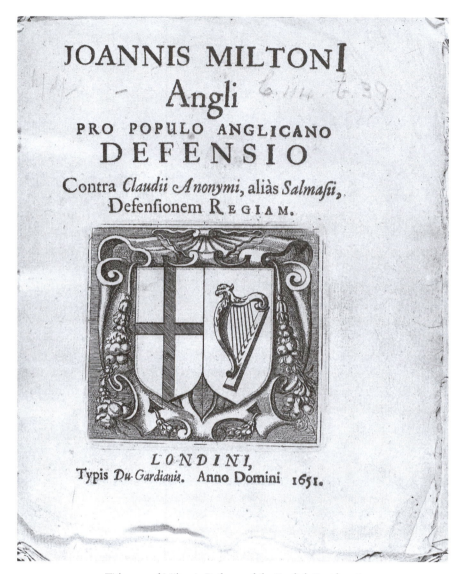

JOANNIS MILTONI
Angli
PRO POPULO ANGLICANO
DEFENSIO
Contra *Claudii Anonymi*, aliàs *Salmasii*,
Defensionem REGIAM.

LONDINI,
Typis *Du-Gardianis.* Anno Domini 1651.

2 Titlepage of Milton's *Defence of the English People*, 1651.

Milton's militant Protestantism, fiery prose and aggressive polemic are evident throughout these early tracts where he justifies using 'a sanctifi'd bitterness against the enemies of truth' (*CPW*, 1:901). *Of Reformation* (May 1641) is infused with violent millenarian rhetoric and imagery inspired by the Book of Revelation: there Milton introduces the startling image of the bishops giving 'a Vomit to GOD himselfe' (a more graphic rendering of Revelation 3:16: 'I will spue thee out of my mouth'), envisions the 'shortly-expected King', and relishes the apocalyptic destruction of the Laudian prelates 'throwne downe into the *darkest* and *deepest Gulfe* of HELL' (1:527, 616–17). In *Animadversions*, however, Milton modulates from the 'rougher accent' of his sharply written prose to offer a fervent prayer to the dazzling heavenly light and to Christ whose 'kingdome is now at hand' (1:662, 704–7). Zeal and art often reinforce each other: in *Animadversions* Milton yearns to sing the apocalyptic Christ 'an elaborate Song to Generations' (1:706); and in *An Apology against a Pamphlet* (April 1642) he takes 'leave to soare . . . as the Poets use' as he envisions Zeal ascending his fiery chariot 'drawn with two blazing Meteors figur'd like beasts' (1:900). This vivid apocalyptic passage – inspired by the visionary chariot of Ezekiel 1 and anticipating the Son's apocalyptic chariot in *Paradise Lost*, Book 6 – reveals how Milton's visionary prose could express 'a well heated fervencie' (1:663) and a poetics of vehemence as he waged polemical warfare against the Laudian episcopacy: 'the invincible warriour Zeale shaking loosely the slack reins drives over the heads of Scarlet Prelats . . . brusing their stiffe necks under his flaming wheels' (1:900). Later, in his divorce tracts, Milton would admire the contentious Christ who responds to the Pharisees 'in a vehement *scheme*' and with a '*trope* of indignation' (11:664) – evidence again of the literary and poetic terms in which he conceived vehement polemic.

Scornful laughter, derision and vehemence: these are among the most notable dimensions of Milton's prophetic voice in the early revolutionary prose. The contentious, zealous polemicist justifies indignation, derides lukewarmness, and admires martyrs unsparing in their derision of their superstitious persecutors. Sustained mockery and satire of the clergy are among the polemical weapons he skilfully exploits; thus, having been accused by his polemical attacker, the Modest Confuter, of having visited playhouses and bordellos, Milton strikes back in *An Apology* by scornfully recalling the pretentious future divines at university foolishly 'prostituting' themselves as they overacted in bad stage performances before courtiers:

> in the Colleges so many of the young divines, and those in next aptitude to Divinity have beene so oft upon the Stage writhing and unboning their Clergie limmes to all the antick and dishonest gestures of Trinculo's, Buffons, and Bawds; prostituting the shame of that ministry which either they had, or were nigh having, to the eyes of Courtiers and Court-Ladies, with their Groomes and *Madamoisellaes*. There while they acted, and overacted, among other younger scholars, I was a spectator; they thought themselves gallant men, and I thought them fools. (*CPW*, 1:887)

The zealous Puritan relishes this memory and exploits it for polemical ends as he scorns Laudian prelates who appeal to shows of outward worship, elaborate vestments and ceremonial religion – conducted, Milton observes, 'in an antick Coape upon the Stage of a High Altar' (1:930).

The crisis in religion in the early 1640s manifested itself in an extensive literature about church government. The longest of Milton's five antiprelatical tracts, *The Reason of Church-Government* (published in early 1642), aimed at opposing forms of episcopal power and church hierarchy by responding to *Certain Briefe Treatises . . . Concerning the Ancient and Moderne Government of the Church* (1641), a collection of essays assembled by Archbishop James Ussher. A complex and provocative polemic, Milton's *Church-Government* weaves together public religious polemic and personal vocational testimony. Like the previous antiprelatical tracts, it is fiercely anti-Laudian; whereas Laud stressed that 'the external worship of God . . . might be kept in uniformity and decency, and in some beauty of holiness',[1] Milton asks: 'Did God take such delight in measuring out the pillars, arches, and doores of a materiall Temple? was he so punctuall and circumspect in lavers, altars, and sacrifices soon after to be abrogated?' (*CPW*, 1:757). Such innovative ceremonialism and sacramental worship only fuelled religious divisions in the nation, leading Milton to conclude that 'Prelaty is a schisme it selfe from the most reformed' churches (1:791). Milton emphasizes instead the inner temple where the Spirit dwells (as in 1 Cor. 3:16). He emphasizes, moreover, a church built on self-discipline arising from the authority of the Word and the Spirit; consequently he says little – and certainly less than his Presbyterian allies might like – about a visible, hierarchical church. A Presbyterian-style government is clearly less important to Milton than individual piety. True discipline does not encourage 'cloyed' repetition or ceremonial observance. So Milton suggests in an elaborate metaphorical passage that draws upon the language of planetary orbits: 'Yet it is not to be conceiv'd that those eternall effluences of sanctity and love in the glorified Saints should by this meanes be confin'd and cloy'd with repetition of that which is prescrib'd, but that our happinesse may orbe it selfe into a thousand vagancies of glory and delight' (1:752). Milton's astronomical language about 'vagancies' or deviations and eccentricities within the church anticipates one of his most polemical points: his provocative defence of sectarianism.

Indeed, not only were the prelates fuelling fears of religious sects and divisions (hoping thereby to discourage Milton's reformist-minded countrymen from changing 'the present deformity of the Church' (*CPW*, 1:794)), but the more mainstream godly – i.e. the Presbyterians – were becoming increasingly alarmed by the fragmentation of zealous Protestantism and its more radical manifestations; within a few years massive catalogues of sects and popular heresies would appear (Milton the 'divorcer' was regularly mentioned among them), including Ephraim Pagitt's *Heresiography* (1st edn, 1645) and Thomas Edwards' *Gangraena* (1646). Milton's *Church-Government* deflates these fears – 'If we go downe, say you, as if *Adrians* wall were broke, a flood of sects will rush in. What sects? What are their opinions? give us the Inventory' (1:786–7) – but responds in a way that would hardly assuage the concerns of the mainstream godly: 'Noise it till ye be hoarse; that a rabble of Sects will come in, it will be answer'd ye, no rabble sir Priest, but a unanimous multitude of good Protestants will then joyne to the Church, which now because of you stand separated' (1:787–8). *Church-Government* thus anticipates Milton's spirited defence of sectarianism and revolution a few years later in *Areopagitica*.

Church-Government, however, is also memorable because of its striking autobiographical digression in the preface to its second book. Vocational and personal crises are interconnected with the religious and political crises of the revolutionary years. Milton justifies the vehement character of his prose – 'sharp but saving words' – as he compares himself to the sad prophet Jeremiah and speaks about the burden of the prophetic, zealous writer who must issue jarring blasts during tumultuous times. Nevertheless, he is also anxious about this burdensome prophetic vocation and about interrupting 'a calme and pleasing solitarynes', including 'the quiet and still air of delight-full studies', to engage in the 'hoars disputes' (*CPW*, 1:821) of occasional polemic. He is sensitive about his age (his 'green yeers') and about being relatively unknown, particularly as he engages in polemical struggle 'with men of high estimation' (1:806) in the Church of England, including Joseph Hall, James Ussher and Lancelot Andrewes. Struggling with his own divided impulses, he deprecates his poetry ('a vain subject'), especially at an urgent time when 'the cause of God and his Church was to be pleaded' (1:805), and he deprecates his prose writing (he sits 'below in the cool element of prose', the product of his 'left hand' (1:808)) as more earthbound than the sublime conceits of the visionary poet. Yet, as we have seen, the controversialist in fact often holds his pen in his right hand – for example, in the sublime passage from *An Apology* envisioning the fiery chariot of Zeal. Indeed, just after apologizing for his poetry and despite the fact that 'time serves not now', he launches into an elaborate literary autobiography that reveals his desire to 'leave something so written to aftertimes, as they should not willingly let it die' (1:810), possibly in the ambitious form of epic. Inspired like the prophet Isaiah, Milton is a poetic *vates* (he alludes to Isaiah 6:1–7 as he does in his 1629 Nativity Ode). He finds himself politically engaged in the religious upheavals of the early 1640s and imagines writing inspired national poetry, including 'Dramatick constitutions . . . doctrinal and exemplary to a Nation', as well as poetry deploring 'the general relapses of kingdoms and

States from justice and Gods true worship' (1:814–15, 817): and so he would in *Samson Agonistes* and in *Paradise Lost* (notably in its final historical books). Milton complains in *Church-Government* about 'the necessity and constraint' imposed by the present moment and the cool element of prose, yet the political/religious crisis had stimulated him to envision a great poetic future and to articulate in polemical prose that highest of literary enterprises.

The politics of divorce and 'free writing'

Milton the controversialist also dared to defend radical beliefs when it came to domestic liberty. As a result of producing four divorce tracts in 1643–5 – including *The Doctrine and Discipline of Divorce*, published in two editions – he was sharply condemned before Parliament in a sermon by the minister Herbert Palmer (in August 1644) and regularly labelled heretical in anti-sectarian writings by the orthodox godly who feared he was destroying the marriage bond and hence the social fabric. The attacks only pressed Milton more firmly towards the camp of the Independent opponents to Presbyterianism (and the recently established Westminster Assembly of Divines). By addressing his first three divorce tracts to Parliament, Milton was politicizing the issue of divorce and stressing interconnections between the tragic yoke of bondage in the household estate and the danger to the godly commonwealth: 'For no effect of tyranny can sit more heavy on the Common-wealth, then this household unhappines on the family' (*CPW*, II:229).

The divorce tracts again show how personal and political crises could intersect in Milton's career – Milton's wife Mary Powell had deserted him in September 1642 (though she would later return) and this triggered a personal crisis which assumed national proportions. A mixture of exalted idealism and anguished bitterness, the divorce tracts thus concern themselves with domestically liberated Englishmen (rather than women) as Milton depicts the bondage and despair of an unfit, unhappy marriage as 'a drooping and disconsolate houshold captivitie, without refuge or redemption' (*CPW*, II:235) – especially for the tragic husband. Engaged in strenuous Scriptural hermeneutics, Milton the Protestant exegete attempts to reconcile contradictory Scriptural passages – the wise, charitable Mosaic law condoning divorce (in Deut. 24:1) and Christ's abolition of Old Testament legislation (in Matt. 5:32 and 19:3–11) – but Milton's heroic efforts (e.g. in *The Doctrine and Discipline*) only highlight irreconcilable tensions. The patriarchal gender politics of the divorce tracts have made them the subject of intense critical interest.[2] Yet however we interpret them to situate Milton's complex (or divided) views of gender and sexuality, we need to remember that the divorce tracts were also products of the tumultuous English

Revolution and thus exceptionally daring texts which further radicalized their author – a dangerous heretic in the eyes of conservative Puritans who feared that, with the breakdown of censorship and the growth of sectarianism, the errors of the times expressed in such wicked books were fuelling social anarchy. Thus in *The Dippers Dipt* (1645), Daniel Featley warned Parliament that Milton's *Doctrine and Discipline* was one of those texts full of 'most damnable doctrines . . . in which the bonds of marriage are let loose to inordinate lust' (epistle dedicatory); embroiled in fierce controversy and stung by accusations of heresy, Milton shot back by accusing Featley's 'equivocating Treatise' of portraying Moses himself as a heretic – 'as one who to a holy Nation, the Common-wealth of Israel, gave Laws breaking the bonds of marriage to inordinate lust' (*Tetrachordon*, in *CPW*, II:583).

In the midst of the divorce controversy, Milton was intensely concerned with the capacity of printed polemics to shape the major debates of the Revolution. Censorship had collapsed with the abolition of the feared Star Chamber (July 1641) – one of those 'Courts of loathed memory' (*CPW*, I:786) – and the overthrow of the bishops' authority, stimulating an ever increasing outpouring of printed texts; the Long Parliament's Licensing Order of June 1643, however, was an attempt to reintroduce a system of censorship. Printed unlicensed and unregistered, Milton's *Areopagitica* offered a spirited challenge to censorship (except in cases when books prove libellous or seditious) and conveyed a new, invigorated sense of authorship stimulated by the Revolution. Authors and their newly empowered readership were actively shaping political debate, as more and more political writings poured out from the presses.[3] These printed texts helped to shape opinions in a radical direction as authors debated issues of popular sovereignty, the supremacy of Parliament, the right of resistance, among other urgent topics; the ferment of political debate and discourse – 'all this free writing and free speaking' (II:559) – was exhilarating. Revolutionary London, 'the mansion house of liberty', itself became in Milton's visionary prose a great 'shop of warre . . . in defence of beleagur'd Truth' – the centre of intellectual energy and ideological warfare where 'new notions and ideas' (II:553–4) were rapidly being generated and circulated by the press.

The striking figurative prose of *Areopagitica*, which interweaves and reinvigorates classical myths and Biblical language, conveys the immediacy of the Revolution and the heightened sense of millennial expectation during the 1640s. Milton writes poignantly about the dismemberment of 'our martyr'd Saint' Truth – evoking the Star Chamber mutilation of Puritan martyrs in the late 1630s[4] – as he explores themes of political fragmentation and unity: he not only urges Parliament to engage in the active search for Truth (as '*Isis* made for the mangl'd body of *Osiris*'), but reminds its members that the pieces of her lovely body will not be fully reassembled until 'her Masters second comming' (*CPW*, II:549–50). Milton's vision of strenuously and artfully building the Temple of the Lord highlights, moreover, that building unity in the chosen nation would not be accomplished without 'many schisms and many dissections': Truth was both one and disparate. Radical sectarians, despite Presbyterian fears, were among the many pieces contributing to the new 'spirituall architecture' of the godly nation (II:555). England at this revolutionary moment was indeed a 'a noble and puissant Nation' – rousing herself like Samson and 'shaking her invincible locks' (II:558) – and Milton was its fiery prophet in this new age of reformation. The crisis of 1649 would challenge this exhilarating vision as Milton harnessed his polemical energies in service of the experimental Republic.

The politics of 1649

The year 1649 was one of climactic revolutionary upheaval. It was preceded by the purging of Parliament (6 December 1648) and followed by the regicide, the abolition of kingship and the House of Lords, and the establishment of the republic – traumatic events supported by many religious radicals and vigorously defended in Milton's polemics. Yet it was also a year of acute internal tensions as Leveller agitation in the Army and the press posed a serious internal threat to the new republic established by a *coup d'état* and lacking popular support.[5] Milton the polemicist positioned himself both boldly and carefully during this year as he used his pen to justify the revolutionary political events and the new regime, but not to attack its radical critics, the Levellers.

Published soon after the execution of Charles I, *The Tenure of Kings and Magistrates* (February 1649) presented a vigorous defence of revolution and tyrannicide, as well as an assault on the counter-revolutionary politics of the Presbyterians. Here Milton insisted, much like the Levellers, that 'the power of Kings and Magistrates is nothing else, but what is only . . . committed to them in trust from the People . . . in whom the power yet remains fundamentally'; and with marvellous bluntness he defended natural rights and liberties since no one 'can be so stupid to deny that all men naturally were borne free' (*CPW*, III:202, 198). Yet Milton does not attempt to reconcile the contradiction between the regime's claim that the people are 'the original of all just power'[6] and the fact that power was being wielded at this critical moment by the Rump Parliament and the Army, by no means representative bodies. Instead, his most pungent prose derives from his polemical engagement with the shifting Presbyterians who had 'juggl'd and palter'd with the world' in a double sense (III:191; echoing *Macbeth* v.viii.19–22): they had first waged zealous war against the King during the 1640s, their fiery preachers invoking the curse upon Meroz in the Song of Deborah (Judg. 5:23) against those who did not; and then they turned around and sought to reconcile themselves to Charles I later in the decade, supporting negotiations with the King (who had agreed to accept Presbyterian religion in Scotland and establish it in England) and inciting sedition against the Rump.[7] The Presbyterians, after all, had claimed their 'discipline' was more demanding than the episcopal government they rejected: so why, Milton scornfully asks, were they absolving the King 'though unconverted, unrepentant' (III:235)? Milton's polemical strategy in *The Tenure* (reinforced in the second edition published before 15 February 1650) involves citing eminent Protestant authorities – including the zealous sixteenth-century John Knox, the original Presbyterian defender of regicide – to blast the present-day prevaricating divines who have assumed their 'new garbe of Allegiance' (III:193). In one striking passage he describes the doubling divines as 'nimble motionists', London militiamen who easily shift ground with 'cunning and dexterity' for their own political advantage-taking; they invoke Providence, as godly preachers and soldiers regularly did in the Civil War years, though in this case to justify equivocal means and covetous ends:

> For Divines, if ye observe them, have thir postures, and thir motions, no less expertly, and with no less variety then they that practice feats in the Artillery-ground. Sometimes they seem furiously to march on, and presently march counter; by and by they stand, and then retreat; or if need be can face about, or wheele in a whole body, with that cunning and dexterity as is almost unperceavable. (CPW, III:255)

Milton's military trope vividly conveys the doubleness of their political behaviour throughout the turbulent years of the Civil Wars as he characterizes these guileful, serpentine clergymen who 'winde themselves' into different positions. Their former revolutionary zeal and Puritan militancy, just like their other various postures, seemed no less calculated.

Milton's attack on counter-revolutionary politics in *The Tenure* no doubt helped to secure his official appointment in March 1649 as the Secretary of Foreign Tongues to the Council of State and as propagandist for the Republic. Among his first polemical assignments on behalf of the fragile new regime was the request 'to make some observations on a paper lately printed, called Old and New Chains'.[8] The first and second parts of John Lilburne's *Englands New Chains Discovered* (February and March 1649) were scathing attacks on Cromwell and the Army leadership for treacherously betraying the Revolution, and the Levellers' new social contract, the *Agreement of the People*. Yet Milton the controversialist remained deliberately silent

rather than use his pen against the Levellers at a moment of mounting tensions when more radical and more conservative forces in the Revolution
were clashing; two months later – in May – Cromwell would crush the
Leveller mutiny at Burford.[9] It is likely (though we cannot know for sure)
that Milton perceived that he could maintain the greatest polemical influence
if he could speak for the new Commonwealth, while restraining from attacking its most vocal and popular radical critics.

During March 1649 Milton was also asked to exercise his polemical
talents to combat the external threat to the Republic believed to emanate
from Ireland. His first official piece of writing on behalf of the new regime,
Observations upon the Articles of Peace with the Irish Rebels (May 1649),
was written in response to a treaty of January 1649 between the King's Lord
Lieutenant, James Butler, the Earl of Ormond, and the Confederate
Catholics of Ireland, an agreement or 'Articles of Peace' which posed a military threat to the new regime and which Milton, with caustic irony, refers
to 'as one of [the King's] last Masterpieces' made 'with those inhuman
Rebels and Papists of *Ireland*' (*CPW*, III:301).[10] Milton's polemical
response to the Irish crisis was partly fuelled by his perception of the late
King's treacherous politics and verbal equivocation since he was inclined to
popery and (Milton asserted in *Eikonoklastes*) 'ever friendly to the Irish
Papists' (III:473). Even when Charles was finally in custody, and
Parliament's supporters 'expected his repentance . . . of all the innocent
blood shed for his meer wilfulness', he engaged (like the unrepentant Satan
of *Paradise Lost*) in 'contriving and fomenting new plots', including plans
to encourage Irish rebels (III:332). Moreover, Milton's portrait of the Irish
rebels as demonic and savage blurs the boundary between the imagined and
the political, conveying the exigencies of polemical propaganda, which
attempted to link the Royalist party and the Irish resistance with popery,
Antichristian tyranny, and monstrous rebellion. Milton's *Observations*
helped to prepare for Cromwell's punitive military expedition in the second
half of 1649 to re-conquer Ireland, combat the forces of Antichrist and
avenge the Protestant massacres of 1641 – a campaign resulting in the
dreadful victories at Drogheda and Wexford. Milton's zealous Republican
tract thus remains one of his most disturbing political texts for readers
today. We may never easily reconcile his militant, nationalistic Protestant
responses to the Irish crisis to our sense of Milton as a towering author of
courageous, often fierce intellectual independence, a fervent defender of
religious freedom and civil liberty, a polemical prose writer who dared (in
Areopagitica, the *Second Defence* and elsewhere) to challenge, test or question political ideologies and regimes even when he praised them.
Nevertheless, his polemical engagement in the politics of the Irish crisis

reminds us that such unsettling inconsistencies are themselves part of his complexity as a godly revolutionary writer.

Milton's most challenging polemical assignment during 1649, however, was to shatter the popular image of the martyred King projected in *Eikon Basilike: The Portraiture of His Sacred Majesty in His Solitudes and Sufferings*, first printed a week after the King's execution. The most important book of Royalist propaganda in its age, the King's book (co-fashioned by the divine John Gauden) went through thirty-five English editions in 1649; its appeal confirmed widespread conservative sentiment and the narrowly based support for the new Commonwealth. One of those 'shrewd books, with dangerous Frontispices' (*CPW*, II:524), *Eikon Basilike* presented the martyred King as a patient Davidic and Christic figure, suffering yet constant in the midst of dark, turbulent revolutionary times; its famous frontispiece by William Marshall showed the pious King kneeling at his prayers in a basilica, gazing at the heavenly crown of glory, while holding the crown of thorns, setting aside his own crown, and treading under foot the things of this world (see Fig. 5).[11] Milton's lengthy response, *Eikonoklastes* (October 1649), attempted to demolish the King's seductive words and image, thereby demystifying the potent language and iconicity of monarchy. The radical Puritan Milton was scornful of the 'Image-doting rabble' who had so easily fallen for the King's book and the clever device of its frontispiece. Recalling themes of dangerous enchantment first dramatized in his *Comus* (1634), Milton depicted the King's book as a form of Circean 'Sorcery' that had bewitched the credulous, deluded people who were running into 'the Yoke of Bondage' (III:601, 488). Such was the enticing power of Royalist representation and Milton responded as a zealous iconoclast. Iconoclasm was itself sanctioned during the 1640s by the Puritan Commons eager to dismantle Laudian innovations: in January 1641 they had determined to get rid of 'all Images . . . superstitious Pictures, Monuments, and Relics of Idolatry', and in 1643 and 1644 they passed further ordinances to purify churches of popish and superstitious objects.[12] Milton's *Eikonoklastes* was itself a vigorous attempt, through verbal polemic, to break to pieces the religious image of the King, as well as to expose the 'glozing words' sustaining the 'illusions of him' (III:582).

Acutely aware of the dramatic appeal of the King's visual and emblematic representation, Milton contemptuously evoked the court masque, that occasional and lavish theatrical art form which had been most instrumental in projecting the power of the Stuart monarchy: 'the conceited portraiture before [the King's] book' was drawn out 'to the full measure of a Masking scene', yet 'quaint Emblems and devices begg'd from the old Pageantry of some Twelf-nights entertainment at *Whitehall*, will doe but ill to make a

Saint or Martyr' (*CPW*, III:343). *Eikon Basilike* was a piece of deceptive 'Stage-work' (III:530). Unlike Marvell whose 'Horatian Ode' movingly depicted the 'royal actor' adorning the 'tragic scaffold', Milton the polemicist responded with only scorn and laughter at the thought that 'he who had trampl'd over us so stately and so tragically should leave the world at last so ridiculously in his exit' (III:364). Milton's aim was to expose the disjunction between seductive image and dangerous reality, between the King's 'fair spok'n words' and 'his own farr differing deeds' (III:346–7); under his mask of martyrdom and behind his 'cunning words' (III:600), the guileful Stuart King, like the theatrical Satan of *Paradise Lost*, was wilful, revengeful, unrepentant, guilty of prevaricating, full of rage and malice, imperious and violent, and monstrous. Responding to an Antichristian King who had shown himself to be so 'doubtful and ambiguous in all [his] doings', the Republic's iconoclast found Scriptural support – as did other religious radicals – in Psalm 149 with its honorific injunction to saints '*To bind thir kings in Chaines, and thir Nobles with links of Iron*' (III:598–9).[13]

Defending the Republic and Protectorate

Milton was soon ordered by the Republic's Council of State to wage his Republican polemical warfare in a wider, international context:[14] the result was his most sustained vituperative work, his *Pro Populo Anglicano Defensio* (*A Defence of the English People*; February 1651), the first of his three Latin *Defences*. Milton was especially proud of *A Defence*, for there he took on one of the most famous of European classical scholars, Claude de Saumaise or Salmasius, author of *Defensio Regia pro Carlo I* (1649). The frontispiece to Milton's text (see fig. 2), displaying its two symbols of the shield with a cross and the harp, conveyed multiple, intersecting meanings associated with its author: the chivalric-warrior defender of England (like St George) was now using his literary, prophetic talents (the harp evokes the figures of Orpheus and the prophet David) to defend the Republic against its enemies at home and abroad. Polemic was warfare: 'our little *English David*', as Milton's nephew put it, was showing that he 'had the courage to undertake [the] great *French Goliath*'.[15] Presenting his discourse as a righteous cause and heroic undertaking (it would 'be of matters neither small nor mean' (*CPW*, IV:302)), Milton savagely attacked his opponent in his various roles as scholar, orator, historian and panegyricist for the late King. The aim of the combative English Protestant polemicist was to confound and crush his opponent, destroying both his professional credentials and his personal character: Milton forms '[his] battle line of Luthers, Zwinglis, Calvins, Martyrs and Paraeuses'; moreover, he writes prophetically of divine wrath and vengeance as he associates Salmasius (as well as Charles I) with the beasts of Revelation 13 (IV: 396, 459, 499, 484, 534). The heroic Samson rising up against the Philistines serves as a crucial model of Biblical tyrannicide and would later achieve fuller realization in *Samson Agonistes* where the militant saint of God destroys 'at one stroke' the superstitious Temple of Dagon 'having first made prayer to God for his aid' (IV: 402). Milton's inspiration as godly Republican writer came from *both* the Scriptures and classical authorities. Thus in *A Defence* he invokes such authorities as Euripides, Sophocles, Alcaeus (via Horace), Seneca, and Pliny the Younger to attack tyrannical rulers and justify tyrannicide (IV: 440–2, 446–9, 455), along with Tacitus and Cicero – the latter the selfless defender and orator of the ancient republic after whom Milton, saviour of the endangered English Republic, partly models himself (see, e.g., IV:536). Milton's Republican *Defence* was immensely successful: though publicly burned in France, it won praise from the Low Countries to Greece; Milton felt particularly vindicated in his polemical battle after the Protestant Queen Christina of Sweden, exemplifying her 'vigorous mind', expressed admiration for his Latin defence (see *CPW*, IV:604–6, 655–6). From a rhetorical standpoint, however, Milton's most varied, brilliant revolutionary defence was yet to come.

Having routed the famous Salmasius and exhilarated by the success of his first *Defensio*, Milton continued to wage polemical warfare on an international front with his next defence, a vigorous response to the anonymously published *Regii Sanguinis Clamor ad Coelum* (August 1652) or *The Cry of the Royal Blood to the Sky*, a reply to Milton's *Defensio* by the English Royalist clergyman, Peter du Moulin. The Republican attacker of the martyred King and great Salmasius (likened to 'our French Hercules') had been viciously maligned as a vile adversary, a depraved wretch, an obscure rabbler and a monstrous Polyphemus.[16] Milton mistook the true author of *Clamor* and, needing to aim his polemic at a definable enemy, attacked instead its editor–publisher, Alexander More, again addressing his text to the European community at large. In his *Second Defence of the English People* (May 1654) Milton responded complexly as he offered a skilful mixture of invective, autobiographical self-justification, panegyric and hard-nosed political advice; his tract celebrated the heroic achievements of a number of virtuous Revolutionary leaders and godly Parliamentarians, including the ardent Republican John Bradshaw – President of the High Court of Justice which had daringly tried the King – and Cromwell himself, leader of the Protectorate, the new regime that assumed power in December 1653. The *Second Defence* thus became a polemical occasion for Revolutionary myth-making; there the controversialist presents himself as a fearless chivalric warrior who has, in his own way, borne arms in the mighty struggle for

liberty and who compares himself to the epic poet creating a literary monu-
ment to extol the glorious deeds of his countrymen (*CPW*, IV:684–5). The
Second Defence reveals Milton's impulse to write an epic based not upon legendary British history (which, as a younger poet, he had planned to do), but
upon the major actors and exhilarating events of the Revolution: Milton presents the tireless Cromwell as a classical-style military hero, as *pater patriae*
('the father of his country', the honorific title given to Romans, like Cicero,
who performed outstanding service to the state) and as a Puritan saint
(known for his 'devotion to the Puritan religion' ['*religionis cultu purioris*']).
His exploits have outstripped not only those of English Kings, but 'even the
legends [*fabulas*] of our heroes' (IV:667, 672). Moreover, identifying his own
personal crises and trials with those of Cromwell and the godly nation at
large, Milton vigorously defends himself against Royalist detractors who
claimed that his blindness, which had become total by February 1652, was
a sign of God's judgement against a writer who had justified the regicide. To
the contrary, the heroic, Revolutionary polemicist presents himself as unre-
proachable, having conducted 'a pure and honorable life' (IV:611); his blindness is a mark of sacredness and an occasion for internal illumination – of
strength made perfect in weakness (see, e.g., 2 Cor. 12:9; the Pauline phrase
became the blind writer's personal motto). Like Cromwell, he remains 'tireless' in his work (indeed, his work for the Council of State continued
unabated during this period) and willing to risk great danger in his polemical combat (IV:591).

Milton counters attacks on the new quasi-regal government, with its
single-person executive, from disenchanted Independents and inflamed sectarians, as well as from religious Presbyterians who were fuelling factions
('men who are unworthy of liberty most often prove themselves ungrateful
to their very liberators' (*CPW*, IV:683)). However, he also advises Cromwell
and their fellow countrymen: though hard won through warfare and the
traumatic events of the Revolution, political liberty remains vulnerable; it
must be vigilantly defended as arduous trials – including internal struggles –
lie ahead in times of peace. Cromwell and his countrymen must therefore
separate church and state, reduce and reform laws, see to the education and
morals of the young, allow free inquiry and a more open press, protect free
conscience, refrain from factions, and resist succumbing to 'Royalist excess
and folly', as well as other vices which would enable corrupt, incompetent
men to assume power and influence in the government (IV:681–2). The
Second Defence thus balances skilful panegyric with a realistic assessment of
the precarious political situation under the experimental Protectorate.
Thousands of radical Puritans – many more than the fiery militant saints
who protested King Oliver was usurping the role of King Jesus – looked to

Cromwell's regime with hope.[17] Milton was one of them. Like a number of notable contemporary writers, including Marvell, George Wither and Marchamont Nedham, he employed his formidable literary talents to help sustain the regime and defend its precarious authority against its enemies at home and abroad.

Radical spiritualism and the Good Old Cause

After the verbal mud-slinging of his final defence (his *Pro Se Defensio* of 1655, a tract further devoted to attacking Alexander More), Milton did not engage in public polemic until the final, unstable two years of the Interregnum. After the death of Oliver Cromwell in September 1658, there followed a period of political flux and upheaval: Richard Cromwell's Protectorate, which antagonized the Army and more radical Independents and sectaries, was short-lived; the Rump returned to power in May 1659, but was no more popular than before and proved ineffective; General George Monck (commander of the Army in Scotland) marched into London in February 1660 and reassembled the Long Parliament which met and dissolved itself in mid-March 1660; with mounting popular enthusiasm for the King's cause, the newly elected Parliament summoned Charles II from exile in May 1660.[18] Despite the conservative, backsliding trends of these late Interregnum years and the failure of the Republican 'Good Old Cause', Milton's radical religious and political voice nevertheless remained 'unchanged / To hoarse or mute' (*Paradise Lost*, 7.24–5); indeed, in some ways it became more radical.

The companion texts he published in 1659 highlighted his radical spiritual convictions: *A Treatise of Civil Power in Ecclesiastical Causes*, addressed to the conservative Puritan Parliament of Richard Cromwell, and *The Likeliest Means to Remove Hirelings out of the Church*, published in August when intensified fears of sectarianism and an escalation of radical pamphleteering (especially from militant Quakers) had led to the pro-Royalist uprising of Sir George Booth. In *Civil Power* Milton reveals his radical Protestantism by vigorously challenging ecclesiastical and political powers when it comes to spiritual matters and inward religion: no church authority or civil magistrate should employ outward force to constrain inward conscience or faith. Inwardness has become Milton's touchstone of integrity and his polemical strategy involves his own 'free and conscientious examination' (*CPW*, VII: 258) of divisive religious terms which had sharply aggravated tensions during the Revolutionary years. Thus he diffuses (as he does in *Areopagitica*) the explosive terms '*heresie* and *heretic*' – 'another Greek apparition' – by defining a heretic freshly: one who maintains the traditions of men or opinions not supported by Scripture; heresy therefore means professing a belief contrary to one's conscientious understanding of and strenuous engagement with Scripture (VII:247–9, 252).[19] Moreover, Milton's emphasis in *Civil Power* on the guidance of the 'inward perswasive motions' of the Spirit (VII:261), rather than on the laws and commandments of men, reminds us of his close relation to contemporary religious radicals – the Quakers among them – who were following the impulses of the Spirit within, while also anticipating the radical spiritualism of his great poems (e.g. expressed in the 'strong motion' by which Jesus is led into the wilderness in *Paradise Regained*, 1.290; or the 'rousing motions' Samson feels just before he enters and destroys the Philistine temple of Dagon in *Samson Agonistes*, line 1382). *Civil Power* is marked by its emphasis on internal illumination, by Milton's concise uses of Scriptural proof texts to emphasize our freedom from ceremonies and the servile laws of men, and by the plainness of its style, meant to reinforce Milton's polemical rejection of the learned ministry: for 'doubtless in matters of religion he is learnedest who is planest' (VII:272).

Milton the radical Protestant is not known to have joined a separate congregation; and he remained staunchly opposed to a national church: *Civil Power* and *The Likeliest Means to Remove Hirelings* are notable for neglecting the role of the church in Protestant experience. Milton's biting attack on the hireling clergy as wolves and 'greedy dogs' (*CPW*, VII:296; echoing Isa. 56:11), as well as his firm rejection of tithes (tax-payments of one-tenth of income by the laity to the church) in order to maintain a national established ministry is close indeed to the concerns of radical sectarians, especially the Quakers, who publicly reviled the orthodox, university-trained clergy as hirelings and hypocrites for making a trade of their preaching. Tithes became one of the most contentious religious issues of the English Revolution; religious radicals, including Milton (VII:281–90), argued that they had lost their divine sanction when the ceremonial Law was superseded by the Gospel and the Levitical priesthood by an apostolic ministry. Yet while attacking in 1659 a hireling clergy and their 'seeming piety', Milton never specifically invoked the example and writings of the Quakers (who modelled themselves upon the Apostles) or other contemporary sectarians; rather, he asserted his own polemical independence and authority, as he likewise does in his theological treatise, *De Doctrina Christiana*, where he sets out to establish his independent thinking by eschewing human authorities and by emphasizing his own strenuous exertions. Milton preferred an inwardly inspired ministry, but to remove hirelings and find ministers prepared to preach the Gospel *gratis* (as St Paul did), he tersely remarks in *Likeliest Means*, would not be easy, since 'few such are to be found' (VII:280). Indeed, in an age of 'carnal power' when 'grievous Wolves' succeed for teachers and make the Gospel a cloak of carnal interest, the end of *Paradise Lost* grimly envisions, 'works of faith / Rarely be found' (12.507–37).

As the rising flood of enthusiasm for the monarchy alarmingly increased, Milton the godly Republican produced one of his most daring prose works with its valiantly optimistic (yet ironic) title: *The Readie and Easie Way to Establish a Free Commonwealth*, first hastily published probably in late February 1660 (when the Rump was still sitting), and then revised, enlarged and published in a second edition in April (when the Rump no longer existed), only weeks before Charles II was restored as King and entered London. In these dangerous days Milton showed a reckless disregard for his own safety. As the Commonwealth was rapidly collapsing inwardly – undone by its own internal strife – Milton dared to cry out prophetically against its dangerous and impending backsliding, as he urged his impulsive countrymen to 'consider whither they are rushing' (*CPW*, VII:463). Yet in April 1660 Milton could expect little: his countrymen, with many eager to embrace the thraldom of kingship, would soon begin 'so long a Lent of Servitude' (VII:408). Milton spoke freely one last time before the Restoration, for he wanted his countrymen to be without excuse. Here again the radical voice of *Eikonoklastes* can be heard, as Milton – envisioning the court of Charles II – ridicules the spectacle of semi-divine kingship and absolute power promoted by the Stuarts, 'whereas a King must be ador'd like a Demigod, with a dissolute and haughtie court about him, of vast expense and luxurie' (VII:425). Such regal prodigality only encourages mindless servility among the people. With mocking scorn for 'the new royaliz'd presbyterians', Milton presciently warns that the return of monarchy would fuel a backlash of Royalist revenge – in the form of 'imprisonment, fines, banishments, or molestation' (VII:451) – against not only radical Nonconformists and Republicans but Presbyterians as well. In response to the volatile and grim political situation, Milton proposes a commonwealth whose main foundation would be not a single person (i.e. an authoritarian monarch or even a quasi-regal Protector) but a perpetual senate of meritorious men inspired by such ancient classical and Jewish models as the Areopagus and the Sanhedrin. Moreover, in the second edition Milton the revolutionary managed, with remarkable directness, to justify minority rule if that is the necessary means to preserve endangered liberty, not sufficiently valued by the majority: 'They who seek nothing but thir own just libertie, have alwaies right to winn it and to keep it, when ever they have power, be the voices ever so numerous that opposed it' (VII:455).

Acutely conscious that these were his 'last words of . . . expiring libertie' before the Restoration and the loss of '*the good Old Cause*', Milton evoked the elegiac words of the prophet Jeremiah: '*O earth, earth, earth!* to tell the very soil it self, what her perverse inhabitants are deaf to' (see Jer. 22:29). Milton was bidding farewell to a revolutionary era. He had movingly given voice not only to Republican ideals – the vision that England might be 'another *Rome* in the west' – but also to a generation of radical Puritans who had sought to act according to the divine light: 'after all this light among us', how could his countrymen now choose 'a captain back for *Egypt*' (*CPW*, VII:423, 462–3)? *The Readie and Easie Way* concludes with a sense of great forces rushing out of control. In the Restoration Milton would publish his great epic about the Fall in which a rash act would have tragic consequences for human history; in April 1660, as his countrymen faced 'a precipice of destruction', Milton cried out against 'the deluge of epidemic madness' (VIII:463) and the tragic loss of freedom signified by the impetuous rush towards monarchy.

NOTES

1 J. P. Kenyon (ed), *The Stuart Constitution*, 2nd edn (Cambridge University Press, 1986), pp. 148–9.
2 See, e.g., James Grantham Turner, *One Flesh: Paradisal Marriage and Sexual Relations in the Age of Milton* (Oxford: Clarendon Press, 1987), ch. 6; Mary Nyquist, 'The Genesis of Gendered Subjectivity in the Divorce Tracts and in *Paradise Lost*', in Mary Nyquist and Margaret W. Ferguson (eds.), *Re-membering Milton: Essays on Texts and Traditions* (London: Methuen, 1988), pp. 99–127.
3 See further Sharon Achinstein's chapter above, pp. 50–68.
4 As in the famous cases mentioned on p. 71 above.
5 On Leveller tracts, see Thomas N. Corns' discussion above, pp. 72–5.
6 Kenyon (ed.), *Stuart Constitution*, p. 292.
7 *CPW*, III:234–5, 242, IV:334–5; Robert Ashton, *Counter-Revolution: The Second Civil War and its Origins, 1646–48* (New Haven, Conn.: Yale University Press, 1994), ch. 8.
8 On 26 March 1649: see Gordon Campbell, *A Milton Chronology* (Basingstoke: Macmillan, 1997), p. 98.
9 For the political tensions during 1649, see Brian Manning, *1649: The Crisis of the Revolution* (London and Chicago: Bookmarks, 1992).
10 See *Articles of Peace Made and Concluded with the Irish Rebels, and Papists . . . in behalfe of the late King* (May 1649), in *CPW*, III: 259–91; see also the related correspondence to which Milton responds: III:291–5.
11 On *Eikon Basilike*, see Isabel Rivers' discussion in chapter 11 below, pp. 205–6, and Lois Potter, *Secret Rites and Secret Writing: Royalist Literature, 1641–1660* (Cambridge University Press, 1989), pp. 10–12, 60–5, 169–87.
12 *Journals of the House of Commons*, 2:72; Firth and Rait, *A&O*, 1:265, 425; John Morrill, *The Nature of the English Revolution* (Harlow: Longman, 1993), pp. 73, 154.
13 See also *CPW*, IV:359; Bernard Capp, 'Popular Millenarianism', in J. F. McGregor

and B. Reay (eds.), *Radical Religion in the English Revolution* (Oxford University Press, 1984), p. 175.

14 On Milton's Republicanism see David Armitage, Armand Himy and Quentin Skinner (eds.), *Milton and Republicanism* (Cambridge University Press, 1995); David Norbrook, *Writing the English Republic: Poetry, Rhetoric and Politics, 1627–1660* (Cambridge University Press, 1999).

15 Helen Darbishire (ed.), *The Early Lives of Milton* (London: Constable, 1932), p. 70.

16 Selections from the *Clamor* may be sampled in *CPW*, IV:1041–81.

17 Austin Woolrych, *Commonwealth to Protectorate* (Oxford: Clarendon Press, 1982), p. 390.

18 For an excellent account of the politics of these years, see Austin Woolrych's introduction to *CPW*, VII. See also Godfrey Davies, *The Restoration of Charles II, 1658–1660* (1955; Oxford University Press, 1969), and Ronald Hutton, *The Restoration: a Political and Religious History . . . 1658–1667* (Oxford: Clarendon Press, 1985).

19 See also *Of True Religion*, *CPW*, VIII:421, 423.

FURTHER READING

For individual editions of primary texts cited or discussed, please see the notes above.

Achinstein, Sharon, *Milton and the Revolutionary Reader*, Princeton University Press, 1994.

Armitage, David, Armand Himy and Quentin Skinner (eds.), *Milton and Republicanism*, Cambridge University Press, 1995.

Barker, Arthur E., *Milton and the Puritan Dilemma, 1641–1660*, University of Toronto Press, 1942.

Cable, Lana, *Carnal Rhetoric: Milton's Iconoclasm and the Poetics of Desire*, Durham, N.C.: Duke University Press, 1995.

Corns, Thomas N., *The Development of Milton's Prose Style*, Oxford: Clarendon Press, 1982.

   Uncloistered Virtue: English Political Literature 1640–1660, Oxford: Clarendon Press, 1992.

   John Milton: The Prose Works, New York: Twayne, 1998.

Dobranski, Stephen B., and John P. Rumrich (eds.), *Milton and Heresy*, Cambridge University Press, 1998.

Fixler, Michael, *Milton and the Kingdoms of God*, London: Faber, 1964.

Hill, Christopher, *Milton and the English Revolution*, London: Faber, 1977.

Kranidas, Thomas, 'Milton's *Of Reformation*: The Politics of Vision', *ELH*, 49 (1982), 497–513.

   'Style and Rectitude in Seventeenth-Century Prose: Hall, Smectymnuus, and Milton', *Huntington Library Quarterly*, 46 (1983), 237–69.

Lewalski, Barbara, 'Milton: Political Beliefs and Polemical Methods, 1659–60', *PMLA*, 74 (1959), 191–202.

   The Life of Milton: A Critical Biography, Oxford: Blackwell, 2000.

Lieb, Michael, *Milton and the Culture of Violence*, Ithaca, N.Y.: Cornell University Press, 1994.

Lieb, Michael, and John T. Shawcross (eds.), *Achievements of the Left Hand: Essays on the Prose of John Milton*, Amherst: University of Massachusetts Press, 1974.

Loewenstein, David, *Milton and the Drama of History: Historical Vision, Iconoclasm, and the Literary Imagination*, Cambridge University Press, 1990.

Representing Revolution in Milton and his Contemporaries: Religion, Politics and Polemics in Radical Puritanism, Cambridge University Press, 2001.

Loewenstein, David, and James Grantham Turner (eds.), *Politics, Poetics, and Hermeneutics in Milton's Prose*, Cambridge University Press, 1990.

Norbrook, David, *Writing the English Republic: Poetry, Rhetoric and Politics, 1627–1660*, Cambridge University Press, 1999.

Nyquist, Mary, and Margaret W. Ferguson (eds.), *Re-membering Milton: Essays on Texts and Traditions*, London: Methuen, 1988.

Skerpan, Elizabeth, *The Rhetoric of Politics in the English Revolution, 1642–1660*, Columbia: University of Missouri Press, 1992.

Smith, Nigel, *Literature and Revolution in England, 1640–1660*, New Haven: Yale University Press, 1994.

Stavely, Keith, *The Politics of Milton's Prose Style*, New Haven: Yale University Press, 1975.

Von Maltzahn, Nicholas, *Milton's 'History of Britain': Republican Historiography in the English Revolution*, Oxford: Clarendon Press, 1991.

Webber, Joan, *The Eloquent 'I': Style and Self in Seventeenth-Century Prose*, Madison: University of Wisconsin Press, 1968.

Wilding, Michael, 'Milton's Areopagitica: Freedom for the Sects', in Thomas N. Corns (ed.), *The Literature of Controversy: Polemical Strategy from Milton to Junius*, London: Frank Cass, 1987, pp. 7–38.

6

ANNABEL PATTERSON

Andrew Marvell and the Revolution

Introduction

This chapter describes the reactions of Andrew Marvell to the English Revolution. From the famous 'Horatian Ode upon Cromwel's Return from Ireland', whose message continues to be debated by literary scholars and historians alike, and the almost contemporaneous 'Tom May's Death', where the matter in dispute is whether Marvell really wrote it, through to the Restoration satires which often hark back to the Commonwealth and Protectorate era, his writings (and their history of publication) suggest one simple, and to many, unpalatable truth: that Marvell, after initial reluctance, committed himself absolutely to the Revolution, in so far as it could be identified with the leadership of Oliver Cromwell. Another unpalatable truth will emerge in the course of the argument: that for Marvell, one of the chief values of the Revolution and its extraordinary leader was the re-emergence of England, after the pacific Caroline period, as a power in international relations, power being expressed primarily through military force and reputation. If we face the facts, as expressed by all of Marvell's writings, before, during and after the Cromwellian period, the urbane treasures of his pastoral poems (a contradiction I intend) are eccentric rather than self-defining; though he could not have been so intelligent a celebrator of Cromwell without some internal conflicts and ironies.

This view means that I reject the complacency with which, over and over again, critics who much prefer the pastoral and lyric Marvell to the politically committed Marvell turn to the *Second Part* of his *Rehearsal Transpros'd* (1673), and cite as his final verdict on the Revolution a verdict that seems to be a recantation of earlier allegiances: 'upon considering all, I think the Cause was too good to have been fought for. Men ought to have trusted God; they ought and might have trusted the King with the whole matter. *The Arms of the Church are Prayers and Tears*, the Arms of the Subjects are Patience and Petitions'. [1] In fact, this paragraph often seems to substitute for a thorough reading of Marvell's Restoration writings, which deliver, in the aggregate, far less pacificist advice.

By substituting 'and' for 'in' in my title, I extend the chronological reach of this topic into the Restoration, and indeed through the 1670s. Not to do so would seriously distort the account of Marvell's experience and working agenda. In 1675, for example, he wrote (we think) and circulated anonymously an outrageous verse satire against the Stuarts, past and present: the 'Dialogue between the Two Horses', which develops from the comic premise that the horses in the two equestrian statues, representing Charles I and Charles II respectively, can speak.[2] To get a quick sense of this poem's tone and audience, it is worth quoting the heading provided by a female compiler of a commonplace book:

> A Dialogue between the two horses . . . that of Marble the new Kings and stands at Woolchurch, set up by Sir Robert Vinner [Viner]. the other of Brass the Lait Kings and stands at Charing Cross set up by Sir Thomas Osbourn [Osborne], Supposeing the two riders in a dark night on their severall occasions to bee absent. The while the two horses make a visset [visit] to each other and discourse and dispute with each other.[3]

The horses produce a catalogue of complaints, embracing the 'Priest-ridden' policies which led Charles I ultimately to war against his subjects; Charles II's disreputable financial dealings and sexual libertinism; the public conversion to Roman Catholicism of the King's brother, James, Duke of York; and the corruption by bribery of the House of Commons – all issues about which Marvell would issue extensive critiques elsewhere. The horses argue as to which of their riders is the worst. 'The Debauched and the Bloody since they Equally Gall us', says Charles I's mount, 'I had rather Bare Nero than Sardanapalus.' Charles II's horse replies:

> I freely declare it, I am for old Noll.
> Tho' his Government did a Tyrants resemble,
> Hee made England great and it's enemies tremble.
>
> (*P&L*, 1:212)

Thus Oliver Cromwell emerges, in retrospect, as very much the lesser evil, the standard insult contained in the nickname 'Old Noll' (meaning drunken person, a reference to Cromwell's being the son of a brewer) converted to affectionate loyalty, the standard critique of his authoritarian government revalued in terms of an effectively strong and militaristic foreign policy. A few lines later, this horse adds a still more radical challenge:

> A Commonwealth a Common-wealth wee proclaim to the Nacion;
> The Gods have repented the Kings Restoration.
>
> (*P&L*, 1:212)

It is important to insist on Marvell's retrospective commitment to the Revolutionary period, his determination to do it justice in a culture that prohibited and prosecuted such statements. All three of his most explicitly 'Cromwell' poems were in fact suppressed by those who arranged for the posthumous publication of his *Miscellaneous Poems* in 1681, a remarkable matter to which we shall return. The Restoration satires had to negotiate in their own day a maze of printing restrictions, and in ours a fog of disputes about their authorship. The 'Dialogue between the Two Horses' speaks defiantly to the seventeenth-century end of this problem:

> Tho' Tyrants make Laws which they strictly proclaim
> To conceal their own crimes and cover their shame,
> Yet the beasts of the field or the stones in the wall
> Will publish their faults and prophesy their fall.
> When they take from the people the freedome of words,
> They teach them the Sooner to fall to their Swords.
>
> (*P&L*, 1:213)

Though a largely unread poem, then, the 'Dialogue' sets up very nicely the characteristics of Marvell's Revolutionary poetry that deserve our attention: first, the scope of his political analysis, which includes the still red-hot topic, the 'causes' of the English Civil War – the relation, as Marvell saw it, between Charles I's autocracy and the high-church policies of Archbishop Laud; second, the courage and directness of his address to the issues of his day; third, the broad and deep education, classical and Scriptural, which allowed him to wield the names of Nero and Sardanapalus as codes respectively for despotism and debauchery, or to cite Habakkuk's prophetic judgement against the Chaldeans ('For the stone shall cry out of the wall', 2:11) as an indictment still relevant to the Stuarts. Fourth, and always most difficult to demonstrate in words other than his own, there is Marvell's inimitable wit. Despite its loose and galloping form, so different from his Commonwealth precision, the 'Dialogue' exhibits the same inventiveness and sardonic humour as 'Upon Appleton House' and other poems that, certainly or tentatively, we assign to the 1650s.

Revolutionary poems

The next and equally important point to make about Marvell *during* the Revolutionary period is that the poems we can certainly or even probably assign to the years from 1640, when the Long Parliament became in effect the government, through to 1658, the year of Cromwell's death, are remarkably few. Let us list them here in chronological order (which is not the order in which they appeared in the *Miscellaneous Poems* or in *Poems and Letters*, the great and so-far-unexcelled edition by H. M. Margoliouth, Pierre Legouis and E. E. Duncan-Jones.[4]

1. **'Fleckno, an English Priest at Rome'**. Margoliouth dated this poem as referring to Richard Flecknoe's visits to Rome between 1645 and 1647, and it is therefore the first of the Civil War poems chronologically, though in its focus (Rome, Catholicism and bad poetry) it could scarcely be further detached from what was happening in England during those years.

2. **'To his Noble Friend Mr. Richard Lovelace, upon his Poems'**: one of a number of commendatory poems in Lovelace's *Lucasta*, finally published after political difficulties in 1649. Since Lovelace was eminently a Cavalier, whose problems with the Long Parliament, resulting in the sequestration of his estate, stemmed directly from his activism, this poem is often deployed to argue that Marvell was at this phase something of a Royalist himself. It is undeniable, however, that the poem sets writing and fighting against each other, and condemns 'our Civill Wars' for their abandonment of the peaceful, civic virtues.

3. **'An Horatian Ode upon Cromwel's Return from Ireland'**. This poem specifies its own date, since Cromwell returned from the Irish Campaign in May 1650. Though written only a year later than the poem to Lovelace, therefore, the 'Ode' revisits the values opposed in the previous poem, and makes its choices entirely differently.

4. **'Tom May's Death'**. Tom May, translator of the first-century Latin poet Lucan, playwright and historian, died on 13 November 1650. Though not printed at this time, it seems more likely to have been written then than after May's exhumation from Westminster Abbey in September 1661, although the latter date is a possibility. The poem's appearance in the *Miscellaneous Poems* obviously attached it to Marvell, but its seemingly anti-Republican views, combined with its excision from the Popple manuscript,[5] render the attribution debatable.

5. **'To his worthy Friend Doctor Witty'**, in both Latin and English. Both were published in 1651 as commendatory poems to Witty's translation of the *Popular Errors*. Witty was a Hull physician, who translated the work of another Hull physician; the errors were medical, both by doctors and home remedies.

6. **'In Legationem Domini Oliveri St. John ad Provincias Foederatas'** (On Oliver St John's Embassy to the United Provinces). Marvell's complimentary poem to Oliver St John on his 1651 embassy to the United

Provinces of Holland. The embassy began on 17 March and ended, with no results, in June.

7, 8 and 9. The three 'Fairfax' poems, '**Epigramma in Duos montes . . . Farfacio**', '**Upon the Hill and Grove at Bill-Borow To the Lord Fairfax**', and '**Upon Appleton House, to my lord Fairfax**'. All three, we can very reasonably assume, were written while Marvell was working as tutor of Mary Fairfax, from (perhaps) early 1651 to February 1653.

10. '**On the Character of Holland**'. This bellicose satire against the Dutch, motivated by the war between the English and the Dutch Republic, is internally dated by virtue of its reference to the joint generalship of Richard Deane, George Monck and Robert Blake from November 1652 to June 1653. It was therefore written either during Marvell's period of employment at Sir Thomas Fairfax's estate at Nunappleton (startling thought) or shortly after his departure. Possibly it led to his next appointment (and poem).

11. '**Bermudas**'. This gorgeous poem, escapist in at least two senses, was probably, but by no means certainly, written while Marvell was tutor to Cromwell's ward William Dutton. The two resided in the house of John Oxenbridge, Fellow of Eton College, from July 1653; and, so far as we know, Marvell remained thus loosely in Cromwell's domestic service through to 1657, when he was appointed to a post in the office of Cromwell's Secretary of State, John Thurloe.[6]

12. '**A Letter to Doctor Ingelo, then with my Lord Witlock, Ambassador from the Protector to the Queen of Sweden**'. Another poem motivated by English diplomacy in Europe, this identifies itself as belonging to the next stage of the history of the Revolution, when the Republic gave way to Cromwell's Protectorate. The embassy took place between November 1653 and 16 June 1654, and Marvell's letter (written in Latin, the language of diplomacy, despite its English title) was clearly intended to be read aloud during the embassy.

13 and 14. '**In Effigiem Oliver Cromwell**' and '**In eandem Reginae Sueciae transmissam**'. Closely connected to the previous poem, these two short poems comment on the portrait of Cromwell sent to Queen Christina of Sweden to celebrate the conclusion of the treaty of April 1654.

15. '**The First Anniversary of the Government under O.C.**' This panegyric celebrating the first year of Cromwell's Protectorate, which was completed in December 1654, was published, anonymously, in 1655.

16. '**On the Victory obtained by Blake over the Spaniards . . . 1657**'. Another panegyric to Cromwell, as head of a militaristic state. Whether by Marvell or not, it appeared in his papers and hence in the

Miscellaneous Poems, though excised from Popple. Thematically, it too is a militarist Cromwell poem, ending with the direct address: 'Whilst Fame in every place, her Trumpet blowes, / And tells the World, how much to you it owes' (*P&L*, 1:124).

17. **'Two Songs at the Marriage of the Lord Fauconberg and the Lady Mary Cromwell'**. Self-dating by virtue of the marriage of Cromwell's daughter on 19 November 1657.

18. **'A Poem upon the death of O.C.'** Self-dating by virtue of the fact that Cromwell died on 3 September 1658.

All the above, with 'Bermudas' constituting a marginal case, can be located in time either by the events to which they refer or by what we know of Marvell's location in a particular place. There are two additional poems whose date of composition cannot even be guessed, but which might place themselves in the Revolutionary period by the more fragile strategies of allusion and allegory. 'The Nymph complaining for the death of her Faun' alludes in its very first line to 'the wanton Troopers' (*P&L*, 1:23), a term that came into use only in about 1640 and was primarily applied to the Parliamentary armies in the North. 'The Unfortunate Lover', with its images of storm and shipwreck, and the allusion to the good King Josias in Ecclesiasticus 49:1, could be taken as an emblematic portrait of the isolated heroism of Charles I, between his captivity at Hampton Court and his actual execution in January 1649. Or perhaps the poem's last emblematic line, 'In a Field Sable a Lover Gules', alludes to the execution itself (*P&L*, 1:31), at which Charles appeared theatrically clothed in black velvet. If so, the poem's macabre images are maddeningly evasive; but at the century's exact midpoint, Marvell would offer Charles' execution the ultimate tribute of a poem without any indirection, without a moment's lapse of taste or integrity.

Now, listing the Commonwealth and Protectorate poems in this way has, or ought to have, a galvanic effect on the critical consciousness. The first surprise is the small number of poems in the list: of the eighty poems attributed to Marvell by Margoliouth, only twenty were definitely or even probably written during the Revolutionary period. (This does not, of course, mean that others, more gratifying to many readers, were not; only that we cannot prove or disprove such a hypothesis.) The second: how few of these confront the central issues of the Revolution. Two of them are of doubtful attribution. Three, the poems about Flecknoe (the earliest of the sequence), Lovelace's *Lucasta* and Dr Witty's translation, are themselves literary criticism, although the poem to Lovelace clearly situates itself and its values in the era of the Long Parliament's dominance. The three poems written on the Fairfax estate take an enigmatic, pastoral position on the great events occurring outside it, such that the readers of 'Upon Appleton House' cannot agree as to whether Lord Thomas Fairfax is praised or blamed for absconding from the cause. The two marriage songs are only tied to the time by the name 'Cromwell'. Half of these poems, therefore, while written during the Revolutionary period, are not directly 'about' it. It would almost be tempting to suggest that Marvell usually *avoided* the topic, and hence reinstate him in the role that I and others[7] have worked so hard during the last half of the twentieth century to rescue him from: the poet of disengagement, pastoral solitude, neo-Platonic philosophy, and virtually Cavalier dalliance. Those who prefer this version of Marvell will by now be pointing energetically to all the poems, unmentioned hitherto, that *could* have been written between 1640 and 1658: the Mower poems, 'On a Drop of Dew', 'Musick's Empire' (whose last stanza pays 'Homage' to a 'gentler Conqueror' than music itself, and so probably identifies itself either as a 'Fairfax' or a 'Cromwell' poem (*P&L*, 1:51)), or, the favourite candidate for defining the 'green' Marvell, 'The Garden'. Yet even this beloved work has been persuasively shown to be a Restoration poem[8] and there is nothing to prevent the same hypothesis being applied to any of the undatable poems. That Marvell's lyric poetry was mostly written on Fairfax's estate is an entirely unfounded assumption.

If we refuse the comfort of that assumption, however, something else of considerable interest appears to replace it. For once reorganized chronologically, the poems that we know Marvell wrote during the Revolutionary period begin to look more coherent than they did when scattered through Margoliouth's arrangement. Poems almost never mentioned in assessments of Marvell's concerns rise to the surface of our consciousness, and offer a surprising argument: Marvell was genuinely concerned with the foreign policy of the Commonwealth and Protectorate era. The Latin poem on Oliver St John's embassy to the United Provinces thus appropriately anticipates 'On the Character of Holland', which expresses English irritation at being forced to go to war with the United Provinces; Oliver St John is connected both by his 'great Name' and his present mission to Oliver Cromwell, but both poems are explicitly Commonwealth poems. The 'Letter to Doctor Ingelo' explores the embassy to Queen Christina of Sweden in terms of an analogy between Cromwell's Protestant Crusade in Europe, for which this Swedish alliance was crucial, and Godfrey of Bullogne's leadership of the first Crusade. The poem is connected to those just mentioned because Christina does not lend a 'Batavian ear' to the English ambassadors (*P&L*, 1:107, l. 121); that is to say, she does not refuse an alliance with England as had the Dutch.[9] The two short Latin poems on Cromwell's portrait as sent to Queen Christina connect backwards to the portrait of Christina mentioned in the 'Letter' ('Vidimus Effigiem, mistaque Coloribus Umbras'; 'we see his face, and the shadows mixed with colours') and actually sent to Cromwell in May 1653. This emphasis on international relations in the 1650s connects seamlessly with Marvell's three Restoration verse satires generated by the Second Dutch War,[10] and with his prose *Account of the Growth of Popery and Arbitrary Government* (1677), where Charles' breaking of the Triple League between Sweden, the United Provinces and England – whose architect was Sir William Temple – was described as a ploy aimed at bringing about the Third Dutch War. And, of course, these were the interests that took him to Russia, Sweden and Denmark for a full year and a half in 1663–5, as secretary to Charles Howard, Earl of Carlisle.[11]

The Cromwell poems

So we can now turn to what might be called the hard core of Marvell's Revolutionary poetry: the three 'Cromwell' poems: the 'Horatian Ode upon Cromwel's Return from Ireland', 'The First Anniversary of the Government under O.C.' and the 'Poem upon the Death of O.C.', and we must return to the striking historical fact that all three were cancelled from the *Miscellaneous Poems* of 1681 while the volume was actually in press, surviving only in two known copies. Even in those copies, the second half of the elegy for Cromwell (*P&L*, 1:134–9, lines 185–324) is missing and may never have been set by the printer. They were, however, written into the Popple manuscript, from whence they passed into Captain Edward Thompson's 1776 edition of Marvell's works. In addition, of these three undeniably 'Cromwell' poems, only one, the 'First Anniversary', was previously published, and that anonymously. The elegy was advertised in a volume including elegies by John Dryden and Thomas Sprat, but it was mysteriously withdrawn and replaced by a poem by George Wither. There seems to be something slightly perverse, however, in thus restoring to central position poems that Marvell himself and some of his friends (the Popple family being an exception) did not wish to highlight. On the other hand, we simply cannot understand the later Marvell unless we do so.

As I understand it now, the story is one in which Marvell, one of the most intelligent observers of his time, did not actually *want* to write about it, any more than he wished to be drawn into the debate about toleration exacerbated by Samuel Parker in the early 1670s, an exigency that led nevertheless to his writing both parts of the *Rehearsal Transpros'd*. Except for a few brief moments, he did not conceive of the Revolutionary era as his personal topic – during the Revolutionary era, that is: when it was over, however, it was forever the home of his allegiance and his touchstone for later, inglorious events. When, however, Marvell did at the time force himself to confront the unprecedented events of the 1640s and 1650s, especially, as in the 'Horatian Ode' and the 'First Anniversary', he produced the most shrewd and the most philosophical comments upon it that the poetry of the moment has to show.

With these spectacles on, as distinct from those which showed us only ambiguity or ambivalence in the 'Horatian Ode', let us now look back at its all-too-well-known opening lines:

> The forward Youth that would appear
> Must now forsake his *Muses* dear,
> Nor in the Shadows sing
> His Numbers languishing.
> 'Tis time to leave the Books in dust,
> And oyl th'unused Armours rust:
> Removing from the Wall
> The Corslet of the Hall.
>
> (*P&L*, 1:91)

It is hard to decide, either from the syntax or the metre, which of the dozen words in the first couplet carries the most weight with the least linguistic fanfare. This aspect of Marvell's style, his extraordinary capacity to reenergize the English monosyllable, to reinvest with significance words that we tend to use merely as fillers, has not been sufficiently appreciated – in part, perhaps, because of our admiration for phrases like 'vegetable Love', 'manacled in Hands', 'Magnanimous Despair' or 'the brotherless Heliades / Melt in such Amber Tears as these'. 'Now', of course, signifies the moment of 1650, an amazing moment, at exact mid-century, when the English had to decide how to live without a king (and a House of Lords and a voting episcopate). It may also signify, and seems to, a change of direction. Can we tell from this opening whether Marvell himself identifies with the forward or the backward youths of 1650 (he himself being twenty-nine)? With 'restless Cromwel' or with Charles I's 'helpless Right'? That other small word, *must*, however, acquires greater force as the poem continues. The sense of Necessity, perhaps undesirable, undergirds the poem, from that normally unstressed 'Must' (competing with 'now' for emphasis), through to the central philosophical proposition, that 'Nature . . . must make room / Where greater Spirits come', and thence to the final exhortation to Cromwell to keep his military prowess alive: 'The same Arts that did gain / A Pow'r must it maintain'. Later, Marvell was to resist arguments drawn from Necessity. In *The Rehearsal Transpros'd: the Second Part* he reproves Samuel Parker for his use of that verb form ('Still *must, must, must* . . . Why, *must* again, eight times at least in litle more than one page'; 'You may please hencefor-ward to write your self Mr *Necessity Bayes*'.[12]) What justifies the appeal to

Necessity in the 'Horatian Ode', however, is the last section of the poem – less compelling to readers today than its 'memorable' and pathetic centre – where Marvell justifies the use of violent restlessness in terms of an imperialist Protestant (and republican) crusade in Europe:

> What may not then our *Isle* presume
> While Victory his Crest does plume! . . .
> A *Caesar* he ere long to *Gaul*,
> To *Italy* an *Hannibal*,
> And to all States not free
> Shall *Clymacterick* be.
>
> (lines 97–8, 101–4)

In other words, the quieter imperatives of the poem's opening lines are retrospectively justified, and subsumed under the authority of a mission that in its modernity and reforming zeal rests securely on classical precedent. Much as we may now dislike the emphasis, this ending matches the last eighteen lines of the 'Character of Holland', where Cromwell has become 'our Neptune' shaking a trident 'Steel'd with those piercing Heads, Dean, Monck and Blake' (*P&L*, 1:103).

Written for December 1654, the anniversary of Cromwell's first year as Protector of England, the 'First Anniversary' had a number of different tasks to perform: the first, to comment on the main events and accomplishments of 1654; the second, to discuss the legitimacy of Cromwell's single rule, the nature of his title, and his first decision to refuse the crown of England; the third, to anticipate the future. Whereas in the 'Horatian Ode' Marvell had selected the unusual but entirely appropriate adverb 'indefatigably' (l. 114) to anticipate what Cromwell should do in Europe after his victory over the Irish, now four years later he can claim it as the proper, the proven definition. In contrast to the 'heavy Monarchs' who preceded him, who 'neither build the Temple in their dayes, / Nor Matter for succeeding Founders raise' (*P&L*, 1:109, lines 33–4):

> indefatigable *Cromwell* hyes,
> And cuts his way still nearer to the Skyes.
>
> (lines 46–7)

More hyperbolically, Marvell asserts, he 'in one Year the work of Ages acts' (l. 14). But what, precisely, has he accomplished? If we look to history, Cromwell has put an end to the First Dutch War, and diverted one of his fleets to the conquest of Jamaica; summoned his first Parliament, in September, and by December excluded ninety members from it for refusing to sign a loyalty oath to himself; struggled with the Levellers and the Fifth

Monarchy Men, some of whom were executed; and had an embarrassing coaching accident at the end of September. The naval victories against Spain belong to the following year. Given this record, it is surprising how much of the poem, quantitatively speaking, is devoted to the idea of Cromwell as military conqueror. There is a longish digression dedicated to the coaching accident (lines 176–222), which Marvell transforms from an embarrassment into an opportunity to reflect on the appalling but inevitable prospect of Cromwell's actual death. There are paragraphs devoted to discrediting the Levellers and Fifth Monarchy Men (lines 259–310). And there is, of course, the wonderfully stirring, mythical account of the Instrument of Government (lines 49–98), in which Marvell fully develops the architectural metaphor for church- and state-building that he had found in Milton's *Areopagitica*, a typically inventive piece of borrowing. Where Milton had merely stressed the variety of materials out of which the architects of the new Temple must learn to create a stable structure, Marvell turned the 'resistance of opposed Minds' which Cromwell had discovered in his first Parliament into a scientific principle, whereby the centrifugal pressures of disagreement and sectarianism are contained and turned to good by the downward pressure of 'the Roofs Protecting weight' (l. 98), that is to say, by Cromwell's personal domination.

All this, however, amounts to about 150 lines out of a total of 400. It is easy, diverted by the imaginative strategies Marvell uses for his more apologetic sections, to overlook the sheer amount of space devoted to restating the imperialist premises broached in the 'Horatian Ode'. To begin with, Marvell's complaint against the 'heavy Monarchs' who have preceded Cromwell in the leadership of Europe includes a complaint about their lack of military successes:

> Yet some more active for a Frontier town
> Took in by Proxie, beggs a false Renown;
> Another triumphs at the publick Cost,
> And will have Wonn, if he no more have Lost;
> They fight by Others, but in Person wrong,
> And only are against their Subjects strong;
> Their other Wars seem but a feign'd contest,
> This Common Enemy is still opprest;
> If Conquerors, on them they turn their might;
> If Conquered, on them they wreak their Spight.
>
> (lines 23–32)

These complaints, difficult to pin down today as specific referents to the reigns of the first two Stuarts, would have acquired a new topicality in the reign of the third, when Charles II's pretext of the Second Dutch War,

Marvell argued, was designed as a move in his secret campaign to undermine his subjects' rights and liberties.

Next, and immediately following the justification of the Instrument of Government, comes Marvell's fuller development of the crusading theory of the 'Ode', coloured now by millenarian texts and metaphors. In fact, it appears that the preceding section – on constitutional innovation at home – was merely preparatory to surveying the wider theatre of international relations; for 'When for his Foot he thus a place had found, / He hurles e'r since the world about him round' (lines 99–100). Returning to the theme of Cromwell's difference from other princes, Marvell invokes the lines from Revelation and the Book of Daniel that promise the passing away of all human kingdoms. 'Observing Princes' court Cromwell as the forerunner of the Apocalypse, yet fail to read the Biblical prophecies correctly:

> O would they rather by his Pattern won
> Kiss the approaching, nor yet angry Son; . . .
> How might they under such a Captain raise
> The great Designes kept for the latter Dayes!
>
> (lines 105–6, 109–10)

It is at this point in the poem that Marvell inserts himself, as Cromwell's self-appointed interpreter (a harbinger of the harbinger), in a most uncharacteristic statement of literary intention:

> Unhappy Princes, ignorantly bred,
> By Malice some, by Errour more misled;
> If gracious Heaven to my Life give length,
> Leisure to Time, and to my Weakness Strength,
> Then shall I once with graver Accents shake
> Your Regal sloth, and your long Slumbers wake:
> Like the shrill Huntsman that prevents the East,
> Winding his Horn to Kings that chase the Beast.
>
> (lines 117–24)

For many reasons (some of them hinted at within this poem) Marvell would never keep this promise during Cromwell's lifetime; but after his death he would savagely attack the secular ambitions of Louis XIV of France, in his *Account of the Growth of Popery*, not to mention those of Charles II; and into the *Second Part* of the *Rehearsal Transpros'd* he introduced a cannily modified version of the doctrine of Revelation, here designed to remind Charles II that the institution he represents does not have Scriptural sanction:

> Indeed although Christ did not assume an earthly and visible kingdome, yet he
> by the Gospel gave Law to Princes and Subjects . . . And he knew very well that

without dethroning the Princes of the World at present, yet by the constant preaching of that benevolous and amiable Doctrine, . . . all opposition would be worn out, and all Princes should make place for a Christian Empire.[13]

Putting these passages from 1654 and 1673 side by side helps to explain the seeming contradictions in Marvell's thinking between militaristic and pacificist imperatives; for only Oliver Cromwell had seemed for a moment to provide that impossible merger of cross and sword, that rationale for fighting (and now, in 1655, for writing as well) in the service of a just war underwritten by Christian prophecy.

Seemed for a moment; because in the very next paragraph of the 'Anniversary' Marvell admits the doubts in this central hypothesis. He admits that a millenarian explanation for Cromwell's remarkable prowess is only a hope:

> But a thick Cloud about that Morning lyes,
> And intercepts the Beams of Mortal eyes,
> That 'tis the most which we determine can,
> If these the Times, then this must be the Man.
>
> (lines 141–4)

The two most crucial words in these lines, again, as in the 'Ode', carrying far more stress than their syntactic and metrical position would suppose, are 'If' and 'must', this being the first time that the word of Necessity has appeared in this longer poem. There are two other weight-bearing 'musts' in the 'Anniversary', one at the end of Marvell's apology for Cromwell's firm dealings with the sectarians ('Him as their Father must the State obey' (l. 282)) and the final lament of the foreign princes about Cromwell's naval supremacy ('Needs must we all their Tributaries be, / Whose Navies hold the Sluces of the Sea' (lines 367–8)). In the passage where Marvell subjects the dreams of millenarianism to his own scrupulous intelligence, however, the 'must' is completely dominated by the 'if', the condition that we cannot as yet tell whether the latter days are indeed upon us, or if, as indeed it proved, the Cromwellian state was itself to disintegrate.

This brings us to the remarkable structural fact that the 'First Anniversary' ends by giving the last say on Cromwell not to his dependent poet but to the foreign princes whom 'his' navy or his diplomacy have challenged since 1651: fifty-two lines of reluctant compliment, expressed as military fear and epistemological confusion as to how such power can be embodied in someone not a king. Marvell even admits, in his close, that the kings of Europe can, as he imagines their responses, surpass himself in giving the measure of the man, if only man he be.

It is worth quoting half of this tribute, partly because it illustrates the mastery of contradiction within the pentameter line that Marvell would later use for his praise of *Paradise Lost*, and that Alexander Pope would learn from; partly because it sets up my last hinge between the Cromwellian and the Restoration Marvell, proving that they are indeed the same person. The issue is control of the sea, which stands for control of the world:

> The Ocean is the Fountain of Command,
> But that once took, we Captives are on Land.
> And those that have the Waters for their share,
> Can quickly leave us neither Earth nor Air.
> Yet if through these our Fears could find a pass;
> Through double Oak, & lin'd with treble Brass;
> That one Man still, although but nam'd, alarms
> More then all Men, all Navies, and all Arms. . . .
> The Nation had been ours, but his one Soul
> Moves the great Bulk, and animates the whole.
> He Secrecy with Number hath inchas'd,
> Courage with Age, Maturity with Hast;
> The Valiants Terror, Riddle of the Wise;
> And still his Fauchion all our Knots unties.
>
> (lines 369–76, 379–84)

The last four lines attempt the same feat of oxymoronic definition as would Marvell's lines about Milton's heroic act of writing *Paradise Lost*, where 'At once delight and horrour on us seize, / Thou singst with so much gravity and ease' (*P&L*, 1:138). In the sphere of theology as well as poetry, delight and horror are caused by the normally incompatible qualities of gravity and ease – qualities that Marvell himself had attempted to combine in the *Rehearsal Transpros'd*, though there he called the second of the pair 'levity'. In the sphere of international relations, Cromwell's uniqueness consists in part of being able to manifest courage, the quality of rash youth, with the authority of age, maturity with the capacity to make speedy decisions, to act the work of ages in a single year. The interweaving of 'Secrecy with Number', however, is more enigmatic. Does it reject the *arcana imperii* (secrets of state) of the Stuarts as against the Cromwellian use of even a constricted form of democratic council in the decision-making process? Or are the words deliberately Old Testament in their resonance, without being tied to a particular Biblical text?

This passage also supports, remarkably, my hypothesis that Marvell, during the Restoration, continued to write about the Revolutionary period, as it were by default. Occasionally he did so by deliberate, parodic echo of his own earlier tributes. The complaints of the foreign monarchs about Cromwell's naval supremacy, for example, reappear in the *Third Advice to a Painter* (1666) as a critique of the naval strategy of the Second Dutch War.

The charge is that Charles II, having withdrawn his brother from command of the fleet because it was too dangerous to risk the heir to the throne in open warfare, made a fatal mistake in dividing that command in 1666 between Prince Rupert and General Monck (who had earlier been praised as part of a divided command, one of the three points of the Cromwellian trident in the 'Character of Holland'). Apart from revealing how much Marvell was willing to change his mind, if not his principles, the interest of this critique lies in its character of self-quotation:

> First paint me George and Rupert, ratling far
> Within one box, like the two Dice of War:
> And let the terrour of their linked Name
> Fly through the aire like chainshot, tearing Fame. . . .
> United Gen'ralls! sure the only spell
> Wherewith United Provinces to quell.
> Alas, ev'n they, though shell'd in treble Oake
> Will prove an addle Egge with double Yolke.
>
> (lines 11–14, 17–20)[14]

Readers should be able to see how deftly Marvell has reorganized the quantitative component in the complaint of the foreign monarchs, so that epic becomes mock-heroic. Whereas in the earlier poem Europe fears Cromwell's navy 'could find a pass; / Through double Oak, & lin'd with treble Brass', now 'double Oak' becomes a 'double Yolke', protected by something as flimsy as eggshell. And it now takes two Restoration generals with their 'linked Name' to attempt, against one small country, what 'That one Man . . . although but nam'd' accomplished in his foreign policy and colonial ventures throughout the better part of Europe.

Space does not permit extending this analysis to the elegy for Cromwell, although the reader who revisits it in the light of this argument may be surprised to discover, despite the more domestic framework of the lament, and the insertion of new values, Love and Grief, how much of the poem remains a praise of Cromwell's militarism. It is easy, for instance, to overlook the brief reprise of Marvell's claim that there is room in literary history for a Cromwellian epic:

> Thee, many ages hence, in martial verse
> Shall th'English souldier, ere he charge, rehearse;
> Singing of thee, inflame themselves to fight,
> And with the name of Cromwell, armyes fright.
>
> (P&L, 1:136, lines 277–80)

In conclusion, however, it would be best to glance back at the lines in the 'First Anniversary' that follow Marvell's millenarian hypothesis, 'If these the Times, then this must be the Man'. What follows is this:

> And well he therefore does, and well has guest,
> Who in his Age has always forward prest:
> And knowing not where Heavens choice may light,
> Girds yet his Sword, and ready stands to fight.
>
> *(P&L*, i:112, lines 145–8)

Especially recalling the opening injunction to 'the Forward Youth' of the 'Horatian Ode', there is reason to apply these lines not only to Cromwell but to Marvell himself, and to the programme that he was only just beginning to imagine in 1650. Good guesswork, the ability to keep a good many secrets of his own, and a particularly touching brand of courage kept Marvell at work during the Restoration for causes of which, he might have thought, Cromwell would not have disapproved. Writing in May 1673 to Sir Edward Harley about his plans to finally close down Samuel Parker's campaign against the Nonconformists, Marvell claimed to be 'drawn in, I hope by a good Providence, to intermeddle in a noble and high argument' (*P&L*, ii:328). In October 1674 he wrote to Sir Henry Thompson a letter still passionately focused on international diplomacy:

> There are strong indevors by us & the Swedes towards a Peace this Winter And I know not whether we shall haue a mind to spend some of our Treasury in an Army to force the victorious French to accept of a Peace or whether we shall be able to put the Scotch upon rebellion and make another good Old Cause of it.   *(P&L*, ii:330)

Perhaps most tellingly, in an earlier letter to Thomas Rolt, a friend in Persia and hence in need of a newsletter from England, he wrote: 'We truckle to *France* in all Things, to the Prejudice of our Alliance and Honour.' He also wrote, however, 'in this World a good Cause signifys little, unless it be well defended' (*P&L*, ii:325, 324).

NOTES

1 D. I. B. Smith (ed.), *The Rehearsal Transpros'd and The Rehearsal Transpros'd: the Second Part* (Oxford: Clarendon Press, 1971), p. 135.
2 For debates about the attribution of this poem to Marvell, see *P&L*, i:414–15.
3 *P&L*, i:415. Margoliouth was citing from a manuscript volume in his own possession.
4 I.e. *P&L*. A major new edition, edited by Nigel Smith, is forthcoming from Longman.
5 For an account of the Popple manuscript, Bodleian Ms. Eng. Poet. d.49, and its claims to authenticity, see Annabel Patterson, *Marvell: The Writer in Public Life* (Harlow: Longman, 2000), pp. 6 and 77–8.
6 The appointment was as assistant to John Milton, the Commonwealth's Secretary for Foreign Tongues responsible for the regime's Latin correspondence with foreign states and dignitaries. Milton had first recommended Marvell for this post

in 1653; for the remainder of Milton's life, Marvell would remain his admiring friend (William Riley Parker, *Milton: A Biography*, rev. Gordon Campbell, 2nd edn (Oxford: Clarendon Press, 1996), 1:425, 427, 451–2, 506).

7 Critics who have focused on the politically engaged Marvell include Warren Chernaik, *The Poet's Time: Politics and Religion in the Work of Andrew Marvell* (Cambridge University Press, 1983); Patsy Griffin, *The Modest Ambition of Andrew Marvell* (Newark: University of Delaware Press, 1995); David Norbrook, *Writing the English Republic* (Cambridge University Press, 1999); and the various contributors to Warren Chernaik and Martin Dzelzainis (eds.), *Marvell and Liberty* (Basingstoke: Macmillan, 1999).

8 By Alan Pritchard, 'Marvell's "The Garden": A Restoration Poem?' *Studies in English Literature*, 23 (1983), 371–88.

9 In Latin literature, the inhabitants of the area which later became Holland were called *Batavi*.

10 For a restatement of my case that Marvell wrote, in addition to the *Last Instructions to a Painter*, the *Second* and *Third Advice to a Painter*, see Patterson, *Marvell*, pp. 77–97.

11 For this episode, and for Marvell's biography more generally, see Pierre Legouis, *Andrew Marvell: Poet, Puritan, Patriot* (Oxford: Clarendon Press, 1968).

12 Smith (ed.), *Rehearsal Transpros'd*, pp. 190, 231.

13 Smith (ed.), *Rehearsal Transpros'd*, p. 236 (italics added).

14 For the text of the *Advices*, see Patterson, *Marvell*, which transcribes these poems as registered in the Popple manuscript in an appendix.

FURTHER READING

For individual editions of primary texts cited or discussed, please see the notes above.

Chernaik, Warren, *The Poet's Time: Politics and Religion in the Work of Andrew Marvell*, Cambridge University Press, 1983.

Chernaik, Warren, and Martin Dzelzainis (eds.), *Marvell and Liberty*, Basingstoke: Macmillan, 1999.

Condren, A. D., and Tony Cousins (eds.), *The Political Identity of Andrew Marvell*, London: Scolar Press, 1990.

Legouis, Pierre, *Andrew Marvell: Poet, Puritan, Patriot*, Oxford: Clarendon Press, 1968.

Patterson, Annabel, *Marvell: The Writer in Public Life*, Harlow: Longman, 2000.

3
FEMALE VOICES

7

SUSAN WISEMAN

Women's poetry

Introduction

Women writing poetry during the English Civil Wars did not think of women, or of poetry, in the ways which are familiar to us. The idea of the 'woman poet', if it can be said to have existed at all, would have had little resemblance to the way in which we understand those words today. The frames of interpretation brought to poetry, and more specifically to poetry by women, were very different. What we have come to think of as 'self-expression' was not important until after the Romantic era; the poets examined in this chapter (with the possible exception of Margaret Cavendish) wrote in a world where poetic skill was measured by emulation of Classical and other texts, by use of form, by elaboration of image. Women's poetry, however, was also interpreted in terms of what made a good or bad woman, so frames of interpretation linked women's poetry to feminized standards of intellectual achievement and to assumptions about the place of women in the public eye – in short, to what Jonathan Goldberg calls the legend of good (or bad) women.[1] While women were not necessarily discouraged from writing by their families they certainly were not expected to participate in public literary culture; women's poetry had to make difficult negotiations amongst institutions, audiences and texts.[2]

Current critical approaches inevitably address women's poetry in ways influenced by contemporary interests in cultural and gender politics, but women's writing from the Civil War period has been the focus of several different kinds of arguments. Some critics have sought the origins of feminism in seventeenth-century texts – texts arguably situated at the inaugural moment of modernity. Thus, Hilda Smith and Catherine Gallagher have argued for a connection between Royalism and proto-feminism. For Elaine Hobby, however, radicalism as much as Royalism offered women a chance to write. She sees the 1640s as a moment at which all political ideologies were challenged and she traces in the Civil War period a flowering not necessarily of feminist writing, but of writing by women in a wider sense.[3] For Hobby, the Restoration of the monarchy brought a silencing of these voices. The process of writing about 'women' is, thus, far from simple; as Margaret Ezell argues it is problematic to understand seventeenth-century poetry through ideas of authorship and publication which developed in the nineteenth century.[4] In the seventeenth century, poems which circulated in manuscript were neither completely 'public' nor completely 'private'; rather, they imagined and were addressed to a specific and politically designated audience.[5] Often what might at first sight look like a self-enclosed poem, as the lyric is understood to be in the post-Romantic period, turns out to have been pressed into polemical service. What is shared between early modern and contemporary understandings of women's poetry is, perhaps, only the sheer force of the expectations brought to bear on it.

The responses of women poets to the events and ideas of the English Civil War, although inflected by their sex and its cultural constraints, were also determined by other equally complex factors: politics, status, geography. Civil War poetry was, for women no less than for men, a poetry of argument and controversy. In tracing the very different responses – poetic, aesthetic and political – of women's poetry to the war this chapter examines the work of four poets who, in different ways, saw politics as central to the poetic enterprise: Katherine Philips (1632–64) and Margaret Cavendish (1623–73), who are both usually understood as Royalist poets; and Anne Bradstreet (1612–72) and Lucy Hutchinson (1620–81), both supporters of the Long Parliament in the 1640s.

Katherine Philips

Katherine Philips wrote from an early age, but a substantial proportion of her poetry was written when she was living in Wales in the 1650s. Although she came from a middle-class London family with Puritan views and with connections to John Milton, Philips identified with the Stuart cause and with the Prayer-Book worship of the episcopal church.[6] Her husband, Colonel James Philips, held very different views from her: he worked for the Commonwealth and served Cromwell's Protectorate. His wife's political views caused him problems during the 1650s when her poetry circulated in manuscript in Wales, but the fact that, at the Restoration, contemporaries recognized her as loyal and pro-Stuart significantly changed the shape of her career as a poet.

As far as Katherine Philips was concerned, true poetry had been banished under the Republic. In her commendatory verse for the 1651 volume of William Cartwright's posthumously published works she wrote:

3 Engraved frontispiece portrait to Katherine Philips' *Poems*, 1667.

But when those happy powers that guard thy dust,
To us and to thy memory shall be Just,
And by a flame from thy blest Genius lent,
Rescue us from our dull imprisonment,
Unsequester our fancys, and create
A worth that may upon thy glory wait;
We then shall understand thee, and descry
The splendour of restored Poetry.

(*Works*, I:143)

William Cartwright, who died in Oxford in 1643, had been a Royalist soldier and a poet and playwright. The memorial volume, which carried fifty or so prefatory verses, both commemorated Cartwright and asserted Royalist modes of poetry. Philips deliberately associates herself with this Royalist poetic by putting in play tropes associating wit with Royalism – or, as she puts it, 'Such horrid ignorance benights the times / That wit and honour are become our crimes.' Continuing this analogy between true wit and Royalism, the poem's concluding assertion that it would be 'Treason to debase thy coyn' sees in Cartwright's verse an example of the best in poetry and in politics, so that to 'debase' its true currency is to commit 'treason' against both wit and the beleaguered Stuart cause. Elsewhere, in a commendatory verse to a volume of poems by her associate Henry Vaughan, Philips reiterates her disgust at the vulgar spirits of the Republic, suggesting that, had she 'adored the multitude', she would have caught 'an antipathy to wit and sence' (1:96). Like Cartwright, Vaughan is described as one whose poetry 'Restor'st the golden age when verse was law' (1:97). In 1651 Philips' fusion of loyalty and wit, rendering aesthetics indistinguishable from politics, marked her poetry as Royalist and aligned her with others who longed to reinstate a monarchical golden age.[7]

Besides using the shared vocabulary of Royalist poetry, Philips established a highly charged poetic discourse on friendship which worked to political ends. Poems to her friends, addressed under names taken from romances and from Cartwright's works, were circulated in manuscript in the 1650s, making wit and friendship tokens of poetic exchange in a semi-private counter-culture opposing the Commonwealth and Protectorate. Thus, 'Friendship in Emblem, or the Seale, to my dearest Lucasia', Philips' epistolary name for Mrs Anne Owen whom she met in 1651, opens 'The hearts thus intermixed speak / A Love that no bold shock can break' and continues, 'That friendship hearts so much refines, / It nothing but itself designs' (*Works*, 1:106). The charged language of self-enclosure here establishes a sealed and self-sufficient association between the friends which stands in opposition to the 'lower ends', 'smoak or hurt' and 'grossness' of the world. Friendship, and more specifically the imagined exchanges of that friendship between women within Philips' own poetry, offers a bastion against the degenerate standards of the unrestored world and – at least imaginatively – draws others into this alternative world where 'friendship governs actions best, / Prescribing Law to all the rest'. Thus, widely shared tropes of Royalist poetry are elaborated by Katherine Philips to provide not only an aesthetic bulwark against the world she was forced to inhabit, but also to invoke the sense of an oppositional community – moral, political and aesthetic – strictly limited to loyal friends by the boundaries of epistolary and manuscript circulation. Manuscript circulation, in the case of the poems of the 1650s, is bound up with the project of establishing an alternative world, both withdrawn from, and challenging, the wholly public sphere of print.

At the Restoration, it was Philips rather than her husband who was politically in favour. She established court connections, particularly with Sir

Charles Cotterell, Charles II's Master of Ceremonies. After the success of her translation of Corneille's *Pompey* (performed in Dublin in 1663 and published in the same year), Philips was sufficiently well known for a pirated edition of her poems to be published. She responded to this with her own selection, posthumously published after her death from smallpox, which began with a poem ostentatiously calling attention not only to her loyalty to the Stuarts under the republic but also to her active struggle with writers of different political views. The first poem in this 1664 volume, 'Upon the double murther of K.Charles, in answer to a libellous rime made by V.P.', is a polemical poem which justifies Philips as a woman writer commenting on politics. It asserts her status as a poetic controversialist writing in support of the Stuarts during the Interregnum:

> I thinke not on the state, nor am concern'd
> Which way soever that great Helme is turn'd,
> But as that sonne whose father's danger nigh
> Did force his native dumbnesse, and untye
> The fettred organs: so here is a cause
> That will excuse the breach of nature's lawes.
> Silence were now a Sin: Nay passion now
> Wise men themselves for merit would allow.
> What noble eye could see, (and carelesse passe)
> The dying Lion kick'd by every asse?
>
> (*Works*, 1:69)

The 'asse' in question had been Vavasour Powell, a preacher with strong sympathies with the Fifth Monarchist group and with whom her husband had had connections in the 1650s.[8] Thus, at the Restoration, Philips' manuscript poetry written in the 1650s worked to ensure her place as an acknowledged, Royalist, poet.

Margaret Cavendish

Although she is often associated with Philips as a Royalist poet, the poetry of Margaret Cavendish, Duchess of Newcastle, has little of Philips' sense of a Royalist endeavour expressed in a shared vocabulary. Where Philips' poetic persona is bound up with her invention of an imagined oppositional network of friendship and Royalism, Margaret Cavendish insists on her own uniqueness and singularity. This leads her to present a very different version of the early modern idea of the woman writer, openly promoting her individual identity in a bid for applause and lasting fame. Cavendish is further distinguished from the other poets considered here in that she had acquired only a little education before she met her future husband, William

Cavendish, Duke of Newcastle. They met at the court of Henrietta-Maria in France where she was a lady-in-waiting when her future husband joined the Royalist exiles following his defeat at the battle of Marston Moor. It was only after her marriage that Cavendish began to write and to publish. Indeed, a feature of Cavendish's first book, *Poems and Fancies* (1653), and one which came to characterize her work, is the participation of her husband in the process of composition. His contribution of a commendatory verse is extended to the inclusion of poems and, in later texts such as the play *The Publique Wooing* (1662), to the collaborative writing of scenes.[9]

Poems and Fancies has an ambitious range of concerns. It deals with government, with what we would now call scientific discourse (many of the poems develop Cavendish's theory of atoms), with social status, relations amongst men and women and between women, and with romance. As in most of Cavendish's work, the themes are given an almost entirely secular treatment. She uses the poems to work through opinions – often highly tendentious opinions – on issues from politics to the physical nature of matter. For example, although her assertion that, when 'rough Seas, whom highly Windes inrage, / Assault a Ship', a ruler needs to be 'like skil'd *Mariners*' to guide it 'to a *Haven* safe' is in part a platitude, the simile nevertheless engages critically with the need for a ruler to have specific skills, not simply status (*Poems and Fancies*, p. 147).

Cavendish became a prolific writer, publishing poems, prose romances, letters, orations, scientific speculations as well as what are now her best-known texts, the prose *The Description of a New World, Called The Blazing World* (1666) and her plays, including *The Convent of Pleasure* (1662). Despite this publication record, however, Cavendish continued to have a vexed relationship to her intellectual aspirations and to her ambitions as a poet. Throughout her life, her writing is characterized by paradox and contradiction: an unusual insistence on her status as an author cohabits with assertions of her lack of training in formal thought. As her sympathetic biographer notes, amongst poets she seems to have known mainly Ovid, Shakespeare, Jonson, Donne and Davenant.[10] Yet, even in her first volume, Cavendish is keen to be widely recognized as an author and throughout her career circulated her folio volumes to the eminent. She writes, 'so if my *Writing* please the *Readers*, though not the *Learned*, it wil satisfie me; for I had rather be praised in this, by the *most*, although not the *best*. For all I desire, is *Fame*, and *Fame* is nothing but a *great noise*, and *noise* lives most in a *Multitude*; wherefore I wish my *Book* may set a worke every *Tongue*' (*Poems and Fancies*, sig. A3r). Although she was writing from the exile she shared with her husband, Cavendish envisaged a substantial audience, embracing the universities, individuals to whom she sent her book, and 'noble ladies'. However, in terms of her understanding of the role of the woman author, Cavendish is characteristically contradictory. While asserting her own importance, Cavendish's preface to *Poems and Fancies*, 'To All Noble and Worthy Ladies', simultaneously places a high and a low value on women's imaginative faculties, arguing that '*Poetry*, which is built upon *Fancy*, *Women* may claime, as a *worke* belonging most properly to themselves' (sig. A3r).[11] She characterizes her own efforts both as feminine (and therefore minor) and as having all the importance of a production of that newly fledged creature, the author.

Despite having had little formal education, Cavendish took full advantage of the opportunity to meet leading natural scientists of the day when exiled with her Royalist husband in Antwerp. Her first volume of poetry is marked by a fascination with theories of matter which she was to pursue into the Restoration. Thus, at times, as in 'Of Burning', she writes with a combination of vivid originality, strong opinion and learning which is both partly digested and partly challenged:

> The cause why Fire doth burne, and burning smarts,
> The reason is of *Numerous* little *parts*.
> Which *parts* are *Atomes sharpe*, that wound like Stings,
> If they so far do pierce into our Skyns;
> And like an angry *Porcupine*, doth shoot
> His fiery *Quils*, if nothing quench them out.
>
> (*Poems and Fancies*, p. 27)

Cavendish continued to include poetry in later volumes. Thus, *Natures Pictures Drawn By Fancies Pencil* (1656) includes a selection of narrative poems introduced with the conceit that they are told when 'In Winter cold, a company was met / Both Men and Women by the fire set' (p. 1).

For all that Cavendish, describing the triumph of 'the Commons' in 'A Description of the Civil Wars', had written of how 'then astride / Fierce Tyrannie on Noble Necks did ride' (*Natures Pictures*, pp. 88–9), the difference between Philips' Royalism and Cavendish's politics is illuminated most clearly at the Restoration. Philips wrote a sequence of panegyrics to royal figures, made connections at court, and saw her poems from the 1650s published.[12] Cavendish, however, lived on after Philips' death into a time when the restored monarchy was to seem tawdry. Her concerns in the Restoration continued to be with the new science (she visited the Royal Society), with writing and with status, but her post-war writings also develop a critique of courts and of royal favourites. Her *Life* of her husband (1667) she called a 'short History', 'as full of Truths as words'. Its account of her husband's 'Actions and Su'fferings' specifies the debts he had incurred through his commitment to the Royalist cause and is indignant at his neglect and ill-treatment by Charles II and the restored regime.

Anne Bradstreet

In contrast to Cavendish and, particularly, to Philips, Anne Bradstreet and Lucy Hutchinson both supported Parliament in the 1640s. Bradstreet's first volume of poetry, *The Tenth Muse Lately Sprung up in America*, was published in 1650 in England. It is not clear how much control she had over the volume's publication or structure, or even whether she wanted her poems to appear in print; it was her brother-in-law who in 1647 took the poems which appeared in *The Tenth Muse* to England for publication, without, so he stated in its preface, Bradstreet's knowledge and contrary to her wishes.[13]

Bradstreet's critical reception has for some time been influenced by Adrienne Rich's valuation of *The Tenth Muse* as 'remarkably impersonal even by Puritan standards', and her preference for Bradstreet's later, more 'personal' domestic and familial lyrics. Rich's view of Bradstreet implies a particular conception of the woman writer: she is critical of the fact that 'personal history – marriage, childbearing, death – is . . . excluded from the book'. It implies, too, a particular understanding of the 'American' writer: she claims that 'New England never enters' *The Tenth Muse* and holds that 'These long, rather listless pieces seem to have been composed in a last compulsive effort to stay in contact with the history, traditions, and values of her former world.'[14] What Rich's account of *The Tenth Muse* misses is the volume's active engagement with Civil War genres, its sense that the two sides of the Atlantic are linked, and that Old and New England are playing different, though connected, roles in the pattern of Protestant history. *The Tenth Muse* positively invites interpretation as an intervention in Civil War poetics and as a volume which initiates an Atlantic (rather than 'English' or 'American') perspective on the conflict.[15] Once we recognize that, in the 1650s, an 'American' identity was not available and that *The Tenth Muse* makes a highly self-conscious intervention in the political and aesthetic debates of the Civil War, debates which had implications for English speakers and others on both sides of the Atlantic, a reconsideration of Bradstreet as a poet of the Civil War becomes possible.

Critical opinion notwithstanding, *The Tenth Muse* does emphasize Bradstreet's location. The topics, genres and themes indicate that the volume as a whole addresses Puritanism and government in New and Old England. In 1650 the political identity of New England was bound, though not exclusively, to the histories of the Old World just as it was tied to, and partly disavowed, the geography of the New. Bradstreet begins her volume with a poem to her father, to whom her poems were 'humbly presented'. She acknowledges that it was her father's poem, now lost, on the 'four parts of the world' which inspired her to write.[16] This opening is often interpreted solely as a gesture of modesty by Bradstreet, and it does indeed serve to acknowledge her father's precedence. However, in acknowledging him through his poem on the 'four parts of the world' she also recognizes the importance of spatial positioning, including, implicitly, her own as 'Tenth Muse', and begins to signal her own contrasting turn to history. In 'The Prologue', the very next poem and another poem usually interpreted as evidence of Bradstreet's genuine deference to masculine authority, she asserts that she is unworthy 'To sing of Wars, of Captaines, and of Kings, / Of Cities founded, Common-wealths begun', 'Let Poets, and Historians set these forth, / My obscure verse shall not dim their worth' (*Works*, p. 6); but 'Wars', 'Captaines' and 'Kings' are exactly the main poetic focus of the first section of the volume. Clearly, Bradstreet's disclaimer must be treated with some caution. Indeed, as I will show, Bradstreet sometimes asserts modesty and ignorance at the very moment she is making a comment that might be construed as transgressing feminine decorum.

Taking its lead from her father's poem the first part of *The Tenth Muse* analyses elements in fours: humours, ages of man, seasons and, most significantly, in the longest (though unfinished) poem in the book (over a hundred pages), 'the Four Monarchies of the World' (*Works*, pp. 65–179), that is, the four ancient empires of Assyria, Persia, Greece and Rome. Constitutional imbalance and political history, which these poems deal with, offered frames of reference within which the crisis of Civil War and regicide were currently being interpreted. Bradstreet's poems, written in the colonial context, engage with ways of thinking and with genres central and current in the metropolis. 'The Foure Monarchies', usually read by critics as a bookish imitation of Sir Walter Raleigh's *History of the World* (1614), positively demands to be read as an original exercise in Protestant poetic historiography and a striking meditation upon contemporary affairs. That it ends with the rape of Lucretia, the death of the last Roman king, Tarquin, and the founding of the Roman Republic was inescapably suggestive in relation to mid seventeenth-century English politics.

How are we to read this long poem by a woman first published in England the year after the regicide and clearly addressing questions to do with monarchy, with Protestantism, and with Republicanism? A poem using the four ancient monarchies to interpret history was far from remote to a seventeenth-century reader. It was a strategy which combined interest in the Classical world and in Biblical narratives by applying the prophecies of Daniel to world history. The successive empires, degenerating to the end of the Roman empire after which would come the millennium, offered a pattern to history which, by the 1640s, had become an important topic of political and religious debate: when would the end be? Such questions invited comparison between the prophecies of Daniel and the present state of England during the crises of war, and, to many, the chaos of war suggested that the end might come in the near, rather than the distant, future.[17] Bradstreet puts this motivating pattern to work within the shape of a history poem which also draws on Raleigh and, to an extent, on Joshua Sylvester's translation of Du Bartas' creation epic *Devine Weekes and Workes* (1605). In such a poem aesthetic concerns are clearly subordinate to an understanding of past and recent history, a point which Lucy Hutchinson makes quite explicitly in her later investigation of divine time, *Order and Disorder* (published in part in 1679).[18] Bradstreet's poem is not only, in Gerald MacLean's term, an 'appeal' to history, but also an appeal to the divine pattern hidden therein.[19] Tracing a succession of crises generated by monarchy, much of the poem foregrounds examples of inadequacy or tyranny, leaving the reader to infer the connection between degeneracy and the fading of each empire.

That Bradstreet's use of examples invites dialectical reading, by which the reader draws parallels between past incidents and the contemporary crisis of monarchy, is indicated by the text's opening passages:

> When Time was young, and World in infancy,
> Man did not strive for Soveraignty,
> But each one thought his petty rule was high,
> If of his house he held the Monarchy:
> This was the Golden Age, but after came
> The boysterous Son of *Cush*, Grand-child to *Ham*,
> That mighty Hunter, who in his strong toyls,
> Both Beasts and man subjected to his spoyls.
> The strong foundation of proud Babel laid,
> *Erech, Accad,* and *Calneh* also made.
>
> (*Works*, p. 53)

In opening her poem with Nimrod, Bradstreet's account of the birth of political time fuses Biblical and Classical accounts of a time before empire and political hegemony, a time destroyed by 'boysterous' Nimrod, the 'mighty Hunter' of Genesis, dark descendant of Ham, builder of cities, the first King, who dispels the Golden Age. For Bradstreet, as for other contemporary writers, Nimrod's rule represented the start not merely of kingship but of tyranny.[20] As David Norbrook indicates, Nimrod's presence, associated with the Tower of Babel, echoes through the anti-monarchical writings of the Commonwealth and the Restoration, most significantly – in terms of placing

Bradstreet's poem in a tradition of Protestant poetry – in *Paradise Lost*.[21] Tracing, like Bradstreet, the shift from post-Edenic quietude to the rule of Nimrod, Michael's prophecy of the future in *Paradise Lost* dramatizes the change:

> Long time in peace, by families and tribes,
> Under paternal rule: till one shall rise,
> Of proud, ambitious heart, who not content
> With fair equality, fraternal state,
> Will arrogate dominion undeserved
> Over his brethren, and quite dispossess
> Concord and law of nature from the earth.
>
> (XII; 23–9)

Milton's politicization of Nimrod's epithet, 'mighty hunter' (XII:33), as implying 'empire tyrannous' (XII:32), is more direct than Bradstreet's; yet the poets clearly share a Protestant interpretation of postlapsarian history in which labour 'reaping plenteous crop / Corn wine, and oil' is violently disrupted by the arrival of the rule of kings. Structurally positioned at the very opening of Bradstreet's poem, her account of Nimrod's career suggests simultaneously the awesome power of great empire and the destructive potential of that very power.

The example of Nimrod is typical of the implicit way Bradstreet's presentation of particular cases in 'The Four Monarchies' builds an indictment of monarchy. Yet there are moments at which explicit political commentary appears, as in 'The Inter-Regnum between Cambyses and Darius Hyslapes' which leads to the Persian Darius' kingship by election:

> A Consultation by the States was held.
> What forme of Government now to erect,
> The old, or new, which best, in what respect,
> The greater part, declin'd a Monarchy.
> So late crusht by their Princes Tyranny;
> And thought the people would more happy be,
> If governed by an Aristocracy.
> But others thought (none of the dullest braine,)
> But better one, then many Tyrants reigne.
> What arguments they us'd, I know not well,
> Too politicke (tis like) for me to tell.
>
> (*Works*, p. 73)

Bradstreet's withdrawal from opinion here coincides as markedly as in the 'Prologue' with an assertion of political views. Whilst the text makes clear that, within a frame of criticism of monarchy, aristocratic government is to be understood as highly problematic, it does so using a combination of assertion and withdrawal which marks many of the moments of Bradstreet's political interventions in *The Tenth Muse*. Perhaps the most significant of these oscillations is to be found in her treatment of the Roman monarchy.

Within the eschatology of the four monarchies Rome stands at the end, and its end signals the end of the world. That the Roman monarchy is the last brings the poem near to the present, troubling the relationship between Bradstreet's moment of composition and time's end. Opening with 'Stout *Romulus*, *Romes* Founder, and first King', Bradstreet tracks his transformation of pastoral into city:

> Where Shepheards once had Coats, and Sheep their Folds,
> Where Swaines, and rustick Peasants made their Holds.
> A Citty faire did Romulus erect:
> The Mistris of the World in each respect.
> His brother *Remus* there, by him was slaine,
> For leaping o're the Walls with some disdaine;
> The Stones at first was cimented with bloud,
> And bloudy hath it prov'd, since first it stood.
>
> (*Works*, p. 136)

Rome's associations with the 'Citty faire' which replaces Babylon, but also with fratricide, civil strife and the Roman church, 'cimented with bloud', indicates clearly that discussion of this fourth monarchy is bound to touch on contemporary religious and political issues.

Concluding the third, Greek, monarchy Bradstreet writes:

> With these Three Monarchies now have I done,
> But how the fourth, their kingdoms from them won;
> And how from small beginnings it did grow,
> To fill the world with terrour and with woe.
>
> (*Works*, p. 135)

She recognizes that the fourth monarchy demands that she bring political problems within the frame of contemporary history; her 'tired braine', therefore, should defer to 'better pen, / This taske befits not women, like to men' (pp. 135–6). However, between the third and fourth monarchies a passage offers an account of her decision to continue, '*After some dayes of rest, my restlesse heart, / To finish what begun, new thoughts impart*' despite '*inability*,' causing '*confus'd brevity*'. She asks that:

> *What ere is found amisse, take in best part,*
> *As faults proceeding from my head, not heart.*
>
> (*Works*, p. 136)

It would appear that the desire to tackle the politically contentious Roman monarchy is set against modesty and against the difficulty of dealing with the subject, a conflict that the last line addresses by attributing error to weak and unable reason, not to a 'heart' which is politically true, though exactly what that is, remains open. Calling attention to the problem of the fourth monarchy, Bradstreet invites the reader to take careful notice and, as I have indicated, she took the poem no further than Tarquinius Superbus and Sextus, his son, who did:

> *Lucretia* force, mirrour of chastety;
> She loathed so the fact, she loath'd her life,
> And shed her guiltlesse blood, with guilty knife,
> Her Husband, sore incens'd to quit this wrong,
> With *Junius Brutus* rose, and being strong,
> The *Tarquins* they from *Rome* with speed expell,
> In banishment perpetuall, to dwell;
> The Government they change, a new one bring,
> And people sweare, ne're to accept of King.
>
> (*Works*, p. 139)

The poem which started with the earliest tyrants, Nimrod and Semiramis, ends with Tarquinius Sextus' tyranny defeated by Lucretia's chastity and the foundation of the Roman Republic. That the conclusion of the poem is preceded by a sequence of disclaimers of competence and adequate learning, and is further supplemented in the 1678 edition by a subsequent 'Apology' for the poem's incomplete state, claiming 'Essays I many made, but still gave out, / The more I mus'd the more I was in doubt', indicates, I would suggest, that the treatment of the fourth monarchy, though truncated, is highly considered and self-conscious. Leaving the story at the establishment of the Roman Republic allows Bradstreet to avoid direct engagement in contemporary controversy, but the patterning of Nimrod against the Republic was hardly without implications for the attentive reader. When the poem travelled to England in 1647, it might well have been construed as an ominous comment upon the fortunes of the defeated and captive Charles I. When the poem was published in 1650, England *was* a republic, with a reading public highly alert to the contemporary significance of arresting the four monarchies at a moment when the defeat of monarchy might seem to prefigure the contemporary English crisis and the Commonwealth.

The question of the divine pattern in history was pressing for writers in the 1640s and 1650s, including poets. Immediately following 'The Four Monarchies', 'A Dialogue between Old *England* and New, concerning their present troubles. Anno 1642' addresses the question of contemporary England, representing the relationship between past and present in a dialogue between mother and daughter. Taking up the popular Civil War form of the dialogue, the poem uses analysis of the crisis of the Civil War to throw into relief different ways in which the relationship between Old and New England could be understood at the outbreak of war in the 1640s. Using a mixture of bodily, medicinal and religious vocabulary, Old England claims New England's loyalty. For Old England's sins in failing the Protestant cause, allowing the 'scorning of the Saints of the most high', she finds that she is to be punished: 'Now sip I of that cup, and just 't may be, / The bottome dregs reserved are for me.' New England's reply, 'Your fearful sinnes, great cause there's to lament, / My guilty hands (in part) hold up with you, / A sharer in your punishment's my due' (*Works*, p. 145), carefully distances her from full responsibility for maternal sin. An independent voice is established by the end of the dialogue when, saying farewell to Old England, New England foresees that if 'Parliament prevail, / . . . in a while you'l tell another tale' (p. 148). This commitment to a Puritan future recurs through the final section of the volume in a sequence of elegies on exemplary Protestant heroes, each of them an inspiration to those engaged in the contemporary struggle to secure the true path of Protestantism: Sir Philip Sidney (the warrior), Du Bartas (the Protestant poet of Joshua Sylvester's translation), Elizabeth I, 'the pride of Queens, pattern of Kings'. The choice of subjects to commemorate is itself eloquent testimony to the poet's allegiance, and her eulogizing of them resonant with implications for the reader recently emerged from Civil War.

Although Bradstreet may have had no control over the volume's publication, the poems and their arrangement indicate a precise use of genre and topic to shape their reader's consciousness of the historical patterns and discursive breadth of a tradition of reforming Protestant poetics, embracing both millennial history and contemporary political commentary. *The Tenth Muse* articulates the political crisis of the Civil War and differentiates the responses of the Old and New worlds. England's abandonment of true Protestantism, acknowledged by those Puritans who fled to the New World in the 1630s, is forcibly brought to the attention of Old England. Through millenarian discourse, contemporary political commentary and elegies for Protestant heroes the volume enables its readers to build a dialectic with the past and to set current affairs in a historical context which inescapably vindicates the policies of the English Parliament and of New England.

Lucy Hutchinson

Poets who supported Parliament during the actual wars of the early 1640s might take up very different positions in the 1650s. Lucy Hutchinson's memoir of her regicide husband, Colonel John Hutchinson, written in the 1660s, perhaps in response to Cavendish's *Life*, makes clear that she fully shared his Republican views. Although she supported the Civil War, she contrasts with Bradstreet in terms of the kinds of poetry that she wrote, its circulation and – possibly – her political position. Where Bradstreet might be seen as rewriting the genres of Tudor Protestantism from the viewpoint of a Parliamentarian position in the English Civil War, Lucy Hutchinson turned to the Classical discourses and genres used by Royalists, as well as to Biblical and Platonic imagery, to articulate a political position in the world of the 1650s. Under the Protectorate Lucy and John Hutchinson retired to their estate at Owthorpe in Nottinghamshire. At the Restoration, John Hutchinson was imprisoned in Sandown Castle on the coast of Kent on suspicion of plotting against the new Stuart regime. He eventually died in prison, weakened by the harsh conditions. It is to these events, as well as to the public events of the Civil War and Interregnum, that his wife responded with political poems in the 1650s, elegies for her husband after his death and, her best-known work, the *Memoirs of the Life of Colonel Hutchinson*, as well as with the late work, *Order and Disorder*, on the Biblical theme of creation.[22]

Thus, where *The Tenth Muse* engages with Protestant and millenarian thinking, Lucy Hutchinson engages with the equally politicized field of Classical – Roman – history. As David Norbrook has noted, Hutchinson made poetic replies to a range of her Royalist contemporaries. The survival of her commonplace book makes it possible to track her adversarial and political procedures and interests as a writer. The book contains long passages from John Denham's *The Destruction of Troy* (1656) and from Sidney Godolphin's *The Passion of Dido for Aeneas* (1658), copies which indicate her interest in how the poetry of Virgil was appropriated by Royalist poets.[23] Most significantly, it contains Edmund Waller's *Panegyrick to my Lord Protector* (1655), a poem to which Hutchinson made a sustained parodic riposte.[24] John Hutchinson remained steadfastly committed to the ideals of the Republic, in contrast to Waller's ever-changing allegiances. Though he had earlier been critical of Charles I, in 1643 Waller was involved in a Royalist plot; but when Cromwell took power, Waller greeted the Protector as a military leader, close to Caesar and Augustus:[25]

> Whilst with a strong, and yet a gentle hand
> You bridle faction, and our hearts command,
> Protect us from our selves, and from the Foe,
> Make us unite, and make us conquer too.[26]

As Norbrook indicates, the characterization of Cromwell as rescuer, builder of national unity and strong military leader was guaranteed to infuriate all who opposed him. These included Lucy Hutchinson who fully shared with her husband the view that Cromwell's personal rule as Protector was a betrayal of the Republic. Thus Lucy Hutchinson parodies Waller's poem line by line, to devastating effect:

> Whilst with a smooth yet a servile Tongue
> You Court all Factions, and have sweetly sung
> The Triumphs of yo͏ͬ Countreys Overthrow
> Raysing the Glory of her treacherous Foe.[27]

Hutchinson has Waller in her sights and particularly the treacherous servility with which he has deployed his 'sweet' and 'smooth' poetic style, the style which, following the Restoration, led to his reputation as *the* poet of the seventeenth century.

What Lucy Hutchinson's attack on Waller also indicates is that, in the 1640s and 1650s, poetic style and the choice of topic were both highly tendentious matters and signals of political allegiance. As N. H. Keeble has noted, in a poem dating probably from the 1650s we see Hutchinson criticizing courts through the deployment of pastoral conventions, drawing on both Classical and recent pastoral poetry, including Ben Jonson's 'To Penshurst'.[28] Possibly influenced by Horace's poem on country life, the poem is a study in the psychology of ambition and kingly power, and in the possibilities of finding within available poetic languages an analysis of power-relations. It opens:

> All sorts of men through various labours press
> To the same end, contented quietness;
> Great princes vex their labouring thoughts to be
> Possessed of an unbounded sovereignty;
> The hardy soldier doth all toils sustain
> That he may conquer first, and after reign.[29]

Enumerating the desires of the King, soldier and merchant who 'ploughs the angry seas', Hutchinson replaces Virgilian pastoral's emphasis on the pastoral world's easy fruitfulness with a vision of labour. The opening (while invoking Georgic poetry with its emphasis on country labour in terms such as 'ploughs') directs the reader's attention to labour as worldly endeavour, predominantly concerned with power over others ('sovereignty', 'reign'), expansion of the self at cost to others, unequal relations and, in the broad sense, empire. For Hutchinson, to be subject to another is to be constrained by 'tyranny', to be willingly so subject is to be not only a servant but, like Waller, 'servile'.

As these poems indicate, Hutchinson opposed Cromwell as much as the monarchy. Furthermore, while Bradstreet, Cavendish and Philips each address the question of what it means to be a 'woman writer', Hutchinson, often writing anonymously and in manuscript, eschews direct engagement with the question. Hutchinson, as both Keeble and Norbrook note, had little sympathy with women who transgressed the expectations of femininity and her poetry and prose writing, though explicitly concerned with virtue and Republicanism, holds at bay the connections between questions of virtue and femininity which the other three writers render explicit.

Reputations and contexts

On Cromwell's death a poet, apparently a woman, lamented him:

> Our England's victor dead who can express
> Laments sufficient for such worthyness
> Immortal fame must be the trump which may
> Unto eternity thy deeds display.[30]

None of the poets examined here could have written this poem. Their views were polarized around support for Parliament and King, and it is in part these polarized positions that have affected their subsequent reception.

Several factors have affected the ways in which women's poetry of the 1640s and 1650s has been received and passed into current critical writing: assumptions and expectations about the kind of text generated by a 'woman writer', assumptions about authorship as a practice and, particularly, women's political position at the Restoration. After 1660, the Royalist Cavendish continued to publish, but she wrote several pieces highly critical of courts and retired to her husband's estates. The Royalist Katherine Philips, by contrast, moved from an oppositional writer to one who at the Restoration came to enjoy establishment status. Bradstreet continued to write and a revised version of *The Tenth Muse* was printed in 1678, six years after her death. This edition, as it stands, adapts some of the stronger aspects of the potentially Republican or regicidal sentiments of the earlier volume so that, for example, the end of the 'Dialogue', 'Farewell dear Mother, Parliament Prevail' becomes 'rightest cause prevail'.[31] We cannot know for certain whether this was her adaptation. Hutchinson continued to write and published the anonymous poem recently reattributed to her by David Norbrook, *Order and Disorder* (1679). Thus, at the Restoration, Cavendish (a returning exile) and Philips (a Royalist) had most purchase on an audience and continued to be read (and in Cavendish's case ridiculed). Bradstreet, though remembered, was later considered an 'American' writer. Lucy Hutchinson, the writer whose Republican politics left her out on a limb, much of whose work remained in manuscript, and who conformed, perhaps, least to the twentieth-century critical expectation that women poets should address their feminine status, dropped from sight as a poet (though her *Memoirs* of her husband were published in the nineteenth century). Until relatively recently, then, the politics of the reception of writing – by men and women – at the Restoration had some impact on their subsequent fortunes.

Each of these four poets can be understood as an author. Each is susceptible to the modern use of signature and biography to ground and (problematically) to 'explain' texts.[32] Each left a substantial body of writing and left biographical and other traces which enable a critic to situate them, and the reception of their texts, fairly precisely. In this, though, the examples I have chosen to examine contrast markedly with much – perhaps most – of the women's poetry of the 1640s and 1650s. Much less is known, for example, about An Collins, the author of a volume of poetry and spiritual autobiography published in 1653,[33] than about Margaret Cavendish, whose *Poems and Fancies* came out that same year. Similarly, another volume of poems almost certainly by a woman, *Eliza's Babes* (1652), though it includes a poem highly critical of Charles I, is relatively neglected because, we may conjecture, so little is known about its author and provenance.

Furthermore, the fact that each of the poets studied here belonged to some form of social elite has been instrumental in ensuring, first, that they had access to particular forms of cultural capital and were able to learn their techniques as poets, and secondly, that material about them has survived. Other poets, such as many of the sectarian writers, came from backgrounds of lower status. Anna Trapnel, a Fifth Monarchist, was the daughter of a shipwright from Poplar in London.[34] The case of Trapnel interestingly complicates our sense of seventeenth-century authorship, for her long poetic vision, *The Cry of a Stone* (1654), was first spoken by her in a state of trance and written down by a relator. It is a prophecy, drawing on the Bible and, because of the trance in which she delivered this and her other prophecies, the words are not 'hers' in any straightforward sense.[35] As these examples suggest, while the authors examined here offer a range of political positions and poetic practice, in having had writing 'careers', having drawn on cultural and educational capital and having enjoyed elevated social positions, they are not wholly typical of women's poetic writing of the English Civil War.

NOTES

1 Jonathan Goldberg, *Desiring Women Writing: English Renaissance Examples* (Stanford University Press, 1997), p. 5. Goldberg further asserts, more tendentiously, that some contemporary literary criticism continues to judge women's poetry in this way and he uses the term 'legend of good women' to trace continuities between the early modern period and the present, seeing recent scholarly

work which focuses on 'the work of recovery of women writers' as 'tantamount to the recovery of morally pure, suffering subjects whose goodness is legible' in their essentially feminine virtues (pp. 4–6).

2 Ann Rosalind Jones, *The Currency of Eros* (Bloomington: Indiana University Press, 1990), pp. 1–4.

3 Hilda Smith, *Reason's Disciples: Seventeenth-Century English Feminists* (Urbana: University of Illinois Press, 1982); Catherine Gallagher, 'Embracing the Absolute: The Politics of the Female Subject in Seventeenth-Century England', *Genders*, 1 (1988), 24–39; Elaine Hobby, *Virtue of Necessity* (London: Virago, 1988), pp. 11–19.

4 Margaret Ezell, *Writing Women's Literary History* (Baltimore: Johns Hopkins University Press, 1993), pp. 1–38.

5 See for example Arthur F. Marotti's discussion of manuscript circulation: *Manuscript, Print, and the English Renaissance Lyric* (Ithaca: Cornell University Press, 1995), pp. 1–2.

6 Patrick Thomas (ed.), *The Collected Works of Katherine Philips* (Stump Cross, Essex: Stump Cross Books, 1990), 1:1–9.

7 Recent studies of Royalist poetry include Carol Barash, *English Women's Poetry 1649–1714* (Oxford University Press, 1996) and James Loxley, *Royalism and Poetry in the English Civil Wars: The Drawn Sword* (Basingstoke: Macmillan, 1997).

8 A sample of Powell's writing on Charles I, from 'Of the late K.Charles of Blessed Memory, by Vavaser Powell', is given by B. S. Capp, *The Fifth Monarchy Men* (London: Faber, 1972), p. 51: '*He disobeyed his parent, all men know, / It was a sin, although but soe & soe*'; '*of all Kings I am for Christ alone, / For he is King to us, though Charles be gone*'.

9 *Poems and Fancies* (1653; rpt. Menston: The Scolar Press, 1972).

10 Douglas Grant, *Margaret the First* (London: Rupert Hart-Davis, 1957).

11 On Cavendish's prefatory material see Jeffrey Masten, *Textual Intercourse: Collaboration, Authorship, and Sexualities in Renaissance Drama* (Cambridge University Press, 1997).

12 Lois Potter, *Secret Rites and Secret Writing: Royalist Literature, 1641–1660* (Cambridge University Press, 1989), p. xiii.

13 For biographical and critical discussion of Bradstreet see Elizabeth Wade White, *Anne Bradstreet, 'The Tenth Muse'* (New York: Oxford University Press, 1971); Pattie Cowell and Ann Stanford, *Critical Essays on Anne Bradstreet* (Boston, Mass.: G. K. Hall, 1983).

14 Jeannine Hensley (ed.), *The Works of Anne Bradstreet*, foreword by Adrienne Rich (Cambridge, Mass.: Harvard University Press, 1967), pp. xiv, xv.

15 Wendy Martin, *An American Triptych* (Chapel Hill: University of North Carolina Press, 1984), for example, uses the second, posthumous, edition of Bradstreet's poems to trace the development of Bradstreet's 'personal' voice.

16 *The Tenth Muse* (1650), p. 1. Subsequent references are to Joseph R. McElrath and Allan P. Robb (eds.), *The Complete Works of Anne Bradstreet* (Boston: Twayne, 1981).

17 Bernard Capp, *The Fifth Monarchy Men: A Study in Seventeenth-century English Millenarianism* (London: Faber, 1972), pp. 20–1.

18 Recently reattributed by David Norbrook, 'A Devine Originall: Lucy Hutchinson

and the "woman's version"', *Times Literary Supplement*, 5007 (19 March 1999), 13–15.

19 Gerald MacLean, *Time's Witness: Historical Representation in English Poetry* (Madison: University of Wisconsin Press, 1990), pp. 157–8; see also Achsah Guibbory, *The Map of Time: Seventeenth-Century English Literature and Ideas of Pattern in History* (Urbana and Chicago: University of Illinois Press, 1986).

20 Discussing the 'widespread preoccupation' with the Biblical prophecies of Daniel and Revelation, Capp, *Fifth Monarchy Men*, pp. 20–1, notes the popularity of Daniel's vision of the rise and fall of four successive monarchies (Babylon, Assyria, Greece, Rome) and that the concept 'blended with the widespread theory of a Roman Golden Age from which all later history represented a continuous decline lasting till the world's end'. Raleigh, one of Bradstreet's sources, arguing that the 'Storie of mankind was not allegoricall' but historical, makes connections between the Golden Age, paradise and Babylon (Sir Walter Raleigh, *The History of the World* (1614), pp. 37–8).

21 David Norbrook, *Writing the English Republic: Poetry, Rhetoric and Politics 1627–1660* (Cambridge University Press, 1999), pp. 290, 296, 411, 463–7.

22 For further discussion see: David Norbrook, 'Lucy Hutchinson's "Elegies" and the Situation of the Republican Woman Writer', *ELR*, 27 (1997), 468–521; N. H. Keeble, '"The Colonel's Shadow": Lucy Hutchinson, Women's Writing and the Civil War', in Thomas Healy and Jonathan Sawday (eds.), *Literature and the English Civil War* (Cambridge University Press, 1990), pp. 227–47.

23 Lucy Hutchinson, Commonplace Book, Nottinghamshire Archives.

24 David Norbrook, 'Lucy Hutchinson versus Edmund Waller', *Seventeenth Century*, 11 (1996), 61–86.

25 Norbrook, *Writing the English Republic*, p. 306.

26 Norbrook, 'Hutchinson versus Waller', p. 72, which, pp. 72–85, prints Waller's poem in parallel with Hutchinson's reply, 'To Mr Waller upon his Panegirique to the Lord Protector'.

27 Norbrook, 'Hutchinson versus Waller', p. 73.

28 Printed in Lucy Hutchinson, *Memoirs of the Life of Colonel Hutchinson*, ed. N. H. Keeble (London: Dent, 1995), pp. 339–40, with discussion of the poem on pp. 375–6. Loxley, *Royalism and Poetry*, pp. 202–3, notes that Classical characterizations of *otium* are not 'as uniformly celebratory as has sometimes been assumed'.

29 Keeble (ed.), *Memoirs*, p. 339.

30 Elianor Harvey, 'An Acrostick Eligie on the death of yt. no less prudent then virtuous prince Oliver Lord protector', National Library of Scotland, Advocates MSS 19.3.4, fol. 87r.

31 See also Wade White, *Anne Bradstreet*, p. 169.

32 For a fuller discussion of early modern women and authorship, see Margaret W. Ferguson, 'Renaissance Concepts of the "woman writer"', in Helen Wilcox (ed.), *Women and Literature in Britain 1500–1700* (Cambridge University Press, 1996), pp. 143–168.

33 An [Anne] Collins, *Divine Songs and Meditacions* (1653), most readily available in a selection edited by Stanley N. Stewart, Augustan Reprint Society 94 (Los Angeles: Clark Memorial Library Publication, 1961).

34 See also Elspeth Graham, Hilary Hinds, Elaine Hobby and Helen Wilcox (eds.), *Her Own Life* (London: Routledge, 1989), pp. 14–20, 71–86.

35 See Elaine Hobby's chapter, pp. 162–78 below. For a full discussion of the question of authorship in prophetic texts see Hilary Hinds, *God's Englishwomen: Seventeenth-century Radical Sectarian Writing and Feminist Criticism* (Manchester University Press, 1996), pp. 80–107.

FURTHER READING

For individual editions of primary texts cited or discussed, please see the notes above.

Barash, Carol, *English Women's Poetry 1649–1714*, Oxford University Press, 1996.

Cowell, Pattie, and Ann Stanford (eds.), *Critical Essays on Anne Bradstreet*, Boston Mass.: G. K. Hall, 1983.

Ezell, Margaret, *Writing Women's Literary History*, Baltimore: Johns Hopkins University Press, 1993.

Ferguson, Margaret W., 'Renaissance Concepts of the "woman writer"', in Helen Wilcox (ed.), *Women and Literature in Britain 1500–1700*, Cambridge University Press, 1996, pp. 143–68.

Gallagher, Catherine, 'Embracing the Absolute: The Politics of the Female Subject in Seventeenth-Century England', *Genders*, 1 (1988), 24–39.

Goldberg, Jonathan, *Desiring Women Writing: English Renaissance Examples*, Stanford University Press, 1997.

Grant, Douglas, *Margaret the First*, London: Rupert Hart-Davis, 1957.

Hinds, Hilary, *God's Englishwomen: Seventeenth-century Radical Sectarian Writing and Feminist Criticism*, Manchester University Press, 1996.

Hobby, Elaine, *Virtue of Necessity: English Women's Writing 1649–88*, London: Virago, 1988.

Keeble, N. H., '"The Colonel's Shadow": Lucy Hutchinson, Women's Writing, and the Civil War', in Thomas Healy and Jonathan Sawday (eds.), *Literature and the English Civil War*, Cambridge University Press, 1990, pp. 227–47.

Loxley, James, *Royalism and Poetry in the English Civil Wars: The Drawn Sword*, Basingstoke: Macmillan, 1997.

Masten, Jeffrey, *Textual Intercourse: Collaboration, Authorship, and Sexualities in Renaissance Drama*, Cambridge University Press, 1997.

Norbrook, David, 'Lucy Hutchinson versus Edmund Waller', *Seventeenth Century*, 11 (1996), 61–86.

'Lucy Hutchinson's "Elegies" and the Situation of the Republican Woman Writer', *ELR*, 27 (1997), 468–521.

'A Devine Originall: Lucy Hutchinson and the "woman's version"', *Times Literary Supplement*, 5007 (19 March 1999), 13–15.

Writing the English Republic: Poetry, Rhetoric and Politics 1627–1660, Cambridge University Press, 1999.

Potter, Lois, *Secret Rites and Secret Writing: Royalist Literature, 1641–1660*, Cambridge University Press, 1989.

Smith, Hilda, *Reason's Disciples: Seventeenth-Century English Feminists*, Urbana: University of Illinois Press, 1982.

White, Elizabeth Wade, *Anne Bradstreet, 'The Tenth Muse'*, New York: Oxford University Press, 1971.

8

HELEN WILCOX AND SHEILA OTTWAY

Women's histories

In 1648, the Duke of York, second son of Charles I, made a dramatic escape from St James' Palace in London to the safety of the Low Countries. This successful Royalist intrigue was partly made possible by the assistance of one Anne Murray – later Anne, Lady Halkett – whose knowledge of women's clothing was particularly helpful in constructing the Duke's cross-dressed disguise. The record of her involvement in this exciting but dangerous escapade – history in the making – is not to be found in the formal histories of the period of the English Revolution, but in her own autobiographical memoir, an apparently private text which remained in manuscript until 1875.[1]

Anne Halkett's experience, unusual though it may seem, is nonetheless illustrative of what we might call women's relationship to history in mid-seventeenth-century England. The startling and unprecedented turmoil of the 1640s and 1650s brought events of public historical importance to the domestic doorstep and led many women to undertake hitherto 'masculine' activities: the sole running of households, the management of goods and finances, the writing of Parliamentary petitions, and the judging of events for posterity. In other words, women made history in this period. 'Women's histories', the title of this chapter, is a term which not only encompasses the historical lives and interventions of women during this period, but also reminds us that these were inscribed in the women's own texts. As a consequence, our notion of 'history' itself may need adjusting, not only from male to female but also from public to private (if such a divide can ever be upheld), and from interpreted past to immediate present.

What forms did women's written histories take in the mid seventeenth century? Not surprisingly, in view of women's socially determined identity as daughters, wives and mothers, substantial elements of women's experience were recorded indirectly – in the biographies that they wrote of others (particularly men) around them. However, there was also a notable increase in women's own memoirs in and after the mid-century, suggesting just how

4 Unknown artist, Lady Anne Clifford, 1646.

important the Revolutionary years were in empowering women as writers and participants in history. 'Autobiography' as a recognized mode of writing, however, was not formally defined until well into the nineteenth century; thus the written inscription and exploration of individual identity must be sought in more indirect or obliquely expressive modes in the early modern period.[2] Two forms of special importance to the women of mid seventeenth-century England were the sociable letter, combining a personal voice with a topical response to events, and the private diary or journal, often remaining incomplete and unpublished. The experience of civil war and social upheaval transformed these intimate modes of writing into vehicles for history.

In this chapter, a range of women's histories will be discussed in the generic sequence outlined in the previous paragraph. We begin, therefore, with biographies and autobiographical memoirs, examining the instinct to self-examination which is inseparable from the chronicler's vocation in this period. Both of these forms, biography and memoir, constitute the writing of history with hindsight. The second half of the chapter moves on to a consideration of women of the English Revolution as letter-writers and keepers of diaries, recording history close to the moment at which it was experienced.

Histories in retrospect: biographies and memoirs

The English Revolution deeply affected the lives of two women who wrote about their personal experiences in both biographical and autobiographical texts: Margaret Cavendish, Duchess of Newcastle, and Lucy Hutchinson. Cavendish was a staunch Royalist, while Hutchinson was a fervent Republican; each of them wrote a brief autobiography as well as a much fuller biography of her own husband. It is striking that both women, whether consciously or unconsciously, project a positive image of their own histories not only via the medium of their own autobiographical writings, but also in their biographies of their spouses.

Margaret Cavendish was a prolific and versatile writer, whose published works cover a wide variety of genres. She was an autobiographer before she became a biographer: her autobiographical sketch, *A True Relation of My Birth, Breeding, and Life*, appeared in 1656, long before the publication of her *Life of the Duke of Newcastle* (1667). *A True Relation* is a brief account of Cavendish's childhood and youth in England, and of her experiences as a Royalist exile in Paris and the Low Countries when she accompanied her husband, William Cavendish, then Marquis and afterwards Duke of Newcastle, the Royalist commander in the North, who left England after his defeat at Marston Moor in the summer of 1644. She was evidently aware of the fact that, in publishing this personal history – the earliest known secular autobiography by an Englishwoman – she was exposing herself to public vilification; in the seventeenth century, for a woman to write about herself in a non-religious context was tantamount to a display of immodesty. Cavendish precludes adverse criticism of her self-display in *A True Relation* by laying excessive emphasis on her chastity and her bashfulness. At the same time, she purposely diverts attention from herself by describing, in biographical mode, the noble characters of her various relatives, with special reference to their experiences during the Civil War. Her own history is embedded in the histories of her family and cause.

A True Relation testifies to the devastating impact of the Civil War in England; Cavendish asserts that 'this unnatural war came like a whirlwind', leading to the death of all three of her brothers.[3] There is, moreover, an almost hagiographical account of how Cavendish's widowed mother suffered for her devotion to the Royalist cause:

> She made her house her cloyster, inclosing herself as it were therein, for she seldom went abroad, unless to church; but these unhappy wars forced her out, by reason she and her children were loyall to the king; for which they plundered her and my brothers of all their goods, plate, jewels, money, corn and cattle, and the like, cut down their woods, pulled down their houses, and sequestered them from their lands and livings; but in such misfortunes my mother was of an heroick spirit, in suffering patiently where there is no remedy, or to be industrious where she thought she could help.
>
> (*Life of Newcastle*, p. 196)

Cavendish perpetuates the memory of her mother by portraying her as a suffering saint; at the same time the ideals of the daughter/autobiographer are also reflected in the mirror of her biographical portrait of her mother. Private history here comes into sharp focus, defined not only by immediate personal experience but also by the larger frameworks of political loyalties and long-established traditions of life-writing.

Cavendish's brief autobiography was published somewhat inconspicuously, almost as a postscript to a collection of pieces of prose fiction entitled *Nature's Pictures* (1656). When a second edition of *Nature's Pictures* appeared in 1671, *A True Relation* was not included. It would seem that the experience of exile had been liberating for Cavendish, prompting her to write and publish her own personal history. After the Restoration, when Cavendish returned to live in England, she continued to be a productive writer but was never again to write about herself so candidly as in *A True Relation*. Evidently her autobiographical imperative became superseded by a biographical one, resulting in the publication, in 1667, of *The Life of the Duke of Newcastle*. In this biography of her husband, she portrays the Duke as a valiant Royalist hero who has not yet received due recompense for his services to the Crown during the Civil War. In glorifying her husband, Cavendish presents herself, albeit obliquely, as a faithful wife who has shared her husband's tribulations during their years of exile. Cavendish thus speaks out in both her historical texts as a woman claiming attention for those of her relatives who have suffered affliction and injustice as a result of the Revolution. In recording and interpreting the recent past, Cavendish also ensures that her own personal history will be preserved for posterity and that no-one will 'mistake', as she puts it in the closing lines of her autobiography, who she herself was.

It is possible that the publication of *The Life of the Duke of Newcastle* prompted Lucy Hutchinson to write, probably in the late 1660s, a biography of her own husband, the Parliamentarian Colonel John Hutchinson, who had also played an important role as military leader during the Civil War. Lucy Hutchinson never published this biography; she probably intended it to be read in manuscript by her family and close friends.[4] It was clearly written to preserve the memory of her husband as a deeply committed Republican and Puritan, and as a man of unimpeachable integrity. In particular, its aim is to vindicate John Hutchinson's reputation as a regicide and to lament his untimely death as an innocent victim of injustice.

The *Memoirs of the Life of Colonel Hutchinson* is an important historical document, providing much detailed information about events in the Civil War and during the Commonwealth period.[5] At the same time, it is a testimony to Lucy Hutchinson's exemplary support for her husband's political and moral convictions. National and personal history are closely interwoven; a clear parallel is drawn between John Hutchinson's devotion to the Republican cause and Lucy Hutchinson's devotion to her husband. It is as a dutiful and submissive Puritan wife that Lucy Hutchinson portrays herself in this text. This allows her implicitly to contrast herself, in a digressional account of recent English history, with the Queen Consort of Charles I, Henrietta Maria, who is depicted as having been largely responsible for the catastrophe of the Civil War:

> But above all these the king had another instigator of his own violent purpose more powerful than all the rest, and that was the Queen, who, grown out of her childhood, began to turn her mind from those vain extravagancies she lived in at first, to that which did less become her and was more fatal to the kingdom, which never is in any place happy where the hands that are made only for distaffs affect the management of sceptres. (p. 70)

However antifeminist this passage may seem to the modern reader, it nevertheless bears witness to a remarkable preoccupation with the historical significance of women in positions of power. Bearing in mind the more positive impact of Elizabeth I, Lucy Hutchinson adds:

> If any one object the fresh example of Queen Elizabeth, let them remember that the felicity of her reign was the effect of her submission to her masculine and wise counsellors; but whenever male princes are so effeminate as to suffer women of foreign birth and different religions to intermeddle with the affairs of state, it is always found to produce sad desolations. (p. 70)

The hierarchy of commitment here is clear: Protestant nationalism is of far greater significance to Lucy Hutchinson than any sense of common femininity. The contrasting conduct of the two queens is described in terms which impose the orderliness of the Protestant patriarchal household, in which the woman submits to 'masculine and wise counsellors', on to the historical narrative of the nation.

Lucy Hutchinson was also the author of an autobiography, of which only an initial fragment has been preserved (if indeed it was ever completed).[6] Here, too, individual history unfolds against the backdrop of national events, contextualizing the personal and demonstrating how individuals, whether male or female, have distinctive roles to play in wider history. However, the fact that Lucy Hutchinson produced a complete and detailed biography of her husband but only an apparently unfinished autobiography suggests that she was not at ease with writing overtly about herself. By portraying herself obliquely in the *Memoirs of the Life of Colonel Hutchinson*, she draws attention to her submissive role and constructs a self-image with appropriate decorum. It would seem that, for Lucy Hutchinson, biography was a means of containing her autobiographical impulse, enabling her to establish her own place in history without exposing herself to moral condemnation or to the question of the imagined readers of Margaret Cavendish's *True Relation*: 'Why hath this lady writ her own life?'[7]

Among the other Englishwomen who were indeed doing precisely that – writing accounts of their own lives during the mid seventeenth century – were Anne, Lady Halkett (whose daring Royalist escapade was mentioned in the introduction to this chapter), and Ann, Lady Fanshawe. *The Memoirs of Ann, Lady Fanshawe* were written for her son in 1676. They were never intended for publication, but were seen rather as a means of passing on a detailed family history spanning the turbulent mid-century years. A superficial impression of Ann Fanshawe's account suggests that it is largely a glowing account of her husband – the Royalist ambassador and distinguished translator, Sir Richard Fanshawe – written for their only surviving son. However, the *Memoirs* in fact contain a vivid mixture of public and private life – from politics to seasickness and pregnancy – comprising factual accounts of the Civil War and its aftermath as well as memorable, novelistic dialogue reconstructing her personal encounters.

Fanshawe's narrative depicts a woman who experienced the harsh daily reality and witnessed the crucial political moments of the Revolutionary years. She found herself on the road as part of the Prince of Wales' military retinue in 1645 'with a dying child, which did dye 2 days after, in a garrison town, extream weake and very poor'.[8] She spoke with the imprisoned Charles I not long before he died:

> The last time I ever saw him, when I took my leave, I could not refraine weeping. When he had saluted me, I prayd to God to preserve His Majesty with long life and happy years. He stroked me on my cheek and sayd, 'Child, if God pleaseth, it shall be so, but both you and I must submitt to God's will, and you know in what hands I am in.'   (p. 120)

After Charles' death, Lady Ann and her husband were at various times in France, Ireland and Spain, but they were back in England in time for Sir Richard to be taken prisoner at the Battle of Worcester in 1651. Lady Ann later made petitions to Cromwell on behalf of her imprisoned husband, though it was only after Cromwell's death that Sir Richard 'got loose of his fetters' (p. 137) sufficiently to travel abroad again. That, however, enabled Sir Richard and Lady Ann to sail into Dover with the returning Charles II at the Restoration: 'The sea was calme, the moon shined at full, and the sun suffered not a cloud to hinder his prospect of the best sight, by whose light and the mercifull bounty of God hee was sett safely on shore at Dover in Kent upon the 25th of May, 1660' (p. 141). Despite the rejoicing, however, Lady Ann had a deeply practical sense and knew that the preceding years had cost her family 'above an hundred and thirty thousand pounds' (p. 110).

Fanshawe's *Memoirs* are pioneering in their effortless combination of the public and the private. She describes herself as having been a 'hoyting girl', loving 'riding . . . and running, and all acteive pastimes' (p. 110), and the energy shows itself in her hugely demanding later life. During the years of war, travel and danger, for example, she was pregnant no less than twenty times, and the fourteen babies carried to full (or nearly full) term are all described and named, and in nine cases their place of burial is precisely recorded. Meanwhile, when her husband was imprisoned she would go each day

> when the clock struck 4 in the morning, with a dark lanterne in my hand, all alone and on foot from my lodging in Chancery Lane . . . [to] under his window and softly call him. He, that after the first time expected me, never failed to put out his head at first call. Thus we talked together, and sometimes I was so wet with rane that it went in at my neck and out at my heels. (p. 135)

During the war she came by accident within two inches of being shot as she leant against a tree in the garden of St John's College, Oxford. She records having seen, in her chamber in Limerick in 1649, the ghost of a woman 'leaning into the window through the casement, in white, with red hair and pale, ghastly complexion', causing her such a fright that 'my hair stood on end and my night clothes fell off' while her husband slept through the whole commotion (p. 125). This is history in its full idiosyncratic and stirring mixture of grand and trivial, strange and moving material.

Without the Revolution, and without her husband's dramatic career, Fanshawe's life would no doubt have been significantly different. Her *Memoirs* are made from the combination of those public elements with the detail of a marriage, motherhood, strong opinions and a deep sense of adventure. She sums up the moment of her marriage with typical astuteness, noting that she and her husband had so little money between them that they were like 'marchant adventurers' (p. 112), which indeed they were in terms of their practical approach and ingenuity, and the dangerous voyages to come. She develops the image in a way that is most revealing of their embattled generation: 'But, however, it [twenty pounds] was to us as a little piece of armour is against a bullet, which if it be right placed, though no bigger than a shilling serves as well as a whole sute of arms' (p. 112). The metaphor derives from war, and mingles financial security with physical safety, yet refers to the beginning of married life. Romance and practicality, danger and survival are the stuff of this woman's history.

Histories in process: letters and diaries

Women's histories from mid seventeenth-century England are recorded in a wide variety of texts which intermingle personal and political experience, drawing on both the immediacy of events and the interpretative power of memory. While biography and autobiography are consciously presented narratives, the genres now to be considered – letters and diaries – allow us to glimpse history in a more fragmented and everyday manner. In the private letters written by Lady Brilliana Harley and Dorothy Osborne, for instance, we find a vivid record of the fears and frustrations of two women, both of whom found themselves in situations of agonizing uncertainty during the Revolutionary years. While Harley's concerns as expressed in her letters are largely maternal, and Osborne's are predominantly romantic, both are played out against a context of close and threatening conflict.

Lady Brilliana Harley, a devoutly Protestant gentlewoman, regularly wrote letters to her son Edward ('Ned') between 1638 and 1643. In her early letters, written while her son was a student at Oxford, Harley fondly expresses maternal concern for his physical and spiritual well-being. By the summer of 1642, however, the tone of the letters changes dramatically as the Civil War endangers her family at their castle – Brampton Bryan in Warwickshire. At this time her husband and son were away from home, serving the Parliamentary cause, and, in a letter of 2 July 1642, she tells Ned of her determination to defend the family home to the best of her ability:

> My dear Ned, at first when I saw how outrageously this cuntry carried them-
> selfes against your father, my anger was so vp, and my sorrow, that I hardly had
> patience to stay; but now, I have well considered, if I goo away I shall leave all
> that your father has to the pray of our enimys, which they would be glad of;
> so that, and pleas God, I purpos to stay as long as it is poscibell, if I live; and
> this is my resolution, without your father contradict it. I cannot make a better
> use of my life, next to sarving my God, than doo what good I can for you.[9]

Harley's letter shows women's history in the making. Knowing that Brampton Bryan may soon be besieged, she affirms her calling as a mother, doing 'what good I can' for her son, but also as a householder, taking over the traditionally male role of withstanding an attack on the family home. She writes determinedly of '*my* resolution' and the proper use of '*my* life', prompted by the urgency of the situation into a new awareness of her own role. Despite the provisional phrases which surround her 'resolution' (such as 'and pleas God' or 'without your father contradict it'), Harley's letter is an emblem of that moment when female devotedness to family and religion in the Civil War context led to a shift in women's roles and self-construction.

As the uncertainties at Brampton Bryan continue into 1643, Lady Brilliana Harley's letters become increasingly anxious. In January she writes to Ned: 'I am threatened every day to be beset with soulders. My hope is, the Lord will not deliver me nor mine into theair hands; for surely they would use all cruellty towards me, for I am toold that they desire not to leave your father neather roote nor branch. You and I must forgive them' (p. 187). Here Harley speaks up for all women caught up in the horrors of war; without being too explicit, she expresses her fear of the rape and murder not only of herself but also of her younger children. It is remarkable that, in a situation as desperate as this, Harley avows her total commitment to Christian principles by her statement that she and her son must both forgive their assailants. In the face of imminent death, Harley takes on the language, and perhaps implicitly the role, of a Christian martyr.

Lady Brilliana Harley survived the siege of Brampton Bryan, which took place in 1643, but died shortly afterwards, her death undoubtedly hastened by the stresses of the Civil War. Her letters to Ned remain a poignant testimony to the closeness of the bond between mother and child in a life-threatening situation.

Another close bond, namely that between lovers, is attested in the letters written by Dorothy Osborne to her future husband Sir William Temple during the period of their courtship. These letters were written between 1652 and 1654, during which time there seemed little possibility of a happy future for them as a married couple. Osborne was the daughter of a Royalist gentleman who had lost much of his wealth during the Civil War; not surprisingly, her family hoped that she would make a financially advantageous marriage. In this respect, Temple seemed an unpromising suitor, and Osborne's older brother, Henry, was fiercely opposed to the match. Osborne's letters to Temple demonstrate how a young woman's pursuit of personal happiness could be antagonized by the shrinking of family fortunes as a result of the Civil War.

The courtship letters written by Osborne to Temple are not simply concerned with affairs of the heart; they also present an insider's view of upper-class English society in the 1650s. In Osborne's opinion, this is a ruthlessly materialistic society obsessed with the acquisition of wealth. It seems likely that the immense social upheaval of the Revolution, and the wide-scale redistribution of wealth that this entailed, did indeed give rise to a feverish anxiety over money during the Commonwealth period. In her letters, Osborne repeatedly makes sardonic comments on the insincerity of those who pursue a marriage partner purely to consolidate family fortunes. There is clearly an ulterior motive here: in thus condemning those who marry for financial gain, Osborne emphasizes her own virtuousness as a woman who will marry for love. There are, then, two sides to Osborne's epistolary self-representation: while showing herself to be a shrewd and witty observer of contemporary society, she is also able to present herself as an emotionally sensitive lover.

In Osborne's letters there are no overt references to the devastation brought about by the Civil War; nowhere does she express any desire to contextualize her existence as an individual in national history. It is revealing, however, that Osborne uses the image of a war-torn landscape to describe the state of her 'heart' (that is, her self), in a letter to Temple written in a mood of abject melancholy:

> I have noe End's nor noe designes nor will my heart ever bee capable of any, but like a Country wasted by a Civill warr, where two opposeing Party's have disputed theire right soe long till they have made it worth neither of theire conquest's, tis Ruin'd and desolated by the long striffe within it to that degree as twill be usefull to none, nobody that know's the condition tis in will think it worth the gaineing, and I shall not cousen any body with it.[10]

Osborne thus draws on the memory of recent historical events to accentuate the depth of her despair at a moment when she sees no possibility of achieving personal happiness. Civil war becomes a metaphor for the personal experience of a long drawn-out mental conflict that no longer seems worth resolving and has devalued what it sought to achieve.

In her brighter moods, Osborne escapes from historical reality altogether by imagining herself as a fictional character, notably as a heroine of romance. Osborne and Temple were both avid readers of the French romances that were popular in 1650s England – fanciful prose narratives generally set in exotic surroundings and in the remote past. It seems that, in her letters, Osborne took delight in creating a world of fictional history – a textual world that she could share imaginatively with William Temple. Indeed, she envisages Temple and herself as the archetypal star-crossed lovers of fictional romance as she wonders, wishfully, 'can there bee a more Romance Story than ours would make if the conclusion should prove happy'.[11] Unlike Lady Brilliana Harley's letters to her son, which provide an immediate account of a woman's personal history in the political context, Dorothy Osborne's letters to William Temple reveal a rhetorically gifted woman writer who is continually engaged in the process of turning private history into an art of fiction.

If the rhetorical framework that appealed to Dorothy Osborne was the romance, the principles around which the diary of Lady Anne Clifford was ordered were the repeated patterns of time and place over a century of family and national history. Clifford was the only surviving child of Margaret (1560–1616) and George (1558–1605) Clifford, the Earl and Countess of Cumberland, and successively the wife of Richard Sackville, Earl of Dorset (1589–1624), and of Philip Herbert, Earl of Pembroke (1584–1650). She outlived both her husbands, as well as her male rivals as heir to the northern estates of the Clifford family, and spent much of her later life reclaiming and restoring their castles in Westmorland. She kept diaries for most of her long life – at least from 1603 (when she was thirteen) until just before her death in 1676 – and the history of a remarkably determined woman emerges from their pages.

Ironically, Clifford notes that the Civil War years were among the quietest of her life, free from marital or legal conflict:

> And when the Civill Warres between the King & Parliament began to grow hotter and hotter in England, my 2nd Ld & I came together from Wilton ye 12th October in 1642, with my younger Daughter the Lady Isabella Sackville. And the next day we came to London where my 2nd Lord went to lye in his lodgings in ye Cockpitt in St James Park . . . But I and my Daughter went to lye at Baynards . . . where I continued to lye in my own Chamber without removing 6 yeares & 9 monthes, which was ye longest time I continued to lye in all my life, the Civill Warres being then very hott in England. So I may say that it was a place of refuge for mee to hide myself in till these troubles were over-passed.[12]

The passage makes clear that, even as the wars surrounding them were at their height, Clifford and her daughter enjoyed a stable period of residence together, trapped in the splendour of Baynards Castle but set free from the direct influence of the Earl of Pembroke, her '2nd Lord', who chose to live at his own lodgings 'to be near the Parliament' (p. 95). The extract also demonstrates that, although Clifford's history is recorded in a series of notebooks with a diary-like emphasis on chronological detail and retrospective summing-up, nevertheless it does not have the immediacy and local scale which one might expect of a diary; one paragraph surveys a period of more than six years of her life. The historical instinct evinced here, however, is still the diarist's desire to record and order the facts of the past in fragments or snapshots framed by the calendar of months and years.

After the execution of Charles I in January 1649, Clifford was able to leave London and travel northwards, noting with startling precision the dates when she came into her inheritance and when she was actually able to take up residence:

> So the 8th day of August in 1649 I came into Appleby Castle ye most auncient seat of myne inheritance, and lay in my own chamber there. And I continued to lye till about ye 13th of February following.
> So various are ye pilgrimages of this human life. (Eccles. 3.5)
> And from the death of my Coz. german Henry, Earl of Cumberland, till this my first coming into Appleby Castle was just 5 yeares 8 months wanting three days. (p. 100)

Clifford found many of her properties in ruins, but noted defiantly of Cromwell, 'Let him destroy my Castles if he will, as often as he levels them I will rebuild them, so long as he leaves me a shilling in my pocket' (p. 101). This strikes a tone of such determination that it is no surprise to find a diary entry for 1651 expressing satisfaction with her life in 'the ancient Houses of mine Inheritance' where she has, as a woman (in her words, as 'a Wife and Lady oneself'), made the houses 'the place of Selfe fruition' (p. 112).

While national history may be measured in terms of reigns and battles, the woman's history contained in Anne Clifford's diaries centres around coincidences of place and the anniversaries of family births and deaths. Typical of these preoccupations is the account of the autumn of 1654:

> And whilst I now lay here in Brougham Castle in my owne Chamber, where my father was borne, and my Mother died, I had the joyfull newes howe that on the second day of this September (being a Saturday) my Grandchilde ye Lady Margarett Coventry, wife of Mr George Coventry, was delivered of her first Childe, that was a Sonne . . . This being the first Child that made me a Great Grandmother, which I account a greate Blessing of God. (p. 123)

For Clifford, history comprises not only the stones of the castles built by her forebears, and the knowledge that she sleeps in a room so closely connected to her parents, but also her own genealogical place as she looks with pride on the three generations coming after her.

In this discussion we have been able to mention only a very small sample of women's histories from the extensive experiences recorded in varied written genres during the period of the English Revolution. We have, however, tried to suggest the range of significance carried by the term 'history' for the women of those decades, from active involvement in political or military activities to self-analysis against a background of conflict and uncertainty. We have encountered women taking on formerly male tasks in the home or in public life, women identifying themselves with historical processes through their husbands or children, or, at the other end of the spectrum, women using the language of revolution as a source of metaphors for private or emotional life. We have seen women in the roles of daughter, fiancée, wife, widow, mother and even great-grandmother, but also in the roles of political plotter, defender of home or family, rebuilder of castles, Christian martyr and upholder of religious, marital or political integrity. Perhaps most significantly from the literary perspective, we have observed the rise of the woman historian, inscriber of images of personal and national experience.

This chapter will have served its purpose if it has aroused in its readers the curiosity to read more of the texts written by these fascinating women or to reconsider what is meant by 'history' itself. The very parameters of history shift in this early modern period as the urgency of immediate experience forced historians to move away from a preoccupation with ancient events towards a concern for the contemporary, and from a public male historic order towards a vision which is more inclusive in terms of gender and social context. Women not only made history in this era; they also began to *re-make* it.

NOTES

1 See John Loftis (ed.), *The Memoirs of Anne, Lady Halkett and Ann, Lady Fanshawe* (Oxford: Clarendon Press, 1979), pp. 23–5.
2 See Henk Dragstra, Sheila Ottway and Helen Wilcox (eds.), *Betraying Our Selves: Forms of Self-Representation in Early Modern English Texts* (Basingstoke: Macmillan, 2000).
3 Margaret [Cavendish], Duchess of Newcastle, *The Life of the Duke of Newcastle, Memoirs of Her Own Life [A True Relation] and Certain Sociable Letters* (London: Dent, 1915), p. 192.
4 Lucy Hutchinson, *Memoirs of the Life of Colonel Hutchinson: With a Fragment of Autobiography*, ed. N. H. Keeble (London: Dent, 1995).
5 See on this aspect of the text David Norbrook's chapter below, pp. 238–40.
6 Included in Lucy Hutchinson, *Memoirs of the Life of Colonel Hutchinson*, pp. 3–15.
7 This self-doubting rhetorical question, from the final paragraph of *A True Relation*, inspired the title of the anthology edited by Elspeth Graham, Hilary Hinds, Elaine Hobby and Helen Wilcox, *Her Own Life: Autobiographical Writings by Seventeenth-Century Englishwomen* (London: Routledge, 1989), and appears on p. 98 of that volume.
8 Loftis (ed.), *Memoirs of Halkett and Fanshawe*, p. 114.
9 Thomas Taylor Lewis (ed.), *Letters of the Lady Brilliana Harley*, Camden Society, 1st ser. 58 (London: Royal Historical Society, 1854), p. 185. For a selection of

these letters, see Eva Figes (ed.), *Women's Letters in Wartime* (London: Pandora, 1994), pp. 34–52.

10 Dorothy Osborne, *Letters to Sir William Temple*, ed. Kenneth Parker (Harmondsworth: Penguin, 1987), p. 156.

11 Osborne, *Letters*, p. 164. For further discussion of Osborne's literary influences, see Sheila Ottway, 'Dorothy Osborne's Love Letters: Novelistic Glimmerings and the Ovidian Self', *Prose Studies*, 19 (1996), 149–59.

12 *The Diaries of Lady Anne Clifford*, ed. D. J. H. Clifford (Stroud: Alan Sutton, 1990), p. 95.

FURTHER READING

For individual editions of primary texts cited or discussed, please see the notes above.

Clarke, Danielle, and Elizabeth Clarke (eds.), *'This Double Voice': Gendered Writing in Early Modern England*, Basingstoke: Macmillan, 2000.

Davies, Stevie, *Unbridled Spirits: Women of the English Revolution: 1640–1660*, London: The Women's Press, 1998.

Dragstra, Henk, Sheila Ottway and Helen Wilcox (eds.), *Betraying Our Selves: Forms of Self-Representation in Early Modern English Texts*, Basingstoke: Macmillan, 2000.

Healy, Thomas, and Jonathan Sawday (eds.), *Literature and the English Civil War*, Cambridge University Press, 1990.

Hobby, Elaine, *Virtue of Necessity: English Women's Writing, 1649–88*, London: Virago, 1988.

Keeble, N. H. (ed.), *The Cultural Identity of Seventeenth-Century Woman: A Reader*, London: Routledge, 1994.

'Obedient Subjects? The Loyal Self in Some Later Seventeenth-Century Royalist Women's Memoirs', in Gerald Maclean (ed.), *Culture and Society in the Stuart Restoration: Literature, Drama, History*, Cambridge University Press, 1995, pp. 201–18.

Mendelson, Sara, and Patricia Crawford, *Women in Early Modern England*, Oxford: Clarendon Press, 1998.

Morrill, John (ed.), *Revolution and Restoration: England in the 1650s*, London: Collins and Brown, 1992.

Ottway, Sheila, 'Dorothy Osborne's Love Letters: Novelistic Glimmerings and the Ovidian Self', *Prose Studies*, 19 (1996), 149–59.

Desiring Disencumbrance: The Representation of the Self in Autobiographical Writings by Seventeenth-Century Englishwomen, University of Groningen Press, 1998.

Plowden, Alison, *Women All On Fire: The Women of the English Civil War*, Stroud: Alan Sutton, 1998.

Wilcox, Helen (ed.), *Women and Literature in Britain, 1500–1700*, Cambridge University Press, 1996.

9

ELAINE HOBBY

Prophecy, enthusiasm and female pamphleteers

When war broke out in 1642, British women's place was clearly defined in both ideology and law as subordinate to men's. Their central concern was supposed to be their reputation for chastity, and their goal, marriage and motherhood. In a culture where existing hierarchies were supposedly the will of God, and so beyond question, key Bible texts were cited to reinforce the status quo: since Eve's rebellion had resulted in the Fall, women were divinely commanded to obey their husbands (Gen. 3:16). The New Testament expands this subordination into a requirement that women not even speak on matters of public concern: 'Let your women keep silence in the churches: for it is not permitted unto them to speak; but they are commanded to be under obedience, as also saith the law. And if they will learn any thing, let them ask their husbands at home: for it is a shame for women to speak in the church' (1 Cor. 14:34–5).[1]

In the excited bevy of ideas set loose by the Revolutionary years, arguments used to justify intervention in public affairs by those men previously excluded from politics proved particularly adaptable to support the idea that women, too, could act. If Britain really was living through the Biblical 'last days' before Christ's return, then God's promise of a great overturning meant that women, as well as men, could be called to speak on God's behalf. Indeed, since 'God hath chosen the weak things of the world to confound the things which are mighty' (1 Cor. 1:27), the weaker vessel, woman (1 Pet. 3:7), might be thought particularly likely to carry God's word. As a result, women were involved in establishing the new congregations of Baptists, sometimes outnumbering the men; and the earliest Quaker prophets included many women, who abandoned their secular role as wives and mothers to travel and suffer imprisonment as they spread the new ideas.[2]

In the early years after the Restoration, some of these women continued to press for change, the Quaker Dewans Morey, for instance, publishing in about 1665 *A True and Faithful Warning from the Lord God, sounded through me, a poor despised earthen vessel, unto all the Inhabitants of*

England, who are yet in your sins.[3] As she describes how she has 'been made to fast, hunger and pine, to groan, weep and cry bitterly' for the imminent dreadful fate of the nation, and calls on Charles II to 'come down from his Throne and sit in the Dust' (p. 1), she presents herself as the image of an Old Testament prophet, and in doing so continues the traditions of the Revolutionary years. This presentation of the self as God's vessel or instrument, who is required to deliver his message to the world, quickly became unacceptable in the land of restored monarchy, however; and, as the sects organized self-protective regulations and structures, the role of the woman prophet was largely squeezed out. Quaker Women's Meetings, for instance, defined the female role according to the frame set in St Paul's Epistle to Titus: older women 'may teach the young women to be sober, to love their husbands, to love their children, To be discreet, chaste, keepers at home, good, obedient to their own husbands, that the word of God be not blasphemed' (Titus 2:4–5).[4]

It is, however, fortunate that, as the early radicals reorganized, they also collected and preserved pamphlets written by their members. Although most of the female-authored texts have not been republished since, feminist scholars have recently brought a selection back into print; this chapter therefore mostly focuses on works the modern reader can obtain.[5]

Breaking silence

'I thought to have beene silent, but this is a time of warre', declared Sarah Jones, arguing for the establishment of Independent congregations in 1644.[6] On the copy of her pamphlet in the Thomason collection, George Thomason has noted that she was 'a diars wife'; this small detail is more than is known about many of her female contemporaries. Women prophets and pamphleteers did however exist in large numbers: published writings by more than 80 radical women have survived from the period 1640–80, and Phyllis Mack has found evidence of as many as 300 female prophets active between 1640 and 1660, most of whom appear not to have published at all.[7] They were inspired by the divine promise that in the last days before Christ's second coming, 'I will pour out of my Spirit upon all flesh: and your sons and your daughters shall prophesy' (Acts 2:17). In the great overturning, women could imagine for themselves a role not wholly circumscribed by chastity, obedience and silence.

A few of these women gained notoriety. When fifteen-year-old Sarah Wight stopped eating and fell into a trance lasting more than two months in 1646, for instance, many people, including a Sarah Jones, visited her to listen to the advice she proffered on God's will.[8] Details of these events were collected by her Fifth Monarchist congregation and published by Henry Jessey as *The Exceeding Riches of Grace*, a 160-page book which must have sold well, as it passed through six editions between 1647 and 1652. She also published her own account of her life subsequent to the trance: *A Wonderful Pleasant and Profitable Letter* (1656). More prominent yet was Elizabeth Poole, who was twice granted an audience by the New Model Army's General Council of Officers to deliver to them God's messages. It is possible that her first appearance before them, on 29 December 1648, was at the behest of Oliver Cromwell: her declaration that God had blessed Parliament's victory was most welcome as preparations began for Charles I's trial.[9] When she returned on 5 January 1649, however, it was with a prophecy less convenient for the Council, and somewhat startling to any modern reader anticipating that a woman bold enough to express opinions on matters of national politics would also be a defender of women's autonomy in the domestic sphere. Poole, on the contrary, used the ubiquitous analogy between the position of the king in the land and that of the father or husband in the family to warn the Council not to execute Charles. Were they to do so, she insisted, they would undermine their own rights over their wives: 'He is the Father and Husband of your bodyes, as unto men, and therefore your right cannot bee without him, as unto men' (*A Vision*, p. 4). Just as a wife must remain faithful to her husband even if she 'suffereth his terrour to her flesh' (p. 5), she continued, so the country should not overthrow their king. The violent husband could be left for the law to deal with, and Parliament should leave the King's punishment to God.

Comparable cases for the King's exemption from punishment were also presented by Mary Pope, and by the Presbyterian Elizabeth Warren, the author of several learned works of Scriptural exegesis published between 1645 and 1649.[10] Having made the claim (soon thereafter also made by the Royalist poet Katherine Philips) that the extraordinary national events had forced her, like Croesus' dumb son, to break silence, Warren presented herself as a highly learned and analytical figure.[11] Her attacks on the 'blasphemous boldnesse, and brazen faced impudence' of those rejecting the guidance of ordained ministers are thus implicitly contradicted by her breaking of connected injunctions to female silence and subservience, for all her assertion of her 'mental and Sex deficiencie'. With their extensive Latin marginalia and mobilizing of wide-ranging reading, her works were as likely to alarm conservatives as to be embraced by them, despite her insistence that God's law 'prohibiteth rebellion and acts of violence, both in Children to their Parents, and in Subjects to their Prince'.[12] Although her books are recommended to the reader in prefaces by Presbyterian divines James Cranford and Robert Cade, she, like Elizabeth Poole, proved not to be the convenient vehicle for masculinist thought that she might have been expected to be.

The gender politics of Elizabeth Poole's attempted intervention on the King's side are further complicated by the fact that when Poole's Particular Baptist church elders, led by William Kiffin, circulated a letter to other congregations condemning her, it was a disobedient wife, Thomasina Pendarves, who sprang to her defence. She intercepted Kiffin's letter to her husband, and called on the church to recognize that 'you may not judge right in this thing', soon thereafter acting on her threat to publish her rebuke to them if they did not withdraw their accusations.[13] A key issue for Pendarves in deciding where to ally herself in this dispute seems to have been Poole's economic position: Kiffin's church was damaging Poole's reputation, leading to people withdrawing business from her. 'You cannot be ignorant', Pendarves wrote, 'that she hath no livelihood amongst men, but what she earns by her hands: and your defaming her in this manner cannot in an ordinary way but deprive her of that and so at last bring her blood upon you' (*An Alarum*, pp. 8–9). This series of events suggests that the modern reader has much to learn about how to read these materials: alliances which might seem contradictory today made perfect sense to our forebears, who perceived matters through their own, not our, cultural framework.

The often-argued interdependence of kingly and paternal power none the less had the effect that, when women intervened in the public issues of the day, supposedly men's province, questions about correct female behaviour were inevitably raised. A particularly interesting example of this is the career of Katherine Chidley. A member of a separatist congregation in the 1630s, she campaigned against many of the practices of the national church, including the requirement that women be 'churched' (blessed in church for a fee) after giving birth. In 1641 and 1645 she published detailed rebuttals of Thomas Edwards' attacks on the radicals, and in the latter year also presented a petition against Presbyterian reorganization of the national church, *Good Counsell*, in which she declared that 'the truly godly ought to arise and be doing'. After the arrest of the Leveller leader John Lilburne in 1653, she was one of many women who engaged in campaigning for his release.[14] The published women's petitions that survive from this time cast an interesting light on how widespread the questioning of women's subordination was becoming. Though presenting themselves conventionally as women whose 'hearts [are] melting in tendernesse', they also insisted on 'our undoubted Right of Petitioning', and cited both Biblical texts and incidents from English history in their support.[15]

The most remarkable instance of this kind of collective female petitioning was not to occur until 1659, as the sense grew that women had an interest in questions of national politics, and a right to intervene. Quaker women organized a mass attack on the hated tithes, the tax system under which those who disagreed with and had left the Anglican church were still legally required to support its ministers financially. *These Several Papers Was Sent to the Parliament* was signed not only by hundreds of Quakers from all over the country, but also by a wide range of women from other radical congregations. As the published petition's preface asserts, the time had come for women to act: '*But now arise and shine O daughter of* Sion, *shake thy self from thy dust*' (sig. pv; *Hidden in Plain Sight*, p. 59).[16]

Quaker women writers

That Quaker women should have organized a nationwide petition against tithes is characteristic of their role within the Society of Friends. From the beginning, women were active ministers in the Society, setting up local meetings, sharing ideas and working to forward the Revolution. Friends' belief that each human being had within them a Light that could reveal divine will both made it possible for them to circumvent traditional ideas about female inferiority, and made it important to reach out to 'that of God' in any person: change in the world would come through a great returning to the Light.[17] As a result, early Friends travelled to spread the Word, and many of their first published writings were composed in prison. Anne Audland is a typical example. A mother of two small children, she travelled from her Westmorland home to Banbury, where she was gaoled for interrupting a church service. From prison she published *A True Declaration* (1655), the titlepage of which cites God's promise in Acts 2:18, 'And on my servants, and on my handmaidens, I will pour out in those days of my Spirit; and they shall prophesy'. The pamphlet displays joyful confidence, as Audland tells her story and reproves William Allen JP for persecuting Friends. Within weeks, Audland's text had been incorporated into the collectively written *The Saints Testimony*, which gives details of the prosecution of several women and men Friends: Audland herself was accused in court of blasphemy, and sent back to prison without formal charges being levelled. The pamphlet also includes William Allen's contemptuous order to Sarah Timms that, instead of engaging in prophesying, she should be '*sweeping the house and washing the dishes*' (p. 8), before the Quaker authors go on to justify women's speaking.

The early appearance in *The Saints Testimony* of what, derived from Galatians 3:28 but variously phrased, was to become the standard Quaker retort on the issue of women's silence – '*in Christ Jesus the spirit of God in male and female is both one*' (p. 15) – demonstrates neatly what is also shown by many other pamphlets: the challenge to the traditional injunction that women should 'keep silence' was an integral part of female Friends' theology, and Scriptural justification of their behaviour emerged from the need to defend what they were doing. In prison in Exeter later that same year, 1655, Priscilla Cotton and Mary Cole playfully pushed the case for their speaking out to its logical conclusion: they are permitted to speak, they insist, because they are inspired by the Light. The church ministers exhorting them to silence, by contrast, are clearly not divinely inspired, since if they were, they would not try to interfere with God's messengers. The conclusion they gleefully press is that the male ministers are therefore themselves 'the women forbidden to speak in the church'.[18]

The anthology *Hidden in Plain Sight*[19] includes several pamphlets typical of the kinds of writing women prophets produced as they evaded their traditional role as silent helpmeets. Sarah Blackborow's *A Visit to the Spirit in Prison* (1658) deals with metaphorical, not actual, imprisonment, as she appeals to her reader to realize that 'a Witnesse hath the Lord God in you, which is faithful and true' (p. 1; *Hidden in Plain Sight*, p. 48). She weaves together Biblical texts that would have been familiar to her readers with examples drawn from her own experience, in order to present herself as a living sign of the joy and community that can be experienced by those who follow her example and 'return to the light'. Alluding to the Song of Solomon, she urges, 'Oh! love truth and its Testimony, whether its Witness be to you, or against you, love it, that into my Mothers house you all may come, and into the Chamber of her that conceived me, where you may embrace and be embraced of my dearly beloved one, Love is his Name' (p. 10; *Hidden in Plain Sight*, p. 55).[20] In her later tracts, *Herein is Held Forth the Gift* (1659) and *The Just and Equal Balance* (1660), she expands on these themes, in the latter celebrating the new possibility of community offered by Quaker practices, before ending with a defence of women's role as preachers.

The energy that pervades Blackborow's writings is also typical of the excited immediacy of one of the most prolific Quaker prophets, Dorothy White. For Quakers, human activities and the Bible function at a symbolic level as well as at a literal one, so, for instance, all people should be addressed as 'thou', not the more formal and respectful 'you', to signify that all are equal in God's sight; tithes should not be paid because they both literally and symbolically support the national church. The Bible, therefore, can be used as a source of living metaphors that directly apply to present-day concerns, with the result that, as White declares in *A Trumpet* (1662), '*this* is the Glorious Day of the Lord God, wherein he hath appeared in great power, for the gathering of the Sons of Men from far, and the bringing of his Daughters from the ends of the Earth' (p. 8; *Hidden in Plain Sight*, p. 142). Within this theology, the common female similes and metaphors that occur in the Bible (evil-doers are symbolically harlots, strumpets, the Whore of Babylon; see for example Ezekiel 16, Revelation 17) can also be revivified to provide a new role for women, one not delimited by negative images of female sexuality, or by their traditional functions as wives and mothers. Drawing on Isaiah 54:1 and Galatians 4:27, for instance, White exhorts her reader to replace the role of mother with a life of ministry: 'now rejoyce thou barren Womb, which hath brought forth the first Begotten of God, for more shall be thy Children than of her that was the married Wife, for the Vine shall yield its increase' (p. 15; *Hidden in Plain Sight*, p. 148). In the fast-changing political landscape of 1659, she then produced several pamphlets concerning God's will for Britain's future.[21] Comparable attempts by women to persuade rulers to change policy are many: Anne Clayton in 1660 and Anne Gilman in 1662 both addressed Charles II in print, as did Margaret Fell, the most prolific and powerful female Friend.[22]

Though writing at all required such women to confront attempts to silence them, their major focus is not on that issue, but on the matters of belief and practice that had prompted them to join the Friends in the first place. A good example of this is Hester Biddle's *Woe to Thee City of Oxford* and its companion piece, *Wo to the Towne of Cambridge* (1655): Biddle's concern is to challenge the system of hierarchies that oppresses the majority of people, reproving the university towns, 'thou art full of filth . . . thou art full of pride and covetousness, thou art polluted in thy blood, and joins house to house, and field to field, until there is no place left for the poor'.[23] After the Restoration she was not deflected from this radical vision, and her pamphlet *The Trumpet of the Lord* (1662) warns that 'he is risen, who will scatter Rulers in his anger, and will pluck down Kings in his Wroth' (p. 9).

Most of these Quaker tracts are quite short – no more than twenty pages in length – but they manage a complex blend of argument about doctrine, autobiography and exhortation for change. Two book-length Quaker works, Katherine Evans's and Sarah Cheevers' *This Is a Short Relation* (1662), and Joan Vokins' *God's Mighty Power Magnified* (1691), contain a comparable variety on a grand scale. Evans's and Cheevers' text, like those of so many of their sisters, was written from prison: in their case, in the Inquisition in Malta, where they had called to spread the Quaker message as they retraced St Paul's journey to Alexandria. On their way across Europe, they also met up with other travelling women Friends, Ann Gargill and Hester Biddle.[24] *This Is a Short Relation* is compiled from a series of writings, including letters, autobiographical narrative, and prophecies which they wrote, both separately and together, from their prison cells. As they describe the friars' attempts to convert them to Roman Catholicism, knit stockings to wear, and mend the clothing of other prisoners (p. 42; *Hidden in Plain Sight*, p. 202), they also switch into periods of ecstatic visions and prophecy. Evans, for instance, records that she 'saw a great wonder in Heaven, the Woman cloathed with the Sun, and hath the Moon under her feet, and a Crown of 12 Stars upon her head, and she travelled in pain ready to be delivered of a Man-child' (p. 12; *Hidden in Plain Sight*, pp. 180–1; *Her Own Life*, p. 123[25]). Whilst her contemporaries would recognize here the direct allusion to Revelation 12:1–2, she also insists that the meaning of her experience cannot be found in a book: she is the living embodiment of God's word, and is recording 'the things which I did hear, see, tasted, and handled of the good Word of God' (pp. 13–14; *Hidden in Plain Sight*, p. 181; *Her Own Life*, p. 124). Evans's and Cheevers' pamphlet thus re-enacts the Quaker conviction that lives could be, quite fully, a 'living testimony': Friends could signify, in their words and activities, the meaning of returning to the Light, setting an example for others to follow.

The transformation that joining the Society of Friends could entail for a woman is shown nowhere more clearly than in Joan Vokins' *God's Mighty Power Magnified* (1691). Vokins looks back on and makes sense of a life in which, leaving behind her husband, seven children and all 'visibles' in 1679, she had travelled around the Caribbean spreading news of 'the Marriage Union with the Lamb of God' (p. 18; *Hidden in Plain Sight*, p. 257; *Her Own Life*, p. 215). Her choice of this metaphor is typical of the framework within which her text makes its story. What God means to her is 'Power' – she uses the term repeatedly; but the power in question is his, not her own. God it is who determines her itinerary, sometimes changing the wind's direction to ensure that ships take her to the islands he has determined she should visit (pp. 39–41; *Hidden in Plain Sight*, pp. 268–9; *Her Own Life*, pp. 219–21). She is thus able, whilst living an extraordinary life, to interpret her experiences as being the result of her perfect obedience to the will of another, her 'Soul's Beloved' (p. 32; *Hidden in Plain Sight*, p. 264). This willing subordination none the less prompts her to rush home to England to defend the existence of separate meetings for women Friends (pp. 29–30, *Hidden in Plain Sight*, p. 263), or to intervene in an Anglican church and insist on a woman's right to minister (pp. 44–5; *Hidden in Plain Sight*, p. 271; *Her Own Life*, pp. 222–3). After the Restoration, as the Society of Friends set up structures that reduced women's role in an attempt to protect themselves from state persecution, narratives like Vokins' show how it was possible for some of the liberating impact of the Revolution to be maintained, within a framework of acceptable feminine obedience.

Eleanor Douglas and Anna Trapnel

Most of the prophetic writings by women from the Revolutionary period are the work of Quakers, no doubt reflecting the particular role women Friends created for themselves in their Society. There are two notable exceptions. One is the maverick aristocrat Lady Eleanor Douglas (earlier, Davies), who published more than sixty tracts between 1625 and 1652. These interpret the events of her own life through Bible promises to God's nation, Zion. Though the elements that make up her pamphlets are comparable to those of other prophets, Lady Eleanor's rank means that her works are fundamentally different from others': she does not need anyone to join her or to accept her case. Instead, she insists that the truly godly will understand the writings that she makes deliberately arcane and allusive.[26]

The other important non-Quaker prophet of the 1640s and 1650s was the Fifth Monarchist and Particular Baptist Anna Trapnel. Like her fellow believer Sarah Wight, she had trances and prophesied in the mid-1640s, and indeed Jessey's *Exceeding Riches of Grace* specifically refers to Trapnel's experiences, presenting their simultaneity with Wight's as itself evidence of God's active work in the world (p. 139). When Trapnel began again to prophesy in 1654, the circulation of her words was at first very much under the control of the congregation who recorded them as *Strange and Wonderful Newes from Whitehall*. In her case, as in Wight's, the conventional association of women with weakness could make her seem a particularly appropriate vessel for God to work through, as 'God hath chosen the weak things of the world to confound the things which are mighty' (1 Cor. 1:27). As her activities expanded, however, she appears to have come into her own. The record of her trial in Cornwall, charged with witchcraft and disturbing the peace, portrays her as a witty and politically adept prophet, one able to retort to the court's implicit reproof, 'I understand you are not married': 'Then having no hinderance, why may not I go where I please if the Lord so will?' (p. 26; *Her Own Life*, p. 91). Her reworking of this episode and her earlier experiences into the extended autobiographical narrative, *A Legacy for Saints* (1654), demonstrates a sophisticated ability to tell the story of a life in terms that give it a specific and radical political force. Though in her *Report and Plea* (1654) she denies a wish to become 'a gazing stock' (p. 49), she actively used the events of her life to demonstrate the truth of her Fifth Monarchist message, promising that 'the strongest Dragons teeth cannot rend Saints asunder' (p. 44).[27]

Autobiographical writings

Trapnel's pamphlets report that she experimented with various radical groups before joining her Baptist congregation, and the high prophetic content of her pamphlets is more typical of Quaker women's writing than of Baptists'. Where the majority of writings published by Quaker women during the aftermath of the Revolution were prophecies, reaching out to others in an attempt to convert, the works of women from other radical sects were more often focused on telling the story of the believer's own life. This difference arose from the theological disagreements that divided the sects: whereas early Quakers confidently insisted that all people could join the forces for good by turning to their Inner Light for guidance, Baptist churches required would-be communicants to examine their own lives for evidence that God had saved them personally. The practice of narrating these 'conversion experiences' led first to the publication of collections of many such short accounts, and longer individual narratives followed.[28] In these, though the experiences of the author are offered as a lesson – usually, that the misery and terror of fearing damnation could be succeeded by confidence in salvation – the life described is not offered as a symbol, but as material evidence of God's work upon the individual soul.

Focus on an individual's life did not, of course, result in autobiographical writings that took their structure from the key events of the author's secular life: the important matters were questions of faith and doctrine, not the births, deaths and marriages that might be thought central to women's concerns. These works do not, therefore, yield easily to modern assumptions about what an autobiography might consist of. *Susanna's Apologie Against the Elders* (1659), for instance, lets us know that Susanna Parr had a baby who died, but the significance of this episode in the story she tells is theological, not purely emotional or personal.[29] As she describes the 'very melting affliction' (p. 13; *Her Own Life*, p. 110) of bereavement, she uses the reader's rush of sympathy to bolster the case she is making against separation from the national church: our father God suffers the same agonies of loss when a congregation leaves the church's body as a grieving parent does when a child dies, she asserts. Parr's conversion narrative is indeed, in a sense, an anti-conversion narrative: this is the story of her leaving the separatist congregation she was involved in forming. A particularly intriguing element of *Susanna's Apologie* is the fact that what might be seen as a conservative retreat from separation is justified by her in part through her refusal to behave in unfeminine ways: just as the Elders in the Apocrypha tried to tempt Susanna to sin (Dan. 13), the elders in her own congregation have persuaded her into the immodest behaviour of speaking in church (pp. 4, 9–10, 13,

75–9; *Her Own Life*, pp. 105, 108, 109–10). Her resultant 120-page book justifies her defying the pastors and moving to a less radical congregation.

Although the over-arching concern of the conversion narrative is matters of doctrine, the requirement to work these out by focusing on the individual's own relationship with God means that these stories engage with a wide range of life events. The usual pattern in a conversion narrative, where the believer is shown to progress from misery to the joy of assured salvation, permits the analysis of a very diverse range of experiences. In *A Wise Virgin's Lamp* (1658), for instance, Anne Venn, daughter of the regicide John Venn, details through 330 pages the churches she and her father visited, and the sermons they heard, in their attempts to find a truly holy congregation. After his death in 1650, her search for a congregation she could join in good conscience continued unabated. That she considered her salvation her own concern, and not under the control of her father's authority, is clear. Though finding the right church could bring community, the journey to find it was a lonely one. Sarah Davy's *Heaven Realized* therefore moves from the lonely despair of bereavement (both her baby brother and her mother die) to joyful union with the congregation of 'one of a sweet and free disposition', the woman she falls in love with.[30] A similar structuring of what might be seen as personal and emotional issues through the logics of faith and salvation is seen in the narrative of Agnes Beaumont, who records the conflict that erupted between herself and her widower father when she wanted to join John Bunyan's church.[31] Hannah Allen and An Collins also tell tales of suffering: Allen repeatedly tries to kill herself in the melancholy that overwhelms her after a childhood and youth of repeated losses; Collins searches for comfort in God's love when her illness leads to sterility (loss of 'flowers' or menstruation) and the single life.[32] Elizabeth Major, too, sees illness as the test given her by God, and the intricate acrostics she comes to write on her name as a proof of her salvation.[33] Katherine Sutton learns the lesson that she is divinely required to obey her husband, and that punishment will follow if she fails to do so.[34] All these texts engage intimately with the Bible and with doctrinal disputes, the authors recording their personal journeys through the arguments over God's will that the Revolutionary years set in motion, and demonstrating a creative capacity to make sense of a life in new religious terms. As a result, most of these works were published posthumously by the authors' congregations, and offered to the reader as exemplary lives. Once in print, however, they are available for interpretation with other priorities in mind.

Perhaps the most startling exploration of the relationship between a woman's secular life as wife and mother and her spiritual journey appears in a series of pamphlets by Anne Wentworth, written between 1676 and 1680, long after the revolutionary events themselves, but still drawing on the expectation of a great overturning.[35] Where in 1649 God had told Elizabeth Poole that a wife must suffer her husband's terror to her flesh, in 1671 Wentworth received a very different message. In *A Vindication* (1677), she explains that God sent an angel to tell her to write and publish the truth about her husband's treatment of her, who 'has in his barbarous actions towards me, a many times over done such things, as not only in the *Spirit* of them will one day be judged a murdering of, but had long since *really* proved so, if God had not wonderfully supported me' (p. 4). This pamphlet and her next, *The Revelation* (1679), are ecstatic in tone and saturated with the Bible language that marks Wentworth out as a prophet in the Revolutionary tradition. Free to prophesy, it is her duty to God, she says, to explain that her husband's behaviour is like the oppression of Zion by Babylon in the Bible: she, the abused wife, is Zion; Babylon is figured in the violent man. God's undertaking to free Zion and punish Babylon is therefore a promise made to all abused women, and the Lord is exasperated by the public's failure to understand this:

> The Lord shewed me why the people did not understand me, nor my work; Because they will not (saith the Lord) go to the root of the matter, but blind themselves with poring so much upon a Man and his Wife, and will look no further: but continue writing all faults in thy forehead, as delusions and disobeyings of thy Husband, and see none in themselves: they are so stark blind that they can see nothing at all of what I the Lord am doing: They will not see, how I have placed the two Spirits in a Man and his Wife, to figure out Zion and Babylon. (*Revelation*, p. 9)

The fact that this message from God was so consistently misunderstood leads Wentworth to conclude that all current churches, including Baptists and Quakers, have lost sight of divine will, and lapsed into a 'formalism' that conceals from them the true interpretation of Scripture (*England's Spiritual Pill*, p. 17).

The society she was writing for had recoiled from 'enthusiasm', and did not seem ready to hear her message. Her Particular Baptist church (led by Hanserd Knollys, who had in 1663 been only too happy to endorse Katherine Sutton's account of how she learned to obey her husband) had intervened in 1674 on her husband's side to urge her silence. Certain that her prophecy was of national importance, however, she wrote to the Lord Mayor of London and to Charles II, who for a while seemed keen to hear from her; probably they expected that her message, like the writings of her minister Knollys, would have some bearing on the Popish Plot furore. When she did not deliver what they expected, the authorities stopped listening.[36]

Her story ends tantalizingly, with Wentworth, having left her husband, sitting in the London house he has tried to rent from under her, waiting for God to pay her rent, safe in his promise that 'when I the Lord come to sit upon my Throne, to rule all Nations: the Man of Earth shall no more oppress, for I King Jesus come to give my children rest, and thou art a free woman, to worship me in spirit and truth'. The ideas set whirling in the great overturning could, thirty years on, justify the dissolution of violent marriages, 'to overthrow *Babylon* with such an overturning, as never was, nor never will be again' (*Vindication*, p. 9; *Her Own Life*, p. 190).

The war released women into the public world of contention, and into speech and writing. This was a consequence of the very inter-relatedness of kingly and masculine power that had long been used to justify both. Once the King's authority was questioned, that of men also came under strain, as women made the radical move of connecting directly with their God, without mediation on the part of a state church and its ministers. Women did not, however, flock to a particular sect, or form their own separate one. Instead, different women made different decisions, based on their own understanding of divine will. The result is a rich variety of published writings.

NOTES

1 Useful anthologies of texts on women's role include N. H. Keeble (ed.), *The Cultural Identity of Seventeenth-Century Woman: A Reader* (London: Routledge, 1994); Kate Aughterson (ed.), *Renaissance Woman: Constructions of Femininity in England* (London: Routledge, 1995); Suzanne Trill, Kate Chedgzoy and Melanie Osborne (eds.), *Lay By Your Needles Ladies, Take the Pen: Writing Women in England, 1500–1700* (London: Arnold, 1997). See also Amy Louise Erickson, *Women and Property in Early Modern England* (London: Routledge, 1993, 1995).

2 See further: Phyllis Mack, *Visionary Women: Ecstatic Prophecy in Seventeenth-Century England* (Berkeley: University of California Press, 1992); Christine Trevett, *Women and Quakerism in the Seventeenth Century* (York: Ebor Press, 1991); J. F. McGregor and B. Reay (eds.), *Radical Religion in the English Revolution* (Oxford University Press, 1984); Patricia Crawford, *Women and Religion in England, 1500–1720* (London: Routledge, 1993).

3 This dating is speculative. The date given by the British Library catalogue is 1665.

4 See Mary Foster *et al.*, *A Living Testimony* (1685), in Mary Garman, Judith Applegate, Margaret Benefiel and Dortha Meredith (eds.), *Hidden in Plain Sight: Quaker Women's Writings, 1650–1700* (Wallingford, Penn.: Pendle Hill, 1996), pp. 523–8, for examples of such definitions.

5 Garman *et al.* (eds.), *Hidden in Plain Sight*; Trill *et al.* (eds.), *Lay By Your Needles*; Elspeth Graham, Hilary Hinds, Elaine Hobby and Helen Wilcox (eds.), *Her Own Life: Autobiographical Writings by Seventeenth-Century Englishwomen* (London: Routledge, 1989); Esther S. Cope (ed.), *Prophetic Writings of Lady Eleanor Davies* (New York: Oxford University Press, 1995).

6 Sarah Jones, *To Sions Lovers* (1644), sig. A3.

7 Mack, *Visionary Women*, p. 24. For published prophets, see Elaine Hobby, *Virtue of Necessity: English Women's Writing 1649–88* (London: Virago, 1988).

8 Henry Jessey, *The Exceeding Riches of Grace* (London, 1647), lists 'Mrs Sar. Jones, wife to M. Th: Jones, Esq. of Towerhil' amongst Wight's visitors (p. 9). See also Diane Purkiss, 'Producing the Voice, Consuming the Body: Women Prophets of the Seventeenth Century', in Isobel Grundy and Susan Wiseman (eds.), *Women, Writing, History 1640–1740* (London: Batsford, 1992), pp. 139–58. An extract from Jessey appears in Trill *et al.* (eds.), *Lay By Your Needles*, pp. 155–61.

9 Rachel Trubowitz, 'Female Preachers and Male Wives: Gender and Authority in Civil War England', in James Holstun (ed.), *Pamphlet Wars: Prose in the English Revolution* (London: Frank Cass, 1992), pp. 112–33. Poole's first pamphlet, *A Vision* (1649), included both messages, and is reproduced in Trill *et al.* (eds.), *Lay By Your Needles*, pp. 164–9. There is a contemporary report of Poole's interviews in C. H. Firth (ed.), *The Clarke Papers* (London: Royal Historical Society, 1992), 2nd pagination, pp. xix–xx, 150–4, 163–70.

10 Mary Pope, *A Treatise* (1647) and *Behold* (1649); Elizabeth Warren, *The Old and Good Way* (1645).

11 Warren, *Old and Good Way*, sig. A3r–v; Philips, 'Upon the double murther of K. Charles', in Patrick Thomas (ed.), *The Collected Works of Katherine Philips the Matchless Orinda*, vol. 1: *The Poems* (Stump Cross, Essex: Stump Cross Books, 1990), p. 69.

12 Elizabeth Warren, *A Warning-Peece* (1649), p. 25 (misnumbered 29), 35 (misnumbered 18); Warren, *Old and Good Way*, sig. A3.

13 Pendarves' letter, signed 'T. P.', was included in Poole's second publication, *An Alarum of War* (1649), and in her fourth, *A Prophesie*. It was omitted from her third work, also confusingly called *An Alarum of War* (1649).

14 Ian Gentles, 'London Levellers in the English Revolution: The Chidleys and Their Circle', *JEH*, 29 (1978), 281–309.

15 *To the Parliament . . . afflicted Women* (1653); *Unto Every Individual Member* (1653). See Patricia Higgins, 'The Reactions of Women, with Special Reference to Women Petitioners', in Brian Manning (ed.), *Politics, Religion and the English Civil War* (London: Arnold, 1973), pp. 179–222.

16 Reproduced in Garman *et al.* (eds.), *Hidden in Plain Sight*, pp. 58–128.

17 Barry Reay, 'Quakerism and Society', in McGregor and Reay (eds.), *Radical Religion*, pp. 145–7.

18 Priscilla Cotton and Mary Cole, *To the Priests and People of England* (1655), pp. 7–8. Reproduced in Hilary Hinds, *God's Englishwomen: Seventeenth-century Radical Sectarian Writing and Feminist Criticism* (Manchester University Press, 1996), pp. 222–6; the relevant section is in Trill *et al.* (eds.), *Lay By Your Needles*, pp. 200–1. See also Elaine Hobby, 'Handmaids of the Lord and Mothers in Israel: Early Vindications of Quaker Women's Prophecy', in Thomas N. Corns and David Loewenstein (eds.), *The Emergence of Quaker Writing: Dissenting Literature in Seventeenth-Century England* (London: Frank Cass, 1995), pp. 88–98.

19 For details, see above, n. 4.

20 The concept of 'community' is discussed in Elaine Hobby, '"Come to Live a Preaching Life": Female Community in Seventeenth-Century Radical Sects', in Rebecca D'Monté and Nicole Pohl (eds.), *Female Communities, 1600–1800: Literary Visions and Cultural Realities* (London: Macmillan, 1999).

21 Dorothy White, *A Diligent Search*; *This to be Delivered*; *Upon the 22 day*; *A Visitation* – all 1659. For Quaker activism in 1659, see Barry Reay, *The Quakers and the English Revolution* (London: Temple Smith, 1985), pp. 81–100.

22 Anne Clayton, *A Letter to the King* (1660); Anne Gilman, *An Epistle . . . Also, A Letter to Charles* (1662), in Garman *et al.* (eds.), *Hidden in Plain Sight*, pp. 463–9. Some of Fell's many pamphlets are in Garman *et al.* (eds.), *Hidden in Plain Sight*, pp. 38–46, 233–54, 453–62. See also Judith Kegan Gardiner, 'Margaret Fell Fox and Feminist Literary History: A "Mother in Israel" Calls to the Jews', in Corns and Loewenstein, *Emergence*, pp. 42–56.

23 An edited version appears in Elaine Hobby, '"Oh Oxford thou art full of filth": The Prophetical Writings of Hester Biddle, 1629(?)-1696', in Susan Sellers (ed.), *Feminist Criticism: Theory and Practice* (London: Harvester Wheatsheaf, 1991), pp. 157–69.

24 According to the Inquisition's own record of their interrogation; see Andrew P. Vella, *The Tribunal of the Inquisition in Malta* (Royal University of Malta, 1964), p. 35; the relevant part is reproduced in Henry J. Cadbury, 'Friends and the Inquisition at Malta', *Journal of the Friends' Historical Society*, 53 (1974), 219–25.

25 For details of this anthology, see above, n. 5.

26 Cope, *Prophetic Writings*. For interpretations, see Esther S. Cope, *Handmaid of the Holy Spirit: Dame Eleanor Davies, Never Soe Mad a Ladie* (Ann Arbor: University of Michigan Press, 1992); and Megan Matchinske, 'Holy Hatred: Formations of the Gendered Subject in English Apocalyptic Writing, 1625–1651', *ELH*, 60 (1993), 349–77.

27 Nigel Smith, *Perfection Proclaimed: Language and Literature in English Radical Religion 1640–1660* (Oxford: Clarendon Press, 1989), sees Trapnel as less independent than this.

28 John Rogers, *Ohel or Beth-shemesh* (1653), extracts in Trill *et al.* (eds.), *Lay By Your Needles*, pp. 182–6; Henry Walker, *Spirituall Experiences* (1653). See Owen C. Watkins, *The Puritan Experience: Studies in Spiritual Autobiography* (London: Routledge and Kegan Paul, 1972).

29 There is an extract in Graham *et al.* (eds.), *Her Own Life*, pp. 103–15, and a discussion in Crawford, *Women and Religion*, pp. 152–9. Susanna Bell also explores her own child's death, which she believed was God's punishment for disobedience to her husband, in *The Legacy of a Dying Mother* (1673), extracted in Trill *et al.* (eds.), *Lay By Your Needles*, pp. 233–9.

30 Sarah Davy, *Heaven Realized* (1670), extracted in Graham *et al.* (eds.), *Her Own Life*, pp. 168–79.

31 Agnes Beaumont, *The Narrative of the Persecutions of Agnes Beaumont* (East Lansing, Mich.: Colleagues Press, 1992).

32 Hannah Allen, *Satan his Methods and Malice Baffled* (1683), extracted in Graham *et al.* (eds.), *Her Own Life*, pp. 200–210; An Collins, *Divine Songs and Meditations* (1653), ed. Sidney Gottlieb (Tempe, Ariz.: Renaissance Text Society, 1996), extracted in *Her Own Life*, pp. 57–70.

33 Elizabeth Major, *Honey on the Rod* (1656); extracted in Germaine Greer, Jeslyn Medoff, Melinda Sansone and Susan Hastings (eds.), *Kissing the Rod: An Anthology of 17th-Century Women's Verse* (London: Virago, 1988).

34 Katherine Sutton, *A Christian Womans Experiences* (Rotterdam, 1663).

35 Anne Wentworth, *A True Account* (1676), *A Vindication* (1677), *The Revelation*

(1679), *England's Spiritual Pill* (c. 1680). *A Vindication* is excerpted in Graham *et al.* (eds.), *Her Own Life*, pp. 183–96. *The Revelation* can be found on the World Wide Web at http://chaucer.library.emory.edu/wwrp/went_web/went_frame.html, edited by Vickie Taft.

36 The correspondence is in *Calendar of State Papers Domestic, 1677*, pp. 279–80, 411, 434–6, 477–8, 528–9. Hanserd Knollys' comments on the Popish Plot are in *Mystical Babylon Unvailed* (1679), p. 31.

FURTHER READING

For individual editions of primary texts cited or discussed, please see the notes above.

Aughterson, Kate (ed.), *Renaissance Woman: Constructions of Femininity in England*, London: Routledge, 1995.

Clarke, Danielle, and Elizabeth Clarke (eds.), *The Double Voice: Gendered Writing in Early Modern England*, Basingstoke: Macmillan, 2000.

Cope, Esther S., *Handmaid of the Holy Spirit: Dame Eleanor Davies, Never Soe Mad a Ladie*, Ann Arbor: Michigan University Press, 1992.

Crawford, Patricia, *Women and Religion in England, 1500–1720*, London: Routledge, 1993.

Davies, Stevie, *Unbridled Spirits: Women of the English Revolution: 1640–1660*, London: The Women's Press, 1998.

Erickson, Amy Louise, *Women and Property in Early Modern England*, London: Routledge, 1993.

Gardiner, Judith Kegan, 'Margaret Fell Fox and Feminist Literary History: A "Mother in Israel" Calls to the Jews', in Thomas N. Corns and David Loewenstein (eds.), *The Emergence of Quaker Writing: Dissenting Literature in Seventeenth-Century England*, London: Frank Cass, 1995, pp. 42–56.

Garman, Mary, Judith Applegate, Margaret Benefiel and Dortha Meredith (eds.), *Hidden in Plain Sight: Quaker Women's Writings, 1650–1700*, Wallingford, Penn.: Pendle Hill, 1996.

Gentles, Ian, 'London Levellers in the English Revolution: The Chidleys and their Circle', *JEH*, 29 (1978), 281–309.

Graham, Elspeth, Hilary Hinds, Elaine Hobby and Helen Wilcox (eds.), *Her Own Life: Autobiographical Writings by Seventeenth-Century Englishwomen*, London: Routledge, 1989

Greer, Germaine, Jeslyn Medoff, Melinda Sansone and Susan Hastings (eds.), *Kissing the Rod: An Anthology of 17th-Century Women's Verse*, London: Virago, 1988.

Higgins, Patricia, 'The Reactions of Women, with Special Reference to Women Petitioners', in Brian Manning (ed.), *Politics, Religion and the English Civil War*, London: Arnold, 1973, pp. 179–222.

Hinds, Hilary, *God's Englishwomen: Seventeenth-century Radical Sectarian Writing and Feminist Criticism*, Manchester University Press, 1996.

Hobby, Elaine, *Virtue of Necessity: English Women's Writing 1649–88*, London: Virago, 1988.

'Handmaids of the Lord and Mothers in Israel: Early Vindications of Quaker Women's Prophecy', in Thomas N. Corns and David Loewenstein (eds.), *The*

Emergence of Quaker Writing: Dissenting Literature in Seventeenth-Century England, London: Frank Cass, 1995, pp. 88–98.

'"Come to Live a Preaching Life": Female Community in Seventeenth-Century Radical Sects', in Rebecca D'Monté and Nicole Pohl (eds.), *Female Communities, 1600–1800: Literary Visions and Cultural Realities*, London: Macmillan, 1999, pp. 76–92.

Keeble, N. H. (ed.), *The Cultural Identity of Seventeenth-Century Woman: A Reader*, London: Routledge, 1994.

Mack, Phyllis, *Visionary Women: Ecstatic Prophecy in Seventeenth-Century England*, Berkeley: University of California Press, 1992.

Matchinske, Megan, 'Holy Hatred: Formations of the Gendered Subject in English Apocalyptic Writing, 1625–1651', *ELH*, 60 (1993), 349–77.

McGregor, J. F., and B. Reay (eds.), *Radical Religion in the English Revolution*, Oxford University Press, 1984.

Mendelson, Sara, and Patricia Crawford, *Women in Early Modern England*, Oxford: Clarendon Press, 1998.

Purkiss, Diane, 'Producing the Voice, Consuming the Body: Women Prophets of the Seventeenth Century', in Isobel Grundy and Susan Wiseman (eds.), *Women, Writing, History 1640–1740*, London: Batsford, 1992, pp. 139–58.

Reay, Barry, *The Quakers and the English Revolution*, London: Temple Smith, 1985.

Trevett, Christine, *Women and Quakerism in the Seventeenth Century*, York: Ebor Press, 1991.

Trill, Suzanne, Kate Chedgzoy and Melanie Osborne (eds.), *Lay By Your Needles Ladies, Take the Pen: Writing Women in England, 1500–1700*, London: Arnold, 1997.

Trubowitz, Rachel, 'Female Preachers and Male Wives: Gender and Authority in Civil War Literature', in James Holstun (ed.), *Pamphlet Wars: Prose in the English Revolution*, London: Frank Cass, 1992, pp. 112–33.

Watkins, Owen C., *The Puritan Experience: Studies in Spiritual Autobiography*, London: Routledge and Kegan Paul, 1972.

4

CONSERVATIVE VOICES

10

ALAN RUDRUM

Royalist lyric

Introduction

In this chapter I consider only work which responded to the Civil War itself.
Those 'Cavalier poets', 'the Mob of Gentlemen who wrote with Ease' (and
published) in the 1630s before armed conflict arose,[1] are excluded, as are
minor figures, such as Rowland Watkyns, whose poems had a local manuscript circulation but were not published until 1662, by which time they had
merely sycophantic point.[2] A more significant omission is Alexander Brome,
whose love lyrics and drinking songs circulated in the 1640s but were not
collected into a book until after the Restoration.[3] Each of the five poets who
are considered participated or suffered in the conflict. Robert Herrick lost
his living as a clergyman; John Cleveland was a notable figure in the Royalist
camp as the war began; Richard Lovelace lost his fortune in the Royalist
cause and was twice imprisoned; Abraham Cowley was a Royalist agent of
some importance; Henry Vaughan fought in the war and was part of a conspicuously Royalist circle in his native Breconshire.

As we might expect, a conflict which divided many families also on occasion led to civil war within the individual. Not all Royalist poets were consistently supportive of Charles I, even in their published utterances. Nor is
there a consistent Royalist poetic, of attitude, theme or of style; such vari-
ables as age, temperament, class, education, experience of battle, sequestration and/or imprisonment, and intensity of religious commitment made for
a wide variety of response. Moreover, in a rapidly changing political landscape, local circumstance and the pressures to which individual poets
responded affected their work, even though their aims might have been consistent and unwavering.

The changing agenda of literary criticism has markedly affected our
reading of the verse of this period. Until quite recently, literary critics paid
little attention to the shifting nature of censorship, which must have concerned the poets and publishers of the time. Verse apparently worried the

authorities less than overtly political or religious prose: twelve licensers were assigned in 1643 to books of divinity, four to law, but only three to 'books of philosophy, history, poetry, morality and arts'.[4] Nevertheless, Royalist poets prepared to attach their names to their publications must have felt themselves at risk, and developed strategies of concealment and encoding so as to reach their intended audiences while keeping the censors at bay.[5] It is not easy to estimate how effective as propaganda their poems actually were; but until quite recent times their concealments rather than their messages tended to shape modern critical responses. Vaughan, for instance, has been read as the author of 'timeless' religious lyrics, whose effects were occasionally marred by ill-tempered contemporary references. Similarly the post-Restoration Milton of *Paradise Lost*, his political cause defeated, has been seen as having withdrawn 'from politics into faith', into 'eternal verities'.[6] Such responses have been ascribed to the a-political readings of the New Critics. No doubt the popularity of 'close reading' in the years after the Second World War, with its concomitant concern that to go beyond the text for enlightenment was to fall into the 'biographical fallacy', helped to perpetuate the view that seventeenth-century lyric poets rose above the conflict of their times. The New Critics did not, however, initiate this view. Their predecessors in the late nineteenth and early twentieth centuries were eager to see what was 'eternal' in works of art, dismissing political reference as dross where it was obvious and not being at all disposed to seek it where it was not. In the last quarter of the twentieth century all this changed: critics have increasingly paid attention to the contexts in which literary works were written and those into which they were published. Historians have engaged with literature and literary critics with history, with the result that poems once seen as 'timeless', or even frivolous, are now seen as having been in close engagement with their times.

Royalist poets, in various ways, continued to be engaged in the war of words after the military cause was lost. Yet the theme of retirement from the fray is pervasive in Royalist verse; it is not surprising that many modern critics have read such verse as making the best of things in a purely private manner, rising above the conflict, retiring to a rural peace, spiced by convivial friends and good wine. In presenting themselves in this way, Royalist poets were conscious of living within a moral debate dating from Classical times and revived by Renaissance humanism: the debate, that is, on the value of *otium* or leisure and *negotium* or an active life. Recent criticism has considered how individual Royalist poets dealt with a retirement imposed by the victors, and the variety of ways in which *otium* issued in *negotium* – in which, that is, the performance of public duties was carried on within an apparently private life.[7] The poets themselves were conscious of the paradox inherent in their situation, as the title of Mildmay Fane's *Otia Sacra* ('The holy fruits of leisure'), balanced against its contents, makes clear.[8] In the preface to the 1655 *Silex Scintillans* Vaughan puts his work 'under the *protection*' of the Church's '*glorious head*' who 'can make it as useful now in the *public*, as it hath been to me in *private*.'[9]

Robert Herrick

The question of what texts respond to the Civil Wars is not entirely straight-forward. Herrick addressed verses to 'the Most Illustrious, and Most Hopeful Prince, Charles, Prince of Wales'.[10] Which is their more meaningful context: 1638, when the future Charles II was made Prince of Wales at the age of eight, or 1648, when the poem was first published and when its dedic-atee, his father in confinement, had become 'a central totem for the renewed active royalism of the second civil war'?[11] In general, when reading these poets, we need to consider both the text and its significance as a speech-act in the circumstances into which it was published.[12] The publication of *Hesperides* in 1648 may fairly be regarded as a political act. Many of Herrick's poems must have been written before the outbreak of the Civil Wars; a volume of his verse was entered in the Stationers' Register in 1640, but never published. However, verse written in the 1630s took on new implications when published in the context of the late 1640s. At the very least it might be said that by 1648 the generally festive tone of *Hesperides* was calculated to evoke the response that 'things were better then'. Such nostalgia may well have had propaganda value. Herrick presents the 'halcyon days' of Charles I's 'personal rule' in the 1630s as a time of innocent mirth and merry-making, which must have seemed appealing to those already wearied of the Rule of the Saints. The late 1640s in fact saw a number of rebellions against the Puritan proscription of just such festivities as Herrick celebrated. H. L. Mencken's definition of Puritanism as 'the haunting fear that someone, somewhere, may be happy' might accurately express a good deal of popular sentiment in Herrick's time as in our own.[13]

Poems which present themselves as innocuous, finely crafted and cheerful celebrations of 'cleanly-*Wantonnesse*' have long been popular with British and American readers.[14] Raised as many were within a tradition of Puritan inhibition, they read Herrick as offering a moral holiday, an experience of 'mirth' which contrived to be essentially innocent. Until quite recently, few modern readers considered these poems in their relation to a prose work both highly political and highly controversial, namely the re-issue by royal command in 1633 of the Book of Sports. The edict is clearly a licence for the people to enjoy themselves on the Lord's Day within strict limits laid down by authority. Similarly, Herrick's 'Corinna's Going A Maying' (*Poetical Works*, p. 67) sets limits on the licence it celebrates. 'Many a green-gown' may have been given, and 'many a kiss, both odd and even'; but the plighting of troth, and the choosing of a priest, is not far away. Herrick was an extraordinary craftsman in the tradition of Ben Jonson, with the ability to find the word ('*tempestuous* petticoat', 'that *liquefaction* of her clothes') that turned a good poem into a magnificent one.[15] To experience 'Corinna's Going A Maying' in merely political terms is to diminish it; nevertheless it is throughout, and especially in its marvellous rendering of Catullus at the end, an implicit argument that political structures created by doctrinaire Calvinists amounted to tyranny. In similar fashion, Herrick's 'Delight in Disorder', opposing a trend to praise simplicity and modesty in female dress, recommends 'a sweet disorder'. Yet the 'winning wave (deserving note) / In the tempestuous petticoat', in which the urbanity of 'deserving note' leads into the 'tempestuous', is not trivial in its implication that sexual imagination is an irreducible component of humanity. Though they were on opposed sides in the political conflict, Milton might have taken a lesson from Herrick in presenting the innocent sexuality of Milton's Eve: 'She as a veil down to the slender waist / Her unadorned golden tresses wore / Dishevelled, but in wanton ringlets waved'.[16] Puritan diaries such as Lady Margaret Hoby's, with its daily rehearsals of private prayer, self-examination, public prayer, hearing the lecture, and so on, suggest what Herrick was confronting.[17] In imagining women with the freedom to dress as they pleased, Herrick is not merely indulging male fantasy, but, as Shakespeare did, demonstrating the possibility of a world in which women need not be entirely at the mercy of a male-dominated social and religious establishment. The 'dishevelled woman' of Cavalier verse is consciously set against Puritan values.

John Cleveland

Until he was ejected from his living in 1647, Herrick had lived at some remove from the conflict, and while his Royalist and Anglican sympathies are perfectly clear and sometimes directly and trenchantly expressed, his poems do not express the engagement of one whose day-to-day existence, or psychological well-being, is bound up with the fortunes of the Royalist cause. In this sense Cleveland, a younger Cambridge poet, might be regarded as the more committed of the two. Cleveland's Royalism cost him his fellowship in 1645, two years before Herrick lost his living. Cleveland was with the Royalist army at Oxford and was at Newark when the Royalist garrison surrendered. His importance for his contemporaries is suggested by the appearance between 1647 and 1700 of twenty-five editions of his poems.

While Cleveland's poems were frequently reprinted, there is no evidence that he had ever intended them to be printed. To imagine them with a mere manuscript circulation, available and read for the most part only within the Royalist camp, raises the question of what kind of effectiveness such manuscript circulation might have had. If Cleveland had survived into the Restoration, and then published, as Henry Vaughan's neighbour Rowland Watkyns published in 1662 poems which until then had only circulated among local Royalists, how would we appraise his poems today? Certainly their value as speech-acts then would have been different.

Modern readers are familiar and even comfortable with the concepts of 'party politics' and religious pluralism, knowing that they can co-exist within a relatively ordered and peaceful state; but our modern system evolved, through the trauma of civil war, from one in which parties and pluralism were unthinkable. The bitterness and savagery of Cleveland's tone is his response to the sheer unthinkability of what was happening as church and state fell before the fury of the King's enemies, in a series of actions every bit as questionable in terms of 'legality' as anything done during the years of Charles' 'personal rule'. He registers this fact in his poem on the execution of Laud:

> The state in *Strafford* fell, the Church in *Laud* . . .
> The facts were done before the Lawes were made,
> The trump turn'd up after the game was plai'd.[18]

On 27 April, 1646, Charles I left Oxford disguised as a gentleman's servant and on 5 May surrendered himself to the Scots. Cleveland's response, in 'The King's Disguise', is that of a man who had internalized Stuart propaganda about the position of the monarch in the scheme of things (as Charles himself had), and who felt disorientated, seeing Charles' disguise as majesty's self-betrayal. The tone of anguish and scorn is palpable, even in passages whose meaning might not be at once clear, like the poem's ending:

> Thus *Israel*-like he travells with a cloud,
> Both as a Conduct to him, and a shroud.
> But oh! he goes to *Gibeon*, and renewes
> A league with mouldy bread, and clouted shooes.

(Poems, p. 9)

Cleveland's contemporaries were more likely than we are to recognize at once the implication that the Scots were no more to be trusted than were the inhabitants of Gibeon who deceived Joshua (Joshua 9:3–15), but serious readers of early modern verse are accustomed to using a Biblical concordance. Other allusions are less easily accessible, referring to matters which are no longer part of the mental stock of the ordinarily well-educated person. Cleveland's ideal reader in his own time would have been the equivalent of a champion cryptic crossword solver in ours. The assertion of intelligence, education and wide general knowledge in such allusions was clearly an aspect of Cleveland's method, a 'putting-down' of an enemy seen as intellectually inferior, but they are not merely ostentatious. Expressing his concern at the King disguising himself, Cleveland refers to quite recent history prefiguring even more recent occurrences:

> What an usurper to his prince is wont,
> Cloister and shave him, he himself hath don't.
> His muffled fabric speaks him a recluse,
> His ruins prove it a religious house.
>
> (lines 7–10)

Here 'fabric' applies both to a building and to the human body; at that time more 'ruins' still stood as reminders of Henry VIII's Reformation. The Reformation history of demolition was repeated as the Roundheads defaced 'idolatrous' decorations in churches.

Richard Lovelace

Richard Lovelace's *Lucasta* was registered for publication in February 1648, but did not appear until the spring or summer of 1649, that is, until after the death of Charles I.[19] The presumption is that its publication was forbidden in the interim. Among those whose complimentary poems preface the volume, Marvell alone addressed this directly, suggesting that 'Censurers' are looking 'like the grim consistory' on the volume and referring to its author's sequestration, his role in presenting the Kentish petition, and his consequent imprisonment in 1642. Clearly Marvell was aware that the volume had been read with an eye to political implication, and expected that it would continue to be so read.[20]

Lovelace and Cleveland were both imprisoned, and both freed after writing a letter to the authorities. Lovelace's to Parliament has been seen as self-abasing, Cleveland's to Cromwell as 'manly and sensible'.[21] The experience of imprisonment and the necessity of submission has been interpreted as climacteric for Lovelace, turning him, early in his writing career, into a neutralist rather than a loyalist. This argument is ingenious and interesting, but rests on selective quotation (for example of Lovelace's 'self-abasing' letter) and strained readings of more than one poem.[22] However, it is true enough that Lovelace's verse cannot be read as a sustained tribute either to Charles I's version of Royalism or to the Church of England. Lovelace is to be distinguished from those poets such as Herrick and Vaughan whose work consistently tended to keep the flame of Royalism and Anglicanism alive. Neither the 1649 *Lucasta: Epodes, Odes, Sonnets* nor the 1659 *Lucasta: Posthume Poems* represents 'a single signifying unit which presents the opportunity for the exploration and maintenance of a poetics of activism'.[23] Nevertheless, the three perfect stanzas of 'To Lucasta, Going to the Wars' (*Poems*, p. 18) would have made an excellent recruiting song. Its reference to 'the nunnery' of Lucasta's 'chaste breast, and quiet mind' is a good example of Royalist coat-trailing, like similar apparently approving references to Roman Catholicism in Herrick and Vaughan. The paradox of the second stanza, and the ascription of transcendental value to 'Honour' of the third, express an idealism which has impelled young men to their deaths in our century as well as in Lovelace's. The poem's evocation of an earlier, 'heroic' age, far removed from the actualities of contemporary combat (the English cavalry did not carry shields, for example), reflects precisely the kind of chivalrous attachment to a cause which bitter experience might later bring one to re-evaluate.

A similar idealism is expressed in 'To Althea, from Prison' (*Poems*, p. 78), which circulated in manuscript for seven years before it was printed. These four exquisite stanzas lend little support to the view that Lovelace's imprisonment in the Gatehouse in 1642 caused him to adopt a 'neutralist' position at so early a date. Nor do they uphold the assertion that 'there is nothing in Lovelace's corpus which proclaims . . . openly Royalist sentiments'.[24] 'To Lucasta. From Prison' (*Poems*, p. 48), less pure in its lyric intensity, has more explicit reference to contemporary events. Lovelace almost certainly composed this poem during his first imprisonment, in 1642, rather than during his second, in 1648. The later date would mean that it had been added to the volume after its registration, which is improbable.[25] I find it difficult to accept that the poem 'refuses to deliver its expected cavalier sentiment' and that 'we can see, in its final stanzas, the beginnings of Lovelace's movement towards "militant neutralism", and a doubt which signals the beginning of Lovelace's abandonment of the King'.[26] The poet asks for Liberty from Lucasta in order to find other objects of love; he lists '*Peace*', '*War*', '*Religion*', '*Parliament*', '*Liberty*', '*Property*', '*Reformation*', the '*Publick Faith*', and concludes that none can be fit objects of his love, and in answer to the rhetorical question of what remains, replies 'th' only spring / Of all our loves and joyes? the KING'.[27] This seems undeniably Royalist. In the three stanzas that follow, Lovelace draws on the familiar analogy between the sun and the King, arguing that when we eclipse the right of the King, 'blinded, we stand in our own light', and asks the King to guide him to a place 'where I soone may see / How to serve you, and you trust me'. The doubt expressed here concerns Lovelace's own trustworthiness, not the King's, and need not be read as ironic. When he wrote it he was possibly already contemplating making his submission to Parliament with a view to obtaining his release.

In 'The Grass-hopper' (*Poems*, p. 38), Lovelace expresses a common topos of the defeated Royalist, the retreat into private life, personal friendship and the cup that cheers; the grass-hopper is an extended metaphor of the impermanence of prosperity, which teaches us to 'lay in' against winter and rain, and to 'poize / Their flouds, with an o'reflowing glasse'. Yet it is not primarily a drinking song but a pæan to friendship. Vaughan's poems of friendship in *Olor Iscanus* address similar concerns: 'why should we / Vex at the time's ridiculous misery?' he asks in one, and in another suggests a meeting 'while this world / In wild *eccentrics* now is hurled', ending with the thought that 'who in this age a mourner goes, / Doth with his tears but feed his foes'.[28]

Lovelace's work as a whole shows that commitment to a political cause was not his whole existence. Some poems in the posthumous *Lucasta* may register loss of idealism and even some degradation of character. 'Her Muff' (*Poems*, p. 128) has been cited as one such, while 'To a Lady with child that asked an old shirt' (*Poems*, p. 148) is seen as an expression of the poverty into which he may have fallen during his later years. Such poems may well be regarded as reactions to Lovelace's experience in the Civil Wars, expressing a loss of idealism consequent upon the powerlessness and poverty that afflicted many Royalists during the Interregnum. While the second *Lucasta* is considered to be generally inferior to the 1649 volume, the poems in which such creatures as an ant, a snail, a falcon and a fly are discussed as emblems of the human political world are full of interest.[29]

In 'The Ant' (*Poems*, p. 134), Lovelace, at first gently, then with increasing severity, satirizes Puritan thrift, industry and suspicion of festival. The line 'For thy example is become our Law' leaves no doubt as to the ant's emblematic meaning. The poem does not merely *flaunt* Royalist liberality and love of pleasure, but suggests that Lovelace has given real thought to the opposition between the two value-systems. He understands Puritan objection to festivals as based upon their connection to pagan customs and argues that '*Cato* sometimes the nak'd Florals saw', which is historically inaccurate but reflects the fact that, 'rather than prevent a popular custom, [Cato] left the theatre' (*Poems*, p. 300). The fourth stanza comments on the 'workaholic' tendencies of Puritanism:

> *Austere* and *Cynick*! not one hour t'allow
> To lose with pleasure what thou gotst with pain . . .
> Not all thy life time one poor Minute live,
> And thy o're labour'd Bulk with mirth relieve?

In the fifth stanza Lovelace imagines the ant being swallowed by magpie or jackdaw, and in the sixth generalizes his moral:

> Thus we unthrifty thrive within Earths Tomb
> For some more rav'nous and ambitious Jaw . . .
> So scattering to hord 'gainst a long Day,
> Thinking to save all, we cast all away.

Abraham Cowley

Lovelace's 'To Dr F. B. On His Book Of Chess' (*Poems*, p. 190) suggests that what 'Court, Clergy, Commons' 'Bluster'd, and clutter'd for' was no more significant than a game of chess. Chess appears as a metaphor again in Cowley's Pindaric Ode 'Destiny', in which human actions are compared to the moves of chess-pieces in a game played between two angels.[30] Cowley remarks in his note, 'the spectators would have reason . . . to believe, that the pieces moved themselves'. Just so, human actions appear to be autonomous, but '*Destiny plays us all*.' Royalist sympathizers had to contend with the idea of which Cromwell was so fond (and which they themselves had adopted in better times): that victory signified God's favour. In turn, after the Restoration, supporters of the Republic had a similar problem, many concluding that as the cause had been just, its failure must be explained as God's judgement on their sins. In the first stanza of 'Destiny' the speaker, thinking of the pieces as autonomous, blames the losing party 'For those false *Moves* that break the *Game* . . . And above all, th'*ill Conduct* of the *Mated King*'. In the second he discovers that, whereas the pieces appeared to have '*Life, Election, Liberty*', in fact 'An *unseen hand* makes all their *Moves*', and '*Destiny plays us all*.' In the third and fourth stanzas Cowley appears to be solely concerned with how he personally came out of the conflict of the times. Yet the message may be generalized: we must play the part assigned to us, despise '*Fortune*' as she does us, and act honourably even though our actions may be futile in the overall scheme. In considering poems like this, we recall that the outcome of events was not mysterious to the victors: God had been on their side. 'Destiny' answers to Lois Potter's suggestion that 'literary forms which emphasised the ultimate mysteriousness of human and divine purposes' were important to the defeated party, 'enabling communication and consolidating its sense of itself as an elite' – presumably through the implied assertion of superior understanding of the way things are. Also, making Destiny rather than Parliament or the Army responsible for events 'is an obvious way of healing old discords within a comforting myth of the civil war which all sides could accept'.[31]

Cowley prepared the *Poems* of 1656, containing the Pindaric Odes, while he was in prison and under interrogation by Cromwell's officers. The preface became notorious for its suggestion that defeat should be wholeheartedly accepted: 'we must lay down our *Pens* as well as *Arms*, we must *march* out of our *Cause* itself, and *dismantle* that, as well as our *Towns* and *Castles*, of all the *Works* and *Fortifications* of *Wit* and *Reason* by which we defended it'.[32] There is some irony in the fact that this apologia for disengagement cancelled out Cowley's years of Royalist service when rewards and punishments were handed out after the Restoration, since the wording of the preface anticipated the Act of Indemnity and Oblivion. Given the enigmatic quality of many poems in the volume, it remains open to question whether the preface was intended to put the victor off the scent, or whether Cowley had indeed, under the pressure of events, arrived at this view of things. Poems like 'Destiny' and the 'Brutus' ode (*Poems*, p. 195) certainly provoke 'political questions while refusing to supply unequivocal answers'. The latter in particular, printed without notes such as Cowley supplied for 'Destiny' and other odes, comes close to suggesting that in some circumstances the assassination of a ruler could be justified, only swerving from this in the conclusion that if Brutus had lived 'a few years more' the new morality of Christianity would have taught him better. It is as if Cowley has pondered Charles' 'personal rule' and judged against him but refused to endorse his execution. Cromwell and the other regicides took Christianity sufficiently seriously to have taken the end of this poem seriously. Nevertheless Annabel Patterson's view that 'everywhere in the odes and their commentaries is a sense that poetry. . . could not legitimize when the very bases of legitimacy were still in dispute' has force.[33] Whatever we may think of Cowley's attempt to ingratiate himself with Charles II at the Restoration, his Pindaric Odes are the work of someone wrestling to get at the meaning of the times in which he lived, and to do justice to the arguments of both sides. Yet praise of Cromwell is conspicuously absent, and the erotic poems added to the 1656 edition of *The Mistress*, such as 'The Innocent Ill', 'Dialogue. After Enjoyment' and 'Bathing in the River', are more calculated to offend Puritan sensibilities than most of those in the 1647 printing (*Poems*, pp. 145, 147, 150). It is worth noting that the 1656 volume, like that of 1647, was published by Humphrey Moseley, the most significant Royalist publisher of the time. Of the five poets discussed here, Cowley was the most ambitious, perhaps the most frustrated in his poetic ambitions, but also the most highly regarded in his own time.

Henry Vaughan

As suggested above, criticism of Interregnum verse earlier in this century tended to describe it as a-political. F. E. Hutchinson's view of Vaughan, expressed in his brief chapter on *Silex Scintillans*, set the tone for much subsequent criticism.[34] After noting the historical circumstance that 'the outbreak of the Civil War caught [Vaughan] in the impressionable years just as the French Revolution caught William Wordsworth at almost the same age', he goes on to minimize the relevance of this parallel with the remark that he will concentrate on 'those poems which are unspoiled by topical allusion and which are, by comparison, independent of time and place and circumstance'. He ends on a similar note: 'there is a quiet serenity about these timeless poems of Henry Vaughan that is their chief attraction'. At least three of the poems he quotes from, 'Regeneration', 'And do they so?' and 'The Book', have been treated by later critics as very much implicated in time and place and circumstance.[35] However, in spite of several recent essays on the nature of Vaughan's engagement with the political sphere,[36] most book-length studies of literary reactions to the Civil War have largely ignored his work.[37]

This neglect is strange, given the quality of Vaughan's work and the consistency of his commitment to Royalism and Anglicanism, which he would have regarded as indivisible. Vaughan began to publish before the Second Civil War and the execution of Charles, and went on into the Protectorate (from 1646 to 1655). The prefatory epistle to his first volume calls attention to some characteristically Royalist themes. It is addressed to the '*refined spirits*' of 'Gentlemen'; it announces that the longest piece in it, a translation of Juvenal's Tenth Satire, is a product of *otium*, '*borrowed, to feather some slower hours*', but hints strongly that if read with care it will yield its *negotium*, and suggests that contemporaries who might see themselves in its satire are indebted to Vaughan's learning for their 'awakening', since not being 'Gentlemen' they would not know Latin. The acknowledgement that his volume might seem anachronistic is itself couched in political terms: '*I know the years, and what coarse entertainment they afford poetry*'. It seeks for readers who '*soar above the drudgery of dirty* intelligence' – that is, above the stream of propagandistic news-sheets put out by both sides in the conflict (*Complete Poems*, p. 31).

The poems to Amoret, of which Vaughan writes that 'the fire at highest is but Platonic', no doubt represent his sense of what would have been acceptable to Henrietta Maria in happier times, a re-creation of one aspect of the halcyon years. In 'A Rhapsody' (*Complete Poems*, p. 40), however, there is thinly veiled allusion to events leading up to the outbreak of war. In proposing a toast to the deranged Roman emperor Caligula, 'him / That made his horse a Senator', Vaughan is expressing his contempt for Parliament. His reference to Julius Caesar ('he, that like fire broke forth / Into the Senate's face') recalls, and praises, Charles I's attempts to arrest the five members. Similarly, there is much to be read between the lines in the translation of Juvenal (*Complete Poems*, p. 46), a fact signalled to the reader by the poem's epigraph, disclaiming any intention to be a slavish translator. The reference to Pompey, around line 440, is an example of a historical reference functioning as a contemporary one: there is nothing in the original to warrant the words 'our public vows / Made *Caesar* guiltless', and the word 'our' would have signalled to an alert reader that a contemporary allusion was intended. The obvious one is the role played by Charles I in Strafford's downfall, when he consented to the Bill of Attainder in fear that the mob clamouring outside Whitehall Palace might be dangerous to his own family. The bitterness of Vaughan's tone, comparable to that of Clement Paman's reference to 'STRAF-FORD, who was hurried hence / 'Twixt Treason and Convenience', brings home to us that Charles' abandonment of Strafford was a bitter pill for those of Royalist sympathies to swallow.[38]

The titlepage of Vaughan's first volume, the *Poems* of 1646, describes the author merely as Henry Vaughan, Gentleman. The titlepage of *Olor Iscanus*, usually (and reasonably) thought of as his second collection, though published one year after the first impression of *Silex Scintillans*,[39] gives him out as Mr Henry Vaughan, Silurist, a style he was to retain. By 1650, that is, Vaughan was identifying himself by region rather than by class. The Silures were an ancient British tribe, powerful and warlike, but defeated by the Londinium-based Romans, as predominantly Royalist South Wales had been defeated by the London-based Parliamentarians. As Silurist, Vaughan identified with his home region, rather than with the London so skilfully evoked in his first volume; he identified with the defeated; and he identified with the past. The regional identification was emphasized by the title *Olor Iscanus* ('the Swan of Usk').

Olor Iscanus is more or less exactly the book one might expect from a young Royalist of that time and place. Vaughan writes a joking poem on his poverty (the Royalist ruined in his fortunes); he writes verse-letters to his friends (as Royalists scattered by their adversities did); he writes elegies for acquaintances slain in battle; he participates (at one remove in the case of Fletcher and directly in the case of Cartwright) in two of the great Royalist publishing ventures of the time. He treats one Royalist theme with uncommon *gravitas*, that is, the theme of retirement. He treats it mostly through translation, of the poems which Ovid (43BC?–AD17) wrote during his banishment by the Emperor Augustus, and of those written by Boethius (*c.* AD 480–524) during his imprisonment by the Ostrogoth King Theodoric. In his translations of the Polish Jesuit neo-Latin poet Casimir Sarbiewski (1596–1640), too, we see Vaughan coming to terms with his situation. Casimir rejects the Horatian *beatus ille* theme of the Royalist retired to his estates ('Happy the man, whose wish and care, / A few paternal acres bound', in Pope's translation). In Vaughan's translation, Casimir answers Horace's *Beatus ille* ode with the reflection that the 'worldly he . . . Ploughing his own *fields*, seldom can / Be justly styled, *the blessed man*', for 'That title only fits a *Saint*', who 'can gladly part / With *house* and *lands*, and leave' the 'loud strife / Of this world for a better life' (*Complete Poems*, p. 127). A man of intense religious commitment, at least in this period of his life, Vaughan understood defeat as a divine correction, intended to recall him to a life of grace.

The translations were probably written between 1647 and 1651, not merely to 'bulk out' the volume, but in the cause of self-examination, seen as an aspect of the *negotium* which should issue from *otium*. In them we find a deepening of the theme of retirement. In *Silex Scintillans* (1650 and 1655) this was transformed into the themes of hiddenness and potentiality, the themes of 'hermetic' Christianity which became Vaughan's extraordinary contribution to Anglican thought and sensibility while the Anglican church was in abeyance.

In *Silex Scintillans* we see the theme of hiddenness in such poems as 'The Book', where the world of all that has lived within nature is hidden within an artifact, the book, waiting for that day when God will 'make all new again'; we see it in the alchemical imagery of 'Holy Scriptures', when Vaughan, addressing the Bible, says 'In thee the hidden stone, the *manna* lies, / Thou art the great elixir, rare and choice'; we see it in 'The Timber', where Vaughan relates death to new life, to the growing up of fresh groves and the shooting of green branches, 'While the low *violet* thrives at their root'; we see it in 'The Seed Growing Secretly', with its so typical reference to that 'Dear, secret *greenness*!' which is nursed below the level of tempests and winds, and whose growth is apparent only to God; we see it even more movingly expressed in the elegiac poem 'I walked the other day', in which the poet represents himself as digging in winter time in a place where he had once 'seen the soil to yield / A gallant flower', and there 'saw the warm recluse alone to lie / Where fresh and green / He lived of us unseen'. We see it, finally, in the hidden God of 'The Night', in whom there is a deep but dazzling darkness, and in whose night the poet wishes to 'live invisible and dim' (*Complete Poems*, pp. 309, 198, 262, 277, 240, 290).

In virtually all such examples, the theme of hiddenness is linked with that of potentiality, as expressed through notions like new growth, alchemical transmutation, resurrection of the dead. If 'our lives are hidden with Christ in God' then the possibility of new life, of transfiguration, is there. It is as if Vaughan brings together the notion of potentiality as expressed through alchemical philosophy and the same notion as expressed through the Parables of the Kingdom, in which mustard seeds grow into great trees, or a little leaven works on three measures of meal, or scattered seed brings forth a hundredfold, in which, that is, hidden and apparently insignificant things gather to a greatness. Vaughan's is of course a religious and spiritual response rather than a directly political one in such poems as these. Nevertheless it is a spiritual response to a political situation. Whether from Dante or from more ancient sources, Vaughan had plenty of opportunity to know about the polysemous possibilities of poetry; there is so much in his world that is hidden, quietly biding its time, waiting for a new life, that the sympathetic contemporary reader may, if nearly subliminally, have read into such images hidden and buried Royalism and Anglicanism waiting for *their* potentialities to be actualized, for *their* new day to dawn. In the last poem of *Silex Scintillans* Vaughan prayed for a world in which 'like true sheep, all in one fold / We may be fed, and one mind hold' (*Complete Poems*, p. 313). Long before the Restoration, he had settled into the obscure life of a rural physician with an interest in wild flowers and their medicinal properties. There is no record of his view of the court of Charles II, or of the persecution of Dissenters which followed the return of the Anglican bishops. His work lives on today for its aesthetic quality certainly – his best poems challenge the finest religious lyrics of the age. It lives too because his sense of God's indwelling in all the creatures, and of the value placed by God upon the non-human creation, foreshadows our modern knowledge of the relationship between all forms of life, and speaks to our modern sense that the wanton destruction of natural habitat is also a kind of civil war.

NOTES

1 Alexander Pope, *The First Epistle of the Second Book of Horace Imitated*, line 108, quoted from John Butt (ed.), *The Poems of Alexander Pope* (London: Methuen, corrected rpt 1973), p. 639.

2 See Rowland Watkyns, *Flamma Sine Fumo (1662)*, ed. Paul C. Davies (Cardiff: University of Wales Press), 1968.

3 See Alexander Brome, *Poems*, ed. Roman R. Dubinski (University of Toronto Press, 1982).

4 F. S. Siebert, *Freedom of the Press in England, 1476–1776* (Urbana: Illinois University Press, 1952), p. 187.

5 See Annabel Patterson, *Censorship and Interpretation: The Conditions of Writing and Reading in Early Modern England* (Madison: University of Wisconsin Press, 1984); and Lois Potter, *Secret Rites and Secret Writing: Royalist Literature, 1641–1660* (Cambridge University Press, 1989).

6 Blair Worden, quoted in David Norbrook, *Writing the English Republic: Poetry, Rhetoric and Politics, 1627–1660* (Cambridge University Press, 1999), p. 433. As Norbrook remarks, 'innumerable critics' took the same view.

7 See especially Thomas N. Corns, *Uncloistered Virtue: English Political Literature 1640–1660* (Oxford: Clarendon Press, 1992); and James Loxley, *Royalism and Poetry in the English Civil Wars: The Drawn Sword* (Basingstoke: Macmillan, 1997).

8 See Mildmay Fane, *Otia Sacra*, ed. Donald Friedman (New York: Scholars' Facsimiles and Reprints, 1975).

9 Alan Rudrum (ed.), *The Complete Poems of Henry Vaughan*, rev. rpt (Harmondsworth: Penguin, 1983), p. 142.

10 L. C. Martin (ed.), *Herrick's Poetical Works*, corrected edn (Oxford: Clarendon Press, 1963), p. 3.

11 Loxley, *Royalism and Poetry*, p. 227.

12 See Sandy Petrey, *Speech Acts and Literary Theory* (New York: Routledge, 1990).

13 *The Oxford Dictionary of Quotations*, 4th edn (Oxford University Press, 1992), p. 457.

14 The phrase is from line 6 of 'The Argument of his Book', *Herrick's Poetical Works*, p. 5.

15 'Delight in Disorder', 'Upon Julia's Clothes': *Herrick's Poetical Works*, p. 28, p. 261.

16 *Paradise Lost*, 4: 304–6.

17 See Dorothy M. Meads (ed.), *The Diary of Lady Margaret Hoby* (London: Routledge, 1930); and Joanna Moody (ed.), *The Private Life of an Elizabethan Lady: The Diary of Lady Margaret Hoby 1599–1605* (Stroud: Sutton, 1998).

18 Brian Morris and Eleanor Withington (eds.), *The Poems of John Cleveland* (Oxford: Clarendon Press, 1967), p. 39.

19 See C. H. Wilkinson (ed.), *The Poems of Richard Lovelace* (Oxford: Clarendon Press, corrected rpt, 1953). This one-volume edition, first published in 1930, is used as the more readily available. However, some interesting material contained in Wilkinson's two-volume edition of 1925 is omitted from it.

20 Marvell, 'To his Noble Friend, Mr Richard Lovelace, upon his Poems', in *P&L*, 1:2–4.

21 Both are printed by Wilkinson in *Poems*, pp. xxxviiiff.

22 Gerald Hammond, 'Richard Lovelace and the Uses of Obscurity', *Proceedings of the British Academy*, 71 (1985), 203–34.

23 Loxley, *Royalism and Poetry*, p. 223.

24 Hammond, 'Lovelace and Obscurity', p. 213.

25 The point was made by H. M. Margoliouth in an important review of C. H. Wilkinson's first (1925) edition of Lovelace's poems in *RES*, 3 (1927), 89–95.

26 Hammond, 'Lovelace and Obscurity', p. 216.

27 In his review (see n. 25) Margoliouth writes that the lines on '*Peace*' and '*War*' are quite general, but he relates those on '*Parliament*', '*Liberty*' and '*Property*' to various clauses of the Kentish Petition and those on '*Reformation*' to one of the aims of the other side. Margoliouth relates the poem in detail to the events which resulted in Lovelace's imprisonment of 1642.

28 'To His Retired Friend, an Invitation to Brecknock', lines 77–8; 'To my Worthy Friend, Master T. Lewes', lines 23–4 in *Complete Poems*, pp. 79 and 95 respectively.

29 See Erna Kelly, 'Richard Lovelace's Separate Peace', in Claude J. Summers and Ted-Larry Pebworth (eds.), *The English Civil Wars in the Literary Imagination* (Columbia and London: University of Missouri Press, 1999), pp. 81–101.

30 A. R. Waller (ed.), *Abraham Cowley: Poems* (Cambridge University Press, 1905), p. 192.

31 Potter, *Secret Rites*, pp. 113, 202.

32 Quoted by Corns, *Uncloistered Virtue*, p. 257. As Corns notes, Bishop Sprat omitted this part of the preface in his Restoration edition; the omission is perpetuated by Waller.

33 Patterson, *Censorship and Interpretation*, p. 156.

34 F. E. Hutchinson, *Henry Vaughan: A Life and Interpretation* (Oxford: Clarendon Press, 1947).

35 Claude J. Summers and Ted-Larry Pebworth, 'Vaughan's Temple in Nature and the Context of "Regeneration"', *Journal of English and Germanic Philology*, 74 (1975), 351–60; Alan Rudrum, 'Henry Vaughan, the Liberation of the Creatures, and Seventeenth-Century English Calvinism', *Seventeenth Century*, 4 (1989), 33–54.

36 A number of essays on Vaughan's involvement in the politics of the Civil War and Interregnum are listed in note 2 of Alan Rudrum's 'Resistance, Collaboration and Silence: Henry Vaughan and Breconshire Royalism', in Summers and Pebworth (eds.), *The English Civil Wars*, pp. 102–18. See also P. W. Thomas, 'The Language of Light: Henry Vaughan and the Puritans', *Scintilla*, 3 (Usk Valley Vaughan Association, 1999), 9–29.

37 Vaughan is not mentioned in the index of Michael Wilding, *Dragons Teeth: Literature in the English Revolution* (Oxford: Clarendon Press, 1987); nor in that of Corns' *Uncloistered Virtue*; he scarcely figures in Raymond A. Anselment, *Loyalist Resolve: Patient Fortitude in the English Civil War* (Newark, N. J.: University of Delaware Press, 1988); there are scattered references in Potter's *Secret Rites*.

38 This poem has been regarded as possibly by Cleveland. For discussion, see Cleveland's *Poems*, p. xxxiii. For the attribution to Clement Paman (1612–64), see Peter Davidson (ed.), *Poetry and Revolution* (Oxford: Clarendon Press, 1998), pp. 363 and 547.

39 Its prefatory epistle is dated 'this 17 of *Decemb.* 1647'.

FURTHER READING

For individual editions of primary texts cited or discussed, please see the notes above.

Anselment, Raymond A., *Loyalist Resolve: Patient Fortitude in the English Civil War*, Newark, N. J.: University of Delaware Press, 1988.

Corns, Thomas N., *Uncloistered Virtue: English Political Literature 1640–1660*, Oxford: Clarendon Press, 1992.

Hutton, Ronald, *The Rise and Fall of Merry England: The Ritual Year 1400–1700*, Oxford University Press, 1994.

Loxley, James, *Royalism and Poetry in the English Civil Wars: The Drawn Sword*, Basingstoke: Macmillan, 1997.

MacLean, Gerald, *Time's Witness: Historical Representation in English Poetry, 1603–1660*, Madison: University of Wisconsin Press, 1990.

Norbrook, David, *Writing the English Republic: Poetry, Rhetoric and Politics, 1627–1660*, Cambridge University Press, 1999.

Parry, Graham, *Seventeenth-Century Poetry: The Social Context*, London: Hutchinson, 1985.

Patterson, Annabel, *Censorship and Interpretation: The Conditions of Writing and Reading in Early Modern England*, Madison: University of Wisconsin Press, 1984.

Post, Jonathan, *Henry Vaughan. The Unfolding Vision*, Princeton University Press, 1982.

Potter, Lois, *Secret Rites and Secret Writing: Royalist Literature, 1641–1660*, Cambridge University Press, 1989.

Raylor, Timothy, *Cavaliers, Clubs and Literary Culture*, Newark, N.J.: University of Delaware Press, 1994.

Rollin, Roger B., and J. Max Patrick (eds.), *Trust to Good Verses: Herrick Tercentenary Essays*, University of Pittsburgh Press, 1974.

Rudrum, Alan, *Henry Vaughan*, Cardiff: University of Wales Press on behalf of the Welsh Arts Council, 1981

   (ed.), *Essential Articles for the Study of Henry Vaughan*, Hamden: Archon Books, 1987.

Summers, Claude J., and Ted-Larry Pebworth (eds.), *The English Civil Wars in the Literary Imagination*, Columbia and London: University of Missouri Press, 1999.

Trotter, David, *The Poetry of Abraham Cowley*, Basingstoke: Macmillan, 1979.

Zwicker, Stephen N., *Lines of Authority: Politics and English Literary Culture, 1649–1689*, Ithaca, N.Y.: Cornell University Press, 1993.

ISABEL RIVERS

Prayer-book devotion: the literature of the proscribed episcopal church

Introduction

In the years from the Long Parliament to the Restoration, the Church of England underwent an extraordinary and violent series of changes. As a result of legislation – Parliamentary ordinances in the 1640s, reinforced by Parliamentary acts and the Protector's declarations in the 1650s – the government, liturgy, ceremonies and fabric of the reformed Church of England, established by law in the reigns of Edward VI and Elizabeth I, were all transformed. Archbishops, bishops and cathedral deans and chapters were abolished; the Book of Common Prayer was suppressed, its place officially taken by the *Directory for Public Worship*, and its use made a crime; the ancient pattern of the Christian year and the Church festivals of Christmas, Easter and Whitsun were eliminated; many of the surviving medieval crucifixes and images of the persons of the Trinity and of angels and saints in stone, wood, paint and glass were destroyed or defaced, as were organs, fonts and priests' vestments; rails in front of altars were removed and raised chancels levelled; cathedrals were damaged and used for secular purposes, and their complete demolition was considered, though not carried out.[1] However, none of these drastic changes meant that the Church of England had ceased to exist. The Puritan iconoclasts who enacted these measures and tried to ensure (with varying success) that they were carried through regarded themselves as the true Protestant reformers: they thought it imperative to free the English church, only partly reformed in the sixteenth century, from the surviving vestiges of popery and especially from its backsliding and increasing entanglement in popish superstition under the influence of Archbishop Laud. Those on the other hand (long described as Anglicans, though this label was not often used at the time), who were loyal to the Church of England as governed by bishops under the authority of the monarch, and to its doctrines and ceremonies as defined in the Thirty-Nine Articles, the Homilies, the Book of Common Prayer, and the Canons of

5 William Marshall, engraved frontispiece to *Eikon Basilike*, 1649.

Convocation, regarded these measures not as freedom from superstition but as descent into barbarism, the contemporary equivalent of the Babylonian captivity of the Jews. Ironically they now found themselves in a similar position, though for opposite reasons, to that of the Puritans in the 1630s who had reacted with horror to the general beautifying of churches with images, candles and embroidered altar cloths, and who had refused to accept the Laudian insistence on ceremonies such as bowing at the name of Jesus and kneeling for communion at the rails of an elevated, closed-off altar.[2]

An important consequence of the attack on the episcopal church was that its supporters in the period 1645–60 wrote a number of defences of its organization, ceremonies and liturgy, and in some cases tried to provide alternative forms of worship suitable for use in a period of proscription. In effect, they developed a new kind of Anglican devotional literature, closely tied to the Prayer Book, which served a very specific purpose at the time but which remained enormously influential after the re-establishment of the episcopal church at the Restoration and throughout the next century. The attempt to suppress ceremonial worship thus had the paradoxical effect of strengthening it. This chapter is concerned with the literary implications of the Anglican defence of the liturgy. Before exploring the significance of the Book of Common Prayer, the defences that were mounted and the most important contributions to prayer-book devotion, it sets out the options that were open to episcopal Anglicans from 1645 to 1660: exile, retirement, compromise or acquiescence.

Episcopal Anglicans in the Interregnum

Beginning with the work of John Walker in the early eighteenth century, a number of historians have investigated what happened to the Interregnum Anglicans, and how far they were affected by the penal laws directed against them.[3] In theory, 'scandalous' or 'malignant' or 'ill-affected' or 'delinquent' ministers or schoolmasters (the labels covered those who were hostile to Parliament or persisted in using the Prayer Book as well as the simply incompetent) were supposed to be ejected or sequestered from their livings.[4] (*Sequestered* is a technical term meaning deprived of the income of a benefice.) Matthews calculated that about 2,425 parish clergy (out of a national total of about 8,600), 650 clergy of the cathedral and collegiate churches, and 829 fellows and heads of houses at Oxford and Cambridge lost their livings. Though the effects were severe for the last two categories, the majority of parish clergy were unaffected.[5] This was either because the large numbers involved were difficult to oversee, or because blind eyes were turned to the use of the Prayer Book, or because most of the clergy conformed to the new requirements more or less willingly. In the mid 1650s, because of increasing Royalist resistance to the Protectorate government, attempts were made to lessen the influence of episcopal Anglicans on Royalist gentry. Orders in Council 'for securing the peace of the Commonwealth' in September 1655 banned Royalists from keeping any of the ejected clergy in their homes as chaplains or schoolmasters, and these were followed by a Declaration of the Protector in November to the same effect.[6]

How far did the most prominent defenders of the Episcopal church suffer? The most obvious victim was Laud: after over three years' imprisonment in the Tower of London he was attainted of high treason and condemned to death on the same day that the Prayer Book was abolished, 4 January 1645, and executed six days later. Matthew Wren, Bishop of Ely and formerly of

Norwich, one of the strongest imposers of conformity in the 1630s, was imprisoned in the Tower from 1642 to 1660. Jeremy Taylor, Rector of Uppingham and one of Charles I's chaplains, was imprisoned in 1655 for three months in Chepstow Castle and in 1657 or '58 in the Tower of London for offences caused by his publications. Some went into exile. John Cosin, Prebendary of Durham, Master of Peterhouse (in succession to Wren), and Vice-Chancellor of Cambridge, who was attacked by Puritans for his love of ritual and church ornamentation, was impeached by the House of Commons in 1641 but escaped to Paris, where he remained until the Restoration as chaplain to the Protestants in Henrietta Maria's household. George Morley, Canon of Christ Church, Oxford, and Rector of Mildenhall, who as one of Charles I's chaplains briefly attended him in captivity, left the country in 1648 for exile in France and Holland, and served as chaplain to Charles I's sister, the Queen of Bohemia, at the same time keeping in touch by correspondence with the like-minded at home. Richard Allestree, Student of Christ Church, travelled between England and the continent as an agent for Charles II and on one occasion was captured and briefly imprisoned.

Others remained in England after ejection, and used their retirement as a base for furthering the Anglican cause. The most important of this group was Henry Hammond, Canon of Christ Church, Rector of Penshurst, and another of Charles' chaplains, who, together with Gilbert Sheldon, ministered to the King during his captivity in 1647; after a period of imprisonment in Oxford and house arrest in Bedfordshire he spent the years from 1650 until his death in 1660 as chaplain to Sir John Pakington at Westwood in Worcestershire. He corresponded about the state of the episcopal church with friends such as Morley and Sheldon, Warden of All Souls College, Oxford, who, like Hammond, was ejected and briefly imprisoned, and who spent the Interregnum living in retirement. One aspect of the lives of this group was captured in Izaac Walton's fishing manual *The Compleat Angler* (first published in 1653 and enlarged in 1655, 1661 and 1676): Walton, a friend of Morley who became his steward after the Restoration, and who served a very important function as biographer of leading churchmen, stressed Sheldon's skill in angling, linking the patience of the fisherman implicitly with that of the sequestered clergyman and explicitly with the piety of prayer-book devotion.[7] Hammond was anxious to secure the succession of the episcopal church, made difficult by the demoralization of the remaining deprived bishops; only Brian Duppa, Bishop of Salisbury, who lived in retirement at Richmond, seems to have exerted himself. So Hammond set about providing for the future. His friend and biographer John Fell, also ejected from Christ Church, said that 'he projected by Pensions unto hopeful persons in either University, to maintain a Seminary of Youth instituted in Piety and Learning upon the sober Principles and old establishment of the *Anglicane* Church'. Hammond sent money to the clergy in exile, the sequestered clergy at home, and their wives and children, and acted as an agent for the gentry, providing them with schoolmasters and chaplains.[8] This last arrangement was precisely the relationship the Cromwellians feared: 'The importance of this training can hardly be exaggerated, for it cemented an alliance between the High Church clergy and the Squires or "Country Party" which was to figure in politics for the next hundred years.'[9]

Some episcopal Anglicans, however, kept their posts as parish clergy, and struggled to remain loyal to the liturgy while at the same time avoiding legal sanctions. Robert Sanderson, Rector of Boothby Pagnell, Lincolnshire, Canon of Christ Church and Regius Professor of Divinity at Oxford, also one of Charles' chaplains and a friend of Hammond, Morley and Sheldon, attempted to continue reading the Prayer Book in his church. This he was unable to do, because he was interrupted by soldiers who 'forc'd his Book from him, and tore it, expecting extemporary Prayers'. He therefore devised his own version of the liturgy to avoid sequestration.[10] Sanderson took the conciliatory view (not shared by Hammond) that it was better for congregations to be offered an attenuated form of the Prayer Book than none at all. This approach was also taken by John Gauden, Dean of Bocking, the likely author of *Eikon Basilike*, who despite his initial Presbyterian sympathies became a strong supporter of the episcopal church, yet continued in his post throughout the Interregnum. Several sequestered clergy who supported the episcopal church were prepared to appear before the Triers to have their fitness for ordination tested and to be admitted to new posts, for example the church historian Thomas Fuller. Conversely, several of the younger generation of clergy who later rose to prominence after the Restoration were ordained under the new regime, the only one officially open to them, but became persuaded of the legitimacy of the proscribed church and sought out and obtained illegal ordination from the deprived bishops.

The Book of Common Prayer and the King's Book

Why was the Prayer Book such a cause of dissension? Why did it arouse such contrary feelings of hostility and loyalty?[11] The Parliamentary *Ordinance for taking away the Book of Common Prayer, and for establishing . . . the Directory for the publique worship of God* of January 1645 repealed the Acts of Edward VI and Elizabeth that had established uniformity of prayer and administration of the sacraments and had made use of the Prayer Book mandatory. The Preface to the *Directory* explains that the liturgy used in the

Church of England has given offence to the godly at home and the reformed churches abroad because of 'the many unprofitable and burdensome Ceremonies', and because preaching of the word has been made inferior to the reading of the Prayer Book. In addition, the Papists have boasted that the service largely complied with theirs, and as a consequence of all these things the godly have been driven away from the ministry. Instead of set forms, the *Directory* therefore provides (somewhat paradoxically) very full instructions for the reading of Scripture, the content of public prayer (by the minister only) and the method of the sermon. Ceremonies are notable by their omission: communion is to be taken sitting at or round the table; there is no reference to the ring in marriage or the sign of the cross in baptism; the burial service for the dead is dismissed as superstitious; there is no calendar for the church year and there are no festivals.[12]

What was the character of the book that the *Directory* was intended to replace?[13] The Book of Common Prayer appeared in three versions in the sixteenth century: the first and second books of Edward VI (1549 and 1552) and that of Elizabeth (1559); it was reissued under James I (1604), and a revised version was forced on the Scots in 1637 and then withdrawn. This last version had a considerable influence on the most important and long-lasting book of all, the revised book of Charles II (1662). The principal compiler of the first two books was Thomas Cranmer (1489–1556), Archbishop of Canterbury under Edward and burned in the reign of the Catholic Mary. Much of the material was compressed and translated by Cranmer from the numerous medieval Latin service books in use before the Reformation, though he also drew on the work of his contemporaries in England and in the continental reformed churches; the use of Catholic ceremonies is justified in the detailed statement 'Of Ceremonies, why some be abolished, and some retained', which still forms part of the prefatory material of the Prayer Book. Cranmer is best remembered for his wording of the numerous collects (short prayers spoken by the minister) and general prayers, phrases from which have entered the language (e.g. 'the devices and desires of our own hearts', 'whose service is perfect freedom', 'lighten our darkness', 'read, mark, learn, and inwardly digest').[14] The characteristic pattern (then and now) is of prayers spoken by the minister, responses by the people, prayers spoken by the minister and people together, readings from the Old and New Testaments, and the singing of psalms. The Christian year consists of two halves, from Advent to Trinity, commemorating the life of Christ, and from Trinity to Advent. The Prayer Book prescribes the service for daily morning and evening prayer, and the collects and portions of Scripture to be read and psalms to be sung on successive Sundays and holy days throughout the year; it also prescribes the order of communion, baptism, matrimony, the burial of the dead, and other significant services.

The first full analysis of the Prayer Book was provided by one of the sequestered Anglicans, Anthony Sparrow, in *A Rationale upon the Book of Common Prayer* (1657). Sparrow goes through each section, explaining its origin and its function. He suggests that the collects are so called either because they are made by the priest on behalf of the congregation, '*Super collectam populi*', or 'because the Priest doth herein *collect* the Devotions of the people, and offer them up to God', and emphasizes that it has been a constant practice from the beginning of Christianity for the people to bear a vocal part in the public service of God, hence the name Common Prayer. He helpfully explains the shape and meaning of the church year. There are two sorts of festivals:

> The *First* commemorate the signal Acts or Passages of our Lord in the Redemption of mankinde, His incarnation and Nativity, Circumcision, Manifestation to the Gentiles, his Fasting, Passion, Resurrection, and Ascension, the sending of the Holy Ghost, and thereupon a more full and expresse manifestation of the sacred Trinity. The *Second* sort is of Inferiour dayes that supply the Intervals of the greater, . . .wherein without any consideration of the sequence of time . . . the holy Doctrine, Deeds, and Miracles of our Lord are the chief matters of our meditations.

In all these days 'some respect is had to the season, and the holy affections the Church then aimes at, as Mortification in Lent, Joy, Hope, Newnesse of Life &c. after Easter; the Fruits, and Gifts of the Spirit & preparation for Christs Second coming in the time between Pentecost and Advent'. Sparrow insists on the crucial function of the Prayer Book as a means of infusing Christian knowledge through ordered repetition, and quotes Hammond on the disastrous long-term effect of its abolition:

> *it may well be feared* (as a Reverend Person [Hammond] hath forewarned) that *When the Festivals and Solemnities for the Birth of Christ and his other famous passages of life, and death, and Resurrection, and Ascension, and Mission of the Holy Ghost, and the Lesson, Gospells (and Collects) and Sermons upon them, be turned out of the Church, together with the Creeds also, twill not be in the power of weekly Sermons on some head of Religion to keep up the knowledge of Christ in mens hearts.*[15]

Sparrow is quoting from Hammond's *A View of the New Directory and a Vindication of the Ancient Liturgy of the Church of England; In Answer to the Reasons pretended in the Ordinance and Preface, for the abolishing the one, and establishing the other* (1645, with two further editions the following year). Hammond's text was prefaced by the King's Proclamation, dated 13 November 1645 at Oxford (the royal headquarters), '*Commanding the use of the Book of* COMMON-PRAYER *according to Law*'. One of the arguments in the Proclamation was that the *Directory* would 'mislead People into sinne and Rebellion'.[16] The events of the next few years meant that the fate of the Prayer Book and the King became inevitably intertwined. The perceived relationship is set out schematically by the sequestered clergyman James Harwood in his *Plea for the Common Prayer Book* (1657):

> It came in with the fall of Papacy.
> It went out with the fall of Monarc[h]y.
> It came in with the rise of Protestant Bishops.
> It went out when Presbyter *John* came in.
> It received Christendom from a Prince.
> It suffered Martyrdom by the People. (n.p.)

The relationship is nowhere more evident than in the book that was to take on the status of a sacred or devotional text, *Eikon Basilike: The Pourtraicture of His Sacred Majesty in His Solitudes and Sufferings*.[17] It was published shortly after the King's execution and was an astonishing bestseller: in 1649 there were thirty-five editions in England and twenty-five more in Ireland and abroad. It was translated into Latin, French, German and Danish, and even set to music as *Psalterium Carolinum* (Charles' book of psalms). Milton's *Eikonoklastes*, commissioned to break the King's image (the meaning of *Eikon Basilike*) just as church iconoclasts had broken the images of Christ and the saints, could do nothing to hinder the book's popularity, nor could the Council of State's threats to its printers. Though probably written by Gauden with the help of other clergy, including Duppa, based in part on papers belonging to the King, *Eikon Basilike* purports to be Charles' autobiography, his justification for his conduct in the war and his spiritual legacy to the Prince of Wales. Later editions included lengthy additional documentation – speeches, messages and letters by the King in the early stages of the war at the beginning of the book, papers about church government, prayers used by the King in his captivity, his last words to his children and his speech on the scaffold at the end – but the core of the book consists of twenty-eight chapters of self-exculpation and self-examination, beginning with the calling of the Long Parliament and ending with meditations on death. Each chapter contains two sections, a defence of the King's conduct in a specific situation and a long formal prayer (only chapters 25 and 27 lack this structure). Throughout there is an antithesis between reason, moderation, discretion, honour, innocency, conscience, piety and religion on the King's side, and faction, passion, prejudice, partiality, madness, slavery and policy on that of his opponents. The association between the King and the Church of England and between the King's book and the Book of Common Prayer becomes increasingly apparent. In chapter

16, 'Upon the Ordinance against the Common Prayer Book', Charles defends the use of set forms of prayer, points out the illogicality of the *Directory's* instructions, and prays for truth, unity, constancy and order against error, novelty and variety. In chapter 25, 'Penitential Meditations and Vows', he explicitly compares himself with David, both as King and as author of the Psalms. In chapter 27, 'To the Prince of Wales', he urges his son not to suffer any disaffection in his heart 'from the true religion established in the Church of England'. The King continues with a traditional characterization of the Church's unique virtue: 'I tell you I have tried it, and after much search and many disputes have concluded it to be the best in the world, not only in the community, as Christian, but also in the special notion, as reformed, keeping the middle way between the pomp of superstitious tyranny and the meanness of fantastic anarchy.' The final chapter, 'Meditations upon Death', associates the King's suffering with Christ's: 'If I must suffer a violent death with my Saviour, it is but mortality crowned with martyrdom, where the debt of death which I owe for sin to nature shall be raised as a gift of faith and patience offered to God.'[18] These Biblical and liturgical associations are anticipated in the emblematic frontispiece (see Fig. 5), in which the kneeling King grasps a crown of thorns representing grace, tramples his splendid but weighty earthly crown, and looks up to a heavenly crown of glory. To his left are shown a rock unmoved by raging waves, and palm trees laden with weights; the accompanying verse explains 'Palma *ut* depressa, *resurgo*' ('Palm-*like* Depress'd, I *higher rise*'). Political as well as Christian resurrection can be understood here. The emblem of weighted palm trees with the motto 'Depressa Resurgo' recurs on the titlepage of Gauden's lengthy folio defence of the episcopal church, *Ecclesiae Anglicanae Suspiria: The Tears, Sighs, Complaints, and Prayers of the Church of England*, published in 1659 by Richard Royston, one of the publishers of *Eikon Basilike* (and also of books by Hammond and Taylor). Church and King will rise again. Charles is the martyred Church of England and the martyred Christ, yet he is also David the psalmist, whose book of meditations brings consolation to its grieving readers just as the Prayer Book does.

Devotional literature

The final indignity visited on the dead King was that William Juxon, Bishop of London, who had assisted him at the scaffold, was forbidden to read the burial service from the Prayer Book over him.[19] However, despite its illegality, the Prayer Book continued in use in many places, while the Presbyterian *Directory* became increasingly irrelevant in a church largely controlled by Independents.[20] Unofficial Prayer-Book services were tolerated in Oxford, despite the ejection of so many episcopal and Royalist Fellows.[21] The diarist John Evelyn recorded his frequent visits to such services in London in the 1650s: on 16 April and 7 May 1654, for example, he heard Jeremy Taylor preach at St Gregory's by St Paul's and at the Earl of Rutland's chapel at Exeter House, both frequent resorts of Anglicans.[22] After Cromwell's Declaration of 1655, however, there was less informal tolerance.[23] Evelyn describes how he and other members of Peter Gunning's congregation at Exeter House chapel were arrested by soldiers while they were taking communion on Christmas Day, 1657: before his release he was asked 'why contrarie to an Ordinance made that none should any longer observe the superstitious time of the *Nativity . . .* I durst offend, & particularly be at *Common prayers*, which they told me was but the *Masse in English*'. [24]

Defenders of the Prayer Book answered such questions in different ways, polemical, historical or more oblique. One tactic (used in Harwood's pamphlet quoted above and by Taylor)[25] was to link Papists and Presbyterians: the former had martyred the makers of the Prayer Book, the latter had martyred the book itself. Other writers drew on George Herbert's *The Temple. Sacred Poems and Private Ejaculations*, published after his death in 1633. Although Herbert was also admired by Puritans and antinomians,[26] in his celebration of the 'perfect lineaments' of 'The British Church' and inclusion of Prayer-Book festivals and services ('Easter', 'Whitsunday', 'Mattens', 'Even-song', 'Trinitie Sunday', 'Christmas') he was properly seen as a forebear by the Interregnum Anglicans. This side of *The Temple* was elaborated by the clergyman Christopher Harvey, the second edition of whose collection *The Synagogue or, The Shadow of the Temple* (1657) was usually bound with it; Harvey's 'Church Festivals' is an imitation of Herbert's 'Prayer', and Harvey systematically provides a sequence of poems for the festivals of the first half of the church year, from 'The Annunciation' to 'Trinitie Sunday'. The second edition further contains a sequence on church furniture (paralleling Herbert's 'Altar'), including 'The Font', 'The Book of Common Prayer' and 'The Communion Table'. In the last of these the lines 'In uniformity / There's greatest decency' sum up one aspect of the Anglican case.[27] Harvey, a friend of Walton, contributed a commendatory poem to the 1655 edition of *The Compleat Angler*, alerting the reader to its underlying emphasis: '*Here sits in secret blest* Theologe'. In turn, Walton added Harvey's 'The Book of Common Prayer' to chapter 5, following Herbert's 'Virtue' (present in the first edition), thereby making the bias of his book more obvious. Part of the last stanza reads:

> *Devotion will add Life unto the Letter,*
> *And why should not*

> That which Authority
> Prescribes, esteemed be
> Advantage got?
> If th' prayer be good, the commoner the better.[28]

Further ammunition for the Anglican cause was the publishing in 1652 by the sequestered clergyman Barnabas Oley of *Herbert's Remains*, containing *A Priest to the Temple*, Herbert's account of 'the Form and Character of a true Pastour'. In the anonymous preface of 1652, Oley (who was identified as the author in Walton's *Life* of Herbert in 1670) argued that Herbert's chief aim was '*to win those that disliked our Liturgy, Catechisme, &c: by the constant, reverent, and holy use of them*' (n.p.). Chapter 13, 'The Parson's Church', stresses the importance of order and decency: for example, the parson should ensure that 'at great festivalls [the church is] strawed, and stuck with boughs, and perfumed with incense' (compare Herbert's 'Easter'), and that the books appointed by authority and a communion cloth of fine linen are present, 'not . . . as putting a holinesse in the things, but as desiring to keep the middle way between superstition, and slovenlinesse'.[29]

The most significant literary contribution to Prayer-Book devotion was the development of a literature of private prayer and meditation and of handbooks for the conduct of the whole Christian life.[30] Such books had a very long history, and were widely distributed in the sixteenth century, both before and after the Reformation. Pre-Reformation lay people had official Primers for private devotion; the Book of Common Prayer, once it became available in cheap duodecimo editions, could be used for private as well as the *common* prayer for which it was devised.[31] In addition a large number of unofficial collections of prayers and meditations was published – there were more than eighty such books in Elizabeth's reign. An important Protestant development was the handbook that combined theological instruction and prayers with directions for private and public duties. Lewis Bayly's *Practice of Pietie* (*c.* 1612) combined Calvinist doctrine with a detailed guide to daily walking with God, prayer and meditation, and preparation for death; it was enormously popular with Puritans and Nonconformists (Bunyan had a copy) and was still being reprinted in the nineteenth century. At the other end of the religious spectrum Cosin's *Collection of Private Devotions* (1627, reissued in 1655), which Charles I commissioned as a Protestant alternative to the Roman Catholic books used by his wife, resembled a Primer (it reinstated the canonical hours of devotion dropped at the Reformation) and was vehemently attacked by Puritans as Papist.[32]

The Interregnum Anglicans developed both kinds of literature, the book of private prayers and meditations and the handbook. A small pocket translation from Lancelot Andrewes' manuscript prayers in Greek was published in 1647 and '48 as *Private Devotions*; Andrewes, Bishop of Winchester, who died in 1626, was the leading reviver of ceremonial worship in the Jacobean church. Among new collections were those by Fuller, *Good Thoughts in Bad Times* and *Good Thoughts in Worse Times* (1645 and '47), and by the poet and layman Henry Vaughan, *The Mount of Olives: Or, Solitary Devotions* (1652). In the Preface to his second book Fuller observed: '*I perceive controversal writings (sounding somewhat of* Drums *and* Trumpets,*) do but make the wound the wider. Meditations are like the* Minstrel *the Prophet called for, to pacifie his mind discomposed with passion.*'[33]

The most important contributor to both genres was Jeremy Taylor. During the Civil War, Taylor lived in Wales as a schoolteacher and as chaplain to Richard Vaughan, Earl of Carbery, at Golden Grove, Carmarthenshire; in the late 1650s he moved first to London and then to Ireland with a new patron, the second Viscount Conway. He was a prolific and important writer of works of theology and controversy: his interest in toleration in *The Liberty of Prophesying* (1647) and rejection of the doctrine of original sin in *Unum Necessarium* (1655) got him into trouble with Anglican colleagues. This aspect of Taylor links him with the development of moral theology after the Restoration and the rise of freethinking. As a member of the proscribed episcopal church Taylor vigorously defended its liturgy in *An Apology for Authorized and Set Forms of Liturgy* (1649) and the preface to *A Collection of Offices* (1658), and he saw it as vital to continue its traditions in private. In *The Golden Grove* (1655), a brief collection of prayers, hymns and devotional guidance, he urged that 'we must now take care that the young men who were born in the captivity, may be taught how to worship the God of Israel after the manner of their forefathers, till it shall please God that religion shall return into the land' (*Works*, VII: 589). In his devotional handbooks, *The Rule and Exercises of Holy Living* (1650) and *The Rule and Exercises of Holy Dying* (1651), Taylor was writing specifically for those deprived of ministerial help, 'that by a collection of holy precepts they might lesse feel the want of personal and attending Guides, and that the rules for conduct of soules might be committed to a Book which they might alwayes have'. Yet these books, like *The Whole Duty of Man* attributed to Richard Allestree and first published in 1658, were by no means tied to their original context and were to remain enormously influential and popular for the next 150 years. The longevity of these texts can be attributed partly to the confidence with which Taylor describes the capacities of the individual Christian; his optimistic portrait of human nature in the first lines of *Holy Living* was to be developed in many Anglican sermons of the later seventeenth and eighteenth centuries: 'It is necessary that every Man should consider, that since

God hath given him an excellent nature, wisdom and choice, an understanding soul, and an immortal spirit, having made him Lord over the Beasts, and but a little lower than the Angels; he hath also appointed for him a work and a service great enough to imploy those abilities.'[34]

The Restoration

The Restoration of the monarchy in 1660 brought with it the re-establishment of the episcopal church and, after much debate and some revision, its liturgy.[35] The iconoclasts of the 1640 and '50s would have been astonished at the longevity of the institutions and practices they sought to suppress. To this day, bishops sit in the House of Lords (a Royal Commission is currently considering their position), Anglican cathedrals and churches are instantly recognizable by their elevated chancels and railed altars, and, though alternatives may be more popular, the Book of Common Prayer is still the official service book of the Church of England, and versions of it are in use in episcopalian churches throughout the world. Most of those discussed in this chapter rose to high office in the Restoration Church: Sheldon was made Archbishop of Canterbury after Juxon's death, and Morley, Cosin, Sanderson, Taylor, Gauden and Sparrow were all made bishops; Allestree became Regius Professor of Divinity at Oxford. Several were involved in the unsuccessful negotiations with the Presbyterians at the Savoy Conference over reform of the liturgy, and Wren, Cosin and Sanderson were largely responsible for the revisions to the final version approved by Parliament and attached to the Act of Uniformity of 1662. Perhaps the most striking of the additions was 'A General Thanksgiving' by the former Presbyterian Edward Reynolds, one of the new Restoration bishops, which thanks God 'for all thy goodness and loving-kindness to us, and to all men'. The Prayer Book, however, could not regain its inclusive pre-Civil War status. In Anglican thought *common* prayer – the public joining together of priest and people in a set form – must be *uniform*. No other public form of worship could be tolerated, but the experience of the 1640s and '50s made uniformity impossible to achieve. In response to the Act of 1662 about 2,000 ministers left the church; Presbyterians, Independents, Baptists and Quakers acquired the new legal status of Nonconformists, liable to persecution (far worse than that suffered by Interregnum Anglicans) for failure to worship according to the Book of Common Prayer. This position was to be significantly altered by the so-called Toleration Act of 1689, which suspended the penal laws against Protestant dissenters and allowed them freedom of public worship. Common prayer and uniformity were never again to be legally associated.

NOTES

1 For the relevant ordinances in chronological order see Firth & Rait, *A&O*, 1:265–6, 425–6 (demolishing of monuments of superstition or idolatry, 26 August 1643, 9 May 1644); 1:582–607, 755–7 (abolition of Book of Common Prayer and substitution of *Directory*, 4 January 1644/5, 26 August 1645); 1:879–93 (abolition of archbishops and bishops, 9 October 1646); 1:954 (abolition of festivals, 8 June 1647); 11:81–104 (abolition of deans and chapters, 30 April 1649). For the proposed demolition of cathedrals see Gardiner, *HCP*, 11:22–3, and, for the damage they suffered, Stanford E. Lehmberg, *Cathedrals under Siege: Cathedrals in English Society, 1600–1700* (University of Exeter Press, 1996), ch. 2.

2 For different perspectives on these changes see Peter Lake, 'The Laudian Style: Order, Uniformity and the Pursuit of the Beauty of Holiness in the 1630s', in Kenneth Fincham (ed.), *The Early Stuart Church, 1603–1642* (Basingstoke: Macmillan, 1993), and Kevin Sharpe, *The Personal Rule of Charles I* (New Haven and London: Yale University Press, 1992), ch. 6.

3 See A. G. Matthews, *Walker Revised, Being a Revision of John Walker's 'Sufferings of the Clergy during the Grand Rebellion' 1642–60* (Oxford: Clarendon Press, 1948, 1988); Robert S. Bosher, *The Making of the Restoration Settlement: The Influence of the Laudians, 1649–1662* (London: Dacre Press, 1951), chs. 1–2; Peter King, 'The Episcopate during the Civil Wars, 1642–1649', *EHR*, 83 (1968), 523–37; John W. Packer, *The Transformation of Anglicanism 1643–1660, with Special Reference to Henry Hammond* (Manchester University Press, 1969); I. M. Green, 'The Persecution of "Scandalous" and "Malignant" Parish Clergy during the English Civil War', *EHR*, 94 (1979), 507–31; John Spurr, *The Restoration Church of England, 1646–1689* (New Haven and London: Yale University Press, 1991), ch. 1. Details of all the clergy discussed are in *DNB*.

4 Firth & Rait, *A&O*, 1:371–2, 413, 431, 449, 457, 510 (1644); 11:977–8, 984–90 (1654).

5 Matthews, *Walker Revised*, pp. xiii–xv; Bosher, *Restoration Settlement*, p. 5; Packer, *Transformation*, pp. 10–12; Green, 'Persecution', p. 508; Spurr, *Restoration Church*, pp. 6–7.

6 Gardiner, *HCP*, 111:175–8, 190–2; John Evelyn, *Diary*, ed. E. S. de Beer, 6 vols. (Oxford: Clarendon Press, 1955), III. 163. Bosher, *Restoration Settlement*, p. 42, disputes Gardiner's assumption that Cromwell's Declaration was not enforced.

7 Izaac Walton, *The Compleat Angler, 1653–1676*, ed. Jonquil Bevan (Oxford: Clarendon Press, 1983), pp. 325, 203. See B. D. Greenslade, 'The Compleat Angler and the Sequestered Clergy', *RES*, n.s. 5 (1954), 361–6; Jonquil Bevan, *Izaac Walton's 'The Compleat Angler': The Art of Recreation* (Brighton: The Harvester Press, 1988), chs. 1 and 3.

8 John Fell, *The Life of the Most Learned, Reverend and Pious Dr H. Hammond* (1661), pp. 74–7, 92, 142.

9 Bosher, *Restoration Settlement*, pp. 39–40.

10 Izaac Walton, 'The Life of Dr Robert Sanderson' (first published 1678), in *The Lives*, intro. George Saintsbury (London: Oxford University Press, 1927; rpt 1966), pp. 382–3. Sanderson's manuscript liturgy, from which Walton quotes, was published in William Jacobson (ed.), *Fragmentary Illustrations of the History*

of the Book of Common Prayer, from Manuscript Sources (London: John Murray, 1874).

11 For a full consideration of the rival positions on the liturgy see Horton Davies, *Worship and Theology in England*, vol. II: *From Andrewes to Baxter and Fox, 1603–1690* (Princeton University Press, 1975).

12 Firth & Rait, *A&O*, I: 582, 583–4, 586–94, 597, 601, 604.

13 For an excellent account of the development of the Prayer Book see G. J. Cuming, *A History of Anglican Liturgy*, 2nd edn (Basingstoke: Macmillan, 1982).

14 From the General Confession; the Second Collect, for Peace (Morning Prayer); the Third Collect for Aid against all Perils (Evening Prayer); the Collect for the Second Sunday in Advent. See Diarmaid MacCulloch, *Thomas Cranmer* (New Haven and London: Yale University Press, 1996).

15 Anthony Sparrow, *A Rationale upon the Book of Common Prayer of the Church of England* (1657), 'The Collects', p. 80; 'Of HOLY-DAYES', pp. 110–13. Sparrow's book is the ancestor of the much revised and reprinted early twentieth-century handbook known as Proctor and Frere: Francis Proctor, *A New History of the Book of Common Prayer*, rev. Walter Howard Frere (London: Macmillan, 1901), Part 2 of which is entitled 'The Sources and Rationale of its Offices'.

16 Proclamation prefacing Hammond, *View of the Directory*, 2nd edn (1646), n.p. Hammond's arguments are summarized in Packer, *Transformation*, pp. 132–5.

17 For a publishing history and an acount of the authorship see Francis F. Madan, *A New Bibliography of the Eikon Basilike of King Charles I* (London: Bernard Quaritch, 1950), also the introduction to the edition by Philip A. Knachel (Ithaca, N.Y.: Cornell University Press, 1966). For an interesting interpretation see Lois Potter, *Secret Rites and Secret Writing: Royalist Literature, 1641–1660* (Cambridge University Press, 1989), ch. 5.

18 Knachel (ed.), *Eikon Basilike*, pp. 95–6, 98, 100, 149, 167, 179. Duppa was probably the author of ch. 16 (see p. 94n.). Knachel includes only a small amount of the additional material.

19 Gardiner, *HGCW*, IV:324.

20 For the popularity of the Prayer Book, hitherto underestimated by historians, see John Morrill, 'The Church in England, 1642–49', in *The Nature of the English Revolution* (Harlow: Longman, 1993), pp. 148–75; Judith Maltby, *Prayer Book and People in Elizabethan and Early Stuart England* (Cambridge University Press, 1998).

21 Nicholas Tyacke (ed.), *The History of the University of Oxford*, vol. IV: *Seventeenth-Century Oxford* (Oxford: Clarendon Press, 1997), pp. 595–6, 768.

22 Evelyn, *Diary*, III:94–5; C. J. Stranks, *The Life and Writings of Jeremy Taylor* (London: SPCK, 1952), p. 139; Bosher, *Restoration Settlement*, pp. 11–12.

23 See n. 6 above.

24 Evelyn, *Diary*, III:203–4.

25 Preface to *A Collection of Offices*, later transferred to *An Apology for Authorized and Set Forms of Liturgy* in Reginald Heber (ed.), *The Whole Works of the Right Rev. Jeremy Taylor*, rev. Charles Page Eden, 15 vols. (London: Longman, 1847–54), V:237, 249.

26 See F. E. Hutchinson (ed.), *The Works of George Herbert* (Oxford: Clarendon Press, 1941), pp. xliii–xliv; Nigel Smith, *Literature and Revolution in England, 1640–1660* (New Haven and London: Yale University Press, 1994), p. 266.

27 Harvey, *The Synagogue*, 2nd edn (1647), pp. 33–45 (festival sequence); the added sequence is unpaginated. Harvey does not figure in Matthews, *Walker Revised*.

28 Walton, *Compleat Angler*, pp. 260–1. Bevan does not include the commendatory poems.

29 Hutchinson (ed.), *Works of Herbert*, pp. 224, 246, 556, 559.

30 See C. J. Stranks, *Anglican Devotion: Studies in the Spiritual Life of the Church of England between the Reformation and the Oxford Movement* (London: SCM Press, 1961), chs. 1–3; C. John Sommerville, *Popular Religion in Restoration England* (Gainesville: University Presses of Florida, 1977), ch. 3; Isabel Rivers, *Reason, Grace, and Sentiment: A Study of the Language of Religion and Ethics in England, 1660–1780*, vol. I: *Whichcote to Wesley* (Cambridge University Press, 1991), ch. 1; Spurr, *Restoration Church*, ch. 6.

31 Stanley Morison, *English Prayer Books: An Introduction to the Literature of English Public Worship* (Cambridge University Press, 1949), p. 73.

32 See editor's Introduction to P. G. Stanwood (ed.), *A Collection of Private Devotions* (Oxford: Clarendon Press, 1967); Evelyn, *Diary*, III:44–6.

33 *Worse Times* (1649 edn), A3v. The reference is to Elisha in 2 Kings 3:15.

34 P. G. Stanwood (ed.), *Holy Living and Holy Dying*, 2 vols. (Oxford: Clarendon Press, 1989), I:6, 17.

35 See Geoffrey F. Nuttall and Owen Chadwick (eds.), *From Uniformity to Unity, 1662–1962* (London: SPCK, 1962), chs. 1–2; I. M. Green, *The Re-Establishment of the Church of England, 1660–1663* (Oxford University Press, 1978); Davies, *From Andrewes to Baxter and Fox*, ch. 10.

FURTHER READING

For individual editions of primary texts cited or discussed, please see the notes above.

Bevan, Jonquil, *Izaac Walton's 'The Compleat Angler': The Art of Recreation*, Brighton: The Harvester Press, 1988.

Bosher, Robert S., *The Making of the Restoration Settlement: The Influence of the Laudians 1649–1662*, London: Dacre Press, 1951.

Cross, Claire, 'The Church in England 1646–1660', in G. E. Aylmer (ed.), *The Interregnum: The Quest for Settlement 1646–1660*, London: Macmillan, 1972.

Cuming, G. J. *A History of Anglican Liturgy*, 2nd edn, Basingstoke: Macmillan, 1982.

Davies, Horton, *Worship and Theology in England*, vol. II: *From Andrewes to Baxter and Fox, 1603–1690*, Princeton University Press, 1975.

Fincham, Kenneth (ed.), *The Early Stuart Church, 1603–1642*, Basingstoke: Macmillan, 1993.

Green, I. M., *The Re-Establishment of the Church of England, 1660–1663*, Oxford University Press, 1978.

'The Persecution of "Scandalous" and "Malignant" Parish Clergy during the English Civil War', *EHR*, 94 (1979), 507–31.

Greenslade, B. D. *'The Compleat Angler* and the Sequestered Clergy', *RES*, n.s. 5 (1954), 361–6.

Jacobson, William (ed.), *Fragmentary Illustrations of the History of the Book of Common Prayer, from Manuscript Sources*, London: John Murray, 1874.

King, Peter, 'The Episcopate during the Civil Wars, 1642–1649', *EHR*, 83 (1968), 523–37.

Lehmberg, Stanford E., *Cathedrals under Siege: Cathedrals in English Society, 1600–1700*, University of Exeter Press, 1996.

Maltby, Judith, *Prayer Book and People in Elizabethan and Early Stuart England*, Cambridge University Press, 1998.

Matthews, A. G., *Walker Revised, Being a Revision of John Walker's 'Sufferings of the Clergy during the Grand Rebellion' 1642–60*, Oxford: Clarendon Press, 1948, 1988.

Morison, Stanley, *English Prayer Books: An Introduction to the Literature of English Public Worship*, Cambridge University Press, 1949.

Morrill, John, 'The Church in England, 1642–49', in *The Nature of the English Revolution*, Harlow: Longman, 1993, pp. 148–75.

Nuttall, Geoffrey F., and Owen Chadwick (eds.), *From Uniformity to Unity, 1662–1962*, London: SPCK, 1962.

Packer, John W., *The Transformation of Anglicanism 1643–1660, with special reference to Henry Hammond*, Manchester University Press, 1969.

Potter, Lois, *Secret Rites and Secret Writing: Royalist Literature, 1641–1660*, Cambridge University Press, 1989.

Proctor, Francis, rev. Frere, Walter Howard, *A New History of the Book of Common Prayer*, 3rd edn, London: Macmillan, 1914.

Rivers, Isabel, *Reason, Grace, and Sentiment: A Study of the Language of Religion and Ethics in England, 1660–1780*, vol. I: *Whichcote to Wesley*, Cambridge University Press, 1991.

Sharpe, Kevin, *The Personal Rule of Charles I*, New Haven and London: Yale University Press, 1992.

Smith, Nigel, *Literature and Revolution in England, 1640–1660*, New Haven: Yale University Press, 1994.

Spurr, John, *The Restoration Church of England, 1646–1689*, New Haven: Yale University Press, 1991.

Stranks, C. J., *The Life and Writings of Jeremy Taylor*, London: SPCK, 1952.
Anglican Devotion: Studies in the Spiritual Life of the Church of England between the Reformation and the Oxford Movement, London: SCM Press, 1961.

Tyacke, Nicholas (ed.), *The History of the University of Oxford*, vol. IV: *Seventeenth-Century Oxford*, Oxford: Clarendon Press, 1997.

12

PAUL SALZMAN

Royalist epic and romance

Epic and romance

This chapter deals with the least read and, in some cases, least studied writing of the period of the English Revolution. In recent years, literary scholars have been drawn towards radical writing of all kinds, in part following on from historians and in part due to a salutary change in political and cultural sympathy. The two obviously canonized writers of the period, Milton and Marvell, are readily accommodated to this radical bias. Their dominance is hardly challenged by the Royalist sentiments of the 'B' list of 'cavalier lyricists' (Herrick, Lovelace, Suckling, Waller) and Anglican religious poets (Vaughan, Traherne), still less by two other kinds of Royalist writing which have been all but invisible in literary discussion of the period: epic poetry, although this has at least never been entirely invisible, and romance, which has pretty much vanished from the sight of all but a handful of scholars. Recently Timothy Raylor has pointed to the limitations of our understanding of cavalier culture, in comparison to 'the sophisticated appreciation we now have of the ideological complexities of those traditionally labelled "Puritans"'.[1] Epic and romance are perfect candidates for just such a sophisticated appreciation of the complex ideological agendas of Royalist writing. I will argue here that epic ultimately became a form of oblique political commentary for Royalist writers, while romance was, by the mid seventeenth century, a genre that was used by Royalist writers for a much more direct engagement with a complex political situation.

Royalist epic and romance are both particularly grounded in history – indeed, they make little sense studied in isolation from their historical contexts, and never could have had the vogue of the cavalier lyric or religious poem back in the days in the first half of the twentieth century when a good deal of literary criticism isolated the literary text and subjected it to a narrow, exegetical gaze. Despite the increasing historical sensitivity of criticism of the last century, there are some problems involved in an account of Royalist epic and romance writing. Because the works discussed here are generally both very substantial and (in the case of the romances) almost entirely unavailable to anyone other than a scholar, I will have to spend rather more time summarizing than analysing. One important point that I want to make is that the terms 'Royalist epic' and 'Royalist romance' imply a homogeneity that is quite misleading. I hope, in the account that follows, to show how a very wide variety of political gradations are subsumed under these two headings.

There is a clear distinction between the genres of epic and romance in terms of their appropriation by particular political groups during the English Revolution. While epic was a genre available to writers with a very wide range of political sympathies, romance was, virtually without exception, a Royalist genre. Some evidence of the political diversity associated with epic is attested to by the fact that Virgil's *Aeneid* was translated in the mid seventeenth century by the Republican James Harrington as well as the Royalists John Denham and Edmund Waller.[2] Similarly, the epic form was open to adaptation by Milton, as well as by the Royalist writers I discuss in detail here. Nigel Smith notes the importance of Lucan's incomplete *Pharsalia* during the Civil War, as an example of an ironic, pro-Republican epic.[3] *Pharsalia* was written around AD 62 and was originally entitled *The Civil War*. It was translated in the seventeenth century by Thomas May. Gerald MacLean points out that the critical debate over *Pharsalia* in the seventeenth century was 'a struggle for control over the status and meanings of historical poetry'.[4] The Civil War transformed the whole question of how political criticism might be expressed through literature, given that writers found themselves actively engaged in an escalating political crisis. The example of *Pharsalia* was debated because it was presented (especially through May's translation and continuation) as a key example of how literature and 'history' (including contemporary political/historical events) might interact.[5]

Abraham Cowley: *The Civil War* and *Davideis*

The most significant example of Royalist epic poetry, influenced to some degree by *Pharsalia* and directly engaged with the Civil War, is an incomplete poem written by Abraham Cowley in Oxford in 1643. Cowley left Cambridge (where he was a Fellow of Trinity College) at the beginning of the Civil War and took up residence at Oxford, where the court had retreated after the outbreak of hostilities. There, in anticipation of a Royalist victory, he began writing *The Civil War* some time around the middle of 1643. However, Cowley's anticipation of a Royalist triumph which would, presumably, have been celebrated at the conclusion of the poem, was dashed by the series of Royalist reversals following the Battle of Newbury in September 1643. In 1644 Cowley left Oxford to join Queen Henrietta Maria in exile in Paris. He returned to England a decade later as, it has been conjectured, a Royalist spy, but after a brief imprisonment in 1655 he engaged in a fairly conciliatory series of manoeuvres, including the preface to the 1656 publication of his *Poems*. There, Cowley refers back to *The Civil War* in the context of a general repudiation of what we might call politically oriented (for which one might read 'politically dangerous') poetry:

> I have cast away all such pieces as I wrote during the time of the late troubles, with any relation to the differences that caused them; as among others, *three Books of the Civil War it self*, reaching as far as the first *Battel of Newbury*, where the succeeding *misfortunes* of the *party* stopt the *work*; for it is so uncustomary, as to become almost *ridiculous*, to make *Lawrels* for the *Conquered*.[6]

Cowley indeed recommends a kind of willed amnesia about the very events addressed by *The Civil War*, suggesting (in what was regarded as a direct gesture of appeasement) that 'We ought not sure, to begin ourselves to revive the remembrance of those times and actions for which we have received a General Amnestie, as a favor from the Victor' (Cowley, *Complete Works*, 1:cxxviii–cxxix). Finally, he claims that he destroyed his politically engaged poetry: 'I would have it accounted no less unlawful to rip up old wounds, than to give new ones; which has made me not onely abstain from printing any thing of this kinde, but to burn the very copies' (1:cxxix). While a single book of *The Civil War* was first published in 1679, twelve years after Cowley's death, the remainder of the poem was assumed to have been burnt until the discovery of manuscripts, which included Books Two and Three, by the scholar Allan Pritchard in the 1960s.[7]

One cannot presume that Cowley abandoned *The Civil War* for the same reasons that he later renounced it. Whatever sense of political expediency motivated the preface to the 1656 *Poems*, the incompletion of *The Civil War* is not necessarily a simple result of Cowley's anticipation of impending Royalist defeat. In David Trotter's reading of Cowley's development, *The Civil War* was an unsustainable venture because of a kind of generic bottleneck which is a reflection of the internal political divisions of the Civil War itself; that is, the events of the Civil War simply could not be accommodated to the epic form. From this perspective, Trotter argues, 'Cowley found the epic frame increasingly inhospitable.'[8] It is certainly true that, in its engagement with the concrete historical detail of the Civil War, Cowley's poem shifts between genres. It begins in a clear epic mode, taking a sweeping view of both England's current conflict ('What rage does England from it self divide') and its previous military triumphs under past rulers (Edward III;

Henry V; Elizabeth).[9] By Book Three, Cowley resorts to satire in an attempt to belittle the Parliamentary forces, when he has to tackle the very events which undermine Royalist hopes of overall victory.

In contrast to Trotter's sense of *The Civil War* as a generic unravelling, Nigel Smith offers an important positive interpretation of this generic mix as a reflection of the 'power divisions of the Civil War itself', with the flexibility of epic allowing for 'a conflict between masque and elegy (royalism) and satire/scatology (Parliamentarianism, puritanism)'.[10] I think that most readers of the poem would acknowledge an edgy and at times confusing shift of tone, as Cowley moves from an account of the conflict's origins to a detailed engagement with some of the actual battles. At the beginning of Book One, Cowley offers a rather delimited explanation for the events of the Civil War. It is as if the nation has been literally 'blown' from peace to conflict: 'Sixteene Yeeres we endur'd our Happinesse: / Till in a Moment from the *North* we find / A *Tempest* conjur'd up without a *Wind*' (p. 116). This is the rhetoric of astonishment expressed by many Royalists, not perhaps as a serious explanation for the Civil War, but rather as a kind of propaganda: an attempt to persuade people that a time of peace and prosperity had been wantonly and for no good reason overturned: 'Thus into War we scar'ed our selves' (p. 117). This is a reading of the poem endorsed in considerable detail by Gerald MacLean, who also sees its incomplete state as a paradigm for later Augustan poetry, given that, in MacLean's view, Cowley's difficulty was not with the generic capacities of epic form, but with the way that his incorporation of a heroic past conflicted with the historical particularity of the present.[11] From this perspective, the poem can only end (as it does) as an elegy for the dead Royalist Lucius Cary, Viscount Falkland, with the Royalist fortunes representing a kind of heuristic impasse for the poet. The elegiac conclusion follows the second book, where Cowley turns to the depiction of Parliament as a meeting of fiends in 'Bel-zebubs Hall' (p. 142), and where the conflict is viewed as the product of a purely vindictive evil.

However one interprets Cowley's stalled epic, it is significant that *The Civil War* seems, for Royalists, to have spelled the end to a direct depiction of the Civil War within the epic genre. From this point on, Royalist epics approach aspects of the conflict more obliquely. For Cowley himself, this occurred with a second incomplete epic, but this time one which he did publish in the 1656 *Poems – Davideis: A Sacred Poem of the Troubles of David*.[12] Significantly, Cowley took some material from *The Civil War* and reworked it into parts of *Davideis*, but by its very nature *Davideis* is simultaneously politically suggestive and politically opaque. Based on the Biblical account of David, Cowley's poem is copiously annotated with his own notes, many of them displays of Biblical/historical scholarship and musing. Given

Cowley's remarks in the preface (quoted above), in which he essentially renounced political poetry, *Davideis* is at first sight a retreat to an uncontroversial subject. However, David's story, and the poem, constantly evoke questions of power and dynastic struggle. The poem seems to have been written in the early 1650s, and its appearance in 1656 evokes many potential parallels with Cromwell's position as Protector. Recent political interpretations of the poem have tried to grapple with the whole question of how Cowley might be commenting on both the current political situation in England, and on the aftermath of the Civil War in general.

The key aspect of *Davideis* for this purpose is the relationship between David and Saul. Both characters are treated with considerable complexity, with Cowley, at some level, intending an oblique association to be drawn between Saul and Cromwell and between David and Charles II. While this association has been seen as a clear allegory, I think that most readers would be more persuaded by Thomas Corns' subtle reading (following on in part from David Trotter's), which stresses the fact that 'no simple equations obtain', and sees the poem as a whole as a 'Royalist fantasy' which, just like *The Civil War*, was not able to be completed because political circumstances would not allow for the successful realization of such a fantasy.[13]

Cowley, however, always seems to be hedging his bets. In Book Four, when David explains why the Jews demanded a monarchy, Cowley offers a complex account of the need for the 'remedy' of a King:

> They saw the State and glittering Pomp, which blest,
> In vulgar Sense, the *Scepters* of the *East*.
> They saw not *Pow'r's* true *Source*, and scorn'd t' obey
> Persons that *look'd* no *dreadfuller* than *they*.
> They miss'd *Courts*, *Guards*, a gay and num'rous Train;
> Our *Judges*, like their *Laws*, were rude and plain.
> (Cowley, *Complete Works*, ii:95, lines 156–61)

Published close to the moment when Cromwell was offered the throne, this passage can be interpreted either as a critique of monarchical power or as a Hobbesian explanation for its necessity. In the poem, Samuel wryly notes: 'You're sure the first (says he) / Of *free-born* Men that begg'd for Slavery' (lines 232–3). The choice of Saul as King may well be seen, in an oblique reading of the political possibilities, as paving the way for David, yet David/Charles II and Saul/Cromwell are both placed in an uneasy relationship with the notion of monarchical legitimacy and questions of succession.

The political indirection of *Davideis* points to what might be seen as the norm for political commentary in early modern England. Annabel Patterson has argued that early modern writing was invariably conscious of censorship and had an abiding interest in ways of expressing political comment indirectly.[14] This is of particular relevance to the romances which I will discuss below, but it is also evident in the way that a work like *Davideis* exemplifies a technique by which an author might protect him or herself from open political declaration, while still engaging in suggestive political commentary. This situation is equally evident in the other major Royalist epic of the period: Sir William Davenant's *Gondibert*.

Sir William Davenant: *Gondibert*

Gondibert may also serve as a bridge to the second genre discussed here, because it has been seen as being allied much more with romance than with epic. Davenant wrote much of *Gondibert* in exile in Paris; like Cowley's work, it remained incomplete. Davenant wrote a postscript to the incomplete third book from prison on the Isle of Wight in October 1650, where he had been captured en route to America. He expected to be taken to the Tower and executed, but was reprieved and eventually released. The preface to *Gondibert* had been published in Paris in 1650 in advance of the poem itself. Both the preface and the 'answer' to it by Thomas Hobbes are now the only parts of *Gondibert* read by most people. From a generic point of view, Davenant offers a careful defence of an epic poem which eschews the supernatural. From a political point of view, however, the preface offers a considered argument for what Stephen Zwicker has named a 'political culture', particularly through Davenant's theory that true poetry would have, at its source, wit, rather than an 'inspiration' associated with superstition and, by implication, with the kind of religious zealotry that Royalists saw behind the Revolution.[15] In particular, Davenant associates the court with a civilizing influence largely, in his opinion, lost upon the common people who 'looke upon the outward glory or blaze of Courts, as Wilde beasts in darke nights stare on their Hunters Torches'.[16]

The poem itself is particularly oblique in its depiction of a political situation which, based as the narrative is upon obscure Lombard history, makes direct identification of contemporary parallels quite difficult. Lois Potter has argued that this was exactly Davenant's intention, noting that 'if *Gondibert* is a coded narrative, the point of the code is not its precise equivalence between fictitious characters and events and those of Davenant's own time but rather its creation of a world where, as in Royalist propaganda, private motives are privileged over public consequences'.[17] One aspect of *Gondibert* that has been noted as bearing specific political significance is a section in Book 1, canto 2, describing a stag hunt. The link of a stag hunt to the fortunes of King Charles I was something of a commonplace, the most prominent example being John Denham's *Cooper's Hill*, a poem which was first published in 1642, but was then much revised, notably after Charles I's execution. *Cooper's Hill* is a development of the pastoral genre which allowed Denham to invest the landscape with Royalist ideology (especially in the revised versions). Davenant in particular echoes Denham's image of the stag disdained by the herd; in Denham's more politically pointed image, the stag is 'Like a declining States-man' (which has been seen as an evocation of Strafford as much as of Charles).[18] For Davenant, the herd is significant as an example of the common people whose taste as well as judgement he so disdains:

> We blush to see our politicks in Beasts,
> Who Many sav'd by this one Sacrifice;
> And since through blood they follow interests,
> Like us when cruel should be counted wise.
>
> *(Gondibert, p. 73)*

The narrative of *Gondibert* centres on a romance plot, with the hero torn between his love for Birtha and his planned marriage to Rhodalind, the Princess of Lombardy. In his movement from epic to romance, Davenant might be seen to be searching for a solution to Cowley's problems with the interrelationship between the epic genre and the traumatizing (for Royalists) events of history which stalled *The Civil War*. The example of *Gondibert* might lead one to believe that the romance as a genre implied a kind of political evasiveness. However, romance as a genre was particularly flexible in the mid seventeenth century, and it could also lead to works that were able to engage much more directly with the political events of the time. To understand this use of the genre we need to trace its development earlier in the century.

John Barclay: *Argenis*

At the beginning of the seventeenth century, the form of romance most available for political comment derived from Sir Philip Sidney's *Arcadia*, a prose romance that Sidney began writing around 1580. In a composite version which joined together the original version of *Arcadia* and an incompleted, elaborate revision (taking it in a more chivalric and epic direction), *Arcadia* was extremely popular in the seventeenth century and, by the reign of King James, was read by at least some people as a dark commentary on monarchical power and its abuse.[19] However, Sidney treats politics and history in the *Arcadia* in an indirect, philosophical manner, with only occasional (and circumspect) glances towards directly identifiable figures. Such treatment is apparent in the major example of a romance directly influenced by *Arcadia*, Sidney's niece Mary Wroth's *Urania* (1621),[20] but a major change towards a more direct treatment of recent history and contemporary politics was fuelled in the 1620s by *Argenis*, a romance written originally in Latin by John Barclay.

Barclay had a Scottish father and a French mother and had attached himself to the court of James I in 1603. After its publication in Latin in 1621, *Argenis* attracted the attention of the King, who asked for it to be translated into English. While this was undertaken by Ben Jonson, his version was lost in a fire that destroyed many of his works, and eventually translations by Kingesmill Long (1625) and Robert Le Grys (1628) appeared (with the poetry translated by Thomas May). Barclay took the romance form and, in Annabel Patterson's phrase, used it for 'an encoded and fictionalised account of European history'[21]. *Argenis* is centred on France under Henry III and Henry IV, but the narrative does also glance at more contemporary English events, such as the Overbury scandal (which surrounded the marriage of James' favourite Robert Carr, Earl of Somerset), and at the reign of Elizabeth. *Argenis* offers an elaborate and detailed depiction of specific historical circumstances (keys to the narrative rapidly appeared in both Latin and English editions), but also a sophisticated series of meditations on current political issues (such as the relationship between a monarch and Parliament – Barclay voices an anti-Parliament line that must have appealed to James) and on the significant contribution that a work like *Argenis* itself might make both to the reformation of morals and to political debate.

By 1645, a number of editions of *Argenis* in both English and Latin were available as examples of how romance might be used as a genre which could incorporate the events of the Civil War. It seems to me that the example of *Argenis* ensured that romance would be a more productive genre for Royalist purposes than epic.[22] A series of prose romances were written and published between 1645 and 1661 which took their lead from *Argenis*. As well as continuing Barclay's combination of detailed historical representation and serious political analysis, the surviving examples are quite diverse, and indicate the complex range of political positions all too easily subsumed under the label 'Royalist'. As each example was published or written at a different stage in the ever-changing political situation from 1645 to 1661 (and after), they also offer a range of responses to the way events might be interpreted, depending upon the writer's distance from them. The romances written or published in 1645, 1653 and 1654 are quite different to those published before or shortly after the Restoration (and I include in this notion of difference the most interesting example, Sir Percy Herbert's *Princess Cloria*, which appeared in two parts in the earlier period and was only published in its complete form after 1660).

Political romances

As an indication of the particular appeal of these romances to those at some remove from the conflict itself, we have Dorothy Osborne's intriguing remark in one of her letters to William Temple, written in September 1653:

> My Lord Broghill sure will give us something worth the reading. My Lord Saye, I am told has writ a Romance since his retirement in the Isle of Lundee, and Mr Waller they say is makeing one of Our Warr's, wch if hee do's not mingle with a great deal of pleasing fiction cannot bee very diverting sure the Subject is soe sad.[23]

I will discuss below the romance *Parthenissa* by Roger Boyle, Baron Broghill. Neither Saye's nor Waller's romances (if they were indeed written) have survived. While from a purely literary point of view we might most regret the loss of Waller's, a romance written by William Fiennes, Viscount Saye & Sele, would be particularly interesting from a political point of view, because he was a strong opponent of Charles I and a supporter of Parliament at the beginning of the Civil War. He progressed to support for the Army in 1647. By 1648, however, he formed part of the group attempting to find some sort of settlement with the King. His 'retirement' followed the execution of the King and his romance would have made fascinating reading. Nevertheless, the first extant romance of this kind that we do have also manifests a complex attitude towards the Civil War.

In 1655, Sir William Sales published a romance entitled *Theophania: Or Several Modern Histories Represented by Way of Romance and Politicly Discoursed Upon*. As the complete title indicates, Sales is interested in explanations as well as events. *Theophania* has at its centre a gentleman named Synesius who has retreated from the chaos of the Civil War to his country estate; but the events of the war are inescapable. Sales contrasts a largely fictional account of the 'romance' between Charles I's daughter, Mary, and William of Orange with a detailed and incisive analysis of the Earl of Essex's involvement in the Civil War. Essex was the initial commander of the Parliamentary army, and his attitudes to the war are explored at length. This involves Sales in an elaborate tracing back of Essex's history, including that of his father (who was executed in 1601 for his attempted rebellion against Elizabeth). This culminates in Essex's downfall during the army reforms of 1644–5. *Theophania* ends inconclusively, reflecting the uncertainty surrounding its time of writing. Its publication in 1655, long after the resolution of the events held in suspension at the end of the romance, points to some of the same problems for these romances as those that faced Cowley when he wrote *The Civil War*: without a clear outcome evident, the war can certainly be contained within the form of romance, and even explained, at least to some extent, but its resolution cannot be foretold.

Sir Percy Herbert: *The Princess Cloria*

What became the most substantial of these works was first published in two parts in 1653 and 1654 and left incomplete, not unlike *Theophania*. This is a romance by Sir Percy Herbert that was first entitled *Cloria and Narcissus*. Herbert had been an MP in the 1620s. A Catholic, in 1639 he was the collector of Catholic contributions in County Montgomery for the war with the Scots. He was called before the Committee for Recusants Convict in 1641 and though he was bailed at that time, his estates were eventually confiscated and sold in 1651. The only piece of writing attributable to Herbert apart from his romance is a collection of essays addressed to his son, published in 1650 as *Certain Conceptions or Considerations*. Parts One and Two of *Cloria and Narcissus* centre a romance narrative on Mary and William, in the same way that Sales does in *Theophania*. However, Herbert engages in a much more ambitious piece of historical contextualizing for the Civil War, interweaving the history of Europe with the history of England. The romance begins with an account of the political chaos surrounding the Thirty Years' War (between Catholic and Protestant powers in Europe).

As *Cloria and Narcissus*, parts One and Two of Herbert's romance offer an account of the first stages of the Civil War and part Two concludes well before the execution of Charles I, so that readers in 1653 and 1654 would, like readers of *Theophania*, have been presented with an unfinished (perhaps even, like *The Civil War*, unfinishable) romance, which ended without facing the defeat of the Royalist cause. What is particularly interesting about this unfinished first version of Herbert's romance is the way it examines the causes of the Civil War; these are presented to readers in the early 1650s who are aware of the disastrous consequences of the conflict (for the King and his followers). Herbert looks closely at James' reign and is particularly critical of James' character:

> The Father of *Euarchus* [Charles I] our now King, being a Prince wholly given, as I may say, to his own pleasure, onely studied wayes to keep himself during his life in a quiet security; and to this purpose he not onely brought up his son, after the death of his elder brother in learning and domestic exercises, under the protect [*sic*] of his own eye and jurisdiction, but when he came to years of consent, he endeavoured with some violence, to marry him to the King of *Egypts* [i.e. Spain's] Daughter, by whose greatnesse he thought to establish his own Regal Power the better in *Lydia* [England]. (p. 168) [24]

In Herbert's presentation, responsibility for the whole Buckingham/Charles episode in Spain rests with James. While Herbert is much more positive about Charles than he is about his father, he also offers some acute criticism of Charles' character during this same passage: 'perhaps some will say, he is more beholding to nature for his inclination, then to resolution for his temperance' (p. 168). Herbert's interest in the pre-history of the Civil War takes the narrative back to the reign of Elizabeth in some detail, as well as leading him to undertake a detailed account of relevant European history. The 'romance' component of *Cloria and Narcissus* is evident in the treatment of Cloria herself as a romance heroine whose activities bear only a slight resemblance to those of the historical character she stands for: Charles I's daughter Mary. This is because Herbert follows Barclay's model and uses Cloria as a composite figure who is more than simply a real person disguised by a romance name. Herbert also offers the reader detailed and careful accounts of many of the Civil War conflicts, but he ensures that the narrative focuses on significant individuals (such as the King). Nigel Smith notes the 'grittiness of the detail' with which Herbert describes notable battles, such as Edgehill.[25]

In contrast to Cowley, Herbert evidently found in the Restoration the inspiration to complete his romance, and in 1661 he published it in five parts as *The Princess Cloria*. The further three parts make it the longest and most ambitious of these political romances. An interesting preface to the reader details the theory behind the use of romance in order to make sense of the events surrounding the Civil War: 'the Ground-work for a Romance was excellent; and the rather, since by no other way almost, could the multiplicity of strange Actions of the Times be exprest, that exceeded all belief, and went beyond every example in the doing' (sig. A1v).[26] This points to the structural flexibility of the romance, which is able to entwine multiple narrative threads and, as a consequence, deal with a complex nexus of explanations for the conflict. Herbert certainly succeeds in offering just such a sophisticated teleology for the outbreak of the Civil War. However, he required the Restoration to turn tragedy into a kind of tragicomedy. As the romance proceeds from the two parts that were published in the early 1650s, Herbert is able to incorporate the King's imprisonment, trial and execution. While Herbert follows historical events with some accuracy, he also, as the preface points out, follows the precedents of classical historians in often producing appropriate speeches for characters, even if they were not made or cannot be recovered. The most interesting example in *The Princess Cloria* is a speech made by Charles at the end of his trial (when Charles was in fact prevented from making such a speech).[27] This has the effect of rewriting certain Civil

War events in order to have them accord with romance expectations of appropriate behaviour. Therefore, the romance genre itself is part of Herbert's account of the events of the Civil War, because it is through the romance treatment of characters and events that Herbert is able to direct our sympathy. At times this does involve a considerable simplification; for example, Cromwell, named Hercrombrotus in the romance, is a largely one-dimensional villain. For a writer with Royalist sympathies (however shaded some of them may be), there is no room for a measured assessment of the political reasons why so many people sided with Parliament.

What Herbert does offer, though, is a sophisticated depiction of political turmoil, seen as a historically situated event. The disruption to Charles' rule is viewed in the context of European conflict. It forms, within the romance, a moral collapse that cannot recognize the common benefits of Charles' reign. Herbert offers vivid accounts of the suffering of ordinary people during the Civil War (especially in part Three), which he describes as unnecessary, given that Parliament never should have rebelled. While Herbert's Catholicism is not especially evident in the romance, he does imply that the religious turmoil following the Reformation is responsible for many political ills which (by implication) would not have happened if Catholicism had remained unchallenged: 'since the first appearing of Herenzius [Calvin], in the confines of Arabia [Europe], the world hath been filled in a manner with nothing but Slaughters, Rebellions, and Impiety, altering their opinions (at leastwise the exercise of their Rites) as often as the Moon doth her garment' (pp. 442–3). This is further emphasized in Herbert's depiction of Charles II (named Arethusius in the romance) as someone struck by the degree of religious and political duplicity and confusion in Europe during his exile there. Herbert moves into a fascinating (if idealistic) account of the political education of Charles II, depicting him as torn between the need for the duplicity which his grandfather (the romance claims) practised so adeptly and a nobler view of a ruler's duties. Arethusius says 'I would have a Prince always to prosecute his designs although with secresie, yet without hypocrisie' (p. 392). Given the Restoration of Charles II, *The Princess Cloria* is able to rest upon a notion of providential conclusions to insoluble political dilemmas. The Restoration is made to seem inevitable simply because the assault on the monarchy was unthinkable, within the terms set up by the romance – criticism is possible, but the execution of the King was simply a moral outrage for which no political explanation seems possible.

Restoration romances

Three other political romances were published around the same time as the complete version of *The Princess Cloria*. Lack of space prohibits me from giving them much attention here, though each is of interest. Richard Brathwait's *Panthalia: Or, the Royal Romance* (1659) appeared as an intervention in political events leading up to the Restoration. As Brathwait wrote, events changed rapidly, so that *Panthalia* has a 'sequel' recounting Cromwell's death and Richard Cromwell's succession, and then a 'postscript' describing Richard's abdication. As Annabel Patterson notes in her discussion of *Panthalia*, Brathwait shifted his intended audience from the Parliaments of 1659 (either Richard Cromwell's or the restored Rump) to the monarch, once the monarch's return seemed imminent.[28] *Panthalia* is interesting from a generic point of view, because, in contrast to the wholly serious *Princess Cloria*, it has a comic and ironic tone, together with its more serious treatment of politics. Brathwait follows the pattern of Sales and Herbert in turning to the pre-history of the Civil War in the reigns of Elizabeth and James. For Brathwait, both James and Charles I have to be criticized for character flaws (much is made of the fate of Strafford, for example, seen as caused by Charles' overly pliant nature), and James in particular is seen, as Patterson acutely notes, to be an 'escapist monarch', named Basilius, after the negligent ruler in Sidney's *Arcadia*.[29]

In 1660 Sir George Mackenzie published *Aretina, or The Serious Romance*. Mackenzie was to become king's advocate in Scotland and was known as 'bloody Mackenzie' for his prosecution of covenanters.[30] This aspect of Mackenzie's character is evident in *Aretina* (published when he was twenty-four), which offers satirical portraits of Protestant sects in the 1650s. The satire is also evident in Mackenzie's detailed treatment of Scotland in the Civil War (including a devastating portrait of Argyll's troops). Book Three encompasses a narrative running through from Charles' execution to the Restoration.

The final extant work that can be placed in this category is really an anti-romance in the guise of a political romance. *Don Juan Lamberto*, which was probably written by Thomas Flatman, was published in 1661 (described as the second edition). *Don Juan Lamberto*, is a piece of broad, effervescent political satire, disguised (right down to the use of black-letter type) as a chapbook chivalric romance. The title is a spoof on Major-General John Lambert, and the work as a whole uses the mock-romance form to poke fun at Cromwell, 'the dread Soldan of Britain', and 'his late Son Ricardus, sirnamed for his great valour the Meek Knight'.[31] *Lamberto* centres wholly upon the collapse of opposition to the return of Charles II from the brief ascent of

Richard Cromwell onwards; previous stages of the Civil War and Revolution are only alluded to in passing, leaving the way free for a Royalist comedy.

What links these romances together is the influence of *Argenis* and the interest in exploring detailed political and historical events under disguised romance names and places.[32] The political stances, while certainly able to be grouped together as Royalist, vary enormously, especially in relation to the perceived flaws of James I and Charles I. Another form of romance that was extremely popular in the 1650s and later has, in England, some links to these political romances. The French heroic romance was read avidly in both the original and numerous English translations. Although French heroic romances were concerned generally with exotic historical settings, the most ambitious English example of the genre – *Parthenissa* by Roger Boyle, Baron Broghill – while not offering a direct representation of the Civil War, does engage with many political issues that seem to be related quite directly to the situation in England in the 1650s. Boyle published *Parthenissa* in five parts between 1651 and 1656 and added a sixth part in 1669, after he had been created Earl of Orrery. Boyle served both Parliament and crown, Cromwell and Charles II, and *Parthenissa* reflects this in its elaborate debates about conflicted loyalty (evident again in the heroic tragedies which Boyle wrote after the Restoration). It is a Royalist romance in so far as it represents, in Nigel Smith's terms, 'a document of the Parliamentary nobility disaffected by the events of 1648–9'.[33]

It is a great shame that, partly because of their sheer size and partly because their generic conventions seem so alien, the 'Royalist' romances considered here remain largely unpalatable to the average modern reader. Yet just as modern readers have gradually come to understand and enjoy radical prophetic writing or Quaker polemic, so I hope that this chapter will encourage the reader to seek out what remain the most detailed, sustained and interesting attempts by Royalist writers to engage with the political upheaval from 1639 to 1660.

NOTES

1 Timothy Raylor, *Cavaliers, Clubs and Literary Culture* (Newark, N.J.: University of Delaware Press, 1994), p. 19.

2 These were all partial translations. For an explanatory account (albeit one that ignores much of the political implication), see L. Proudfoot, *Dryden's Aeneid and Its Seventeenth Century Predecessors* (Manchester University Press, 1960); for a typically acute and politically aware account of epic in general and the Civil War, see Nigel Smith, *Literature and Revolution in England, 1640–1660* (New Haven: Yale University Press, 1994), ch. 7.

3 Smith, *Literature and Revolution*, p. 204.

4 Gerald M. MacLean, *Time's Witness: Historical Representation in English Poetry, 1603–1660* (Madison: University of Wisconsin Press, 1990), p. 44.

5 For this aspect of May's translation, and an important account of Lucan's influence in general, see especially David Norbrook, *Writing the English Republic: Poetry, Rhetoric and Politics 1627–1660* (Cambridge University Press, 1999), ch. 1.

6 Abraham Cowley, *Complete Works in Prose and Verse*, ed. Alexander B. Grosart, 2 vols. (1881: rpt Hildesheim: Georg Olms, 1969), I:cxxviii.

7 Abraham Cowley, *The Civil War*, ed. Allan Pritchard (Toronto University Press, 1973); this edition has been incorporated into the Calhoun *Collected Works*, see below, n. 9.

8 David Trotter, *The Poetry of Abraham Cowley* (London: Macmillan, 1979), p. 21.

9 *The Collected Works of Abraham Cowley*, ed. Thomas O. Calhoun, Laurence Heyworth and Allan Pritchard, vol. 1 (Newark: University of Delaware Press, 1989), p. 114; parenthetical references to *The Civil War* by page number are to this edition.

10 Smith, *Literature and Revolution*, p. 208.

11 MacLean, *Time's Witness*, pp. 177–211.

12 *Davideis* literally means 'of David' and is an epic title modelled on Virgil's *Aeneid*.

13 Thomas N. Corns, *Uncloistered Virtue: English Political Literature 1640–1660* (Oxford: Clarendon Press, 1992), p. 266; see also Trotter, *Poetry*, ch. 5 and Smith, *Literature and Revolution*, pp. 216–18.

14 Annabel Patterson, *Censorship and Interpretation: The Conditions of Writing and Reading in Early Modern England* (Madison: University of Wisconsin Press, 1984).

15 Steven N. Zwicker, *Lines of Authority: Politics and English Literary Culture 1649–1689* (Ithaca: Cornell University Press, 1993), pp. 17–26; see also the discussion along somewhat similar lines in Kevin Sharpe, *Criticism and Compliment* (Cambridge University Press, 1987), pp. 101–8.

16 David F. Gladish (ed.), *Sir William Davenant's Gondibert* (Oxford: Clarendon Press, 1971), p. 12.

17 Lois Potter, *Secret Rites and Secret Writing: Royalist Literature, 1641–1660* (Cambridge University Press, 1989), p. 97.

18 Theodore Banks (ed.), *The Poetical Works of Sir John Denham*, 2nd edn (n.p.: Archon Books, 1969), p. 83; see Smith, *Literature and Revolution*, p. 322.

19 The most recent and elaborate treatment of the political implications of *Arcadia* at the time Sidney wrote is Blair Worden, *The Sound of Virtue: Philip Sidney's Arcadia and Elizabethan Politics* (New Haven: Yale University Press, 1996). *Arcadia* itself is most readily accessible in the Penguin edition, ed. Maurice Evans (Harmondsworth, 1977), but see also the authoritative *New Arcadia,* ed. Victor Skretkowitz (Oxford: Clarendon Press, 1987).

20 For *Urania*'s treatment of politics see Josephine Roberts (ed.), *The First Part of the Countess of Montgomery's Urania* (Binghampton, N.Y.: Medieval and Renaissance Texts and Studies, 1995), pp. xxxix–liv; Paul Salzman, 'The Strange Constructions of Mary Wroth's *Urania*: Arcadian Romance and the Public Realm', in Neil Rhodes (ed.), *English Renaissance Prose: History, Language and Politics* (Tempe, Ariz.: Medieval and Renaissance Texts and Studies, 1997), pp. 109–24.

21 Patterson, *Censorship and Interpretation*, p. 180. For detailed accounts of *Argenis* and its influence, see Patterson, *Censorship and Interpretation*, pp.

180–5; Paul Salzman, *English Prose Fiction, 1558–1700: A Critical History* (Oxford: Clarendon Press, 1985), pp. 149–55.

22 *Pace* Smith, *Literature and Revolution*, p. 235, who does make an interesting case for the connections between epic and romance in relation to the depiction of the Civil War.

23 Dorothy Osborne, *Letters to Sir William Temple*, ed. Kenneth Parker (Harmondsworth: Penguin, 1987), p. 132.

24 References are to *The Princess Cloria* (1661).

25 Smith, *Literature and Revolution*, pp. 237–8.

26 The preface and a very short extract from the romance may be found in Paul Salzman (ed.), *An Anthology of Seventeenth-Century Fiction*, World's Classics (Oxford University Press, 1991).

27 See C. V. Wedgwood, *The Trial of Charles I* (London: Collins, 1967), pp. 185–6; the speech is on p. 333 of *The Princess Cloria*.

28 Patterson, *Censorship and Interpretation*, p. 198.

29 Patterson, *Censorship and Interpretation*, p. 200.

30 See *DNB*, *s.v.* Mackenzie, Sir George of Rosehaugh.

31 *Don Juan Lamberto* (1661), sig. A.

32 I have elsewhere described them as 'political/allegorical' (Salzman, *English Prose Fiction*, pp. 148–9).

33 Smith, *Literature and Revolution*, p. 345. For a detailed account of *Parthenissa* see Salzman, *English Prose Fiction*, pp. 190–201; Smith, *Literature and Revolution*, pp. 244–6.

FURTHER READING

For individual editions of primary texts cited or discussed, please see the notes above.

Corns, Thomas N., *Uncloistered Virtue: English Political Literature 1640–1660*, Oxford: Clarendon Press, 1992.

MacLean, Gerald M., *Time's Witness: Historical Representation in English Poetry, 1603–1660*, Madison: University of Wisconsin Press, 1990.

Patterson, Annabel, *Censorship and Interpretation: The Conditions of Writing and Reading in Early Modern England*, Madison: University of Wisconsin Press, 1984.

Potter, Lois, *Secret Rites and Secret Writing: Royalist Literature, 1641–1660*, Cambridge University Press, 1989.

Raylor, Timothy, *Cavaliers, Clubs and Literary Culture*, Newark, N.J.: University of Delaware Press, 1994.

Salzman, Paul, *English Prose Fiction, 1558–1700: A Critical History*, Oxford: Clarendon Press, 1985.

    (ed.), *An Anthology of Seventeenth-Century Fiction*, Oxford University Press, 1991.

Smith, Nigel, *Literature and Revolution in England, 1640–1660*, New Haven: Yale University Press, 1994.

Trotter, David, *The Poetry of Abraham Cowley*, Basingstoke: Macmillan, 1979.

Zwicker, Steven N., *Lines of Authority: Politics and English Literary Culture 1649–1689*, Ithaca: Cornell University Press, 1993.

5
RETHINKING THE WAR

13

DAVID NORBROOK

The English Revolution and English historiography

Traditions in historiography

The early modern period, it has been claimed, saw a 'historical revolution'.[1] Just how far that term is appropriate, both for the writing of history and for the events of the mid-century themselves, has been much disputed. What is clear is that the political upheavals of our period provoked a wave of remarkable and original writing, stimulated by the authors' sense that they had helped to shape the events they were describing.[2]

From the start of the Renaissance in Europe, humanist scholars with an impassioned commitment to reviving Classical learning had paid particular attention to history-writing.[3] In the Greek writers Polybius and Thucydides, the Romans Livy and Sallust, they found an intellectual coherence and stylistic vividness that they felt to be lacking in the medieval year-by-year chronicles of secular or religious history. They wanted to go beyond the bare facts to the human passions and motivations that had informed them and the underlying causes. Humanist histories like Sir Thomas More's *History of Richard III* (1543) and George Buchanan's *History of Scotland* (1582) might go well beyond their sources to imagine how the leading agents might have spoken and acted, blurring the boundaries between history and fiction: what counted was the general insight into human behaviour that a particular story could convey. This more 'literary' approach was complemented by an emerging school of antiquarian historians such as John Leland (c. 1503–52) and Sir William Dugdale (1605–86) who devoted themselves to broadening the evidential base of history by compiling manuscript and printed evidence. The great Tudor compilations of chronicles by Edward Hall (1548) and Raphael Holinshed (1577) eclectically brought together passages from humanists like More and Buchanan and a huge range of texts and documents, providing a great diversity of approaches to history to a growing reading public.

The revival of Classical scholarship in the early modern period often had a radical edge, combining textual criticism with sharp political criticism of traditional political and religious institutions. Machiavelli's *Discourses* on Livy (translated into English in 1636) were strongly republican, and there was an antityrannical thrust in More's and Buchanan's histories. Milton was true to that tradition in a letter ridiculing chronicles of the victories of princes: 'For what is so remarkable if strong horns spring forth in the land of mutton-heads which can powerfully butt down cities and towns?' (*CPW*, VII:493). For the more radical Classicists, hierarchy and tyranny in state and church had produced a corruption of language: the independent vigour of the language of the forum gave way to the lazy and flattering parroting of superiors' ideas. Protestant scholars like John Foxe (1516–87) who began to explore Anglo-Saxon history helped to create a rather comparable, home-grown myth of a culture of pure religion and civil liberty which became eclipsed by Roman idolatry and Norman tyranny.

The new historiography did not always have such radical effects, however.[4] In a society where custom and respect for elders still carried such weight, antiquarian research could heighten esteem for an idealized 'ancient constitution' from which it would be perilous to depart. This model was politically ambiguous: both sides in the Civil War were to present themselves as defending the ancient constitution, from the encroachments of a usurping Parliament or a tyrannical ruler. Such ambiguity led radical elements on both sides to wish to break away from constitutional arguments based on histor-ical precedent. It was, however, very hard to separate political debate in the period from debates about the true meaning of English history.

The historical 'revolution' is sometimes seen as an aspect of secularization, moving away from a belief in direct divine intervention in history towards 'civil history'. Such a claim is too simple. Defenders of the Reformation saw that momentous event as a sign that God was intervening more directly in history as the last days approached. New, politicized readings of the Book of Revelation identified Biblical prophecies with contemporary political events. Many Protestants believed that God had shown especial favour towards the English people, a belief that informed Foxe's richly documented history of the English martyrs[5] and was also transmitted by Holinshed's chronicles. That apocalyptic vision fuelled the enthusiasm of the Puritan reformers of the 1640s, for whom the presence of the Holy Spirit in their everyday life was as if proved on their pulses.[6] We might, then, expect to find historians on the Parliamentary side emphasizing that the Civil War was really a war of religion – an interpretation that has been advanced by several recent 'revisionist' historians.[7] As we shall see, however, providential inter-pretations always mingled with more secular paradigms; for Parliament's historians, this was to a considerable degree a war for freedom, and even, for some, contained an element of social revolution.

In looking at the impact of the Revolution on historical writing we need to consider not just the content but the social and political context of the writings. When earlier historians of England came up to the present, they were inhibited by political sensitivity: there were mysteries of state into which a mere subject must not pry. The Revolution changed that situation. The introduction to Bulstrode Whitelocke's *Memorials*, a chronicle compiled by a leading Parliamentarian, claimed that with the collapse of Stuart power 'the State cabinet was laid open'; under a republic, 'where the Counsels are all publickly canvassed and debated', it was easier to tell the whole story.[8] With the widening of the public sphere in this period,[9] the people were being encouraged to look on themselves as agents in making and writing history, rather than as clients of their social superiors. As early as 1645, John Corbet, a Puritan lecturer in Gloucester, was able to narrate his city's role in the war with a careful sociological analysis, identifying the 'middling sort' as the chief agent of the cause of liberty. His narrative was also theoretically self-conscious, drawing on Francis Bacon's *De Augmentis Scientiarum*[10] to explain why a local perspective might reveal truths that would be missed in the larger pattern of a national history.[11] For all his local concerns, however, Corbet believed that the issues of the war were universal. Though civil wars were tragic, yet it was still a 'felicity' for Parliament's forces to be 'engaged for the highest interests in this life, which will exalt them, whatever the successe be . . . The Action of these times transcends the Barons Warres, and those tedious discords betweene the houses of *Yorke* and *Lancaster*, in as much as it is undertaken upon higher Principles, and carried on to a nobler end, and effects more universall' (sig. A2v). Corbet can be linked with that confident and articulate civic culture whose emergence in early modern England has been traced by Markku Peltonen.[12]

As the Revolution became more radical, pamphlets by Levellers and other radical groups appealed to Roman and English history, though they also showed themselves ready to depart from precedent when they thought it necessary.[13] At the same time, there was a heightened interest in autobiography and personal writing. Humanism's emphasis on individual motive had helped to encourage memoirs of an individual's contribution to public affairs. Now Puritanism encouraged acute religious introspection, persuading even individuals low down the social hierarchy that their lives formed crucial parts of a providential divine narrative.[14]

The Revolution had consequences for national historiography. The traditional chronicles had arguably encouraged a sense of national identity,[15] but however broad the social range of individual sections, they were structured around the reigns of monarchs, and thus tied in the nation's story to that of particular dynasties. With the fall of the monarchy in 1649, we find the brief emergence of national chronicles in which a specifically English identity came to the fore.[16] The new Republic had scant respect for Scottish or Irish institutions, but in those countries the breakdown of the old unitary state did have an impact on historiography. English Republicans recycled Buchanan's *History* to urge the Scots to be true to their radical heritage, while in a work like Sir Richard Belling's history of the Catholic Irish Confederacy we find new political institutions generating a new historiography.[17]

May, Harrington, Milton and Ludlow

Radical humanist historiography left a mark on the first major Parliamentarian account of the war's origins and early progress. This was commissioned by Parliament from the poet Thomas May (1595–1650), and had something of the caution and guardedness of an official history. May, though, had earlier translated a key Roman republican text, Lucan's anti-tyrannical epic the *Pharsalia*, which versified Livy's history, and he did give a certain Roman flavouring to the history. Like Lucan, he presents the cause of liberty as the underdog, threatened by growing encroachments of royal power, which May traces back to the succession of the Stuart dynasty in 1603; though the work was published in 1647, he ended the story not with Parliament's final victory but only with the victory at Newbury in 1643, which emerges as a providential delivery after near-disaster. May frequently gives the Parliamentarians a Roman colouring by comparisons with classical heroes in their struggle against growing imperial power. Like 'the lower sort of people' who fought with Brutus and Cassius, Parliament's main supporters are those without aristocratic privilege or courtly office, and thus ready to put the public good before 'private interest'.[18] Here May was probably drawing on grassroots local histories like Corbet's.

In 1650 May published an abbreviation and sequel taking the story down to the execution of Charles I in 1649. His death in September 1650 provoked Andrew Marvell's biting satire 'Tom May's Death', which censured his Roman parallels as failing to recognize 'How ill the Measures of these States agree' (*P&L*, 1:96). This was unjust: May was well aware of the differences between Rome and England, and his polemical brief in 1647 was not the discrediting but the reform of the constitution. In the Roman analogy cited above, May leaves it to the reader to decide whether 'the parallel will in some measure fit this occasion or not'. Even the continuation is distinctly muted in touching on the execution of Charles I.

That event, however, could arouse criticism as much because it was not republican enough as because it had put an end to kingship. It had resulted from a military *coup d'état* effected in December 1648 through Pride's Purge, rather than any clear indication of the people's will; torn by internal divisions, the Republic lasted only four years before being displaced by Cromwell's Protectorate, and was seen by the most enthusiastic Classical republican, James Harrington (1611–77), as a botched compromise between older forms of government and a truly grounded republican constitution. Harrington drew a sharp contrast between the 'ancient prudence' of the Classical republics and the 'modern prudence' that had emerged with the collapse of republican institutions under the Roman Empire and then with the union of political and religious institutions that began under the Emperor Constantine and continued in the Anglican church. His utopian fantasy *The Commonwealth of Oceana* (1656) gave a pioneering sociological analysis of English history in which he claimed that the decline in influence and landed power of the ancient aristocracy had made the long-term survival of the monarchy impossible, and imagined Cromwell as recognizing this truth and founding a new republic. Outside the realm of fantasy, however, the Protectorate proceeded to twist and turn between semi-republican and semi-monarchical tendencies. It was very hard for an aspiring historian to set out to trace the genealogy of regimes whose status was so problematical.

We have already seen signs of unease in May's handling of his subject. Similar unease can be found even in one of the most enthusiastic supporters of the regicide, John Milton (1608–74). As with other Puritans and Republicans, the more radical the programme for the future, the more disenchanted a view one was likely to take of the English past. In his first prose tract, *Of Reformation*, Milton had satirized the 'antiquitarians', the devotees of an ancient constitution who liked to trace back an unbroken tradition in church and state from early times (*CPW*, 1:541). For Milton, that unity of church and state had only stifled the true faith. In the early phases of the Revolution, he expressed great confidence in the people's capacity to make up for lost time, notably in his stirring evocation of Revolutionary London in *Areopagitica*, which combines humanist and apocalyptic themes (*CPW*, II:553–5). The divisions of the cause in the later 1640s, however, disconcerted Milton still more than May, and he began work on a *History of Britain* in which his earlier humanist expansiveness gave way to a terse, disillusioned plainness. Insofar as this held a message for the present, it was a bleak one: from legendary times onward, the British had repeatedly become corrupt and each time there was an opportunity for creating new, reformed institutions, they failed to do so. In a section dealing with such a failure after the fall of Rome, Milton digressed at length into parallels with the state of contemporary England, complaining that, while the people had shown martial virtues in the Civil War, they had yet shown no signs of the civil virtues necessary for a good republic (*CPW*, v:449–51). Scholars are still unsure when the 'Digression' was composed,[19] but it is clear that although Milton was ready to defend the Republic of 1649 in his public capacity, on a longer view he was almost as unsure as Marvell whether the measures of the English state could ever be brought to agree with those of Rome.

Milton's worst fears were borne out by the Restoration of 1660, when the English people voluntarily returned to the Egyptian bondage of monarchy. For Republicans this was a nightmare period, not least because for a brief moment in 1659, when the Republic's Parliament was returned to power, it had seemed that there might be an opportunity for a lasting republican settlement. Only at a very late stage did the return of Charles II come to seem inevitable: it was as if the apocalyptic scheme of history had suddenly been wrenched out of gear. One of the most vivid accounts of the period leading up to the Restoration comes from Edmund Ludlow (1617?–92), a Republican who went into exile in 1660 and composed an extensive vindication of his cause. In dealing with the events of 1660, Ludlow tells how he became transformed from a statesman to a fugitive in the space of a few weeks, as the republican party fell apart; people began 'to prosecute a personall interest before the publique' and the result was a Babel-like 'confusion of language'. Ludlow's humanist-republican ideal of a common, non-courtly language has collapsed, and he fears that this is a sign of divine punishment – though he never loses faith in an eventual millennial deliverance. That apocalyptic faith already seemed dated by the late seventeenth century, when the *Memoirs* were edited by the freethinker John Toland. Only when part of the original manuscript came to light fairly recently was it possible, with the aid of Blair Worden's brilliant detective work, to understand Ludlow's original purposes.[20]

Lucy Hutchinson

Toland may have made Ludlow look more secular and 'modern' than he really was, but he was certainly willing to use a secular language of 'interest'. For all their Protestant zeal, most Puritans believed that the Civil War was more than a war of religion, and May had even argued that Parliament had damaged its cause by placing too much emphasis on religious factors (*History*, 1:115–19). For a particularly interesting and complex statement of that position, we can turn to one of the period's leading woman writers, Lucy Hutchinson (1620–81). Her husband John, a Nottinghamshire Parliamentarian who had signed Charles I's death warrant, had recanted his republicanism in 1660, earning the disgust of Ludlow and other Parliamentarians. In 1663, however, he was arrested on suspicion of involvement in a republican plot, and he died in prison in 1664. His widow was already an experienced writer, and she had compiled a lengthy history of her husband's political and military experiences as Governor of Nottingham Castle. After his death she resolved to vindicate his memory with a laudatory biography.

Hutchinson believed as fervently as Ludlow in the second coming of Christ; yet millennialism is not the only element of the biography. She sets her husband's life story in the wider context of the English people's long-term struggles for civil liberty. Like Corbet, she is ready to see the war as the cause of the middling sort – though she also emphasizes the social gulf that divided her and her husband from the ordinary citizens of Nottingham. She locates John Hutchinson in a small, closely knit enclave south and east of Nottingham where the gentry had enough common solidarity to resist the court; his virtue can be traced back to a lineage which had always resisted great wealth, 'as if there had been an Agrarian law in the family' as prescribed by Harrington.[21] Lucy Hutchinson's impressive humanist education accorded with Hobbes' stereotype of the classicizing republican. She and her husband were close friends of the leading constitutional architect of the 1649 Republic, Henry Ireton, who according to Clarendon was 'a scholar, conversant . . . in all that learning which had expressed the greatest animosity and malice against regal government' (HR, v:265, 297). In introducing autobiographical elements into her husband's story, describing how her husband courted her because of her skill as a writer (Memoirs, pp. 46–52), she draws attention to the process by which the work came to be written: like Corbet, she takes pride in the way her circle can represent itself in writing.

Hutchinson's main source for her narrative of national politics was May's History; but she drew on him far from slavishly, telling her children, her first readers, that he had been too indulgent to the King, and offering a different account of the causes of the war. May had begun his analysis with the reign of Elizabeth, who had 'woven the interest of her own State so inseparably into the cause of Religion it selfe, that it was hard to overthrow one without the ruine of the other' (History, 1:3). This, May asserted, was a source of strength to her because she favoured the cause of Protestantism; but the Stuarts had wrongly come to believe that they were better served by an alliance with religious reaction, following James' aphorism: 'No bishop, no King'. May remains within a mainstream Protestant view that a godly magistrate was the best means of protecting the reformed faith against a return to Popery. In analysing Protestant politics in terms of 'interest', May follows the Huguenot theorist the Duc de Rohan. He is convinced that royal interest and the Protestant religion are in principle compatible: when the Stuarts intrigued with continental Catholic monarchs, they were acting against their own interests (History, 1:6).

Hutchinson is not so sure, and her doubts emerge in her striking reworking of May's phrasing: 'When the dawn of the Gospel began to break upon this isle, after the dark midnight of Papacy, the morning was more cloudy here than in other places by reason of the state interest, which was mixing and working it self into the interest of religion, and which in the end quite wrought it [i.e. religion] out' (*Memoirs*, p. 57). Though her analysis is not entirely consistent, from the beginning she is sceptical of May's rather bland synthesis of Protestant and regal interests. She traces the causes of the war back beyond Elizabeth's reign, to the Reformation under Henry VIII. Here she is turning from May to Harrington, for whom the interest of kingship is ultimately incompatible with the interest of the people, who gain new power with the transfers of land at the Reformation.

Hutchinson varies from Harrington as well, however. He had written of the Reformation: 'Nor was there anything now wanting unto the destruction of the throne but that the people, not apt to see their own strength, should be put to feel it, when a prince, as stiff in disputes as the nerve of monarchy was grown slack, received that unhappy encouragement from his clergy which became his utter ruin.'[22] To Hutchinson, the people were left 'only to expect [wait for] an opportunity to resume their power into their own hands, which, had not the different interests of religion divided them among themselves and thereby prolonged the last gasps of expiring monarchy, they had long since exercised it in a free commonwealth' (*Memoirs*, p. 61). Harrington stresses the role of religious reaction in provoking the people into seeking freedom; for Hutchinson, more painfully, the Protestant zeal and apocalyptic enthusiasm which she herself shares may become enemies to freedom. Hers is a providential history only in a very complex sense. The factional conflicts of the Revolutionary period had brought home to her very forcefully that it was hard any longer to speak of a single 'Protestant interest', that some of the fiercest conflicts had involved groups which each claimed to speak for that interest. From the time of the Anabaptist risings in the 1530s, the most zealous defenders of Protestantism had actually undermined civil liberty by provoking political reaction. For Hutchinson, religious reformation would only serve the common interest when it was united with the secular public interest, and this was very hard to achieve. Cromwell might have advanced liberty of conscience, but only at the cost of undermining Parliamentary government. Like Ludlow, in her account of the calamitous events of 1659–60 she shows the quest for a common language collapsing into a Babel. And yet, by taking a very long view, she is able to present a rather less despairing impression of the English people than Milton: they are not wanting in passion for both religious and civil liberty, and one day their difficult negotiations may be resolved.

Edward Hyde, Earl of Clarendon

The defeat of Hutchinson's cause had stimulated a sharper analysis than May had been able to produce in a moment of victory. In a strange way the situation of defeated Republicans like Ludlow and Hutchinson mirrors that of the greatest historian on the Royalist side, Edward Hyde, Earl of Clarendon (1609–74). Clarendon's *History of the Rebellion* was written in two successive stages of defeat and exile. He had served as a propagandist and councillor to the King during the Civil War. In 1646, learning of May's commission for a history, he had begun work on a Royalist retort. He soon realized, however, that he could not write honestly without undermining Royalist morale, which was in any case too low at this stage of defeat for easy repairing. The series of crushing reversals for the Royal cause in 1648–9 led him to break off work for many years. Clarendon did, however, have faith that the English would eventually restore the monarchy, and he offered his services to the young Charles II in exile in the 1650s. He seemed to be vindicated by the Restoration of 1660, when he became Lord Chancellor. By 1667, however, he was again in exile, having alienated a coalition of enemies to his right and his left. Separated from his official papers, he set to work to vindicate himself in the more personal form of an autobiography. When those papers eventually arrived, Hyde returned to his 1640s manuscripts and revised them by inserting or substituting passages from the autobiography.

The result was a work which is remarkably variable in levels of composition, often juxtaposing accounts of the same events written more than twenty years apart and fusing the original first-person voice with the third-person voice of the autobiography. At different phases of composition he had muted or intensified his criticisms of Charles and the Royalists according to his expectations of publication. The passages dating from 1667–71, written largely from memory, often lose in accuracy what they may gain in vividness. Only in the later account are we told that it was 'a very stormy and tempestuous day' when the King first set up his standard at Nottingham, and that a strong wind blew it down: the atmosphere is right for the sense of foreboding Clarendon wishes to convey, but the standard actually blew down a little later.[23] The autobiography as he initially conceived it has never been published as a whole, though it appeared from 1759 onward in a series of editions which omitted the lengthy passages reused in the *History*. W. Dunn Macray's standard edition of the *History* (1888) prints parallel passages from earlier and later versions, which makes it very hard to follow the thread of the narrative. The easiest way in is through G. Huehns' volume of selections (1978), though we thus lose the work's semi-epic scale.

Some of the best-known passages were written late: the affectionate evocations of the social and intellectual world of the 1630s, when Clarendon as a young lawyer had associated with a remarkable group of friends, from the ageing Ben Jonson to the young intellectual Lucius Cary, Viscount Falkland, whom he recalls in mellow character-sketches (*LC*, 1:28–56). These figures represented for him an ideal in which the intellectual independence of Renaissance humanism had combined with antiquarian scholarship to blend into a discourse of loyalty to the traditional institutions of the church and the 'ancient constitution' of the state. His sketches of his friends build into an effect he considered particularly original, a character of a whole historical epoch (*HR*, III:232; *Selections*, p. 7). Personal and political nostalgia went together: in the 1630s the traditional constitution had attained such an exquisite balance between the rival claims of liberty and unity that England in the decade before the Civil War enjoyed 'the greatest calm, and the fullest measure of felicity that any people in any age for so long time together have been blessed with' (*HR*, 1:93; *Selections*, p. 78).

Clarendon is, then, at one with modern 'revisionists' in finding that the Civil War was far from inevitable: in a hit at May, he ridicules the idea of tracing the causes back before the 1630s. Like the revisionists, however, he then has some difficulty in explaining why it happened at all. At the start of the history he ascribes it to a series of 'accidents, not capable of being contrived', with individual vices and blindnesses serving as 'so many atoms contributing jointly to this mass of confusion now before us' (*HR*, 1:3–4; *Selections*, p. 3). Yet a universe governed entirely by accident was not something that Clarendon, as a pious Christian, could finally embrace. There had, he conceded, been many problems in the period of Charles' personal rule, but in themselves they had been eminently soluble. Some of the King's councillors had shown disrespect for the traditional constitution, justifying absolutist tendencies by the plea of necessity, and had thus inflamed understandable anxieties amongst the political nation (*HR*, III:86; *Selections*, p. 229).

To explain why such a constitutional problem then became a disaster, Clarendon turned to the idea of an opportunistic conspiracy by a tiny group of manipulators. In a vicious spiral, revolution feeds on itself as the subversives, Iago-like, gradually push their destructiveness as they find how easy it is to play upon men 'whose minds were in suspense and shaken, as when foundations are dissolved' (*HR*, 1:568; *Selections*, p. 159). In successive revisions he greatly amplified the 'characters'. Short prose sketches of social types had become popular in the seventeenth century,[24] and Hutchinson enlivened her narrative with some sharply satirical characters of her husband's enemies. Clarendon's characters are built on a larger scale, laying out successive dimensions of an individual before summing up with a pithy closing formulation. In his portraits of the Parliamentarian leaders such as

John Hampden, John Pym, Lord Saye & Sele, and Sir Henry Vane, consistent features emerge. They are 'reserved', tending to bottle up their political emotions until they become malign rather than voicing them in ways that might responsibly counsel the King. They cut themselves off from the traditions of the church and become enclosed in private religious fanaticisms. Rather as Richard III emerges as arch-manipulator from the successive stages of Shakespeare's first tetralogy, so does Clarendon portray Oliver Cromwell as the climax of the Revolution, giving him one of his most memorable, and ambivalent, characters:

> he could never have done half that mischieve without great parts of courage and industry and judgment. And he must have had a wonderful understanding in the natures and humours of men, and as great a dexterity in the applying them, who from a private and obscure birth, (though of a good family,) without interest of estate, alliance or friendships, could raise himself to such a height, and compound and knead such opposite and contradictory tempers, humours, and interests, into a consistence that contributed to his designs and to their own destruction; whilst himself grew insensibly powerful enough to cut off those by whom he had climbed, in the instant that they projected to demolish their own building . . . In a word, as he had all the wickednesses against which damnation is denounced and for which hell-fire is prepared, so he had some virtues which have caused the memory of some men in all ages to be celebrated; and he will be looked upon by posterity as a brave bad man.
>
> (*HR*, vi:91, 97; *Selections*, pp. 355, 358)

('[O]f a good family' indicates Clarendon's uneasy recognition that Cromwell's kinship ties did not quite fit into his paradigm of the alienated, isolated radical.)

Clarendon does not, however, place all the blame on the Parliamentarian leaders. He had after all supported their criticisms of the King in the early stages of the Long Parliament. Though he soon became alarmed enough at the prospect of Parliamentary absolutism to go over to the King, he now found himself involved in a struggle against renewed absolutist tendencies amongst the King's advisers. Clarendon insisted that the King would win most support by presenting himself as the champion of the traditional constitution against a clique of Puritan extremists; he should not lay himself open to the charge of being an extremist himself. As the war continued, he held to this position, making himself unpopular with the high-flying 'cavaliers' who placed winning the battle above constitutional niceties. Here is his verdict on two such cavaliers, Lord George Goring and Henry Wilmot, Earl of Rochester (in whom readers will note an anticipation of his more celebrated son John):

Wilmot loved debauchery, but shut it out from his business; never neglected that, and rarely miscarried in it. Goring had a much better understanding, and a sharper wit, (excepting in the very exercise of debauchery, and then the other was inspired,) a much keener courage, and presentness of mind in danger: Wilmot discerned it farther off, and because he could not behave himself so well in it, commonly prevented [anticipated], or warily declined it; and never drank when he was within distance of an enemy: Goring was not able to resist the temptation, when he was in the middle of them, nor would decline it, to obtain a victory. (*HR*, III:444; *Selections*, p. 276)

Both men, in different ways, abuse their 'wit'; in neither does wit become transformed into serious counsel that can intelligently shape royal policy. The passions drive the head, and disaster ensues. Quite apart from the fact that he was a non-combatant, then, it is not surprising that Clarendon's narrative should show more interest in constitutional declarations, in whose composition he was directly involved, than in the fluctuations of the war, where despite his best efforts he was hindered by a shortage of sources. Even Lucy Hutchinson, whose sex precluded her from direct involvement in battle, sometimes gives a more vivid portrayal of the details of warfare (*Memoirs*, pp. 146–7, 201–4). It is with some relief that Clarendon turns from his narrative of the siege of Gloucester to a long elegiac character of one of the battle's victims, his friend Viscount Falkland (*HR*, III:178–90; *Selections*, pp. 49–61).

Clarendon's character-sketches are so compelling that it may take an effort to remember how partial they can be. His attacks on the Royalist war leaders, it has been argued, fail to recognize the practical constraints they faced.[25] His sketches of the Parliamentary leaders lack a crucial dimension, for he has no feeling for the religious vision, the powerful sense of a progressive revelation of the Holy Spirit, that inspired the leading Puritans. He was uneasy with the extent to which that Spirit could cut across traditional social as well as religious hierarchies. The Parliamentarians for whom he has most respect are the aristocrats such as the Earl of Manchester, of whom he writes in a striking phrase that he 'loved his country with too unskilful a tenderness' (*HR*, II:545; *Selections*, p. 204). Patriotism, for Clarendon, is a matter of skill as well as raw emotion, and if he fails to despair of the political nation it is because he believes so many people were unskilful rather than malign. As he proceeds further down the hierarchy, however, his sympathies narrow, and he stresses the crude violence that erupts when the masses interfere in politics. He differs from some modern revisionists, and agrees with political adversaries, in insisting on the revolutionary incursion of the 'middling sort' into power.[26] We can hear the very voice of such a revolution, at least as it struck opponents, in Clarendon's account of the 'pert, shrill, undismayed accent' with which the citizens of Gloucester replied to the King's demand for surrender (*HR*, 1:133). There is a huge gulf here between Clarendon and John Corbet, the colleague and chronicler of those citizens. As for the participation of women, Clarendon frequently expressed his dismay at their growing political influence.[27]

Religion certainly mattered deeply for Clarendon, who could use providential explanations as eloquently as any Puritan,[28] but he never lost sight of its secular dimensions. Hierarchy in the state was inextricably bound up with hierarchy in the church: by this association, political power became ultimately infused with a divine legitimacy, so that rebellion was not just a political disagreement but a sin. The constitution had been 'equally poised' (*LC*, 1:89; *Selections*, p. 31) and any attempt to separate church and state was 'not a shaking (which might settle again) but dissolving foundations'. Once they lost the traditional wisdom of the church, the English fell subject to 'fits of conscience' (*HR*, IV:406; *Selections*, p. 155) and spiralled into a whirlwind of irrational passions. The attacks on the King in printed sermons, even at a very early stage of the war, were such as 'pious men will not look over without trembling' (*HR*, II:320; *Selections*, p. 254). That there might be any kind of political, let alone spiritual, gain in a religious settlement without uniformity, ritual and hierarchy was beyond Clarendon's comprehension; and to that degree, the Revolution remained to him ultimately mysterious – outbursts of incredulity recur throughout his narrative. He never assembles a fully coherent account of its causes. It is perhaps his fear of the consequences of the individual's breaking free from public forms of worship that leaves him so circumspect in religious or other self-revelation in his autobiography; here there is a strong contrast with the personal elements in Hutchinson's narrative, or even with the relatively dry chronicles of Bulstrode Whitelocke.[29] Hence the impression that he was 'one of those rare individuals who possess force of character without force of personality'.[30] Clarendon firmly believed that, once the pre-war church had been properly restored, most former Puritans would be won back to the fold by a mixture of persuasion and coercion. History proved him wrong.

Clarendon's prose style reflects his ideological stance and the difficulty he sometimes had in reconciling it with the course of events. His long sentences with numerous subordinate clauses follow the Latin stylistic model that has been termed 'Ciceronian';[31] but they reflect also his training as a common lawyer, in that sub-clauses are built up so remorselessly that the balance of the sentence as a whole may be lost. Notoriously, the famous opening sentence becomes so entangled in Latinate double negatives that Clarendon's readers have found it hard to disentangle the clauses. However, at a time when the expanding public sphere was encouraging an immediate, colloquial prose style, Clarendon's magisterial periods conveyed a sense of dignity and refusal to compromise. He is less ready to dramatize events than one might expect in a historian steeped in humanist historiography. His diction aims at elevation rather than concreteness: in reworking a source, the bald 'to go into the West' becomes the statelier though wordier 'to attend the service of the West' and active verbs are recast as passive.[32] In revising the *History* he left out events that might seem unseemly, such as exchanges of kisses between the young Charles II and a female friend (*HR*, IV:23).

Thomas Hobbes

To the young Charles II and his favourite wits, Clarendon seemed ponderous and old-fashioned. The younger generation of Royalists responded more eagerly to the self-consciously modern political theory of Thomas Hobbes (1588–1679). As Clarendon went into exile, Hobbes composed his own history of the Revolution, *Behemoth*, on very different principles. The new science, he believed, offered general laws of motion which extended to the political as much as the physical world. He was thus briskly dismissive not only of medieval philosophy but of the humanist idealization of language. In 1628 he had himself published a translation of Thucydides, offering it as a warning of the dangers of a drift to republicanism. As the political crisis escalated, however, Hobbes reacted sharply against humanist scholarship as a 'Trojan horse' for dangerous republican ideas.[33] In the mid-century outpouring of rhetoric and sermonizing, stability in politics as in language had been endangered: Parliament's 'artifice' had defined loyal service of the King as treachery (p. 67). Hobbes' remedy to this crisis was not tradition – he had no respect for the ancient constitution of state or church – but prescription: only an absolute sovereign power could teach 'the science of *just* and *unjust*' (p. 39), fixing meanings in a stable way and thus inducing social cohesion. This power should have absolute control over church as well as state – Hobbes' hostility to any degree of autonomy for the clergy shocked many contemporaries, and confined the work to an underground manuscript circulation until its surreptitious publication after his death.

His politics is reflected in his style. *Behemoth* is in fact cast in the quintessentially humanist form of a dialogue, rather than as a set of semi-scientific propositions; but at a deeper level its movement is ahistorical and deductive: 'A' has worked out the real truth and imparts it to 'B', whose constant questions spring from a kind of disingenuous common sense. Where humanist rhetoric aims to convey the sense of a mind in the process of reaching for an understanding, Hobbes' terse style lays out conclusions that are already known – albeit stylistically sharpened with his characteristic, subversive wit.

Hobbes, though he can show acute generalized psychological insight, lacks the humanist interest in individual character. As for the humanist preference for the pen over the sword, he insists that once war began, 'papers and declarations must be useless' (pp. 116, 125).

Hobbes' assault on humanism was directed in the first instance at the Republicans; but this last comment was calculated to hit a raw nerve in Clarendon as well; and Clarendon's response to Hobbes brings out his own internal divisions. He taunted Hobbes with hypocrisy for having himself climbed into the Trojan horse by translating Thucydides, a work whose cult of liberty taught the 'Science of Mutiny and Sedition'.[34] Yet he could quote Thucydides to his own purposes, arguing in terms very similar to Hobbes that the Revolution had produced a breakdown of language: the Parliamentary leaders were '"holding" (as Thucydides said of the Athenians) "for honourable that which pleased, and for just that which profited"' (HR, 1:86; Selections, p. 75). Furthermore, in his autobiography Clarendon included a warm tribute both to May's character and to his Lucan translation (LC, 1:31–2). He was anxious to reassure himself that there had been no necessary connection between humanist historical studies and political sedition: May's apostasy was caused by a character flaw, not his study of the Romans.

For Clarendon, it could be said, the republican May and the absolutist Hobbes were mirror images: each had been corrupted by severing contact with a world of shared linguistic experience informed by tradition. Only conversation within institutions that respected traditions, both religious and constitutional, would protect men from arbitrariness in their use both of language and of power. A perfect example was the mystical republican Sir Henry Vane (1613–62), who 'was become (which cannot be expressed by any other language than was peculiar to that time) *a man above ordinances*, unlimited and unrestrained by any rules or bounds prescribed to other men, by reason of his perfection' (HR, VI:148; Selections, pp. 150–1). A language peculiar to a revolutionary time was bound to be flawed; and Hobbes, in his own way, had caught the infection.

There was force in both men's views. Hobbes recognized a radical potential in Classical studies that Hyde's deep conservatism failed to acknowledge. The English Republicans, however, had been too aware of the difficulties of translating from ancient to modern conditions to produce the kind of inspirational history of the Revolution that might have galvanized future generations. May perhaps, and Milton certainly, had the literary ability to have done so; but no such work was produced. Ludlow and Hutchinson were left to chronicle defeat. Clarendon's variety of humanism, by contrast, had been so well naturalized in the English polity that he could see himself as the true defender of the constitution, and bring to his polemical royalism something of the tragic sense of the fragility of liberty that had galvanized his republican adversaries. However, the settlement of the 1630s was never restored; in that sense Clarendon's cause, too, was defeated.

NOTES

1 By Frank S. Fussner, *The Historical Revolution: English Historical Writing and Thought, 1580–1640* (London: Routledge and Kegan Paul, 1962).
2 For a full survey see Royce MacGillivray, *Restoration Historians and the English Civil War* (The Hague: Martinus Nijhoff, 1974).
3 On this see J. G. A. Pocock, *The Machiavellian Moment: Florentine Political Thought and the Atlantic Republican Tradition* (Princeton University Press, 1975).
4 See further J. G. A. Pocock, *The Ancient Constitution and the Feudal Law: A Study in English Historical Thought in the Seventeenth Century*, 2nd edn (Cambridge University Press, 1987).
5 Foxe's immensely influential *Actes and Monuments of these Latter Perillous Dayes, touching Matters of the Church*, published in Latin at Strasbourg in 1559, and in English in 1563, with many subsequent enlarged editions, was popularly known as the *Book of Martyrs*.
6 Blair Worden, 'Politics and Providence in Cromwellian England', *P&P*, 10 (1985), 55–99.
7 See, for example, the section on 'England's Wars of Religion', in John Morrill, *The Nature of the English Revolution* (Harlow: Longman, 1993), pp. 33–175.
8 Bulstrode Whitelocke, *Memorials of the English Affairs* (1682), sig. A2v.
9 See Sharon Achinstein's essay above, pp. 50–68.
10 This was published in 1623, but had appeared in an English version in 1605 as *The Advancement of Learning*.
11 John Corbet, *An Historicall Relation of the Military Government of Gloucester from the Beginning of the Civill Warre* (1645), sig. A3v, pp. 9–10.
12 Markku Peltonen, *Classical Humanism and Republicanism in English Political Thought 1570–1640* (Cambridge University Press, 1995).
13 See R. B. Seaberg, 'The Norman Conquest and the Common Law: The Levellers and the Argument from Continuity', *HJ*, 24 (1981), 791–806.
14 See, on the nature and development of this autobiographical genre, Owen Watkins, *The Puritan Experience* (London: Routledge and Kegan Paul, 1972).
15 See further Richard Helgerson, *Forms of Nationhood: The Elizabethan Writing of England* (University of Chicago Press, 1992).
16 David Norbrook, *Writing the English Republic: Poetry, Rhetoric and Politics, 1627–1660* (Cambridge University Press, 1999), pp. 220, 309.
17 Sir Richard Bellings, *History of the Irish Confederation and the War in Ireland, 1641–1643*, ed. John T. Gilbert, 7 vols. (Dublin: M. H. Gill and Son, 1882–90).
18 Thomas May, *The History of the Parliament of England: which began November the third, M.DC.XL* (1647), III:30.
19 See Nicholas Von Maltzahn, *Milton's 'History of Britain': Republican Historiography in the English Revolution* (Oxford: Clarendon Press, 1991).

20 Edmund Ludlow, *A Voyce from the Watch Tower, Part Five: 1660–1662*, ed. A. B. Worden, Camden 4th ser. 21 (London: Royal Historical Society, 1978), p. 114.
21 Lucy Hutchinson, *Memoirs of the Life of Colonel Hutchinson*, ed. N. H. Keeble (London: Dent, 1995), p. 31.
22 James Harrington, *Political Works*, ed. J. G. A. Pocock (Cambridge University Press, 1977), p. 198.
23 *HR*, II:289–91; G. Huehns (ed.), *Clarendon: Selections from 'The History of the Rebellion' and 'The Life of Himself'* (Oxford University Press, 1978), p. 249.
24 For examples see David Nichol Smith (ed.), *Characters from the Histories and Memoirs of the Seventeenth Century* (Oxford: Clarendon Press, 1918).
25 Ronald Hutton, 'Clarendon's *History of the Rebellion*', *EHR*, 97 (1982), 70–88.
26 Christopher Hill, 'Lord Clarendon and the Puritan Revolution', in his *Puritanism and Revolution* (London: Secker and Warburg, 1958), pp. 199–214.
27 See Martine Watson Brownley, 'The Women in Clarendon's Life and Works', *The Eighteenth Century*, 22 (1981), 153–74.
28 Michael Finlayson, 'Clarendon, Providence and the Puritan Revolution', *Albion*, 22 (1990), 607–32.
29 For an account of this, see Blair Worden, 'The "Diary" of Bulstrode Whitelocke', *EHR*, 108 (1993), 122–34.
30 Martine Watson Brownley, *Clarendon and the Rhetoric of Historical Form* (Philadelphia: University of Pennsylvania Press, 1985), p. 95.
31 See, on this style, Neil Rhodes, *The Power of Eloquence and English Renaissance Literature* (Hemel Hempstead: Harvester Wheatsheaf 1992).
32 Brownley, *Clarendon and Historical Form*, p. 41.
33 Thomas Hobbes, *Behemoth, or The Long Parliament*, ed. Ferdinand Tönnies (University of Chicago Press, 1990), p. 40.
34 Edward Hyde, Earl of Clarendon, *A Brief View and Survey . . . of Mr. Hobbes's Book, Entituled 'Leviathan'* (Oxford, 1676), p. 85.

FURTHER READING

For individual editions of primary texts cited or discussed, please see the notes above.

Brownley, Martine Watson, 'The Women in Clarendon's Life and Works', *The Eighteenth Century*, 22 (1981), 153–74.
   Clarendon and the Rhetoric of Historical Form, Philadelphia: University of Pennsylvania Press, 1985.
Chester, Alan Griffith, *Thomas May: Man of Letters, 1595–1650*, Philadelphia: University of Pennsylvania Press, 1932.
Finlayson, Michael, 'Clarendon, Providence and the Puritan Revolution', *Albion*, 22 (1990), 607–32.
Firth, Katherine R., *The Apocalyptic Tradition in Reformation Britain, 1530–1645*, Oxford University Press, 1979.
Fussner, Frank Smith, *The Historical Revolution: English Historical Writing and Thought, 1580–1640*, London: Routledge and Kegan Paul, 1962.
Helgerson, Richard, *Forms of Nationhood: The Elizabethan Writing of England*, University of Chicago Press, 1992.

Hill, Christopher, 'Lord Clarendon and the Puritan Revolution', in *Puritanism and Revolution*, London: Secker and Warburg, 1958, pp. 199–214.

Hutton, Ronald, 'Clarendon's *History of the Rebellion*', EHR, 97 (1982), 70–88.

Keeble, N. H., '"The Colonel's Shadow": Lucy Hutchinson, Women's Writing, and the Civil War', in Thomas Healy and Jonathan Sawday (eds.), *Literature and the English Civil War*, Cambridge University Press, 1990, pp. 227–47.

MacGillivray, Royce, *Restoration Historians and the English Civil War*, The Hague: Martinus Nijhoff, 1974.

Norbrook, David, *Writing the English Republic: Poetry, Rhetoric and Politics, 1627–1660*, Cambridge University Press, 1999.

    '*Memoirs of the Life of Colonel Hutchinson*', in David Womersley (ed.), *The Blackwell Companion to English Literature from Milton to Blake*, Oxford: Blackwell, forthcoming.

Peltonen, Markku, *Classical Humanism and Republicanism in English Political Thought 1570–1640*, Cambridge University Press, 1995.

Pocock, J. G. A., *The Machiavellian Moment: Florentine Political Thought and the Atlantic Republican Tradition*, Princeton University Press, 1975.

    The Ancient Constitution and the Feudal Law: A Study in English Historical Thought in the Seventeenth Century. A Reissue with a Retrospect, Cambridge University Press, 1987.

Raymond, Joad, *The Invention of the Newspaper: English Newsbooks, 1641–1649*, Oxford: Clarendon Press, 1996.

Seaberg, R. B., 'The Norman Conquest and the Common Law: The Levellers and the Argument from Continuity', HJ, 24 (1981), 791–806.

Smith, Nigel, *Literature and Revolution in England, 1640–1660*, New Haven: Yale University Press, 1994.

Trevor-Roper, Hugh, 'The Great Tew Circle', in *Catholics, Anglicans and Puritans: Seventeenth-Century Essays* (London: Secker and Warburg, 1987), pp. 166–230.

Von Maltzahn, Nicholas, *Milton's 'History of Britain': Republican Historiography in the English Revolution*, Oxford: Clarendon Press, 1991.

Watson, George, 'The Reader in Clarendon's *History of the Rebellion*', RES, 25 (1974) 396–409.

Worden, Blair, 'Providence and Politics in Cromwellian England', P&P, 109 (1985), 55–99.

    'The "Diary" of Bulstrode Whitelocke', EHR, 10 (1993), 122–34.

Wormald, B. H. G., *Clarendon: Politics, Historiography and Religion 1640–1660*, Cambridge University Press, 1951; reissued 1989.

14

NIGEL SMITH

Paradise Lost from Civil War to Restoration

Epics and history

Of all the great literary works produced during the Interregnum and the Restoration, *Paradise Lost* – unquestionably the greatest work of literature in the entire century – is the hardest for us to understand as a product of its political and religious context. This is in part because of its very greatness: after its first printed publication in 1667, Milton's epic quickly became the most imitated poem in the English language, and this remained the case until the end of the nineteenth century. That Milton's subject was ostensibly Biblical and hence 'timeless', especially with regard to the local events of mid seventeenth-century England, helped to form a dominant view that the poet gave up politics with the return of the monarchy, and the failure of Puritan and Republican experiments. Through its popularity, *Paradise Lost* slipped the lease that initially shackled it to history.

The degree to which Milton became a quietist after 1660 is now a matter of dispute among critics, as much as they also debate the extent to which *Paradise Lost* was complete before the same date.[1] What is beyond dispute, however, is that no contemporary of Milton's would have read the poem as unrelated to the events of its own time. This is not least because heroic verse – verse written, like *Paradise Lost*, in conscious and artful imitation of the tradition that stemmed from the ancient epicists of Greece and Rome – was widely understood to address public issues.

Much of the most well-known English heroic poem in Milton's time, Spenser's *The Faerie Queene*, was an exposition of Elizabethan polity. Even ancient poems were thought to have the ability to voice contemporary predicaments. Virgil's *Aeneid* was regarded as the greatest literary achievement in the Classical tradition, and as such it became highly regarded in the literary culture of Renaissance courts: in a sense, their special possession. The overarching theme of renewal – from Aeneas' escape from the sack of Troy, to the foundation of a new Troy in Rome – was consonant with the sense of

6 William Faithorne, engraved frontispiece portrait to Milton's *History of Britain*, 1670.

several European monarchies in the period that they too had reached an apogee of civilization.

By contrast, Virgil's parodist, Lucan, wrote not of mythical but of real wars: the civil war between the Roman republican forces led by Pompey and the army of Julius Caesar. Caesar's triumph was the downfall of the Roman republic, and Lucan's poem appealed strongly to those who found themselves in divided and disharmonious worlds. One influential view is that the history of epic from the ancient world down to the late Renaissance is one of a coupled but double awareness offered by the contrary views of Virgil on the one hand and Lucan on the other.[2]

Learning epic began at school, as Greek and Latin were laboriously digested. It is not surprising to find translations of the *Aeneid* into English in the 1620s and 1630s by schoolmasters. It is equally unsurprising to find a schoolmaster teaching Homer in the 1650s as a warning against anti-monarchical rebellion, as represented by the revolt of the Titans against the Olympian gods.[3] One of the schoolmaster translators of the 1630s happened to be a Puritan, and it is clear that he saw his work as reflecting on the huge conflict between Catholic and Protestant princes that was taking place in contemporary Europe: the Thirty Years' War (1618–48).[4] When the English Civil War broke out, reference to Lucan was widespread among writers on both sides of the main political and religious division.[5] Lucan's martial themes and Republican sentiments, however, made his *Pharsalia* the special property of the Parliamentarians, Republicans and supporters of the Protectorate, while Royalists increasingly clung to Virgil's *Aeneid*, initially as a token of hope for the future in desperate circumstances, and then, notably after the Restoration, as a triumphant vindication of their cause. Charles I revered the *Aeneid*: it must have stood only after the Bible and the Shakespeare folio in his estimation. He is even supposed to have opened a copy of Virgil's poem during the siege of Oxford in 1645 to see Dido's curse (*Aeneid*, IV.615–20) predicting military defeat, the slaughter of his friends and followers, submission to unjust terms of peace, exile and death.[6] Not, we can be sure, what he wanted to see. The great English translations of Virgil in the mid and later seventeenth century are without exception works of monarchist affiliation and celebration, and the translation of and allusion to Lucan, Parliamentarian and even Republican, especially that of Thomas May.[7]

The first readers of *Paradise Lost* knew well that here was a Republican and a Puritan speaking.[8] The poem was read as an extensive critique of the ceremony and spectacle that greeted the return of the monarchy.[9] One of those early readers was Milton's associate and former *protégé* Andrew Marvell, who used the allegory of Sin and Death, in Book II of *Paradise Lost*, as a basis for part of a poetic satire of the administration of Clarendon in 1667.[10] Where Marvell was thereby continuing a tradition of anti-court literature, Dryden contrarily harnessed Miltonic energies in *Absolom and Achitophel* (1681) in order to point up the dangers of rebellion.

That *Paradise Lost* was complex, contradictory even, in the way that it voiced its affiliations, was recognized. The earliest documented responses to the publication of *Paradise Lost*, from the late 1660s, understood that the poem addressed one of the crucial public debates of the time. As the administration of Clarendon faltered under the strain of failure in the Second Dutch War, so religious toleration became a burning issue. Those who supported the cause of the ejected Puritans put pressure on the King and both Houses of Parliament to offer a greater degree of toleration, and to lessen the restrictions of the legislation of 1662. *Paradise Lost* was a map for toleration and a rallying cry for educated Dissenters. Milton was aware of this, and sharpened his stance and appeal in the publications of 1671 (*Paradise Regained* and *Samson Agonistes*) and in the second edition of *Paradise Lost* (1674).

Among the next generation, those who rose to prominence after the Glorious Revolution of 1689, the controversial non-juring bishop Francis Atterbury was sure that the character of Satan represented some great figure from Milton's own time.[11] Across the ocean in the American colonies, *Paradise Lost* was being read, along with Milton's prose, during the debates that led to the foundation of the American Republic and the revolutionary war against Britain. The poem became a paradigm for the understanding of how to protect liberties while guarding against human fallibility.[12]

Epic echoes

Atterbury's interest in character is indicative of the primary level on which most readers would have understood *Paradise Lost* as in some sense a commentary on the Civil War and its aftermath.[13] This is because a very large part of Milton's poem, like all epics, was concerned with acts of persuasive speech by various characters. These acts of rhetoric were understood, in the terms set down by ancient theorists, to embody the ethical stances of the characters themselves.

Milton's prose works leave the reader in no doubt that he learned his republicanism from Greek and Roman writers. He had no time for the imperial vision in ancient texts, and much time for the tradition of civic virtue.[14] Imagine the surprise of a fellow Republican reader of the poem, when, not long after the start of Book I, Satan and the fallen angels begin to talk a language not merely of defeat but of lost liberty. Indeed, they form a 'council' to do so, and they use other terms associated with the political discourse of the Commonwealth during the 1650s. This includes precise reference to Machiavellian vocabulary, which found its first serious usage in England among the ideologues of the Commonwealth.[15] In short, Satan and the rebel angels appear to be republicans. The debate in Book II is concerned with whether to form an empire or a commonwealth for increase (a 1650s way of talking about political economy). This has been seen as Milton's castigation of a policy that had failed, or of republican systems that he felt were too elaborate to work in practice. Mammon proposes 'Hard liberty before the easy yoke / Of servile pomp' (II.256–7), but he is the embodiment of the greed that he is supposedly speaking against. Yet Milton cannot be said to be anti-Republican, since the fallen angels embody and are surrounded by monarchical and tyrannical trappings – none more so than Satan, 'Above his fellows, with monarchal pride / Conscious of highest worth, unmoved thus spake' (II.428–9). This reminds us of Death who wears 'the likeness of a kingly crown' (II.673). And of whom is the council in Hell representative other than those who attend it? The assembly is a perversion of liberty's principles, and the veering between monarchical and republican colourings is meant to perplex the reader, as much as Milton himself was challenged by the transformation from Republic to Protectorate to restored monarchy.

Satan articulating a Parliamentary position is like the poet Abraham Cowley using republican Lucan as a model for a Royalist epic (*The Civil War* (1643)) – a principle of reversal operates. Just so, Milton's epic similes can suggest a counter-logic to the imperialist ideology of Virgil's *Aeneid*, which, after all, told the story of the dispossession of a people by foreign invaders, who proceed to found a future empire that would dominate the known world.[16] But Cowley could not finish his epic because the Royalist victory he supposed did not arrive. Milton completed *Paradise Lost* in his time of defeat by making his epic work by more than mere reversal.

Articulating civil war

The English Civil War, and the campaigns fought in Ireland and Scotland, were, in contemporary terms, not so bloody when compared with the carnage of the Thirty Years' War (1618–48) fought on the continent. This is so even of the unpleasant massacres perpetrated by the New Model Army in Ireland. Like the European wars, the fighting in England was modern, using muskets and artillery, and intermixing cavalry and infantry formations according to the recommendations of contemporary military manuals. However, the first confrontation we see in *Paradise Lost* is the one-to-one combat typical of Classical epic, and associated with the ethos of the champion in the ancient world. Just before the War in Heaven (described by Michael as an 'intestine' (VI.259), i.e., civil, war) is fought, Abdiel smites Satan, who staggers back ten paces, thus making a daunting challenge. The passage echoes Virgil's *Aeneid*, IX.599, 635, and nothing could be more arcane. The initial exchange between the two angelic armies looks at first more like a supernatural version of the Hundred Years' War: 'over head the dismal hiss / Of fiery darts in flaming volleys flew, / And flaming vaulted either host with fire' (VI.212–14). The angelic army, however, is driven by an individual conception of heroic action, as opposed to the later conception of units of troops: 'each on himself relied, /As only in his arm the moment lay / Of victory' (VI.238–40).

Later on, the war takes on a different hue. The womb of nature is ransacked by the rebel angels for 'materials dark and crude, / Of spiritous and fiery spume' (VI.478–9) in order to fashion gunpowder for infernal artillery ('hollow engines long and round / Thick-rammed' (VI.484–5); 'a triple mounted row of pillars laid / On wheels' (VI.572)), from which will issue 'implements to mischief' and 'balls / Of missive ruin' that will dismember the enemy.[17] Satan attacks with his cannon in a formation immediately recognizable as part of early modern warfare: 'in hollow cube / Training his devilish enginery, impaled / On every side with shadowing squadrons deep, / To hide the fraud'(VI.552–5).[18] This attribution of the invention of firearms to the rebel angels, and the havoc they wreak with them (VI.584–607), is met by the angelic army discarding its arms and picking up hills and mountains and even promontories, to hurl back at their foe (VI.637–61). We are in a realm that lies outside history. In the mythical wars of the giants against the Olympian gods, hills were used as missiles, and in some of the Latin poets these wars were supposed to be a return to the confusion of chaos. Milton means us to see here a near ruin of the universe – 'horrid confusion heaped/ Upon confusion rose: and now all heaven / Had gone to wrack, with ruin overspread' (VI.668–70) – had not God sent the Son in his chariot to cast Satan and the rebel angels into Hell. We are, as is often the case in the poem, at the limits of human comprehension. We have been given war in its most archaic, and war in its modern guise, war as legend and war beyond all comprehension, before a deliverance that fuses a Biblical vision and the iconography of apocalypse (VI.824–92).[19] It is no surprise that another early reader of the poem should have felt that *Paradise Lost* made the fighting in Homer and Virgil seem mock-heroic.[20]

At the heart of the war is the invention of gunpowder as well as a swordfight, just as seventeenth-century European wars were fought with steel and powder. The infernal artillery is in fact 'levelled' on the angelic army (VI.591), which of course means 'to aim' but which also refers to the radical democrats of the 1640s.[21] And why does Satan accuse the angels of dancing extravagantly and wildly, instead of negotiating for peace (VI.609–19)? The epic parallel goes back to a moment in Homer's *Iliad* (XVI.617f.) when Aeneas taunts Meriones with dancing to avoid his spear-throw, but, through Satan's eyes, the angelic army looks as the Royalists would have done to the Parliamentarians in the late 1640s. They shirk the inevitable consequences of defeat by immersion in their own decadent courtly culture, and evade the necessity of making a settlement for the kingdom.[22]

Equally telling in the battle parleys, but in another sense and setting, is Abdiel's challenge to Satan. This appears to articulate the position of the Dissenters after 1660: 'I alone / Seemed in thy world erroneous to dissent / From all: my sect thou seest, now learn too late / How few sometimes may know, when thousands err' (VI.145–8). 'Sect' takes our attention away from politics and puts it with religion, when, in the 1640s and 1650s, Puritanism fractured into many various versions of self-governing Protestant confession. The 'Dissenters' were all those Puritans who refused to join the Church of England after the Restoration, and who therefore chose to suffer sometimes severe legal penalties. The Dissenters, Milton among them, claimed to have a more truthful way of reading the Bible than their Anglican opposites.

The work of *Paradise Lost*

Milton's first annotator, Patrick Hume, noted many echoes of ancient epic in *Paradise Lost*, but above all he saw the Bible.[23] Mostly Hume wants Milton to be a Biblical poet, even though his dense allusion to different kinds of Scriptural original and commentary stopped him from playing up Milton's originality. Indeed, Hume was far more ready to see (as later eighteenth-century commentators were not) Milton's faithfulness to Scriptural constructions.

Paradise Lost offers above all else a complete theology, and a heretical one at that. Thereby, it remakes the Bible, even as it is often faithful to the phraseology of the English translations. Many of these positions had been formulated, stated and circulated by Milton during the Civil War and Interregnum years, although sometimes the earlier version was more optimistic. At the heart of *Paradise Lost* is free will theology, articulated by the Father, negatively exemplified in Satan, and painfully exposed as too good for mankind by Adam and Eve:

> Such I created all the ethereal powers
> And spirits, both them who stood and them who failed;
> Freely they stood who stood, and fell who fell.
> Not free, what proof could they have given sincere
> Of true allegiance, constant faith or love,
> Where only what they needs must do, appeared,
> Not what they would?
>
> (III.100–6)

> God left free the will, for what obeys
> Reason, is free, and reason he made right,
> But bid her well beware, and still erect,
> Lest by some fair appearing good surprised
> She dictates false.
>
> (IX.352–5)

Milton had advanced his theology of free will in *Areopagitica* (1644), his famous defence of press freedom and religious toleration. He saw what he said as the centre of a description of reformed, Puritan living, at the heart of which was marriage defined as 'fit conversation', and the almost unrestricted reading of books. *Areopagitica* is a rich fusion of Christian and Classical ideas and sources, not all of which fit consistently together. Milton thought that 'reason' was part and parcel of the word 'heresy', since he understood heresy to derive from the Greek 'prohaeresis', which means 'to reason'. To Milton, heresy thus meant 'to choose' rather than 'that which is forbidden'. In *Paradise Lost*, free will is shown to be deeply problematic: Satan abuses it; Eve is given a more radical version of it than Adam, so that it appears to correspond to the theological position of many 1640s radicals. This position was called antinomianism, the belief that if you have grace, God will always be there to catch you if you fall: 'And what is faith, love, virtue unassayed / Alone, without exterior help sustained?' (IX.335–6). To Eve is given a whole range of experiences that correspond with those of mid seventeenth-century religious enthusiasts: dream visions, solitary communions with nature, the desire to separate from the community in order to fulfil one's personal calling. It is indeed the case that many of these kinds of experience were published by women Puritans.[24] Adam is given the more orthodox line on the relationship between faith and reason, and he turns out to have been right all along. Doesn't he? In fact Adam's instruction in free will theology would have made him look a heretic in the eyes of the dominant Calvinism of most Puritans which held that people were predestined by God to salvation or damnation before they were born.

Milton's second heresy, one that is fundamental to his cosmology, was that God created the universe not out of nothing, as most Christian authorities held, but out of himself. Hell is where God chooses not to be:

> Boundless the deep, because I am who fill
> Infinitude, nor vacuous the space.
> Though I uncircumscribed my self retire,
> And put not forth my goodness, which is free
> To act or not, necessity and chance
> Approach not me, and what I will is fate.

(VII.168–73)

And God is everywhere that is not Hell. The universe is an extension of him: God's flesh. When we exercise free will, we are exercising a part of God. The unfallen Adam and Eve learn that if they remain unfallen (and here, Milton wants us to draw a parallel between the innocent first parents and regenerate Christians in his time), they will in time become like angels, by ascending up the scale of being. There is no distinction between flesh and spirit for Milton, but rather a continuity of matter that is more or less refined, depending on its relative distance from the Father (V.469–91). Such a view is called 'monism', and with it Milton held the further heretical view that since matter and spirit were coterminous, the soul did not leave the body after death. Rather, it remained with the body until the general resurrection at the Last Judgement. This was the position known as mortalism.[25]

All these views are carefully mapped out in the course of *Paradise Lost*. Thus, in the creation scenes of Book VII, God's being is divided between a commanding voice (call it the personal God) and an axiomatic supreme being within whom is chaos, the unordered matter from which the world is made. The terminology used to describe the creation suggests many things, some of which will be discussed below. What is clear, however, is that the creation of living beings on the earth is rendered through gendered terms. Once created, mother nature is a pregnant ocean ('The earth was formed, but in the womb as yet / Of waters, embryon immature involved' (VII.276–7)). who waits for the permission of God's command before bringing forth dry land, flora and fauna: 'The earth obeyed, and straight / Opening her fertile womb teemed at a birth / Innumerous living creatures' (VII.453–5). The creation thus reinscribes the gender relationships that were seen earlier in the poem when the theology of free will was explained, and mankind first encountered by the reader ('He for God only, she for God in him' (IV.299)). That is to say that all the male figures in the poem are 'authors' (Satan and Adam) and repetitions of God, while the females (Sin, Eve and the earth) are made from male figures, and have a fecund, wondering intelligence that must be regulated unless a deviation from male authority is to be risked.

When the order of the universe is explained by Raphael to Adam, harmony and balance remain firmly present until Adam's relationship with Eve, or rather, Adam's responses to Eve, are explored in a dialogue towards the end of Book VIII. In Book IV, Milton had fiercely asserted that Paradisal marriage involved sexual intercourse (IV.741–57). Although he emphasized in this passage God's injunction to mankind to increase, the connection with the purpose of marriage as a 'fit conversation', in which there was (through monism) a meeting of minds and bodies, is evident. Now, in Book 8, Adam confesses his sexual desire for Eve, as a force that destabilizes his rationality and hence his capacity to exercise free will. He is in fact confused:

> here passion first I felt,
> Commotion strange, in all enjoyments else
> Superior and unmoved, here only weak
> Against the charm of beauty's powerful glance.
>
> (VIII.530–3)

Raphael enjoins Adam to think of higher things, to show Eve that he, Adam, is her master, and to remember that sexual pleasures are the part of existence that man shares with the beasts; but these injunctions are undermined by Raphael's description of the higher 'intercourse' in heaven where reason meets desire in a utopia of closeness, a description which is abruptly foreclosed:

> Let it suffice thee that thou know'st
> Us happy, and without love no happiness.
> Whatever pure thou in the body enjoy'st
> (And pure thou wast created) we enjoy
> In eminence, and obstacle find none
> Of membrane, joint, or limb, exclusive bars:
> Easier than air with air, if spirits embrace,
> Total they mix, union of pure with pure
> Desiring; nor restrained conveyance need
> As flesh to mix with flesh, or soul with soul.
> But I can now no more.
>
> (VIII.620–30)

This is the high point of Milton's heretical vision: a reconstruction of the body in the perceived order of creation. The vision originated in a fundamental re-conception of domestic relations that Milton saw as a crucial part of reform in the 1640s.

The poem builds up to this glorious, brief moment through a number of moments earlier in the poem. Satan's body is severed by Michael during the first part of the war in Heaven: 'in half cut sheer, nor stayed, / But with swift wheel reverse, deep entering shared / All his right side; then Satan first knew pain' (VI.325–7). Being of 'ethereal substance', however, Satan's body soon unites, unlike the melting bodies of the defeated Romans in their armour in Lucan's *Pharsalia* (IX.761–838). We are to understand pain in its mental dimensions: a condition of disempowerment and hopelessness:

> we find
> Against unequal arms to fight in pain,
> Against unpained, impassive; from which evil
> Ruin must needs ensue; for what avails
> Valour or strength, though matchless, quelled with pain,
> Which all subdues.   (VI.453–8)

This is the kind of mental anguish that we find imparted by the physical enormities of the birth of Sin and the birth of Death from Sin in Book II.

Sin leaping from Satan's head divides him as a being, and viewing a part of himself with self-love can only incestuously bond: 'such joy thou took'st / With me in secret, that my womb conceived / A growing burden' (II.765–7).

This happened just before and during the war in Heaven. The result was the monstrous birth of Death, a distorting violation of Sin's body, and a double violation when Death rapes his mother, only to bring forth endlessly a multitude of noisy monsters who ceaselessly gnaw her bowels. Milton gives us in allegorical terms the trauma delivered by birth (but rendered as Death) on the female body (defined as Sin). The dialogue at the end of Book VIII uneasily shows a way out of this gloomy vision. However, the account of the Fall that follows in Book IX reasserts feminine vulnerability, and inserts pain into human experience, not least in Adam's interior monologue, where he realizes that he must fall with Eve, since he is utterly continuous with her being:

> Should God create another Eve, and I
> Another rib afford, yet loss of thee
> Would never from my heart; no, no, I feel
> The link of nature draw me: flesh of flesh,
> Bone of my bone thou art, and from thy state
> Mine never shall be parted, bliss or woe.

> (IX.911–16)

The politics of interpretation

It is a famous point of interpretation in *Paradise Lost* that everything in the poem that is beyond the reach of fallen human ken (all things connected with Heaven, Hell and Eden) is narrated in a language of accommodation: rendered in terms that fallen human readers will understand. Raphael in particular explains the problem at length: 'what surmounts the reach / Of human sense, I shall delineate so' (V.571–2). In effect, much of the poem is a metaphor for that which we cannot possibly understand. It is here that Milton uses metaphors of kingship to represent divine characters and action (even a feudal kind of kingship), while abhorring earthly kingship after the Fall and tyranny in Hell.

In this way too, the poem demands that we make choices as we interpret the narrative. To cast, for instance, unfallen things in fallen terms invites a double response. On the one hand, the unfallen world appears fallen before the Fall has occurred; on the other, since we understand the technique that Milton is using, we accept that we are, in a sense, looking beyond the horizon of the knowable. Our awareness of the poem points in two contrary directions at once. We look down at the Fall, at the limitations on human potential and at human despair, and beyond it to infernal despair, but we also look at the possibility of regeneration, through the Son's atonement, and among the fellowship of the Holy Spirit (the Comforter of XII.486) – all those believers in free will and a godly republic, in the present and the future, who constitute Milton's ideal readership. Perfected bodies, and fused material and spiritual worlds, made seamlessly continuous in the poem through the widespread use of metonymy, are part of this. In the fallen world, the corresponding blight is disease, physical and mental, described in the compressed and horrified list as Adam looks on at a hospital (XI.478–93).

At the Fall, the confusion of perspective that the language of accommodation has rendered is removed, and human history begins. Books XI and XII (in the second edition of 1674) contain a vision of history that enables Milton to set forth his views on the progress of mankind. It is a Puritan and a republican vision. In the geographically and chronologically comprehensive vision of human history that Michael gives to Adam, a decidedly anti-tyrannical, anti-monarchical view is put across. The initial view contains many worldly empires, and, in consequence, Adam has to have his vision purged of their seductiveness by special herbs. The agrarian and pastoral world that begins the next stage of the vision is immediately interrupted by Cain's murder of Abel: a fratricide that looks forward in its motive of jealousy to the literary example of Claudius' murder of Hamlet – the heart of courtly corruption. The same idyll is vitiated by Venus and her train, who, according to Michael, deprive men of their godly manliness. 'Effeminate slackness' (XI.634) is the absence of the *virtus* that makes for a free state.

After the Flood, people live 'by families and tribes / Under paternal rule' (XII.23–4), a kind of village republicanism ('fair equality, fraternal state' (XII.26)), until Nimrod rises to dispossess and tyrannize. Nimrod was the Biblical name applied to Oliver Cromwell, first as 'mighty hunter', in admiration of his military prowess, but then increasingly, and especially after the Protectorate was instituted, as tyrant. Milton was one of those who, while publicly maintaining his loyalty to the Commonwealth government, secretly harboured grave doubts about the Protectorate. Milton's *History of Britain* (1670) is concerned with a nation that fails to seize the opportunities that Providence puts in its way. The 'Digression concerning the Long Parliament' that was published with the *History*, and which is now thought to have been written in 1649, is clear that Parliament missed its moment in the later 1640s to establish a true godly republic of virtue, an insight that puts Milton in the company of Levellers as well as Republicans.[26] *Paradise Lost* repeats this fear:

> Yet sometimes nations will decline so low
> From virtue, which is reason, that no wrong,
> But justice, and some fatal curse annexed
> Deprives men of their outward liberty,
> Their inward lost.

(XII.97–101)

The Israelite state after the exodus from Egypt is the epitome of liberty, and a fusion of Old Testament and Aristotle: 'In the wide wilderness, there they shall found / Their government, and their great senate choose / Through the twelve tribes, to rule by laws ordained' (XII.224–6). Nevertheless, there will always be the danger of a slide into tyranny, which will be met by 'signs and judgements dire' (XII.175), and there were certainly many of these, such as the recent plague and fire in London, when *Paradise Lost* first appeared. The Israelites go to Canaan through the desert 'not the readiest way' (XII.215), which echoes the title of Milton's desperate plea for a republic on the eve of the return of monarchy (*The Readie and Easie Way to establish a Free Commonwealth* (1660)), while also pointing to the possibility, or the necessity, of hardship in the cause of freedom.

The 'way out' for the reader is the Son, who announces the atonement he will make on behalf of mankind in Book III.227–65. He is the champion who achieves victory over Satan in the War on Heaven, is the messenger for God's Word just after the Fall, and is the assured leader of the future in Michael's prophecy, to say nothing of his part in Milton's anti-trinitarian vision.[27] The appearance of the Son as ideal man, as well as oracle for the Holy Spirit in Milton's sequel poem, *Paradise Regained* (1671), reinforces this view. We have to work hard to understand him. The Son, the narrator says, will inherit a hereditary kingdom (the Millennium, the thousand-year reign of Jesus after his Second Coming), whereas Satan has risen through 'merit', a key republican quality. Satan, however, is a usurper, and ultimately, though not forever, a conqueror. We can never forget the republican moments in Satan's rebellion, even as it is also tyrannical and imperialist. We can never forget the monarchism in Milton's portrayal of God and the Son, even as the general paradigm becomes clear: monarchist in heaven, republican on earth. Within that earthly republicanism, the sentiments of which Michael condones in Adam, is human lordship over the beasts and the gender hierarchy as set out in Books IV, V and VIII. Even those kinds of dominion, however, are questioned by the vegetarian and monist idyll of Paradise in which Milton's heretical cosmos is given full reign.

If all of this sounds difficult, well – it is. *Paradise Lost* makes the politics and religion of the English Revolution more problematic than they already were by removing them into Scriptural narrative space, and by an engagement with Classical epic that refuses uncomplicated allegiances and values. In doing so, it demands of its readers a more thoughtful engagement with the events and expressions of the Civil War, Interregnum and early Restoration than any other text of the period. This is one important reason why the poem is not exhausted by criticism, why the English Revolution has an enduring relevance, and why free will cannot be challenged enough by circumstance.

NOTES

1 Milton planned a drama on the Fall in the early 1640s; some parts of the epic may have been composed in the early 1640s; serious composition probably began in the mid to late 1650s. The weight of opinion now is that, as far as his blindness and his confinement would allow, Milton remained engaged in public affairs: see David Norbrook, *Writing the English Republic: Poetry, Rhetoric and Politics, 1627–1660* (Cambridge University Press, 1999), pp. 433–8.

2 David Quint, *Epic and Empire: Politics and Empire from Virgil to Milton* (Princeton University Press, 1993).

3 George Hickes, *Memoirs of the Life of Mr John Kettlewell* (1718), p. 14.

4 John Vicars, *The XII Aeneids of Virgil, translated into Engish decasyllables* (1632); see also the discussion in Gerald MacLean, *Time's Witness: Historical Representation in English Poetry, 1603–1660* (Madison: University of Wisconsin Press, 1990), pp. 78–119.

5 See Nigel Smith, *Literature and Revolution in England, 1640–1660* (New Haven: Yale University Press, 1994), pp. 204–7, and ch. 13 above, pp. 236, 247.

6 See Peter Davidson (ed.), *Poetry and Revolution: An Anthology of British and Irish Verse 1625–1660* (Oxford: Clarendon Press, 1998), p. 548, n. 285.

7 *Lucan's Pharsalia: Or the Civill Warres of Rome* (1626–7). May's Latin translation of his *Continuation* of *Pharsalia, Supplementum Lucani* (1640) was genuinely critical of the monarchy. (For May, see ch.13 above, pp. 236–7.) The exception to the rule in the case of Virgil translation was the translation by the Republican theorist James Harrington of the first six books of the *Aeneid* (1658–9), which actively engaged with the Royalist understanding of Virgil.

8 Nicholas Von Maltzahn, 'The First Reception of *Paradise Lost* (1667)', *RES*, 47 (1996), 479–99. See, also, Von Maltzahn 'The Whig Milton, 1667–1700', in David Armitage, Armand Himy and Quentin Skinner (eds.), *Milton and Republicanism* (Cambridge University Press, 1995), pp. 229–53.

9 See Laura Lunger Knoppers, *Historicizing Milton: Spectacle, Power, and Poetry in Restoration England* (Athens: The University of Georgia Press, 1994), chs. 3–4. N. H. Keeble, *The Literary Culture of Nonconformity in Later Seventeenth-Century England* (Leicester University Press, 1987) provides many instances where issues dear to Dissenters are addressed in *Paradise Lost*.

10 Andrew Marvell, *The Last Instructions to a Painter*, lines 131–46, in *P&L*, 1:150.

11 As discussed in Steven N. Zwicker, *Lines of Authority: Politics and English Literary Culture, 1649–1689* (Ithaca, N.Y.: Cornell University Press, 1993), pp. 4–5. Atterbury made his comment in a marginal annotation to *Paradise Lost*, II.106–8, in his copy of the 1678 edition of the poem, which is now in the Osborn Collection (pb 9), Beinecke Library, Yale University.

12 See Lydia Dytler Schulman, *Paradise Lost and the Rise of the American Republic* (Boston, Mass.: Northeastern University Press, 1992). See also Annabel Patterson, *Early Modern Liberalism* (Cambridge University Press, 1997), chs. 1 and 8; and Keith Stavely, *Puritan Legacies: Paradise Lost and the New England Tradition, 1630–1890* (Ithaca, N.Y.: Cornell University Press, 1987).

13 For direct correspondences between the poem and Civil War events, see Christopher Hill, *Milton and the English Revolution* (London: Faber, 1977), pp. 371–4.

14 Martin Dzelzainis, 'Milton's Classical Republicanism', in Armitage *et al.* (eds.), *Milton and Republicanism*, pp. 3–24.

15 E.g. 'Occasion' (II.341), taken from Machiavelli's *occasione* – of seizing the optimal moment in a political situation. See Blair Worden, 'Milton's Republicanism and the Tyranny of Heaven', in Gisela Bock, Quentin Skinner and Maurizio Viroli (eds.), *Machiavelli and Republicanism* (Cambridge University Press, 1993), pp. 225–46.

16 See Norbrook, *Writing the English Republic*, pp. 440–1; for structural counterpoints between Virgil and Milton, see Howard Erskine-Hill, *Poetry and the Realm of Politics: Shakespeare to Dryden* (Oxford: Clarendon Press, 1996), pp. 188–9; for imperialism, see David Armitage, 'John Milton: Poet against Empire', in Armitage, *et al.* (eds.), *Milton and Republicanism*, pp. 206–25.

17 The impact of technological developments in warfare on the epic in Europe is considered in Michael Murrin, *History and Warfare in Renaissance Epic* (University of Chicago Press, 1994), ch. 6.

18 See also the angelic 'cubic phalanx' of VI.399, which suggests virtue and stability; 'hollow' suggests untrustworthiness; 'enginery' means artillery. Pictures of battle formations were common in military manuals and accounts of battles: see, e.g., Joshua Sprigge, *Anglia Rediviva* (1647). For further discussion, see James A. Freeman, *Milton and the Martial Muse: Paradise Lost and European Traditions of War* (Princeton University Press, 1980).

19 The Son's 'fierce chariot' is described in language drawn from the Book of Ezekiel, chs. 1 and 10; the passage ends in echoes of the Book of Revelation, chs. 7 and 12. For links with visual traditions of representation, including paintings and *affresci*, see Roland Mushat Frye, *Milton's Imagery and the Visual Arts: Iconographic Tradition in the Epic Poems* (Princeton University Press, 1978), pp. 140ff.

20 Samuel Barrow, '*In Paradisum Amissum Summi Poetae Johannis Miltoni*', lines 38–42, prefaced to John Milton, *Paradise Lost* (1667).

21 Milton is ostensibly silent about the political radicals of the later 1640s in his writings, although he does share some positions with them, and they did occasionally praise him as an exemplary patriot. For an argument that Milton was in dialogue with the Levellers in his *History of Britain*, see Hugh Jenkins, 'Shrugging off the Norman Yoke: *Milton's History of Britain* and the Levellers', *ELR*, 29 (1999), 306–25.

22 See, e.g., Anon., *The Famous Tragedie of King Charles I basely butchered* (1649).

23 Marcus Walsh, 'Literary Annotation and Biblical Commentary: The Case of Patrick Hume's *Annotations* on *Paradise Lost*', *Milton Quarterly*, 22 (1988), 109–14.

24 See, e.g., the narratives published in Henry Walker (ed.), *Spiritual Experiences of Sundry Believers* (1653), and John Rogers, *Ohel, or Beth-shemesh: A Tabernacle for the Sun* (1653). For a modern anthology, see Elspeth Graham *et al.* (eds.), *Her Own Life: Autobiographical Writings by Seventeenth-Century Englishwomen* (London: Routledge, 1989), and see above, pp. 162–78.

25 See Norman T. Burns, *Christian Mortalism from Tyndale to Milton* (Cambridge., Mass.: Harvard University Press, 1972).

26 See Nicholas von Maltzahn, *Milton's 'History of Britain': Republican Historiography in the English Revolution* (Oxford: Clarendon Press, 1991). The

dating controversy, in which 1647, 1648, 1655 and 1660 as well as 1649, are significant years, is debated by Von Maltzahn and Austin Woolrych in *HJ*, 36 (1993), 929–56. Further discussions are listed by Norbrook, *Writing the English Republic*, p. 188, n. 144.

27 Anti-trinitarians were often harshly treated even during the Commonwealth. For the latest literary account of this heresy, see A. D. Nuttall, *The Alternative Trinity: Gnostic Heresy in Marlowe, Milton and Blake* (Oxford University Press, 1998), pp. 136–71.

FURTHER READING

For individual editions of primary texts cited or discussed, please see the notes above.

Achinstein, Sharon, *Milton and the Revolutionary Reader*, Princeton University Press, 1994.

Armitage, David, Armand Himy and Quentin Skinner (eds.), *Milton and Republicanism*, Cambridge University Press, 1995.

Bennett, Joan S., *Reviving Liberty: Radical Christian Humanism in Milton's Great Poems*, Cambridge, Mass.: Harvard University Press, 1989.

Burns, Norman T., *Christian Mortalism from Tyndale to Milton*, Cambridge, Mass.: Harvard University Press, 1972.

Davies, Stevie, *Images of Kingship in Paradise Lost: Milton's Politics and Christian Liberty*, Columbia: University of Missouri Press, 1983.

Erskine-Hill, Howard, *Poetry and the Realm of Politics: Shakespeare to Dryden*, Oxford: Clarendon Press, 1996.

Freeman, James A., *Milton and the Martial Muse: Paradise Lost and European Traditions of War*, Princeton University Press, 1980.

Hill, Christopher, *Milton and the English Revolution*, London: Faber, 1977.

Hoerner, Fred, '"Fire to Use": A Practice Theory Approach to *Paradise Lost*', *Representations*, 51 (1995), 94–117.

Kahn, Victoria, *Machiavellian Rhetoric: From the Counter-Reformation to Milton*, Princeton University Press, 1994.

Keeble, N. H., *The Literary Culture of Nonconformity in Later Seventeenth-Century England*, Leicester University Press, 1987.

Knoppers, Laura Lunger, *Historicizing Milton: Spectacle, Power, and Poetry in Restoration England*, Athens: University of Georgia Press, 1994.

Kolbrener, William, *Milton's Warring Angels: A Study of Critical Engagements*, Cambridge University Press, 1997.

MacLean, Gerald, *Time's Witness: Historical Representation in English Poetry, 1603–1660*, Madison: University of Wisconsin Press, 1990.

Martindale, Charles, *John Milton and the Transformation of Ancient Epic*, London: Croom Helm, 1986.

Norbrook, David, *Writing the English Republic: Poetry, Rhetoric and Politics, 1627–1660*, Cambridge University Press, 1999.

Nuttall, A. D., *The Alternative Trinity: Gnostic Heresy in Marlowe, Milton and Blake*, Oxford University Press, 1998.

Patterson, Annabel, *Early Modern Liberalism*, Cambridge University Press, 1997.

Porter, William M., *Reading the Classics and Paradise Lost*, Lincoln, Nebr., and London: University of Nebraska Press, 1993.

Quint, David, *Epic and Empire: Politics and Empire from Virgil to Milton*, Princeton University Press, 1993.

Rogers, John, *The Matter of Revolution: Science, Poetry and Politics in the Age of Milton*, Ithaca, N.Y.: Cornell University Press, 1996.

Schulman, Lydia Dytler, *Paradise Lost and the Rise of the American Republic*, Boston, Mass.: Northeastern University Press, 1992.

Smith, Nigel, *Literature and Revolution in England, 1640–1660*, New Haven: Yale University Press, 1994.

Stavely, Keith, *Puritan Legacies: Paradise Lost and the New England Tradition, 1630–1890*, Ithaca, N.Y.: Cornell University Press, 1987.

Turner, James Grantham, *One Flesh: Paradisal Marriage and Sexual Relations in the Age of Milton*, Oxford: Clarendon Press, 1987.

Von Maltzahn, Nicholas, *Milton's 'History of Britain': Republican Historiography in the English Revolution*, Oxford: Clarendon Press, 1991.

'The First Reception of *Paradise Lost* (1667)', *RES*, 47 (1996), 479–99.

Worden, Blair, 'Milton's Republicanism and the Tyranny of Heaven', in Gisela Bock, Quentin Skinner and Maurizio Viroli (eds.), *Machiavelli and Republicanism*, Cambridge University Press, 1993, pp. 225–46.

Zwicker, Steven N., *Lines of Authority: Politics and English Literary Culture, 1649–1689*, Ithaca, N.Y.: Cornell University Press, 1993.

15

RICHARD L. GREAVES

Bunyan and the Holy War

The Restoration and nonconformity

The Republic's collapse in 1660 had more to do with disintegration than with the strength of Royalist and episcopalian forces. Unable to agree among themselves on the appropriate form of government or religious expression, and unable to win broad public support, the disparate and often feuding Republicans and sectaries watched almost helplessly as one of their own number, General George Monck, engineered the restoration of monarchy. In its train came the re-establishment of episcopacy, the ousting of Dissenters from the state church and universities, and efforts to curb nonconformity. The Restoration did not mean the loss of an earthly paradise, for the 1650s had fallen far short of the reformers' dreams, but it sharply curtailed opportunities to build a godly society, stopping a work in progress and compelling reform's proponents to shape strategies for survival. In formulating such strategies, the greatest Nonconformist writers, Milton and Bunyan, transcended their individual experiences and the revolutionary heritage in which they were rooted. For Bunyan, the Restoration heralded the commencement of the first of three overlapping periods that would occupy the rest of his life. Extending from 1660 to around 1662, the first period involved Bunyan's struggle with the experience of defeat, which terminated with his defiant attack on the Book of Common Prayer. As his incarceration lengthened, seemingly without hope of cessation, he grappled with the experience of persecution, plunging into renewed depression before finding hope in millenarianism and the strength to persevere by recounting in detail his earlier spiritual struggles. As the conditions of his confinement eased in 1669, he sensed triumph. His first literary expression of this victorious experience was part One of *The Pilgrim's Progress*, composed near the end of his incarceration though not published until 1678. When the country was plunged into the succession crisis beginning in 1679, Bunyan, the spectre of revived Catholicism notwithstanding, retained his belief in ultimate victory, the fundamental message of *The Holy War*.

7 Robert White, pencil drawing of John Bunyan, aged fifty, 1678/9. This image was used for
the engraved frontispiece portrait of the Dreamer in editions of *The Pilgrim's Progress*.

Initially, the government's religious policy was conciliatory and held out
hope of broad comprehension. The Act for Settling Ministers (September
1660) deprived only clergy who had supported regicide, opposed the
Restoration, repudiated infant baptism, or possessed livings that had
belonged to sequestered ministers who were still living. This statute resulted
in the ejection of 695 clergymen, including many of those most opposed to
the restored church. Among them was the Independent John Gibbs, whose
sermons Bunyan had probably heard while he was stationed in the
Parliamentary garrison at Newport Pagnell in 1644–6. Bunyan's pastor in
1660, John Burton, would probably have faced ejection had he not died in
August of that year. In the ensuing months, efforts to achieve a workable

compromise between episcopalians and Presbyterians, especially at the Savoy Conference held in 1661, failed, paving the way for passage of the Act of Uniformity, signed by Charles on 19 May 1662. Under its terms, on St Bartholomew's Day 1662, 936 ministers were ejected, 59 of whom had been deprived in 1660 and subsequently obtained another living. Altogether, approximately 1,760 ministers were ousted between 1660 and 1663, in addition to 120 clergy in Wales and some 200 university dons, lecturers and schoolmasters. Most ejected ministers were Presbyterians who probably would have conformed if a comprehensive settlement had been implemented. Generally, these were quiescent men who were content to attend parish services or worship unobtrusively in households. Neither of these statutes had much impact on the radical Protestant groups, for few Baptists had possessed livings in the Church of England during the 1650s, and the Quakers had never been part of the national church and had no ordained clergy. Comprehension for these groups was never a possibility. Although the Restoration Church of England failed to incorporate 'mere Nonconformists' such as Richard Baxter and committed Presbyterians, who accounted for nearly 90 per cent of the ejected ministers, the number of clergy who did conform – Baxter's estimate of 7,000 is on the high side – gave the new regime a substantial victory.[1]

The Nonconformists' response to the Restoration was anything but uniform. Many shared similar backgrounds and values with conforming clerics, attended their services (though remaining outside during offending parts) and embraced key theological tenets. The Flintshire dissenting minister Philip Henry numbered conforming clergy among his friends, attended Anglican services, and was not deemed a schismatic by the Bishop of St Asaph. On Sunday mornings Arthur Annesley, Earl of Anglesey, worshipped in a parish church, but he sometimes listened to Dissenters preach in his chapel during the afternoon.[2] At the other end of the spectrum were Nonconformists who plotted and sometimes took up arms against the government. The first such uprising occurred in January 1661, when a band of Fifth Monarchists – a group to which Bunyan had been attracted for a while in the 1650s – followed Thomas Venner into London's streets to fight for King Jesus, pledging to bind monarchs in chains and nobles in iron fetters. The revolution they envisioned was international in scope and included political and social reform. Related dissident activity was reported at Newcastle and in Lincolnshire, Cheshire and Flintshire. After quelling the uprising, the government implemented security measures, including a ban on meetings of Fifth Monarchists, Baptists and Quakers. Baptists and Friends (4,230 of whom were arrested) filled the prisons. Other attempts to alter the government or its policies ensued. In Ireland, the Duke of Ormond quashed a plot involving Presbyterians and Congregationalists shortly before they were ready to revolt in May 1663, but that October dissidents, including Nonconformists, rebelled in Yorkshire, Westmorland and Durham.[3] Radical Nonconformists continued to plot as late as 1685, when the Baptist Henry Danvers and others schemed with Monmouth to overthrow James II, and in the ensuing years.[4]

Many Nonconformists occupied the broad middle ground, eschewing plotting while refusing any *modus vivendi* with the established church. Typically, these people defied those laws that inhibited their perceived right to worship as they chose and to publish their literature. To the extent that religious acts were political statements (as were virtually all of them in this period), these Dissenters were not as quiescent as many scholars have suggested. Disobedience to the state and its laws is a profoundly political act that undermines a government's claim to rule by challenging its moral authority. Throughout the Restoration era the Quakers made this abundantly clear by boldly, even brazenly, calling officials to account for their repressive practices. On the one hand the Friends welcomed the Restoration, having been the victims of persecution in the 1650s, but on the other they dared to prescribe the conduct they expected of Charles. In 1660 Henry Fell published *The Copies of Several Letters*, a collection of Quaker letters to the King, an act that underscored their determination to worship and witness openly. In contrast, the less radical Nonconformists often shunned visibility, meeting in homes and barns, sometimes at night, though others gathered in large numbers, clearly making no attempt to conceal their meetings. Whereas the Friends generally made no effort to avoid confrontations with magistrates, other Nonconformists took pains to help their ministers escape.[5] Either way, their defiance undercut the state's claim to impose religious uniformity and the magistrate's ability to enforce the law; such actions cannot be divorced from their political content and context.

Bunyan's arrest and imprisonment

Bunyan's experience of defeat began as an expression of defiance against the state when, in November 1660, he intended to preach to a conventicle at Lower Samsell, Bedfordshire, despite a reported warrant for his arrest. To evade apprehension, he reasoned, would provide a poor example to Dissenters and lead others to conclude that he had blasphemed the Gospel by his cravenness. Arrested by a constable under an Elizabethan statute against conventicles, Bunyan was offered his freedom if he would apologize, promise to cease preaching, and concentrate on his trade as a tinker. This he refused to do as a matter of principle. In an ensuing exchange with the vicar of Harlington, Dr

William Lindale, Bunyan implicitly likened the cleric to the priests and Pharisees responsible for Christ's death, thus suggesting that the Church of England was not a true church. Bunyan stood his ground at the quarter sessions in January 1661, when he was charged with having 'devilishly and perniciously abstained from coming to church to hear divine service' and being 'a common upholder of several unlawful meetings and conventicles, to the great disturbance and distraction of the good subjects of this kingdom'.[6] From the government's perspective, Bunyan's actions had political ramifications, but he refused to acknowledge this, insisting he and his friends had met only for prayer and mutual edification. On this crucial difference in perspective turned much of the debate between conformists and Dissenters. Bunyan was sentenced to three months in prison, after which he could conform or be exiled. When a clerk of the peace asked him to conform in April, Bunyan refused, while insisting that he, unlike the followers of Venner, would not use religious gatherings as a cover for actions against the state. His obedience, he averred, was to a higher law, which adjudged those who refused to use their gift of preaching as traitors to Christ. When his arguments proved unsuccessful in Bedford, Bunyan dispatched his wife, Elizabeth, to London to seek assistance from the Earl of Bedford and two prominent judges, Sir Matthew Hale and Thomas Twisden, but to no avail (GA, pp. 113–29).

These setbacks notwithstanding, Bunyan was still not ready to accept defeat. Indeed, he must have been encouraged by the gaoler's willingness to allow him enough liberty to resume preaching, to participate in the activities of the Bedford church, and even to visit London in October 1661.[7] Undaunted by his earlier arrest, he boldly preached against the Book of Common Prayer in the late summer and early fall of 1661. These sermons provided him with the material for his tract, *I Will Pray with the Spirit*, the first edition of which (now lost) almost certainly appeared in 1662. Turning the tables on his persecutors, he charged that those who used the Book of Common Prayer, with its borrowing from 'the Papistical Mass-Book', engaged in unlawful worship, for God had banned it as a human invention. Extempore prayer, on the other hand, was divinely ordained. Users of prayer books were hypocrites who babbled in a false voice. Those who enforced the Book of Common Prayer were, in Bunyan's judgement, kin to the 'blood-red Persecutor', Edmund Bonner, Mary Tudor's Bishop of London (MW, II:239, 253). This was a powerful indictment – indisputably political in its connotations – of the new regime. The gulf between Bunyan and Nonconformists such as Philip Henry was greater than the breach that separated the latter from many conformists. Bunyan's initial reaction to the Nonconformists' defeat in 1660 was defiance and resolve to brook no compromise with a state church that had turned its back on the Gospel.

As the conditions of his incarceration tightened and the hope of release faded around early 1663, Bunyan's mood changed. Defeat was real, compelling him to ponder the likelihood of dying in prison. Faced with mounting loneliness, Bunyan was exhorted by his friends to hold his head above the flood of fear and gloom – a telling image of his psychological state. He wrote *Christian Behaviour*, intended to be his spiritual last testament, with a sense of urgency, expecting imminent death (*MW*, vi:42, iii:62). Following the tract's completion on 17 June 1663, his pen fell silent as he plunged into the black despair from which he had mercifully been free since the traumatic spiritual struggles of the early 1650s.

The heart of Bunyan's epic battle to survive the invidious psychological effects of sustained persecution was roughly coterminous with the period that extended from Black Bartholomew's Day, 24 August 1662, to the expiration of the first Restoration Conventicle Act on 1 March 1669. A Corporation Act, requiring all borough officials to swear oaths of allegiance and non-resistance, to repudiate the Solemn League and Covenant, and to take communion in the Church of England, had been passed in December 1661, and the Quakers were the target of a May 1662 statute empowering magistrates to imprison, fine or, for a third offence, banish Friends who gathered in groups of five or more. Two years later, Parliament passed another Conventicle Act imposing similar penalties on anyone over the age of sixteen who attended an illegal religious service at which more than six people were present. Fines were imposed on magistrates who were remiss in enforcing the statute. The final persecutory law during this period was the Five Mile Act (1665), which required nonconformist ministers and teachers who refused to swear the required oaths to stay five miles from all cities and towns, and ejected clergymen to stay the same distance from their former parishes. Because Bunyan was already in prison for having violated an Elizabethan statute, these laws did not directly affect him, but they contributed to the repressive spirit that prompted magistrates to keep him in prison far longer than virtually any of his nonconforming contemporaries. Nevertheless, enforcement of these laws was not uniform, even in the year following passage of the 1664 Conventicle Act, when the greatest effort was made in most places to eradicate dissent. Complaints about magistrates who did not enforce the statute were common, and some officials actually supported Dissenters or did little more than arrest and almost immediately release them.[8]

As unpleasant as persecution was, it served a crucial purpose for Nonconformists by validating their religious experience. Suffering was one of the preeminent hallmarks of the godly throughout the Bible. John Foxe traced the history of suffering from the primitive church to the Elizabethan age, and his editors extended the story into the seventeenth century, linking the afflicted of the present with those who had borne the cross in countless earlier generations.[9] In prison Bunyan had a copy of the 1641 edition of Foxe's *Acts and Monuments* that included material stressing persecution's inevitability. Like the Bible, the *Acts and Monuments* helped sustain Bunyan's faith while reinforcing his association of the papacy with Antichrist, and thus the impossibility of compromising with those who enforced the Book of Common Prayer and its vestiges of the Mass. In one important respect, however, Bunyan disagreed with Foxe as he groped for a way to cope with his lengthening incarceration. Foxe had dated the millennium's commencement with Constantine and its termination in 1294, after which Satan was loosed for 300 years, culminating in the last judgement.[10] Bunyan could obviously have recognized that Foxe's dating was erroneous. As Bunyan was feeling 'empty, spiritless, and barren' in 1665, unable to speak 'so much as five words of Truth, with Life and Evidence' to the Dissenters who shared his gaol, he 'providentially' cast his eye on Revelation 21:11, with its depiction of a heavenly Jerusalem glittering like a precious stone (*MW*, III:69).

The Holy City

As Bunyan studied the full passage, Revelation 21:10–27 and 22:1–4, he came to a deeper realization that persecution was but a prelude to the church's ultimate triumph. The millennium was not in the past but in the future, an idea on which he had touched in the 1650s, probably during the period of his attraction to the Fifth Monarchists.[11] Venner's rebellion, which he, like nearly all Nonconformists, repudiated, had tainted the Fifth Monarchists' expression of belief in an earthly millennium during which the saints would rule with Christ. In *The Holy City*, an outgrowth of the Scriptural lesson he propounded to his fellow prisoners in 1665, Bunyan re-conceptualized his understanding of millenarianism, laying out a schema, suffused with hope and light, in which Christ would rule through the saints in an imminent millennium, though Bunyan eschewed any attempt to date it. A crucial key to his ability to retain his faith through the long years of confinement was his new understanding of the place of persecution in the divine schema of the church's history. That history, he concluded, has three stages, the first of which comprises the period of Jesus and his apostles, and the second involves the church's decline and captivity. Near the end of the second era come two sub-periods, altar-work and temple-work. Characterized by the discovery of Christ's priestly office, the former extends from John Wyclif's age through the Reformation. During the time of temple-work, a subsequent wave of reformers gathers churches of visible saints, setting themselves apart from the 'carnal Gospelers, that every where like Locusts and Maggots craul up and down the Nations' (*MW*, III:135). This was the period in which Bunyan thought he lived. At the end of the second epoch, Antichrist will fall and the millennium will commence. Near the end of the thousand years, the satanic agents, Gog and Magog, will attack the church, only to be destroyed by God in a hail of fire and brimstone that paves the way for Christ's second coming and the last judgement. Bunyan concluded his exposition of millenarianism with a poignant quotation from the psalmist (90:14–17), an 'earnest Groan' beseeching God to make him happy during the days of his affliction and confrontation with evil. Above all, Bunyan was now imbued with the conviction that the holy city's descent, marking the millennium's onset, 'MUST SHORTLY be done' (*MW*, III:196).

Grace Abounding

The period of depression over which Bunyan triumphed through his formulation of millenarian hope had been characterized by profound sadness and fear that he would become enmeshed in this state of despair when he mounted the gallows. Such fears were somewhat irrational, for the Elizabethan Conventicle Act prescribed execution only for someone who illegally returned to England after being banished, but they were nevertheless real and enervating. He brooded about his death, afraid he would bring reproach on the Gospel if he failed to acquit himself with a confident faith. While prayers for strength and comfort seemingly went unanswered, 'the tempter' relentlessly assaulted him with doubts about his soul's ultimate fate. '*What evidence have you*', Satan pressed, '*for heaven and glory, and an inheritance among them that are sanctified?*' (*GA*, §336, p. 100). When at last Bunyan found comfort, he looked back on his struggles with appreciation: 'I would not have been without this trial for much; I am comforted everie time I think of it, and I hope I shall bless God for ever for the teaching I have had by it' (*GA*, §339, p. 101). Realization of the pedagogical value of his spiritual battles motivated him to record them in a spiritual autobiography. Such a work would also justify his ministerial calling since he had neither formal training nor legally recognized ordination, and it would simultaneously provide spiritual instruction for the flock to which his ability to minister had been severely diminished. Revisiting his painful spiritual turmoil was facilitated because he had now found the comfort to survive sustained persecution. It is difficult to envision Bunyan having had either the time or the inclination to recount his intense spiritual strife had he not been subjected to the lengthy incarceration that provided not only the necessary time but also the psychological and spiritual need to revisit his earlier trauma and his eventual triumph. The renewed depression of 1663–4 revived memories of his previous dysphoria and his relentless combat with the tempter.

Grace Abounding to the Chief of Sinners was thus the vehicle for Bunyan's therapeutic revisiting of his prior struggles as well as an *apologia* for his ministry. The persecutory context, Bunyan's struggle with renewed dysphoria, and his recovery through a profound, uplifting millennial hope enabled him to transcend the host of contemporary autobiographies, spiritual and otherwise, in depth of psychological insight and literary force. Paul Delany has justifiably adjudged *Grace Abounding* 'the most powerful English work of its kind in the seventeenth century', though conventional in both its structure and, at least superficially, its experiences.[12] Theologically, the certainty of the elect's salvation should emasculate any sense of drama in Calvinist autobiography, but Bunyan overcame this by relentlessly focusing on the doubt that haunted him, driving him obsessively to examine many facets of life to divine his eternal state. For all its seeming typicality, *Grace Abounding* transcends the ritual recounting of expected spiritual experience to unmask the horrific struggles of a man striving to keep his head above the waves of depression washing over him. However, if the reality of Bunyan's illness is denied, the autobiography can justifiably be criticized as artificial and excessively dependent on a perceived pattern of Puritan spirituality. On the tercentenary of Bunyan's death, I warned of the dangers of psychoanalysing Bunyan without understanding the nature of *Grace Abounding*, which he intended partly to serve as a spiritual guide for others, and partly to demonstrate his qualifications to preach. Because the book was written more than a decade after the events it reputedly depicts, its sense of chronology is sometimes vague and its factual accuracy is subject to Bunyan's ability to recall distant events. Moreover, Bunyan was sometimes prone to exaggerate.[13] Simultaneously, however, the work's real force, I have come to believe, stems from its manifestation of Bunyan's affliction with depression and the resulting 'rawness and repetitive misery of Bunyan's lived experience'.[14] What he expresses in *Grace Abounding* is what he experienced – what he felt – and thus not something he controlled, except as he recollected it in writing his spiritual autobiography.

The Pilgrim's Progress and the second Restoration crisis

In the year following the publication of *Grace Abounding*, England entered a second Restoration crisis, the first having lasted from Oliver Cromwell's death in September 1658 to the passage of the Conventicle Act in May 1664. The second crisis was triggered when Parliament began considering a statute to replace the latter act when it expired. Opposed to another such law, Dissenters began demonstrating for freedom of conscience, at least for Protestants, and, by 1670, against the state's power to persecute Protestant Dissenters. These calls for liberty of conscience and limitations on government power in religion revived the mid-century debate over these issues, effectively renewing a holy war of ideas. Among proponents of toleration the earliest shots included John Owen's *A Peace-Offering in an Apology and Humble Plea for Indulgence and Liberty of Conscience* (1667) and his *Indulgence and Toleration Considered in a Letter unto a Person of Honour* (1667); Sir Charles Wolseley's *Liberty of Conscience, the Magistrates Interest* (1668) and his *Liberty of Conscience upon Its True Proper Grounds Asserted & Vindicated* (1668); and Owen's *Truth and Innocence Vindicated* (1669). Although not published at the time, John Locke's first 'Essay on Toleration' was written in 1667. Among other notable assertions of the case for religious liberty were William Penn's *The Great Case of Liberty of Conscience* (1671), Slingsby Bethel's *The Present Interest of England Stated* (1671) and Andrew Marvell's *The Rehearsal Transpros'd* (1672). Against such advocates, conservatives argued that Nonconformists used conventicles to plot seditious activities, that they were responsible for much of the turmoil and bloodshed of the mid-century upheavals, that uniformity is essential for decent, orderly worship, and that compulsion in religion is an effective, justifiable means to educate and persuade. During the second Restoration crisis, such arguments were espoused, *inter alia*, in Samuel Parker's *A Discourse of Ecclesiastical Politie* (1669), Richard Perrinchief's *Indulgence Not Justified* (1668) and *A Discourse of Toleration* (1668), Simon Patrick's *A Friendly Debate* (1669) and Thomas Tomkins' *The Inconvenience of Toleration* (1667).[15]

There is no evidence that Bunyan read any of the books published during this debate, though he was chary about mentioning what he read, apart from the Bible and Foxe. His Bible and concordance, he avouched in *Solomon's Temple Spiritualiz'd*, were the 'only Library in [his] writings'. This was, of course, not true.[16] While there is no proof that he read any contributions to the toleration controversy, he may have discussed the issue with Owen, whom he knew, while in London. In any event, he had ample reminders of the critical importance of toleration. In January, April and June 1666, John Wright of Blunham and other Dissenters were imprisoned in the Bedford gaol for attending conventicles. Around the same time the dissenting ministers William Wheeler and John Donne were in prison with Bunyan. For teaching at a conventicle, Samuel Fenne and Thomas Cooper were incarcerated at Bedford in 1669, and the following year nearly thirty members of the Bedford Nonconformist church, including John Fenne and Nathaniel Coxe, were arrested for meeting at Fenne's house, and fined; the preacher, Coxe, was gaoled. The fines were doubled when the members met again a week later. Bunyan undoubtedly read a report of these doings in *A True and Impartial Narrative of Some Illegal and Arbitrary Proceedings . . . in or near the Town of Bedford* (1670).[17]

Although Bunyan apparently made no attempt to restate his case for religious liberty or defend members of his church during this time of tribulation, his pen was almost certainly not idle. Troubled with *'worser thoughts'* – presumably his fear of dying in prison – he found diversion by writing the first part of *The Pilgrim's Progress* (PP, p. 1), much of which he probably completed by the autumn of 1669, when he received limited freedom, and the rest of the allegory by early 1671. At first he opted not to publish the book, apparently because some of his friends thought it would do no good. Compared to the gravity of the volumes setting forth the case for liberty of conscience or of the second edition of *Grace Abounding*, on which he worked about 1667, *The Pilgrim's Progress* seemed to some to lack 'solidness' (PP, p. 4). For seven years, therefore, the manuscript lay unpublished. Only when the government renewed its efforts to repress nonconformity and Bunyan himself had briefly been re-incarcerated did he give the manuscript to Nathaniel Ponder, reportedly at Owen's suggestion.

The Pilgrim's Progress effectively links the two themes of greatest interest to Bunyan in the late 1660s, namely, his own religious experience, particularly as a pedagogical tool for the conversion and edification of others, and freedom of conscience for Protestants. *The Pilgrim's Progress* was simultaneously an allegory of his own religious development, of Christian experience broadly conceived, and of conscience. His ability to weave these three strands into a seamless whole established him as a master of multiple allegory. The book has been the subject of considerable analysis as an allegory of Bunyan's experience as well as that of Christians more generally, but *The Pilgrim's Progress* has generally not been situated in the context of the second Restoration crisis.[18] While the allegory as a whole is an extended argument for the primacy of conscience and each person's need to adhere to its dictates, the Vanity Fair episode (PP, pp. 88–98) is a powerful, poignant commentary on the crisis over religious freedom. The charges lodged against Christian and Faithful – inciting unrest and division, seducing people with dangerous tenets, and disturbing trade by neglecting one's calling – echo those against Nonconformists. Faithful's defence rested on his adherence to the divinely prescribed worship of God, much as Bunyan had denounced the Book of Common Prayer as man-made and diametrically opposed to the Spirit's leadings. The demand of Vanity Fair's jurors for capital punishment mirrored the penalty of death faced by Bunyan should he return to England after being exiled. Faithful, of course, is executed in Vanity Fair, though he ultimately triumphs as he is transported to Heaven in a chariot amid the sound of trumpets. The Vanity Fair episode is especially chilling because those who persecute Christian and execute Faithful are outwardly godly, law-abiding and industrious folk – the law-and-order Christians who justified their repressive policies by citing the Bible and insisting on the significance of religious uniformity. One's persecutors were one's neighbours, the very people who expressed their faith through the Book of Common Prayer.

Another key theme in *The Pilgrim's Progress* – wayfaring as warfaring – reflects the combative nature of that strand of the Nonconformist tradition to which Bunyan belonged, namely, that which eschewed accommodation with conformists. 'Bunyan's pilgrims', Nicholas Shrimpton has aptly remarked, 'are remarkably pugnacious'.[19] Christian wields a sword, Great-heart leads an assault on Giant Despair, and a band of armed pilgrims seeks a battle with Gyant Slay-good. At root, the pilgrimage is sustained combat against an array of forces, a series of battles that pits warrior-pilgrims against such foes as Bloodyman, Maul, Slay-good and Giant Despair. The obvious source of the militancy is Bunyan's wartime experience in the Newport Pagnell garrison, where several hundred soldiers served in dismal conditions, short of equipment and clothing as well as chronically behind in their pay. As a trooper Bunyan probably learned how to use a musket, sword, and possibly a hand gun and a pike. Troops from his garrison were involved in combat, sometimes on patrol, the sort of action that accounted for nearly half the estimated casualties during the civil wars.[20] Whether Bunyan engaged in the fighting is unknown, but he was clearly interested in the daring and heroism of those who wielded swords in battle, as reflected in both *The Pilgrim's Progress* and *The Holy War*. The model for Great-heart in the less confrontational part Two of *The Pilgrim's Progress* (1684) may have been the Particular Baptist Paul Hobson, a captain in Charles Fleetwood's regiment who was arrested at Newport Pagnell for unauthorized preaching, or the Independent William Erbery, a New Model Army chaplain whose advocacy of Spirit-baptism may have influenced Bunyan. Bunyan was unique neither in his use of the pilgrimage motif nor in his depiction of the Christian life as combat, but he broke new ground by effectively combining what elderly Mr Honest called Christian's '*Travels and Wars*' in a *de facto* religious romance. Indeed, some readers of the first part were offended by the allegory's resemblance to a romance: 'Romance they count it, throw't away as dust.'[21]

The Succession crisis and *The Holy War*

Bunyan returned to the combat motif when the country plunged into a new crisis as a result of the succession struggle and a concomitant intensification of concern about popery and arbitrary government. Disclosures of an alleged Popish Plot in 1678 led to fierce political struggles and recourse to shameless subornation of witnesses as the court and its enemies sought to emasculate each other. Ideological differences divided the two sides as each looked back to the 1640s and 1650s, finding there the grist for the propaganda mills of what became the Whig and Tory parties. Whereas Whigs espoused toleration for Protestant Dissenters and Parliamentary sovereignty, Tories defended the Church of England, the necessity of penal laws, and Parliament's subordination to the monarch. An epic struggle to exclude Charles II's brother, the Roman Catholic James, from the succession, or to sharply curtail his authority should he become King, occurred between 1679 and 1681. During the Parliaments of October 1680 – January 1681 and March 1681, Whig majorities in the House of Commons favoured exclusion, and Charles' efforts to tone down Whig opposition by convening the latter Parliament at Oxford failed. Political groups, the most noted of which was the Green Ribbon Club, disseminated Whig propaganda, and major efforts were made to collect signatures on petitions. On 5 and 17 November 1679 and again the following year, demonstrators burned effigies of the pope. Bunyan must have been aware of these events, though he probably knew nothing of the plans for a general insurrection to compel Charles to exclude his brother. The first such effort, centring around the Earl of Shaftesbury, occurred in 1680. Renewed consideration began in 1681, following the Earl of Argyll's secret arrival in London after his escape from Edinburgh Castle. When the King became ill in May 1682, Shaftesbury, Monmouth, Ford Lord Grey and Sir Thomas Armstrong contemplated a rebellion. The Scottish minister Robert Ferguson, who had been Owen's assistant, was linked to these conspirators, and Monmouth would later confess that Owen, Matthew Meade, George Griffith, '& all the considerable Nonconformist Ministers knew of the Conspiracy'.[22] Apart from Ferguson, the others, if Monmouth was truthful, likely were not apprised until the fall of 1682; however, the charges against Griffith and possibly Owen are probably unfounded. Although Bunyan knew Owen, Griffith and probably Meade, there is no evidence that he knew of the proposed insurrection, but his circle of acquaintances almost certainly would have discussed the perceived threats of arbitrary government and popery.

In this context, Bunyan wrote two of his major works, *The Life and Death of Mr. Badman* (1680) and *The Holy War* (composed in 1681 and very early

1682, and published in the latter year). *Mr Badman*, a handbook by which to assess conduct and a blistering critique of Restoration society, creatively depicted an England divided into two camps, the visible saints and their arch foes, a country without a middle ground. Reflecting this division, *The Holy War* was Bunyan's response to the mounting concern among Whigs and Nonconformists following the dissolution of Parliament in January and especially March 1681. Artistically and thematically, *The Holy War* comprises complex levels of allegory, the most fundamental of which is soteriological: the soul's struggle for salvation and sanctification. At this level the epic essentially parallels *Grace Abounding* and *The Pilgrim's Progress*, completing a trilogy about conversion and the Christian life. At another level, *The Holy War* is a theological overview of history from Satan's fall to the eve of Christ's ultimate conquest. Christopher Hill has suggested that Bunyan's epic can also be read as an allegorical account of the English Revolution, from Charles I's reputed tyranny to Diabolus' return in 1660 and his eventual overthrow.[23]

Bunyan intended that the allegory be read in political as well as theological terms, with the focus on Charles II's reign and the epic's unmistakable references to the remodelling of corporations, the perceived disregard for God's laws, and the alleged disrespect shown to the nation's statutes. When the epic is read as political commentary, the effect is electric. Determined to crush their foes through the rigorous application of the penal statutes, militant Tories appear in *The Holy War* as pernicious Bloodmen. Stuart violence is horrific. When Diabolus' forces overran Mansoul, they expelled lawful inhabitants from their homes, burned part of the town, dashed many children 'in pieces', and slayed the unborn in their mothers' wombs: 'Many in *Mansoul* that were *women*, both young and old, they forced, ravished, and beastlike abused, so that they swooned, miscarried, and many of them died, and so lay at the top of every street, and in all by-places of the Town.' Diabolus devastated Mansoul, turning it into 'a den of Dragons, an emblem of Hell, and a place of total darkness' (*HW*, p. 204). This was satanic work, but the devil's agents were none other than 'home-bred *Diabolonians*' (*HW*, p. 207), reinforcing the primary lesson of the Vanity Fair episode that persecution is the work of one's law-abiding, seemingly religious neighbours. In one respect the unfolding plot of *The Holy War* at first sight has no historical parallel, namely, Emanuel's final conquest of Mansoul. This is Bunyan's affirmation of faith that the godly forces battling arbitrary government and popery will ultimately triumph, just as Christian will finally complete his pilgrimage by entering Heaven. The epic's closing paragraph returns to harsh contemporary reality by recognizing that the godly were endangered in 1681–2; Bunyan left them with Emanuel's exhortation to 'hold fast till I come' (*HW*, p. 250). In addition to the obvious millenarian reading of this passage, was Bunyan expressing hope that the Protestant prince, Monmouth, would soon save Mansoul?

Rethinking warfaring

After the disclosure of Monmouth's cabal in June 1683 and the notorious scheming by the London attorney Robert West and his associates, who plotted to assassinate Charles and James, Bunyan categorically – and prudently – denounced the conspiracies in *Seasonable Counsel* (1684), which he probably wrote between October 1683 and January 1684. Implicitly likening Monmouth to Absalom, he condemned all plotters as 'the looser sort of Christians' and urged his readers to eschew all discourse against those in authority (*MW*, x:32). Against a background of executions that claimed Algernon Sidney, Lord William Russell and others, Bunyan added his voice to those who denounced the plotters: a conspirator's '*cause* will not bear him out, his heart will be clogged with guilt, innocency and boldness will take wings and fly from him' (*MW*, x:104). In fact, Russell and Sidney died resolutely. Nevertheless, Bunyan put as much distance as possible between himself and the conspirators, insisting he had known none who were disaffected to the government, a claim that rings false in light of his relationship with the radical printers Francis Smith and Benjamin Alsop, and probably with Meade. His counsel now was not to let 'talk against Governours, against Powers, against Men in Authority be admitted; keep thee far from an evil matter'. He also took pains in this work to stress the duty of suffering and urge his readers not to castigate persecutory magistrates or be offended if 'by their State-Acts they may cross thy inclinations'. Expressions of discontent, he warned, could lead to one's execution (*MW*, x:38–40). Persecutors, he avowed, are divine instruments, though at the proper time God will wreak vengeance on them (*MW*, x:11–13, 69–73). Against this background, the second part of *The Pilgrim's Progress* focuses on spiritual growth, eschewing the tone of militant engagement that characterizes *The Holy War*.

The militancy of Bunyan's youth, a product of his Civil-War service, contributed to his life-long sense of envisioning the spiritual world in combative imagery. In literary terms, the bellicose outlook, reflected in part One of *The Pilgrim's Progress*, reached its apex in *The Holy War*. *Seasonable Counsel* marked Bunyan's pragmatic repudiation of a political reading of the epic and a concentration instead on the spiritual nature of the conflict in which he continued to engage until his death in August 1688. The most significant rethinking of warfaring for Bunyan arguably occurred between the autumn of 1683 and the summer of 1684, when he publicly rejected any temporal application of the militancy articulated in *The Holy War*.

NOTES

1 John Spurr, *The Restoration Church of England, 1646–1689* (New Haven: Yale University Press, 1991), pp. 34–43; *Richard Baxter's Farewel Sermon* (1683), p. 5.

2 Spurr, *Restoration Church*, pp. 44–5; Geoffrey F. Nuttall, 'The Nurture of Nonconformity: Philip Henry's Diaries', *Transactions of the Honourable Society of Cymmrodorion 1997*, n.s. 4 (1998), 17, 24; Richard L. Greaves, *John Bunyan and English Nonconformity* (London: Hambledon Press, 1992), p. 5.

3 Richard L. Greaves, *Deliver Us from Evil: The Radical Underground in Britain, 1660–1663* (New York: Oxford University Press, 1986), pp. 50–8, 140–50, 174–92.

4 Richard L. Greaves, *Secrets of the Kingdom: British Radicals from the Popish Plot to the Revolution of 1688–1689* (Stanford University Press, 1992), pp. 253–64, 269–89, 295–302, 312–19.

5 N. H. Keeble, *The Literary Culture of Nonconformity in Later Seventeenth-Century England* (Leicester University Press, 1987), pp. 45–55; Greaves, *Bunyan and English Nonconformity*, pp. 14–15.

6 Bunyan, 'A Relation of the Imprisonment', in Bunyan, *GA*, pp. 105–13.

7 *GA*, p. 130; H. G. Tibbutt (ed.), *The Minutes of the First Independent Church . . . at Bedford 1656–1766*, Publications of the Bedfordshire Historical Record Society, 55 (Bedfordshire Historical Record Society, 1976), p. 37.

8 Richard L. Greaves, *Enemies Under His Feet: Radicals and Nonconformists in Britain, 1664–1677* (Stanford University Press, 1990), pp. 129–33, 145.

9 D. Nussbaum, 'Appropriating Martyrdom: Fears of Renewed Persecution and the 1632 Edition of *Acts and Monuments*', in D. Loades (ed.), *John Foxe and the English Reformation* (Aldershot, Hants.: Scolar Press, 1997), p. 191. See also John R. Knott, *Discourses of Martyrdom in English Literature, 1563–1694* (Cambridge University Press, 1993).

10 K. R. Firth, *The Apocalyptic Tradition in Reformation Britain 1530–1645* (Oxford University Press, 1979), pp. 92, 105, 253.

11 Bunyan, *MW*, 1:205; Greaves, *Bunyan and Nonconformity*, pp. 141–53.

12 Paul Delany, *British Autobiography in the Seventeenth Century* (London: Routledge and Kegan Paul, 1969), pp. 89–90.

13 Greaves, *Bunyan and Nonconformity*, pp. 38–40.

14 Leopold Damrosch, Jr, *God's Plot & Man's Stories: Studies in the Fictional Imagination from Milton to Fielding* (University of Chicago Press, 1985), p. 141.

15 Gary S. De Krey, 'The First Restoration Crisis: Conscience and Coercion in London, 1667–73', *Albion*, 25 (Winter 1993), 565–80; Greaves, 'Great Scott! The Restoration in Turmoil, or, Restoration Crises and the Emergence of Party', *Albion*, 25 (Winter 1993), 605–11; De Krey, 'Rethinking the Restoration: Dissenting Cases for Conscience, 1667–1672', *HJ*, 38 (1995), 53–83; Mark Goldie, 'The Theory of Religious Intolerance in Restoration England', in O. P. Grell, J. I. Israel and N. Tyacke (eds.), *From Persecution to Toleration: The Glorious Revolution in England* (Oxford: Clarendon Press, 1991), pp. 331–68.

16 Bunyan, *MW*, VII:9; cf. Gordon Campbell, 'Fishing in Other Men's Waters: Bunyan and the Theologians', in N. H. Keeble (ed.), *John Bunyan: Conventicle and Parnassus* (Oxford: Clarendon Press, 1988), pp. 137–51.

17 W. M. Wigfield, *Recusancy and Nonconformity in Bedfordshire: Illustrated by Select Documents Between 1622 and 1842*, Publications of the Bedfordshire Historical Record Society 20 (Bedfordshire Historical Record Society, 1938), pp. 167–72.

18 For an attempt to do this, see Richard L. Greaves, '"Let Truth Be Free": John Bunyan and the Restoration Crisis of 1667–1673', *Albion*, 28 (Winter 1996), 587–605.

19 Nicholas Shrimpton, 'Bunyan's Military Metaphor', in Vincent Newey (ed.), *The Pilgrim's Progress: Critical and Historical Views* (Liverpool University Press, 1980), p. 205.

20 C. Carlton, *Going to the Wars: The Experience of the British Civil Wars, 1638–1651* (New York: Routledge, 1992), pp. 206–7.

21 Bunyan, *PP*, pp. 171, 248; Shrimpton, 'Bunyan's Military Metaphor,' pp. 209–11.

22 Jonathan Scott, *Algernon Sidney and the Restoration Crisis, 1677–1683* (Cambridge University Press, 1991), pp. 3–82; Greaves, *Secrets of the Kingdom*, pp. 20–32, 99–103; Public Record Office, SP 29/434/98 (quoted).

23 Christopher Hill, *A Turbulent, Seditious and Factious People: John Bunyan and His Church, 1628–1688* (Oxford: Clarendon Press, 1988), p. 240.

FURTHER READING

For individual editions of primary texts cited or discussed, please see the notes above.

Collmer, Robert G. (ed.), *Bunyan in Our Time*, Kent, Ohio: Kent State University Press, 1989.

Cragg, G. R., *Puritanism in the Period of the Great Persecution, 1660–1688*, Cambridge University Press, 1957.

Gay, David, Arlette Zinck and J. G. Randall (eds.), *Awakening Words: John Bunyan and the Language of Community*, Newark: University of Delaware Press, 2000.

Greaves, Richard L., *John Bunyan*, Abingdon, Berks.: Sutton Courtenay Press, 1969.
　Deliver Us from Evil: The Radical Underground in Britain, 1660–1663, New York: Oxford University Press, 1986.
　Enemies Under His Feet: Radicals and Nonconformists in Britain, 1664–1677, Stanford University Press, 1990.
　John Bunyan and English Nonconformity, London: Hambledon Press, 1992.
　Secrets of the Kingdom: British Radicals from the Popish Plot to the Revolution of 1688–1689, Stanford University Press, 1992.

Hill, Christopher, *A Turbulent, Seditious and Factious People: John Bunyan and his Church*, Oxford: Clarendon Press, 1988.

Keeble, N. H., *The Literary Culture of Nonconformity in Later Seventeenth-Century England*, Leicester University Press, 1987.
　(ed.), *John Bunyan: Conventicle and Parnassus – Tercentenary Essays*, Oxford: Clarendon Press, 1988.

Laurence, Anne, W. R. Owens and Stuart Sim (eds.), *John Bunyan and His England, 1628–88*, London: Hambledon Press, 1990.

Mullett, Michael, *John Bunyan in Context*, Keele University Press, 1996.

Newey, Vincent (ed.), *The Pilgrim's Progress: Critical and Historical Views*, Liverpool University Press, 1980.

Nuttall, Geoffrey F., and Owen Chadwick (eds.), *From Uniformity to Unity, 1662–1962*, London: SPCK, 1962.

Swaim, Kathleen, *Pilgrim's Progress, Puritan Progress*, Urbana and Chicago: University of Illinois Press, 1993.

Watts, Michael, *The Dissenters: From the Reformation to the French Revolution*, Oxford: Clarendon Press, 1978.

Absolutism: a political system which holds that the will of the monarch is absolute and that the royal prerogative or authority of the monarch is not limited by law or precedent.

Anabaptists: literally, *rebaptizers*. The term originally referred to the radical Protestants of early sixteenth-century Europe, who practised the baptism of believers (rather than paedobaptism, the baptism of infants), but it came to be used generally to brand any radical groups as fanatical and socially subversive. For this reason, the term *Baptist* came to be preferred by those who in seventeenth-century England practised believers' baptism.

Antinomianism: the view that, since those who are to be saved have been predetermined by God, the moral life has no bearing on their destiny. The assertion that the elect are set free from the moral law is intended to emphasize their dependence upon the grace of God and the inspiration of the Spirit, but it horrified traditional Calvinists as tending to amorality and libertinism.

Arminianism: theological views derived from the Dutch reformed theologian Jacob Arminius (1559–1609) who, rejecting the predestinarianism of Calvin, held that the human will has the capacity to respond to, or to reject, divine grace, and hence that the Atonement is not limited to the elect but is potentially universal. In common discourse in England, however, the term became associated with the high church party of William Laud, and so was used of what were regarded as tendencies towards Popery.

Calvinism: theological views derived from the French reformed theologian Jean Calvin (1509–64) which, stressing the sovereignty of God, allowed no part to the human will or to good works in determining salvation or damnation. These are predestined by the inscrutable will of God in his decrees of election and reprobation. To its critics, this creed appeared to make God responsible for the sin which led to damnation, and led, logically, to antinomianism, since those predestined to salvation could not fall away from grace.

Commonwealth: the Republican state ruled by the Rump from the execution of Charles I in January 1649 until it was turned out by Cromwell in April 1653.

Diggers: the followers of Gerard Winstanley (*fl.* 1648–52) who, maintaining that land should be held in common, in 1649 began communally to cultivate land on St George's Hill in Cobham, Surrey. The experiment was short-lived, but Winstanley's writings articulate a striking egalitarian and mystical vision, millenarian and idealistic.

Enthusiasts: in Christian discourse, the term is used of those who trust in the immediate inspiration and illumination of the Spirit, rather than in reason, tradition or authority. Radical Puritan opinion is hence enthusiastic.

Fifth Monarchy Men: radicals who looked to the establishment of the Fifth Monarchy of King Jesus (after the empires of Assyria, Persia, Greece and Rome) of Daniel 2:44, during which Christ will rule with his saints for 1,000 years. Some believed this would be brought about by armed rebellion against the powers of this world. An unsuccessful rising to this end was led by Thomas Venner in London in 1661.

'Good Old Cause, the': the political cause of Puritanism, that is, depending upon the speaker, either the original intention to limit the royal prerogative or the republicanism which subsequently emerged. In either case, Cromwell's single-person rule as Lord Protector could be seen as having betrayed the Good Old Cause.

Hermeticism: mystical, magical and philosophical beliefs derived from a collection of Greek and Latin writings of the first three centuries AD ascribed to Hermes Trismegistus ('Hermes the Thrice-Greatest'), in fact a mythical figure. Hermetic ideas concern the communion of humankind with the created world as a manifestation of God and the ascent of the soul to the divine.

Humanism: late fifteenth- and early sixteenth-century intellectual movement which, based on a new attentiveness to Classical writings, stressed the powers of reason and the potential of the human spirit.

Humble Petition and Advice, The: the second constitution of the Protectorate, adopted 26 June 1657.

Independents: originally and strictly those Puritans who favoured a Congregational system of church government, which allows autonomy to each separate, independent congregation. They emerged as a discernible and increasingly powerful party in the early 1640s. Since the system allowed no authority to any person, church or region to dictate to a particular congregation, it tolerated diversity of practice and belief. It was therefore opposed to all attempts to compel conformity to a national church, Presbyterian as well as episcopalian. Under the patronage of Cromwell, it became the prevailing view of soldiers in the New Model Army, with their watchcry of 'Liberty of conscience'. It hence acquired a political sense, denoting those who sought the overthrow of the King and who, after Pride's Purge, came to dominate in the Rump.

Instrument of Government, The: the first constitution of the Protectorate, adopted on 14 December 1653.

Levellers: followers of John Lilburne (1614?–57) who in the late 1640s argued for an egalitarian constitution (the *Agreement of the People*). The movement was broken when Cromwell forcibly put down an army mutiny at Burford, Oxfordshire, in 1649.

Millenarianism: belief in a future millennium, that is, a period of 1,000 years preceding the Second Coming of Christ in judgement during which he will reign with his saints on earth, at its conclusion taking them with him to Heaven. The belief, drawing especially on Daniel and the Book of Revelation, was pervasive among Puritans in the seventeenth century, many of whom anticipated an imminent millennium.

Mortalism: the belief that the soul does not leave the body at death. It is a heresy in the Christian tradition.

Nonconformists: those Puritans who, prior to the Civil War, refused to conform to some aspect of worship as laid down in the Book of Common Prayer. After the Act of Uniformity of 1662, those Puritans who worshipped in illegal non-episcopal congregations gathered outside the re-established episcopal Church of England. The term came to be superseded by *Dissenters*.

Ordinance: Act passed by the Long Parliament after 1641 which had not received the royal assent.

Parliamentarians: those committed to strengthening the role of Parliament within the constitution (and to a corresponding reduction of royal power).

Presbyterians: originally, and strictly, those Puritans who favoured the system of church government by committees of lay elders and pastors practised at Geneva and in Scotland, and who therefore opposed the episcopalian government of the Church of England. Since Charles I was committed to this church, and ruled without Parliament but with William Laud, Archbishop of Canterbury, as a chief minister, opposition to episcopalianism became indistinguishable from opposition to the absolutist tendencies of the King. Hence, the term came to denote those Parliamentarians who led the opposition to the King, the majority party in the Long Parliament, and, in the late 1640s, those who favoured a negotiated settlement with the King on condition he agreed to a reformation of the church.

Protectorate: the period during which, and the system of government by which, Oliver Cromwell ruled as Lord Protector from December 1653 until his death in September 1658. The Protectorate was regarded by Royalists as a usurpation of legitimate monarchical rule, and by Republicans as a dictatorship which was a monarchy in all but name.

Puritanism: a loose term used from the 1560s to designate those who sought further reformation of the established episcopal church, which they regarded as still contaminated with Romish practices and beliefs, and who increasingly in the 1630s and 1640s found themselves in opposition to the state authorities which supported that church. In popular usage, the term was used to suggest hypocrisy and absurdity in those who, in the view of the speaker, adopted a needlessly strict course of life.

Quakers: radical Puritans who in the 1650s preached the precedency of the prompting of the Spirit within each individual over all the dictates of all external political or ecclesiastical authorities. They consisted very largely of the socially disadvantaged and marginalized. In the later part of the century, the charismatic George Fox (1624–91) emerged as their leader.

Ranters: amorphous groupings of mystical and antinomian Puritans, who by those horrified at their radicalism were thought to repudiate all decency, especially sexual decency.

Republicanism: a political system which gives supreme power to the elected representatives of the people. It is hence the opposite to hereditary monarchy.

Royalists: both those committed to maintaining the rule of Charles I, and more loosely those committed to monarchical rule. Royalists in this latter sense might disagree on the extent to which the monarch's authority is restrained by the constitution.

Separatists: radical Puritans who gathered themselves into small, self-governing congregations, condemned by upholders of the ideal of a national church.

Solemn League and Covenant, The: the agreement between the Scots and the English by which, in 1643, the Scots entered the Civil War on the side of

Parliament. Its main provisions were the maintenance of Presbyterianism in Scotland, the reform of the English church on Presbyterian lines, and the preservation of the King.

Triers: commissioners appointed in 1654 to approve all applicants for benefices (that is, vicars and rectors) in the Cromwellian church. The intention was to prevent the pastoral laxity which it was believed had prevailed under the episcopal Church of England.

INDEX

Note: literary works are indexed under their author's name, where known; works of unknown authorship are indexed under their titles; periodicals are indexed under their titles.